The Jung Cult

The Jung Cult

ORIGINS OF A
CHARISMATIC MOVEMENT

RICHARD NOLL

PRINCETON UNIVERSITY PRESS

PRINCETON, NEW JERSEY

Library of Congress Cataloging-in-Publication Data
Noll, Richard, 1959–.
The Jung cult : origins of a charismatic movement / Richard Noll.
p.   cm.
Includes bibliographical references and index.
ISBN 0-691-03724-8 (alk. paper)
1. Jung, C. G. (Carl Gustav), 1875–1961—Religion.
2. Psychoanalysis and religion—History.
I. Title.
BF109.J8N65   1994
150.19′54′092—dc20   94-4831

This book has been composed in Palatino

But we can perhaps agree (at least some of us) on one
point this story teaches us: that even in intellectual history the cranks and the fools are important too; that
those whose cleverness is unimpeachable and invulner-
able to every test do not always carry the most important ideas; that even thinkers are human, and must
think with their whole bodies; and that the Truth is to
be grasped from some very odd angles.

Martin Green, The Mountain of Truth

❈ *Contents* ❈

CONTENTS

⊠ *List of Illustrations* ⊠

⊞ *Acknowledgments* ⊞

THIS VOLUME is a distillation of the conclusions of many frustrating years of trying to understand the life and work of C. G. Jung. It marks the transition of my life from a phase of ten years of clinical practice (the last six as a clinical psychologist) to an academic career based on my intellectual interests in psychiatry and psychology from the disciplinary perspective of the history of science. Attempting to understand Jung within his historical context—particularly from the point of view of the history of science and medicine—has been challenging, to say the least.

Along the way I have received useful criticism and encouragement from many wiser than myself. My friend and mentor John Kerr is a primary source of inspiration for this book, and our many discussions no doubt saved me many years of following irrelevant historical leads. He also taught me an invaluable lesson: never serve the mustard before the meat. Mark Micale read an early draft of the text as a reviewer and provided many helpful suggestions for the manuscript's improvement. Peter Swales helped enormously one Sunday afternoon in New York, before this project had even been conceived, by recounting his trip to the Ernst Haeckel museum in Jena. This stimulated my interest in Haeckel and led to my discovery of his importance to Jung. I am also indebted to Peter for his skills as an entertainer by accompanying—wonderfully—a singing Marilyn Monroe (on tape) with his violin bow and handsaw at my Saturnalia party in December 1992.

Others have provided useful research advice in the past. In particular I wish to thank Sonu Shamdasani for generously sharing information about the controversial origins of *Memories, Dreams, Reflections*. His planned intellectual biography of Jung—if and when it appears—will no doubt supplant some of the conclusions I reach in this volume. I am also indebted to him for directing me to the Katz papers at Harvard Medical School, which have proven to be a rich source of material. Eugene Taylor also has been very gracious in sharing his considerable knowledge with me about the history of psychiatry. William McGuire provided me with much new information, and his warm support of this project has been greatly appreciated.

Early readers of this manuscript who provided useful criticism were Leonard George and David Ulansey. Others who have been influential through comments in their correspondence with me or in their published works are Martin Green, Anne Harrington, Roy Porter, Carl Pletsch, Frank Sulloway, Timothy Lenoir, Frederick Gregory, Ernst Mayr, Henri Ellenberger, William Woodward, and George Mosse. The works of Max Nordau also fell into my hands at a critical period and helped me to understand much about the clash between bourgeois and modern consciousness. Much needed amusement and diversion during the writing of this project were provided by Charles Kohlepp, Ian Cosmo Kohlepp, John Suler, Jim Pawlik, George Huey, and Jason Pyrah.

The seeds of the project were planted during the many long discussions over a number of years with my friends in the Jungian movement who dared to question everything, including, in some cases, the contradictory views of their analysts. These friends include Barbara Crawford, Pam Donleavy, Don Zenner, Jeannie Jaffe, Mary Stamper, Virginia Taylor, Anne Malone, Dolores Brien, Jack Giegerich, George Bernato, and Regina Cudemo. Others of the Jungian faith who are analysts and who were supportive of my early efforts are Andrew Samuels and especially John Beebe, who encouraged me to go ahead and "Weberize" the Jungian movement. Useful insights about the social dynamics of the international Jungian community as a charismatic religious movement and business enterprise were provided by the many Jungian analysts I have encountered who were—and remain—deeply mistrustful and resistant to historical interpretations of Jung. I received sage advice from both James Hillman and Charles Boer who both understand my sentiment when I say that, like Nietzsche, my greatest experience was a recovery.

My experiences as a doctoral student in the early 1980s at the Graduate Faculty of the New School for Social Research have proven to be an invaluable interdisciplinary preparation for this work. Only now do I realize how remarkable my education at the New School was when compared with other graduate programs in psychology, and I can only hope it still retains that European spirit that values theory, history, and interdisciplinary research. In particular I wish to thank Mary Henle for introducing me to the history of psychology and for teaching me to think critically. Others who deserve thanks are Michael Harner, L. Erlenmeyer-Kimling, Jerome Bruner, and Bernard Weitzman.

I wish to thank Richard Wolfe of the Francis A. Countway Library of Medicine of Harvard University for giving me permission to reprint the 1916 document from the Fanny Katz collection concerning the founding of the Psychological Club, and for permission to quote from the interviews with Jolande Jacobi, C. A. Meier, and Lilliane Frey-Rohn in the Jung Oral Archives. I also wish to thank Princeton University Press for permission to reprint passages from the Collected Works of C. G. Jung.

The interlibrary loan and reference librarians at West Chester University were extremely helpful and patient with my many requests, especially for the many obscure books in German that they procured for me.

Some of the ideas in this book were presented to the History of Psychiatry Section of New York Hospital/Cornell Medical Center. I wish to thank the members of this distinguished group for enriching my understanding of certain key points from the perspective of psychiatric history. In particular I wish to thank Leonard Groopman for the opportunity to try out my ideas in a public forum.

My editors at Princeton University Press have been wonderful and patient. This work would not be in existence if it were not for the unfailing support of my editor, Deborah Tegarden, who immediately recognized its significance and put up with a sometimes difficult author. Emily Wilkinson has been gracious in her support and also deserves special mention. Eric Rohmann and my copyeditor, Timothy Mennel, likewise have been inspiring in their enthusiasm.

I wish to dedicate this book to my best friend, Susan Naylor, who has inspired me in ways too numerous to recount here. Susan tolerated the many weeks of my intense graphomania this past summer as I forged this book in the study of our 260-year-old stone home, which sits in the fields where the Battle of Brandywine took place in 1777. Ours is a home where the past still lives.

West Chester, Pennsylvania
December 1993

⊞ *Abbreviations* ⊞

The following abbreviations are used in the text:

MDR *Memories, Dreams, Reflections,* by C. G. Jung, recorded
and edited by Aniela Jaffé, translated from the German
by Richard and Clara Winston (New York: Pantheon
Books, 1963).

CW *The Collected Works of C. G. Jung,* edited by Herbert Read,
Michael Fordham, and Gerhard Adler; executive editor,
William McGuire; translated by R.F.C. Hull (Princeton:
Princeton University Press).

1. *Psychiatric Studies*
2. *Experimental Researches* (trans. by Leopold Stein in
   collaboration with Diana Riviere)
3. *The Psychogenesis of Mental Disease*
4. *Freud and Psychoanalysis*
5. *Symbols of Transformation*
6. *Psychological Types* (trans. by H. G. Baynes)
7. *Two Essays on Analytical Psychology*
8. *The Structure and Dynamics of the Psyche*
9. *Part I. The Archetypes and the Collective
   Unconscious*
9. *Part II. Aion: Researches into the Phenomenology of
   the Self*
10. *Civilization in Transition*
11. *Psychology and Religion: West and East*
12. *Psychology and Alchemy*
13. *Alchemical Studies*
14. *Mysterium Coniunctionis*
15. *The Spirit in Man, Art, and Literature*
16. *The Practice of Psychotherapy*
17. *The Development of Personality*
18. *The Symbolic Life: Miscellaneous Writings*
19. *General Bibliography of Jung's Writings*
20. *General Index*

A. *The Zofingia Lectures* (trans. by Jan van Heurck)
B. *Psychology of the Unconscious* (trans. by Beatrice M.
   Hinkle)

The Jung Cult

✦ *Introduction* ✦

In 1873 Ferdinand Tönnies read Friedrich Nietzsche's *The Birth of Tragedy* and came under its spell, reading it "almost with the feeling of a revelation."[1] In the years that followed, Tönnies secretly adopted Nietzsche, then a classical philologist teaching at Basel University in Switzerland, as his *spiritus rector*, his own private spiritual guru. It was only in Tönnies's imagination that he conversed with his genius, the imaginal Nietzsche: after traveling to the town where Nietzsche lived, Tönnies spied on him from afar but was too afraid to speak to him. Imaginary letters written time and time again to Nietzsche were never put to paper or sent. For Tönnies, Nietzsche had become too imbued with the qualities of divinity and hence too Olympian, too unreachable.[2]

During this period it may be said that Tönnies's hero worship of Nietzsche was his "personal religion." A personal religion, in this sense, is precisely what Thomas Carlyle defined in 1841 as the true essence of hero worship: the attribution of divinity to a living or legendary human by a mere mortal individual who did not (or did not *yet*) perceive the sacred spark of "genius" within his or her own personality. Such a "profane" individual, who may indeed have developed talent but may not have been *born* with "genius," may privately or socially enter into a "genius-cult" of hero worship and, by deed if not by word, place this personal religion above his or her nominal organized faith. Carlyle describes this best:

> It is well said, in every sense, that a man's religion is the chief fact with regard to him. A man's, or a nation of men's. By religion I do not mean here the church-creed which he professes, the articles of faith which he will sign and, in words or otherwise, assert; not this wholly, in many cases not this at all. We see men of all kinds of professed creeds attain to almost all degrees of worth or worthlessness under each or any of them. This is not what I call religion, this profession and assertion; which is often only a profession and an assertion from the outworks of the man, from the mere argumentative region of him, if even so deep as that. But the

3

thing a man does practically believe (and this is often enough *without* asserting it even to himself, much less to others); the thing a man does practically lay to heart, and know for certain, concerning his vital relations to this mysterious Universe, and his duty and destiny there, that is in all cases the primary thing for him, and creatively determines all the rest. This is his *religion*; or, it may be, his mere skepticism and *no-religion*; the manner it is in which he feels himself to be spiritually related to the Unseen World or No-world; and I say, if you tell me what that is, you tell me to a very great extent what the man is, what the things he will do is.[3]

Yet, as the intent and style of Nietzsche's works changed, so did Tönnies's faith in him. The Nietzsche of *The Birth of Tragedy* (1872) was not the Nietzsche of *Also Sprach Zarathustra* (1892).[4] Gone was the Apollonian cultural idealist, the lover of the Dionysian in the musical tragedy of Wagner. Nietzsche *was* Dionysus, the pagan god of irrationality, the "loosener," the "breaker of bonds," the catalyst of reversals, the seducer through sudden cacophonies and equally sudden silences, the iconoclast who could proclaim the death of the Judeo-Christian god and dare to overthrow even his own beloved "Divine Hero," Richard Wagner: this was the image of Nietzsche as Dionysian Hero adopted by individuals and groups seeking *Lebensreform* ("life-reform"), whether spiritual or political. The rediscovery of Nietzsche's works after he went mad in 1889 and the subsequent appearance of his later, more daring works throughout the 1890s and early 1900s ignited the flames of cultism.[5] Tönnies, while still very much admiring the Nietzsche of a generation earlier, would have no part of this.

In 1897 Tönnies's now-forgotten book on the "Nietzsche Cult" appeared.[6] *Der Nietzsche-Kultus: Eine Kritik* was a sociological exposition on the inherent contradictions between the "liberation philosophy" of Nietzscheanism as proselytized by its cultists and the *actual* functions that Nietzschean ideas served. The doctrine of Nietzscheanism was seductive: it promised the release of creative powers of genius within the individual, the courage to freely express oneself and to reject authority and moral and social conventions. Through *deeds* one could truly be who one was, and perhaps even achieve symbolic immortality. Yet, part of this Nietzschean faith was also the exaltation of the mastery of the many by the few, a new nobility of the perpetually self–re-creating who would lead the way for the rest of the herd. Tönnies argued that rather than promote widespread liberation, Nietzschean ideas were being used instead to maintain conservative and especially elitist classes in society—precisely those persons and values that Nietzschean cults claimed they were repudiating. For Nietzscheans, disaffection with the frustrating layers of bureaucratic authority and elitism in the governmental or religious hierarchies—did not apparently contradict a belief in the necessity of a noble elite. Indeed, Nietzscheans actively promoted the creation of such an elite, a vanguard that would transform the world with its "higher" values of community and truth. The alarming truth was that the Nietzschean could adopt these "truths" with little or no consciousness of their underlying elitist implications. Tönnies thus found these inherent contradictions between the professed beliefs and the actual behavior of the members of these Nietzschean groups potentially dangerous.

As historian Steven Aschheim astutely observes about the many "varieties of Nietzschean religion" that blossomed in Europe at the turn of the century, "Nietzscheanism was part creator and part beneficiary of a general erosion of traditional belief and dissatisfaction with the established church. For many this dissatisfaction, far from quenching the thirst for religion, gave it renewed impetus."[7]

It is indeed paradoxical that Western spirituality in the twentieth century has been so influenced—indeed, awakened—by a man who declared the death of God and who defined himself as the Antichrist. Yet, Nietzsche's "hammer" of questions has been taken up time and again in the modern age by spiritual seekers who felt their paths were blocked by the walls of convention and dogma, and who have felt compelled to initiate unconventional acts of personal salvation out of a yearning for new nectar to satiate a very old thirst.

When we survey the spiritual landscape of the Western world a century later we find that there is wide cultural interest in a movement that has its origins among these late-nineteenth- and early-twentieth-century Nietzschean currents. This is the international movement centered on the transcendental ideas and the idealized personality of Carl Gustav Jung (1875–1961), the Swiss psychiatrist, psychoanalyst, and founder of the school of analytical psychology. Jung is best known today as Sigmund Freud's ungrateful disciple, breaking with his master in 1913 to go his own way and establish his own movement. The legend is additionally framed in the context of Jung's advocacy of the essential spiritual nature of human beings over the narrow, sexual view of Freud, who was by his own admission "a godless Jew." Those who read Jung and participate in the activities of the Jungian movement are often individuals seeking to increase their own sense of "spirituality."

Most persons who regard themselves as Jungians do not realize that Jung's ideas changed markedly over a number of years. For example, in late 1909 Jung first began to hypothesize that the unconscious mind had a deeper "phylogenetic" or racial layer beyond the memory store of personal experiences, and that it was from this essentially vitalistic biological residue that pre-Christian, pagan, mythological material emerged in dreams, fantasies, and especially psychotic states of mind. Jung's final theories, those of a transpersonal collective unconscious (1916) and its archetypes (1919), marked a transition away from an already tenuous congruence with the biological sciences of the twentieth century and instead returned to ideas popular during his grandfather's lifetime—the age of Goethe.

By this time a metaphysical idea that was somewhat implicit in Jung's earlier thought became explicit: namely, that all matter—animate and inanimate—has a kind of "memory." Such ancient ideas, ironically, are what Jung is best known for introducing as modern innovations. Indeed these essentially transcendental concepts are so widely spread in our culture through their connections to psychotherapeutic practice, New Age spirituality, and neopaganism that they continue to be the subject of innumerable workshops, television shows, best-selling books, and video cassettes, and they form the basis of a brand of psychotherapy with its own trade name: Jungian analysis.[8]

Freud may still be the genius of choice for the learned elite of the late twentieth century, but it is clear that, in sheer numbers alone, it is Jung who has won the cultural war and whose works are more widely read and discussed in the popular culture of our age. There is no grassroots Freudian movement to match the size and scope of the international movement that has formed around the symbolic image of Jung. Freud's fall from grace as a revered cultural icon of modernity has been so serious that even *Time* magazine felt the need to take up Nietzsche's hammer and ask on the cover of its 29 November 1993 issue: "Is Freud Dead?"

When examined from a historical perspective, the contemporary phenomenon of Jungism presents numerous paradoxes. While its practitioners and theoreticians cite its legitimacy as a fruitful psychological theory and a profession of psychotherapy, the far greater numbers of participants in the movement who are not professionals are attracted by its "spirituality." Its caste of professional psychotherapists—Jungian analysts—profess the virtues of eclecticism, and yet claim the validity of a distinctive Jungian identity for their beliefs and techniques. As an institutionalized capitalist enterprise, it includes not only training institutes throughout the world (which parallels the Freudian system), but also hundreds of local psychology clubs (which have no Freudian parallel) that sponsor programs and workshops related to New Age spirituality and neopaganism. Even most Jungian analytic-training institutes, which emphasize their commitment to clinical training and a desire to maintain professional associations with the psychological and medical sciences, nonetheless have been known to offer practical classes or programs on astrology, the I Ching, palmistry, and other practices associated with the occult sciences.

Perhaps the most perplexing paradox of all is how to make sense of Jung himself, who was a noted experimental psychopathologist, psychiatrist, and psychoanalyst, within the contexts of the history of science and the history of psychiatry. Who, indeed, was C. G. Jung? At the present time a resilient cult of personality very much akin to Carlyle's hero worship is in evidence and occludes the historical Jung. Perplexingly, the phenomenon of Jungism has followed a somewhat different course than other cases of immortalization of physicians and scientists.

For example, the inventor of mediate auscultation and the stethoscope, René-Théophile-Hyacinthe Laennec, died in 1826 at the age of forty-five with little acknowledgment from his colleagues, but by 1870 he had been selected as the focus of institutional celebrations as an authentic hero of French medicine.

7

Laennec's reputation as the greatest French physician of the nineteenth century was the product of collective negotiation and political maneuvering by prominent members within the French medical establishment, as historian George Weisz has shown.[9] Although less well documented, a similar inflation of medical reputation via collective negotiation for political and economic institutional motivations can be found in the case of Benjamin Rush (1745–1813), who was lionized by the American psychiatric community in the mid-nineteenth century.[10] In the cases of both Laennec and Rush, nationalism was an additional motivating force.

Even Freud has enjoyed an exalted place in the pantheon of medicine through the teaching of his ideas in psychiatric training programs in American medical schools since the 1920s, due in no small part to the early conversion of William Alanson White (1870–1937) to Freudian theory. White (and several other Freudians) played a key role in formalizing medical training in psychiatry in the United States. Until very recently the oldest and most "official" Freudian psychoanalytic association in North America allowed only American physicians who were graduates of approved medical schools to train as psychoanalysts. Thus through the imprimatur of such respected institutional affiliations—and the writing of histories of psychiatry by graduates of such institutions—Freud's reputation in medical and scientific history loomed large throughout most of the twentieth century, as the center of scientific and medical education gradually shifted from Germany, England, and France to the United States after the First, and certainly by the end of the Second, World War.[11]

In all of the above cases immortality was institutionally conferred and assured by established medical and scientific disciplinary communities. No such mechanism is at the root of Jungism, for Jung and his theories have remained well outside the established institutional worlds of science and medicine, as they have been regarded, with justification, as inconsistent with the greater scientific paradigms of the twentieth century. Additionally, Jung's theories have never received significant attention in the disciplines of academic psychology. Indeed, although a few lines on Jung are often included in most introductory American psychology textbooks, and many such textbooks for "theories of personality" classes contain a full section or a chapter on Jung, the discussion of Jung is invariably less extensive and usually follows in sequence the much more fully articulated ideas and biography of Freud. Something else must account for the widespread popularity of Jung, but what?

Perhaps we can begin to answer this question when we examine the curious relationship between theory and history in the literature on Jung, and by extension, the role of this relationship in the sociological phenomenon of Jungism. The relationship of history and theory in the historiography of the psychological sciences has become a focus of considerable debate in recent years.[12] Not counting his relatively brief period of significant Freudian influence (1906–1912), Jung may be characterized by his combination of six separate but interconnected theories:

1. the complex theory (circa 1902)
2. the theory of psychological types (1913, 1921)
3. the vitalistic theory of a primarily biologically based phylogenetic unconscious (1909, but revised after 1916)
4. the theory of the collective unconscious (1916)
5. the theory of dominants (1917) or archetypes (1919) of the collective unconscious
6. the principle of individuation (1916).

The remainder of this volume is devoted to an exposition of the relationship between the latter four of these Jungian theories and history.

Whereas the psychological objects of Jungism (especially Jung's theories of the collective unconscious and its archetypes) are widely known, their historical origins and their current use "not only . . . *by* but also *for* and *about* people with particular interests and preferences," as Kurt Danzinger expresses it, needs to be clarified. I would indeed argue along with Danzinger that, furthermore, "only when we understand something of this historical embeddedness of specific psychological objects and practices are we in a position to formulate intelligent questions about their possible historical transcendence."[13]

9

PART ONE

THE HISTORICAL CONTEXT OF C. G. JUNG

The Problem of the Historical Jung

UNDERSTANDING THE HISTORY of ideas at play in the nineteenth century is a key to understanding the historical Jung—a vision of Jung not provided in the posthumous "inner autobiography" of *Memories, Dreams, Reflections by C. G. Jung* (hereafter *MDR*) that forms the basis of almost every other biographical account of Jung to date.[1] The search for the historical Jung is necessary if we are to even begin to understand the considerable impact of his life and work on the culture of the twentieth century. To trace the historical context of Jung's life is to also understand the paradoxes of Jungism, a movement that romanticizes and spiritualizes Jung's theories but has demonstrated little interest in documenting the historical facts of his life outside of the information provided in *MDR*.

MDR was primarily written and constructed by Aniela Jaffé, one of Jung's closest associates, and was originally to appear as a biography of Jung under her authorship with only "contributions by C. G. Jung." Jung personally wrote by hand only the first three chapters of the book, which concern his childhood, school days, and university years, and a final section entitled "Late Thoughts" that contains Jung's metaphysical speculations on the nature of God, life, and love. Although these comprise a third of *MDR*, they underwent further editing by Jaffé and others. A chapter that may or may not have been written directly by Jung concerning his intimate companion of forty years, Toni Wolff, was removed from the text early in the editorial process over objections by members of the Jung family while Jung was a semi-invalid in his last years. The book is therefore a product of discipleship.

Memories, Dreams, Reflections is unenlightening to those interested in history but compelling to those drawn to mystery. "The commonplace is so interwoven with the miraculous and the mythical that we can never be sure of our facts," Jung complains about the writings of St. Paul on Jesus, "and the most confusing thing of all is that [the disciple's writings] do not seem to have the slightest interest in Christ's existence as a concrete human being."[2] This criticism may be equally applied to *MDR* and its many imitators.[3] It is now apparent that like the Gospels, *MDR*, too, seems to be the work of many hands other than Jung's own, casting some doubt on its claim to be an autobiography.[4]

The sacralization of Jung's personality and ideas in *MDR* and by his disciples follows familiar patterns, repeated again and again for millennia, that are well known to the sociologist or historian of religion but less familiar to the historian of science or psychiatry. The biographical treatments of Jung more often than not follow a style derived from the pagan biographical tradition devoted to two related charismatic figures of late antiquity: the *theos aner*, or "divine man," and the ascetic holy man.[5]

Jung's dreams, visions, hunches, miraculous cures, psychokinetic and clairvoyant experiences, his musings on life after death and reincarnation, his experiences with the dead, his confrontation in the "Land of the Dead" (the collective unconscious) with gods (archetypes), his ascetic retreats to his stone tower at Bollingen, are all interwoven in *MDR* with the themes of his final theories—those of the collective unconscious and the archetypes—and therefore depict Jung's life as an exemplum of the theory. Jung thus becomes the only icon of complete individuation to be found in Jungian literature. In this respect *MDR* resembles—in instructive intent and style—a pagan biography of a *theos aner* such as the *Life of Apollonius of Tyana* of Philostratus (third century C.E.) or, to a lesser extent, the Christian hagiographies of the saints of the Middle Ages,[6] rather than a modern history of a "great man."[7]

The "divine man" of late antiquity was a charismatic individual, usually with a following of disciples who regarded him "as having a special relationship with the gods."[8] This special relationship allowed the divine man to perform miraculous feats of healing and divination. Apollonius of Tyana, for example, is depicted by Philostratus as having the gift of foreknowledge and could "receive and interpret divine communications in the form of dreams."[9] The divine man often performed wondrous cures, sometimes by exorcisms or by suggesting changes in diet or habits.

The ascetic "holy man" of late antiquity resembles the divine man in that he, too, worked miracles. Healing through ritualized exorcisms was also his stock and trade. "Above everything, the holy man is a man of power," notes classical scholar Peter Brown.[10] The holy man replaced the oracle as the social arbiter and healer of late antiquity. However, unlike the divine man who derived his power from occult sources or the gods, the holy man was empowered by his "close identification with the animal kingdom"[11] and with nature through his ascetic retreats to the desert.[12] In no small comparison to the Freudian and Jungian movements (among many others), some holy men collected hundreds of followers. Furthermore, like the founding of official training institutes for Freudian or Jungian analysts and the proliferation of Jungian social organizations largely comprised of the patients of Jungian analysts, Egypt of late antiquity (third to fifth centuries C.E.) "provides the first evidence of the formation of lay and clerical clientele around the holy man. . . ."[13] A further parallel to modern times can be found in the statement that "the lonely cells of the recluses of Egypt have been revealed, by the archeologist, to have had well-furnished consulting rooms."[14]

Thus, with *MDR* we do not have the human history of a renowned physician and scientist, but instead the myth of a divine hero, a holy man, a saint, a life produced directly by essentially a *religious* community, and therefore a biography as "cult legend." The life of Jung becomes the basis of shared values and beliefs in the Jungian movement concerning the transcendent (the collective unconscious) and redemption (individuation). Yet, we now know how manufactured this image of Jung seems to be (admittedly the tragedy, unfortunately, of any celebrity biography). The cult legend of Jung that has been faithfully maintained after his death by the Jungian movement (especially its analytic elite) resembles the sociological phenomenon of "manufactured pseudocharisma" by which mass media is used by power-seeking elites to promote seductive fantasy images in order to secure and maintain economic and social rewards.[15] To get at the historical Jung one must find a way to reach the "pre-Jaffé" biographical material, a task comparable to trying to discern the true pre-Pauline facts concerning Jesus of Nazareth.[16]

CULT AND CHARISMA

The use of the word "cult" is always problematic.[17] The word has long been used to single out the Other in society: no one wants to ever think of themselves as participating in a cult, with its implications of fanaticism, irrationality, loss of individual will or decision-making ability ("zombification"), and of holding stigmatizing beliefs or unusual practices that set one outside conventional human society. Yet, paradoxically, it is precisely the attraction of being outside society, and indeed of changing society from this outside perspective, that appeals to many who join spiritual, political, or other movements. Coming together on the outside often fuses people together through a strong bond of identity as outsiders, who nonetheless often sadly lament that they are misunderstood or not taken seriously by those who represent authority in conventional society. The bond is even stronger if the group coalesces around a charismatic leader with a certain totalizing worldview. While required to be physically present initially, after the passing of the charismatic leader only the legend or the image of the leader needs to be invoked for group identity. Such has been the case with those who have been attracted to the Jungian movement, starting with its first germinal "Jung cult" in Küsnacht-Zurich, and then in the multitude of regional cults that currently comprise the Jungian movement.

For my purposes here, I offer two different definitions of a cult. Following its use in the History of Religions School, I follow New Testament scholar Wilhelm Bousset's definition of a cult as simply "a community gathered for worship," however broadly defined; in the case of the Jungian movement, this is very much in the spirit of Carlyle's hero worship.[18] A contemporary psychiatrist here defines a charismatic group in a more psychological and especially sociological way, based on the work on "charismatic authority" by Max Weber (1864–1920):

> A charismatic group consists of a dozen or so members, even hundreds or thousands. It is characterized by the following psychological elements: members (1) have a *shared belief system*, (2) sustain a high level of *social cohesiveness*, (3) are strongly influ-

16

enced by the group's *behavioral norms*, and (4) impute *charismatic (or sometimes divine) power* to the group or its leadership.[19]

Jung, by all accounts, was the epitome of a charismatic leader. The power that a charismatic leader wields over his followers is perceived as coming from a supernatural force and Jung is reverently portrayed in these terms by Jungians. In his *Religionssoziologie* (Sociology of Religion) originally written between 1911 and 1913 but published posthumously, Weber observes that, "Already crystallized is the notion that certain beings are concealed 'behind' and are responsible for the activity of the charismatically endowed natural objects, artifacts, animals, or persons."[20] Thus, the charismatic leader is perceived by his followers as the source of universal powers that are focused and intensified like cosmic rays through the lens of his or her individual person. "It is primarily, though not exclusively, their extraordinary powers that have been designated by such special terms as 'mana,' 'orenda,' and the Iranian 'maga'.... We shall henceforth employ the term 'charisma' for such extraordinary powers."[21]

In 1928 Jung would introduce the concept of the "mana personality" to describe essentially the same concept.[22] However, the supernatural forces behind the mana personality are, of course, the archetypes of the collective unconscious. Although Weber's major work on the sociology of religion, in which he discusses the nature of the charismatic leader, was widely available in 1922, it is notable that Jung does not credit Weber for this concept, although he may have based his later concept of the "mana personality" on Weber's "charismatic leader." There is no record of direct contact between Weber and Jung, although Jung may have known Marianne Weber, Max's wife, through his participation as a guest speaker at the German Christian organization *Die Köngener* in the 1930s.[23] Jung certainly knew of Weber at least as early as 1908 through the "renegade psychoanalyst" Otto Gross, who had a disturbing impact on Weber and his immediate circle of intimates in Heidelberg around this time. (Gross's impact on Weber and Jung will be discussed in a later section.)

In addition to the numerous published accounts that attest to Jung's captivating influence as a *pater pneumatikos* ("spiritual father"), there are equally charismatic descriptions of him among the nearly two hundred interviews with persons who knew him that were collected in the late 1960s and early 1970s by Gene Nameche. Transcripts of these interviews comprise the Jung Oral Archives at the Countway Library of Medicine. In a filmed interview Lilliane Frey-Rohm, one of Jung's closest disciples in his last decades said, "When you met him in [the Psychological Club] or when you met him privately or in analysis, it was always a man interested in the, I would like to use the word, in the *spiritual food*. Always. And to the depths."[24] Judging by the literally hundreds of testimonials to his intuition, his extrasensory powers, indeed his personal charisma, Jung fed the multitude of his disciples in abundance.

Jung himself repeatedly reminded his readers that we are all born within a specific historical context and that this gives form to the specific conflicts played out in the individual psyche. Jung would agree with Weber's conviction that we are essentially "historical beings" (*historische Individuen*).[25] Who, then, is the historical Jung?

The Quest for the Historical Jung

It would be impossible to cover the details of Jung's life in depth as this is not a biographical work, but rather a discussion of Jung from the perspective of the history of ideas. For the historian attempting to distinguish the man from the myth, the task is an arduous one. Jung and his ideas are presented as eternal and therefore outside of history, with little or no priority given to historical accuracy or chronological sequence. Unlike Freud's comprehensive *Standard Edition* of his works, which follows a strict chronological arrangement, Jung's *Collected Works* are grouped "topically." As both the Freud and Jung collections are the products of discipleship, this very distinction may point to important differences in the core aims of these two movements: Freudians are interested in securing Freud's place in history as a major cultural figure, a scientific genius as cult-hero, whereas Jungians seem to place more value on preserving an image of Jung as a divinely inspired human vessel for dispensing the eternal truths of the spirit.

The most informative biographical material on Jung can be found in the work of historian of psychiatry Henri Ellenberger, and thus the reader is referred to Ellenberger's works.[26] Ellenberger's treatments are far superior to the relatively scant historical facts provided in the English edition of *Memories, Dreams, Reflections*, although the German edition does contain additional information on Jung's family.

Carl Gustav Jung was born on 26 July 1875 in Kesswil, Switzerland, to Paul Achilles Jung (1842–1896) and Emilie Preiswerk (1848–1923). Ironically, each parent was the thirteenth child in bourgeois families that had undergone considerable financial loss. Hence, they keenly felt the sting of aristocratic decline. The male sides of Jung's family contain an abundance of Protestant ministers and theologians (some with Pietist leanings), physicians, and scholars in classical (Greek and Roman) and Oriental (Hebrew and Arabic) languages and cultures. Paul Jung's doctorate in theology made him a specialist in all of these areas and Jung's early homes contained scholarly books and images relating to antiquity. Not much is known of the women on the paternal side of the family, but the women on the maternal side are characterized by family legends of spiritualist and clairvoyant abilities.

Several aspects of Jung's early family matrix need to be addressed as they are often understated (sometimes deliberately) in biographical treatments of Jung.

First is the fact of Jung's essential German identity. Biographical accounts often accentuate his Swiss nationality, his Swiss patriotism, and so forth. Jung was indeed a proud and devoted citizen of democratically neutral Switzerland. Historically, most Swiss Germans resisted the nineteenth-century Pan-German unification movement so forcefully promoted (and eventually accomplished) by the Prussians, although Pan-Germanism among the Swiss Germans never completely died out as a source of internal Swiss conflict. The tragedy of German imperialism (the Franco-Prussian War, the two World Wars) led most "neutral" Swiss to downplay their Germanness, and Jung was no exception. In terms of politics and nationality Jung was Swiss, and he dissociated himself from the Germans and Austrians. This was especially true in the late 1930s when Jung's association with individuals and organizations strongly linked to

Nazi Germany led to charges that he was a Nazi sympathizer; he and his disciples tried to dispel this image by fervently insisting that Jung was simply a neutral Swiss physician with only humanitarian concerns.[27]

Culturally and biologically, however, Jung identified very strongly with his German roots, or, more specifically, his Germanic ancestors. His famous paternal grandfather, Carl Gustav Jung the Elder (1794–1864) was a German Catholic physician, playwright, scientist, and eventually rector of Basel University (founded in 1460 by Pope Pius II). Jung the Elder was converted to Protestantism by none other than Friedrich Schleiermacher (1768–1834), the great Protestant theologian who emphasized the role of feeling in the experience of God and who had a profound effect on the eighteenth- and early nineteenth-century Romantic movement.

Additionally, Jung the Elder was alleged to be the illegitimate child of Goethe, the epitome of the German genius and Nietzsche's model of an *übermensch*.[28] This family fable was one that Jung told time and time again throughout his life, as he was apparently quite smitten with the romantic idea that he was a direct descendant of the genius Goethe. Therefore, in an age of intense concern over heredity, it was quite apparent to him that the only fruit of hereditary genius in the Jung family's tree was on the German side, not the Swiss. In fact, the maternal side of the family, which boasted multiple generations of Protestant Swiss stock, contained significant evidence of hereditary degeneration. Ellenberger tells us, "In those days considerable stress was put on heredity, and the whole maternal side of the family appeared to be tainted with insanity."[29]

In a 1928 book review of *Das Spektrum Europas* (*The Spectrum of Europe*) by Count Hermann Keyserling, in which Jung is mentioned as a "model Swiss," Jung good-naturedly backs away from this accolade by noting, "I have been Swiss for some five hundred years only on my mother's side, but on my father's side for only one hundred and six years. I must therefore beg the reader to see my 'relatively Swiss' attitude as the result of my little more than a hundred-year-old Swiss mentality."[30] Jung obviously puts greater emphasis on his paternal roots and, tellingly, does not need to emphasize that his greater ancestral influences are specifically from Germany.

Perhaps another way to approach this problem is through the conceptual schema of Oswald Spengler (1880–1936), who distinguishes between "Civilization" and "Culture" in his own vitalistic *Lebensphilosophie* (life-philosophy). For Jung, his experience of *Civilization*, the Weberian "iron cage" that was artificially imposed from without, was Swiss and Christian, but his *Culture* was Germanic. According to Spengler, it is only "Culture" that engenders and reflects soul.[31] Jung's soul was in this sense, therefore, deeply Germanic.

As is evident in the writings and letters of his first sixty years, Jung undoubtedly felt himself to be part of the community of Germanic *Volk* united in its faith in a field of life-energy, with all of its accompanying transcendent spirituality and pantheistic beliefs. In fact, in retrospect, his 1911–1912 reconceptualization of the libido as a generalized life force of psychic energy (which punctuated his break with Freud), his lifelong use of the anthropological concept of the magical bond between self and Other (whether another individual or nature) known as the participation mystique, and his later (1946) speculations about kinship libido,[32] can each be interpreted as a reformulation of the *völkisch* belief in the cosmic "life force" linking each individual German "with every other member of the *Volk* in a common feeling of belonging, in a shared emotional experience."[33] The concept of transference itself takes on völkisch mystical proportions in Jung's hands after he liberated it from its mesmerist and Freuddian traditions by claiming that one can project transpersonal (archetypal) images onto another, thus uniting in a mystical union the cosmic fate of both the projector and the "hook" that is projected upon. This was eventually how Jung psychologized the seemingly mystical "transference" relationship between Hitler and the German masses. In addition, Jung's frequent expositions on the influence of geography—of how the very earth and one's natural environment were formative influences on the soul (and even on physiognomy!) through the directing characteristics of the soil (*Bodenbeschaffenheit*)—also comes from this same nineteenth-century Germanic concept of Volk.[34]

But arguing that Jung undoubtedly considered himself a cell within the living body of the Volk and wrote from a völkisch perspective does not imply that he was a fascist, Nazi, or even an anti-Semite—although evidence for this latter charge is present in many of Jung's private statements and covert actions. Whereas they may be confirmation of Jung's decidedly racialist thinking, which dominated intellectual discourse at the time, they may not necessarily be conclusive evidence of racism as we currently think of it. We are blinded by history and Hitler in this regard. Instead, we should remember that in German Europe in the late nineteenth and early twentieth centuries, as historian Peter Gay observes, "grand old words like *Volk* and *Reich* and *Geist* were now given new meaning by this great crusade for *Kultur*. These are not, as they might seem to be, imaginary effusions; they are the words of Thomas Mann and Friedrich Gundolf, and there were thousands of others, young and old, who sounded precisely like them."[35]

A second aspect of Jung's background that is often understated is his lifelong experience of being part of the elite. Due to the fame of C. G. Jung the Elder, the Jung family was quite well regarded in Basel where Jung grew up and attended *Gymnasium* (1886–1895) and the medical school at Basel University (1895–1900). Basel was still a relatively small city during this time, and the social networks of the Protestant ministry caste (*Pfarrerstand*) made it seem even smaller.[36] The halo of Jung the Elder extended to his grandson in everyday social interactions once Jung the Elder's paternity was revealed.

Jung's father, Paul, lived out his life as a country minister in Switzerland. Although this may seem to be a modest role from our point of view, as Ellenberger reminds us, "The presbytery (*Pfarrhaus*) has been called 'one of the germinal cells of German culture.'"[37] In nineteenth-century German Europe the Pfarrerstand was a social caste of the best and the brightest. Often only the most gifted students were selected for theological training in German, Swiss, and Austrian universities, and for the most part the German cultural intelligentsia were created from the ranks of the Pfarrerstand. They served as the Protestant "old nobility," a bulwark against barbarism, paganism, occultism, and their combined threat in "Papist" Roman Catholicism. (Perhaps as a product of this upbringing, Jung could not bring himself to enter a Catholic church without fear and anxiety until he was a grown man in his thirties, and throughout his life he could never visit Rome despite his many trips to Italy.)[38] Families in this caste tended to intermarry (as in the case of Jung's parents—his mother was the daughter of a prominent Swiss Protestant minister), and they formed a cultural elite that one historian has called "the German Mandarins."[39]

Jung grew up well aware of his status within this elite and, for the first half of his life, generally followed bourgeois paths commensurate with it (becoming a physician, a university professor, a husband and father, etc.). Throughout his life Jung demonstrated a pattern of participating in elites and then, within a short time, rising to the main leadership positions within them and thereby often assuming a dominating influence. He did this within his university fraternity, the 120-member Zofingia fraternity (whose motto was *Patriae, amicitiae, litteris*, "For fatherland, friendship, and literature"—reflecting its goal of promoting higher Pan-Germanic culture, but with a typically Swiss tolerance of divergent political associations),[40] by becoming president in 1897, only two years after entering it; at the Burghölzli hospital, where he became second in command under Eugen Bleuler in 1905, only five years after joining its large psychiatric staff; in the psychoanalytic movement, becoming second only to Freud in importance within a year of meeting him in 1907, and serving as the First President of the International Psychoanalytic Association (1910–1914); and then (beginning circa 1912–1913) leading his own small group that slowly grew into a large cultural movement. Thus Jung's primary leadership experiences came from excelling in small elite groups, highly cohesive and arguably elitist in philosophy, each with specific ideals and aims to transform society at large. Nietzschean ideals of a new nobility were therefore grounded in Jung's personal and practical experience.

Perhaps reflecting on his own life in 1925, one month from his fiftieth birthday, Jung attributes the surprising appearance of leadership qualities in some individuals as possible evidence of a quasi-spiritualist, quasi- biological idea that he considered but never developed: ancestor possession—that is, literally, spiritual possession by one's ancestors. "Another way of putting these ideas of ancestor possession would be that these autonomous complexes exist in the mind as Mendelian units, which are passed on from generation to generation intact, and are unaffected by the life of the individual."[41] Jung may be thinking of his own latent heredity of German genius:

> Let us say that this imaginary normal man we are talking about gets into a responsible position where he wields much power. He himself was never made to be a leader, but among his inherited units there is the figure of such a leader, or the possibility of it. That unit now takes possession of him, and from that time on he has a different character. God knows what has become of him, it is really as though he had lost himself and the ancestral unit had taken over and devoured him.[42]

Hence, matter was always alive for Jung, and in his view our bodies pulse with the emotions and abilities of our racial forefathers. Despite his occasional efforts to distance himself from explicit support of vitalism in his scientific writings after 1916, in order to make his ideas more palatable to a professional readership that had become increasingly skeptical of vitalism and supportive of materialism, vitalistic metaphors and ideas always remained a significant part of his work.

A third relevant but often understated aspect of Jung's early years is the dominance of classical Greco-Roman culture in the educational philosophy and in the schools of German Europe of this era. This "tyranny of Greece over Germany," as Eliza Marian Butler termed it, began essentially with the rediscovery of the aesthetic wonders of the art and literature of pagan antiquity—particularly Greece—by Johann Joachim Winckelmann (1717–1768).[43] Goethe called it Winckelmann's heroic *Gewahrwerden der griechischen Kunst*, his "finding" of Greek art. The image of ancient Greece as an idyllic, serene, rational, golden age of truth and beauty painted by Winckelmann in his works dominated German culture until the end of the nineteenth century. Ancient Greece was pure, never vulgar, the birthplace of genius, not degeneracy, and therefore it became an ideal that German culture sought to emulate. Winckelmann's most famous statement accentuates the rational over the irrational, the Apollonian over the Dionysian, in his idealization of ancient Greece:

> The universal, dominant characteristic of Greek masterpieces, finally, is *noble simplicity and serene greatness* in the pose as well as

in the expression. The depths of the sea are always calm, however wild and stormy the surface; and in the same way the expression in Greek figures reveals greatness and composure of soul in the throes of whatever passions.[44]

Winckelmann's work became the primary source of inspiration for the art and literature of German Romanticism. Greek mythology became a dominating point of reference in the works of literary figures of German high culture, especially in the works of Goethe. Little needs to be said here about Goethe's place in European culture: he was, by all respects, an unusually gifted creative genius who influenced every cultural aspect of his age. Goethe furthermore infused incipient German Hellenism with the first sparks of sensuousness and passion, of *Sturm und Drang*, the first echoes of the subsequent Dionysian torrent of Heinrich Heine (1797–1856) and especially the later fin-de-siècle Hellenism of the classical philologist Nietzsche, who forced a notable cultural shift away from Winckelmann's Apollonian cult of serenity and reason.[45] Goethe's *Faust* in particular became the sacred text of Germanic culture (Jung's first of many readings was at age fifteen), and was memorized and recited by generation after generation of children in German schools.[46] To even begin to understand the Goethe they were memorizing, these young students had to be given a smattering of basic Greek mythology first.

Through Goethe and the German Romantics, and through the widespread adoption of the teaching of Latin and Greek in secondary schools and universities, almost everyone had some familiarity with Greco-Roman mythology and culture, or could cite passages from pagan authors that would be commonly recognized.[47] Such widespread familiarity among persons at many levels of society in German Europe could seem quite mystifying to British or American visitors. British psychoanalyst and Freud biographer Ernest Jones later confessed with no small embarrassment that what struck him most about his initial contacts with first Jung in 1907, then Freud and his Viennese disciples in 1908, was their frequent quoting of "Latin and Greek passages by memory during their conversations and being astonished at my blank response."[48]

Jung's early life, then, is characterized by an immersion in the

culture and mythology of Greek, Roman, and Germanic antiquity; by participation in cultural and spiritual elites promoting
specific ideas about ways to transform culture; and by excep-
tionally important hereditarian concerns. Focusing on heredity
and its consequences in the nineteenth century served as a scientific form of fantasizing about the dead and their influence on
the present. These specific concerns dominated the next phase of
Jung's life, a fin-de-siècle period that, Jung claimed in 1925,
"contains the origin of all my ideas."[49]

The Fin de Siècle

JUNG WAS BORN and developed during an era of European history that referred to itself as the fin de siècle—the end of the century. It was an age of cultural ferment and generational collision in which opposing forces of rationality and irrationality, of social progress and hereditary degeneration, of positivism and occultism, scraped together like great tectonic plates and set off earthquakes and aftershocks that culminated in the Great War and its subsequent revolutions and putsches (Bavaria, Russia, Transylvania, etc.) of 1914–1919 and beyond. These years marked, as the eminent historian George Mosse describes it, the "change in the public spirit of Europe."[1] It has often been said that 1912–1913 saw the intellectual end of the nineteenth century. The years of the Great War were also a period Jung would later refer to as his "confrontation with the unconscious," a time of great personal tumult but also of visionary exploration and self-discovery, indeed an intellectual end to the tyranny of the nineteenth-century *embourgeoisement* of his own psyche.

These years signaled a turning point from one developmental epoch to another in Jung's life. Just as the Great War seemed to confirm the defeat of nineteenth-century conventional bourgeois morality and cultural and artistic art forms and the ascendancy of the "new ethic" of sexuality and aesthetic styles of the "moderns," so, too, do we find Jung during this period completing the process of shedding the remaining skin of a nineteenth-century conservative bourgeois life-style and reinventing himself as a leader of a movement of modernity that promoted the development of individuality. In this sense, during this period Jung attempted to fully become a modern and developed a practical method for realizing the life-philosophy of the generation of the fin de siècle.[2] However, as many who knew him can attest, he never fully abdicated his persona of nineteenth-century bourgeois respectability despite whatever he enacted in his private life.[3]

Of all the extant biographies of Jung, not one of them places him within the historical context of the fin de siècle. Only the brief but masterful historical studies by Ellenberger attempt such an approach.[4] Such a rendering of Jung as a fin-de-siècle man is crucial for understanding his life's work and especially his fascination with the ancient mysteries.

According to Max Nordau (1849–1923), an acclaimed journalist, social critic, alienist, and defender of bourgeois morality and values against the degeneracy of the moderns, the term *fin de siècle* "is a name covering both what is characteristic of many modern phenomena, and also the underlying mood which in them finds expression."[5] The modern phenomena he had in mind could be found in "degenerate" movements in art (e.g., Symbolism), literature (Tolstoism, Symbolism, Decadentism, Naturalism, Realism), music ("the Richard Wagner cult," as Nordau refers to it), and philosophy (Schopenhauer, Nietzsche, von Hartmann, Blavatsky, etc.). Nordau's most famous book, *Degeneration* (1895), is a massive diagnostic assessment of fin-de-siècle European culture according to the prevailing medical and social theories of hereditary degeneration. Nordau's book reflected the overwhelming obsession of the nineteenth century with "hereditary taint" ("bad blood") that could be passed on from the unhealthy existence of one generation to another, in a progressively weaker form, until the family line eventually died out. Modern styles in the arts were seen, by Nordau, as evidence of the extremely prevalent levels of degeneracy in the population of Europe, due to organic brain damage caused by alcoholism, drug addictions, venereal diseases (the continuing legacy of the "sins of the father"), the wear and tear of cramped urban life, and other harmful environmental factors. Although hereditary degeneracy could be slowed in its transmission through "therapeutics" (halting substance abuse, changing living and work conditions, etc.), successive generations were still weakened and would manifest the "stigmata" of physical and especially mental illnesses.

Nordau was perhaps the most famous prophet of doom in an age that was fascinated with ideas of degeneration, decay, and decadence.[6] A common theme that appears again and again in the documents of that time is the idea that European civilization itself was decaying and dying, that industrialization had stolen

the soul of humankind, that disease and death were all that anyone could expect from life. "Tell me, my brothers: what do we
consider bad and worst of all? Is it not *degeneration*?" Nietzsche
asked a generation of young persons who could understand this
sentiment perfectly.[7] Jung certainly did.

The performance arts and literature of this period also reflected the obsession with decay and death. The feeling that one
was living at the end of time was reinforced by such cultural
events as the premiere of Wagner's opera *Götterdämmerung* (*Twilight of the Gods*) on 17 August 1876 at the Festspielhaus, Wagner's temple-theater of Teutonic mysteries in Bayreuth, Germany. Survivors of the brutal Franco-Prussian War of 1870–1871
and the economic depression of 1873 had very recent memories
of fearing whether their time on earth was indeed at hand, as
the war devastated significant areas of Western Europe and the
resulting economic collapse led to further starvation, pestilence,
and political instability. In Central Europe in the late 1890s es-
sayists and novelists, influenced by the rejection of the present
by Nietzsche in his *Also Sprach Zarathustra*, expressed a "dys-
topian condemnation of their own times" that, by the end of the
century, was followed by science-fiction novels containing a
"dark recounting of society's collapse with visions of a völkisch
'reawakening.'"[8] In addition to the French "decadent" movement[9] and Oscar Wilde's unsubtle, self-deprecating novel of the
degeneration of an aesthete, *The Picture of Dorian Gray* (1890),
Irish author Bram Stoker's *Dracula* appeared in 1897 and has
never been out of print since. Dracula, perhaps more than Dorian Gray, is the consummate degenerate, and is described as
such by Stoker in the psychiatric language of Nordau and crimi-
nal anthropometrics expert Caesare Lombroso (1836–1909).
Dracula, king of the vampires, is the perfect fin-de-siècle cultural horror: something living hundreds of years yet dead,
something dead but undead, draining the vitality of the living,
like European civilization itself.

The age was characterized by an emphasis on the individual
to the exclusion of society, exalted to its apogee in the works of
Nietzsche, which was largely unread when they came out but
"rediscovered" only in the 1890s after he had gone mad.[10] Nietzsche himself had a profound effect on European culture after
1890 with his exciting style of using his "hammer" of questions

to smash every cultural idol, including the Judeo-Christian images of God. Like other young persons of the 1890s, Jung himself began reading Nietzsche at the age of twenty-three (circa 1898).[11] After reading an early work of Nietzsche's, Jung reports: "I was carried away by enthusiasm, and soon afterward read *Also Sprach Zarathustra*. This, like Goethe's *Faust*, was a tremendous experience for me."[12] Jung's *Collected Works* are filled with references to Nietzsche, and he devoted an extensive seminar to Nietzsche's *Zarathustra* between 1934 and 1939.[13]

Nietzsche was absorbed by reformists on the left and on the right, and according to Aschheim, Nietzscheanism became a diffuse "protean force" that could be adopted by politicians, theologians, anarchists, philosophers, psychiatrists, psychoanalysts, sexual libertarians promoting the "new ethic"—indeed *anyone* seeking change, renewal, or rebirth. "Nietzscheanism never constituted one movement reducible to a single constituency or political ideology; it was rather a loose congeries of people attracted to different social milieux, political movements, and cultural-ideological agendae."[14] "I am dynamite," Nietzsche himself claimed in *Ecce Homo*, published posthumously in 1908, and the liberal bourgeoisie elite feared him as the dangerous prophet of irrationalism, which in their minds was synonymous with anything modern.[15]

Equally disturbing to staid bourgeois sentiments were the increasingly prominent members of cultural elite captivated by eroticism, mysticism (spiritualism, Theosophy, Wagnerism, völkisch neopaganism), and the pessimistic philosophy of Arthur Schopenhauer and the related ideas of Eduard von Hartmann that contained elements of alien Eastern (Buddhist, Hindu) philosophies. All of these persons, movements, and ideas were known to Jung and many were great influences on him personally and, later, professionally.[16] As Paris and Vienna were the two cauldrons of fin-de-siècle culture, it is not surprising that another major influence on Jung—Freud and his psychoanalysis, with its interest in sexuality and the development of the individual—also arose in this historical setting.

Psychiatry developed as a new specialized area of medicine in the late 1800s, and psychiatrists competed with another new specialty—neurology—for the treatment of "nervous and mental diseases." By mid-century, following the dominance of the field by French *alienistes* such as Philippe Pinel (1745–1826) and J.E.D. Esquirol (1772–1840), whose circle of young disciples became famous in its own right, the Germans took the lead in psychiatric science.[17] Germans such as Wilhelm Griesinger (1817–1868) and Emil Kraepelin (1856–1926) defined psychiatry as a science by insisting that all mental illness was due to an organic dysfunction of the brain, and that a large portion of the work of psychiatrists was not therapeutics, but diagnosis and research into etiology. This was the practice of psychiatry as Jung learned it in medical school and experienced it at the Burghölzli Mental Hospital. It was Kraepelin who took the concept of degeneration from B. A. Morel and in 1893 defined a new psychotic disorder—*dementia praecox*—as a progressively degenerative disorder that would end in death.

A different tradition from the German psychopathologists (and from Freud's psychoanalysis) was represented by the French clinical tradition that was based on (1) a *dissociation* model of the mind and (2) *polypsychism*, the idea that not only does consciousness split, but it splits into autonomous parts or separate streams of consciousness, perhaps even into multiple personalities. Although J. M. Charcot (1825–1893) sparked this interest with his advocacy of the use of hypnosis to treat hysterics in the 1880s, it was primarily due to the work of Pierre Janet (1859–1947) that dissociation became a focus of interest. Jung studied with Janet in Paris in the winter of 1902 and, despite his Freudian period, from a historical point of view he is probably more properly placed within this French clinical tradition with Janet and Jung's own "fatherly friend" and mentor, Théodore Flournoy (1854–1920).[18] Jung's famous "complex theory," which he supported experimentally through his word-association studies, is derived from this French clinical tradition, as it is based on a model of the mind that emphasized dissociation and polypsychism.[19] Jung's first term for his new, post-Freudian psychology (first used in 1913) was "complex psychology."

The fin-de-siècle was also the age of psychical research, the study of which naturally attracted such dissociationists as Flournoy and Jung. Observing spiritualist mediums in trance states, studying crystal gazing, and analyzing automatic writing were viewed by researchers as valid psychological methodologies for studying the unconscious mind.[20] With the founding of the Society for Psychical Research in England in 1882, and the copious publications of its investigators, new models of the unconscious mind emerged. The most respected model was that of the "subliminal self" by Frederick Myers (1843–1901), the "mythopoetic" (myth-making) function of which resembles Jung's later conception of a collective unconscious.[21] Jung read widely in the literature of psychical research in medical school and his 1902 doctoral dissertation cites the work of Myers and others in this school.

Given the fin-de-siècle mood of degeneration and decay and its obsession with individualism, eroticism, mysticism, and the dead, the conditions were ripe for those seeking novel paths of cultural, political, physical, and especially spiritual renewal. The great cultural historian Jacob Burckhardt (1818–1897), admired from afar on the streets of Basel by the student Jung, could observe as early as 1843 that, "Everybody wants to be *new* but nothing else."[22] Neophilia in the form of a quest for new ideas, new experiences, new academic disciplines, new therapeutics, obsessed the imaginations of many in the fin de siècle, not the least of whom was Jung.

PROTESTANT GERMAN THEOLOGY AND THE REJECTION OF THE CHRISTIAN MYTH

By the fin de siècle, traditional Western religions provided fewer and fewer answers to those in spiritual pain. Central European Jews who no longer found solace in religion sought secular pursuits such as professional scientific or medical careers, politics (primarily liberalism and socialism), journalism, or (by the late 1890s) Zionism. Some Jews chose total assimilation into Christian culture—even such "godless Jews" as Freud and Nordau considered it. But the Reconstructionist Zionism movement allowed a way for ethnic Jews to retain their cultural identity without returning to Judaic spirituality.[23]

Secularism influenced a similar dissatisfaction among Christian Europeans, particularly in the Protestant lands of the German-speaking world (Germany, Austria, Switzerland). Starting during the Enlightenment and continuing into the nineteenth century with its positivism, evolutionism, and scientism, the very foundations of the Christian myth were challenged as never before. In a work published posthumously in 1778, the Halle theologian H. Reimarus (1694–1768) presented the first, tentative, historical treatment of the life of Jesus. Described by historian Karl Löwith as reducing Christianity "to a freely created myth,"[24] the sketch caused controversy at the time, but Reimarus was merely reflecting the Enlightenment views privately expressed by the intelligentsia of his own German Europe. For example, in a letter to Herder written in 1788, Goethe remarked:

> It remains true: the fairy tale of Christ is the reason that the world is able to go forward another ten meters without anyone coming to his senses; it takes as much strength of knowledge, understanding, and wisdom to defend it as to attack it.[25]

In primarily Protestant German Europe, theologians who were acutely aware of the antagonism between Christian theology and modern scientific knowledge strayed from the Scriptures and their accessory libraries of commentaries and concordances, and instead sought novel perspectives through the study of contemporary philosophy, history, and even medicine. These historical and comparative methods were first developed into a school by the theological faculty of Tübingen University in the 1860s, and as historian Roy Pascal observes, "this historical research exerted perhaps a profounder influence on theology than the more sensational challenges of Darwinism."[26] These "theological modernists," as Pascal calls them, set out on a Promethean task to steal the fire of divinity from Christ and from Judeo-Christian traditions: "The heart of the Tübingen school was its biblical criticism, and its studies in comparative religion dispersed the solid revelations of Judaism and Christianity into a nebula of pagan sources."[27] During the Nazi era Tübingen became perhaps the dominant center for theology, for it was the base of operations for maverick Protestant theologian Wilhelm Hauer and his German Faith Movement. An English translation of two of Hauer's essays contains an introduction with a section entitled, "Tübingen—The Home of the Neo-Pagan Movement."[28] Hauer was a close associate of Jung's in the early 1930s and participated with him in a seminar on Kundalini yoga in 1934.

The search for the historical Jesus proved to be the turning point for nineteenth-century critical theology and European culture as a whole, for by the end of the century, widespread skepticism about the divinity of Jesus and the truth of the stories in the Gospels of the New Testament opened the way for social experimentation with alternative religious, neopagan, occultist, or atheistic life-styles. These new paths of social action in European culture were, in part, the result of the intellectual climate created by the widely disseminated researches of German critical theologians. These ideas were denounced from the pulpits of many a Protestant minister (and many more Catholic priests) and were debated at both formal and informal events in the highly influential social worlds of the Protestant clergy. For some Protestant ministers—such as, perhaps, Paul Jung—the compelling new image of a historical Jesus led to a secret, shameful loss of faith in Jesus' divinity that had to be hidden from family and flock.

Although European culture as a whole became more openly skeptical of its Christian myth, it was strongest in the Protestant countries where, as Weber so brilliantly argues in *The Protestant Ethic and the Spirit of Capitalism* (1905), individual decision making, belief in the rewards for one's own effort in the here and now, the relative acceptability of original thought, and the pursuit of an active life of faith were emphasized over blind adherence to traditional Roman Catholic authority and dogma. Capitalism, Weber argues, arose from this more liberal social context created by the ideals of the Protestant Reformation.

George Bernard Shaw, recognizing the historical source of these same Protestant qualities, waxed poetic about "Siegfried as Protestant." Siegfried was the very familiar Wagnerian opera hero whom Shaw considered the consummate nineteenth-century symbol of "a perfectly naive hero upsetting religion, law and order in all directions, and establishing in their place the unfettered action of Humanity doing exactly what it likes, and producing order instead of confusion thereby because it likes to do what is necessary for the good of the race."[29]

It was indeed in the Germanic lands of the Teutonic hero Siegfried and of the maturing parson's son C. G. Jung that the most serious challenge to Christianity fermented. Albert Schweitzer (1875–1965) is not shy about his openly Pietist exaltation of the German Volk and their contribution to the world in the introduction to his famous 1906 volume summarizing the research on the historical Jesus:

> When, at some future day, our period of civilization shall lie, closed and completed, before the eyes of later generations, German theology will stand out as a great, a unique phenomenon in the mental and spiritual life of our time. For nowhere save in the German temperament can there be found in the same perfection the living complex of conditions and factors—of philosophic thought, critical acumen, historical insight, and religious feeling—without which no deep theology is possible.
>
> And the greatest achievement of German theology is the critical investigations of the life of Jesus. What it has accomplished here has laid down the conditions and determined the course of the religious thinking of the future.[30]

The two most widely known volumes in this tradition were *Das Leben-Jesu* (1835) by theologian David Friedrich Strauss (1808–1873), the first true historical biography of Jesus, but read primarily only in German Protestant Europe;[31] and Ernest Renan's much more famous *Vie d'Jesu* (1863), which was less diplomatic than Strauss's work since Renan (1823–1892) was a positivist, and therefore his relatively neutral prose was more shocking to nineteenth-century individuals conditioned to reading about Jesus in only the most reverential tone.[32]

Although Renan developed a talent for Semitic philology during his early seminary training, the knowledge he gained about Biblical history conflicted with the dogma of his faith, and after sacrificing his career as a Roman Catholic priest he wrote volume after volume on religion from a positivist perspective.[33] Strauss was fired from his university position after the publication of his book and was never allowed back into academia. He became more and more critical during the remainder of his career, and in later works became a supporter of the monism of Ernest Haeckel, writing social criticism with a more biological and Social Darwinist bent.[34] Although Nietzsche decisively realized his loss of faith in Christianity after reading Strauss's book on Christ in 1865 at the age of twenty-one (indeed, he changed his formal course of study from theology to philology), he viciously attacked Strauss's later Social Darwinist works in the first of his *Untimely Meditations* (1873).[35] It took Jung until he

was thirty-seven (in 1912) to make the same decisive repudiation of Christianity as his imaginal mentor Nietzsche.

Anyone raised in educated Protestant clerical families of the
Pfarrerstand of the latter half of the nineteenth century—such
as Nietzsche (Lutheran) and Jung (Calvinist)—would certainly
know the names and ideas of Strauss and Renan, and would
perhaps have even read their works.[36] They would also at least
be aware of the thrust of the scholarly literature of the Tübingen
school. It is most likely primarily the works of Strauss, Renan,
and the Tübingen school that Jung refers to in a January 1899
Zofingia lecture where he discusses the cultural and individual
moral problems inherent in the theological literature on the historical Jesus. For any individual—particularly a young individual like the twenty-three-year-old medical student Jung—looking for cultural role models of spirituality or genius on which to
base one's own behavior, the theological literature on the historical Jesus would certainly—and ironically—turn one away from
traditional orthodox Christianity:

> I have been listening attentively to theologians for more than two
> years now, vainly hoping to gain a clue to their mysterious con-
> cept of human personality. Vainly I sought to discover where
> human personality gets its motivational force. Apparently the de-
> piction of his [Jesus's] human personality is intended to present
> us with a clearly defined image. The formation of an ethical char-
> acter should result from the holding up of the image, either
> through some secret correspondence inaccessible to perception
> or, more naturally, this image is supposed to serve as a model to
> awaken in us the impulse to imitate Christ. . . . We can find as
> much motivation in any other personality—and even more in
> those modern personalities with whom we are most familiar—
> than in the personality of Christ, who is so widely separated from
> us both in time and through the interpretations. What then is so
> special about Christ, that he should be the motivational force?
> Why not another model—Paul, or Buddha or Confucius or
> Zoroaster? . . . If we view Christ as a human being, then it makes
> absolutely no sense to regard him, in any way, a compelling
> model for our actions.[37]

In this lecture Jung indicates that, although still not willing to
let go of the mystery of Christianity, he has considered opening

the doors of his mind to non-Christian, perhaps even pagan, sources of inspiration. His reasoning was matched by thousands of others his age who asked similar questions that guided them along non-Christian paths. However, at this early age, Jung is still very much the young, bourgeois, Christian idealist, and he ridicules those who say: "'We are throwing out everything that has been built up around the figure of Jesus for eighteen centuries, all the teachings, all the traditions, and will accept only the historical Jesus'—this is not much of a feat, either, for as a rule people who talk this way have nothing to throw out in the first place."[38] However, Jung's later repudiation of orthodox Christianity has its roots in this Protestant critical theology that also redirected Nietzsche to explore pagan paths of regeneration.

In a sense, then, Schweitzer was more right than he realized when he trumpeted that German theologians would determine the course of the religious thinking of the future: Jung's psychological approach to the "God-image" (most fully argued in his *Answer to Job* [1952]), so influential in the twentieth century, rests upon the foundation of these critical theologians from whom Jung "vainly sought" guidance. Through Jung's influence on New Age spirituality, many indeed believe it is an inalienable human right to personally choose the image of one's own god (or gods). Indeed, the development of a scientific or secular psychotherapy independent of religious dogma perhaps would have been slowed without the work of these primarily German theologians.[39]

Furthermore, revising the image of Christ and the development of Christianity also allowed fin-de-siècle classicists to reevaluate pagan religion, especially the ancient Hellenistic mystery cults, which seemed to have many surface similarities with certain aspects of the early Christ cult of the Roman Empire. The ancient mysteries and their pagan gods would no longer seem as satanic and taboo to the average Christian—or at least to the learned scholar, who may even be a man of the Christian cloth himself and who perhaps fears the heretical influence of studying paganism or the social stigma attached to him by his Christian peers who investigated much safer areas of Church history. As recently as 1952 the possible personal taint of paganism was apparently still a concern for some scholars interested in writing about the historical development of Christianity in its pagan context, for as the eminent classicist Arthur Darby Nock optimistically remarks, "We have perhaps reached the point where we can think of these things *sine ira et studio*, with no desire to explain away the rise of Christianity and with no feeling that the suggestion of Hellenistic elements in it would involve something 'common' or 'unclean.'"[40]

If Jesus of Nazareth was no longer outside of time and was in fact a historical person, as these German Protestant theologians argued, how could any thinking Christian turn to Christ or his contemporary representatives in the various Christian churches for redemption or salvation? Many late nineteenth-century individuals came up with creative solutions to these problems and paved new paths to individual fulfillment—in some cases with more than a little help from some very ancient pagan sources. Indeed, philosopher of history R. G. Collingwood interprets the rise of fascism and National Socialism in the twentieth century as the direct result of the popularity of the neopaganism in the late 1800s that worshiped the power of the human will and that, in turn, arose to fill a spiritual vacuum created by this very eclipse of faith in orthodox Christianity.[41] Others, such as Marxian philosopher Georg Lukács (1885–1971), attribute the rise of fascism and Nazism to a related movement that exalted "irrationalism": *Lebensphilosophie*.

Lebensphilosophie

An additional phenomenon of the fin de siècle was the rise of a movement that was generically called *Lebensphilosophie*, or "life-philosophy." It has heretofore escaped notice that Jung was very much a product of the vitalistic Lebensphilosophie tradition that gained ascendency among the bourgeoisie in Wilhelmine Germany and greater Central Europe after 1870. Lukács correctly observes that Lebensphilosophie "nurtured an aristocratic feeling" with its appeal to direct experience and its preference for intuition over reason, since "an experiential philosophy can only be intuitive—and purportedly it is only an elect, the members of an aristocracy, who possess a capacity for intuition."[42] Lukács, who places the history of irrationalism in German philosophy and social life in a Marxian perspective of class struggle, also attributes "the conversion of agnosticism into mysticism, of subjective idealism into the pseudo-objectivity of myth" to such Lebensphilosophie movements. Mythology is thus rediscovered and given a "special type of objectivity" by the *Lebensphilosophen*, observes Lukács. Mythology thus becomes a novel—and potentially dangerous—reference point for claims about the true nature of reality or of one's own subjective experience of life.[43]

Among those in this Lebensphilosophie movement and its appeal to the primacy of direct experience and intuition, Lukács places the following: Nietzsche, von Hartmann, Paul Anton de Lagarde, Wilhelm Dilthey, Otto Weininger, Georg Simmel, Stefan George, Oswald Spengler, Max Scheler, Karl Jaspers, Martin Heidegger, Henri Bergson, and three men that Jung knew personally: Count Keyserling, Leopold Ziegler, and Ludwig Klages (who Lukács says exemplifies "prefascist" vitalism). Several of the above names have either been cited by Jung himself or by others as influences on his thought. The works of Bergson in particular, which were translated into German and published by Eugen Diederichs Verlag circa 1908, were identified by some of Jung's earliest disciples as strikingly similar to his 1912 theory of the libido as generalized psychic energy.[44]

The aristocratic values and social systems that arose logically from groupings of the proponents of Lebensphilosophie came to have a profound effect on German cultural and political life in the early twentieth century. From the fin de siècle until the end of the Nazi era there were multiple cries for new spiritual and political elites to lead the Germanic peoples of Central Europe to new "awakening" through reliance upon the more highly refined "intuitive" faculties of such specialists.[45] Jung's voice, as we shall see, may certainly be counted among them.

Freud, Haeckel, and Jung

NATURPHILOSOPHIE, EVOLUTIONARY BIOLOGY,

AND SECULAR REGENERATION

Evolutionary theory was the topic on everyone's tongue in the latter half of the nineteenth century after the publication of *The Origin of the Species by Means of Natural Selection* by Charles Darwin (1809–1882) on 24 November 1859. With Darwin's work the field of evolutionary biology was born. Darwin's highly articulated mechanistic theories of evolution surpassed all previous efforts and stimulated an interest in origins, in the creative or regenerative processes of ontogeny (individual development), and in phylogeny (the evolution of an entire species, or the birth of new ones) from the perspective of scientific materialism.[1]

Prior to Darwin, at least in the minds of many supposedly skeptical Enlightenment theorists, the only "origins" and "variations" were degenerations from perfect or ideal original types that had been created by the Judeo-Christian God.[2] Between 1790 and 1830, several different schools of *Naturphilosophie* dominated the scientific community in German Europe, in which philosophical and literary speculation was combined with empirical science.[3] These schools of Naturphilosophie have also been generically referred to as "essentialism" or "morphological idealism."

The word *archetype* was used in the mid-1800s in this Romantic biological context by the last great morphological idealist, Richard Owen (1804–1892) in his *On the Archetype and Homologies of the Vertebrate Skeleton* of 1848.[4] For most early biologists, there was no descent, as species did not evolve—especially not from one into another. The search for the *Urform* or original form (or *Urtyp*, the original type or archetype) of each species— studied by comparing similar structures in the different organisms—was known as the idealistic science (*Wissenschaft*) of mor-

phology, a term coined by Goethe in 1807. Goethe used the terms *Urbild* or "primordial image" and Urtyp, and these were later borrowed by Jung. These archetypes were eternal and transcendent, shaping man and the natural world in mysterious, but observable, ways.

Some of Jung's earliest and most powerful influences were among the speculative and metaphysical *Naturphilosophen* of the Romantic era, who after 1800 increasingly confined their studies to medical theory and practice.[5] C. G. Jung the Elder practiced medicine in this metaphysical Romantic mode. The most influential Naturphilosophen included F.W.J. Schelling (1775–1854), Goethe, Lorenz Oken (1779–1851), and a man that Goethe much admired, Carl Gustav Carus (1789–1869), a comparative anatomist who insisted that the divine essence of life would only be recognized through initiation into these insights through spiritual development:

> Insofar as the idea of life is no other than the idea of an eternal manifestation of the divine essence through nature, it belongs among those original insights of reason that do not come to man from outside. . . . These insights open up in the inwardness of man; they *must* reveal themselves and, once a man has reached a certain level of development, they *will* always reveal themselves.[6]

This view is precisely the affirmation of the belief of the Naturphilosophen that, as historian of science Timothy Lenoir succinctly puts it, "when properly trained in the method of philosophical reflection, the understanding is capable, primarily through a higher faculty of judgment, of penetrating and comprehending the structure of the life process itself."[7] Thus, as living beings at the peak of the great chain of being (as historian of ideas Arthur O. Lovejoy called it), humans were uniquely capable of an *intuitive* grasp of the very pulse of life itself in its more elemental forms. Jung's twentieth-century psychological methods—including that of "active imagination"—are direct survivors of this Romantic praxis.

As Ellenberger and others have briefly pointed out, it is with these early Romantic Naturphilosophen that we feel closest to a living tradition—albeit one that was driven underground—that resurfaces in the work of Jung.[8] Jung's own biological position and his fascination with the Urtyp seem to place him directly

within the speculative or metaphysical schools of Naturphilosophie, despite his later attempts to integrate this idealism regarding mechanistic evolutionary concepts with his own phylogenetic theories.[9] Jung mentions Carus throughout his life, in the
same breath with von Hartmann, as a major influence on his
idea of a collective unconscious, and he read both men during
his student years.[10] Jung was particularly taken with Carus's
Psyche (1846). In *Mysterium Coniunctionis* (1955–1956), a late
work that comprises *CW 14*, Jung says:

> the psychology of the unconscious that began with C. G. Carus
> took up the trail that had been lost by the alchemists. This hap-
> pened, remarkably enough, at a moment in history when the ap-
> paritions of the alchemists had found their highest poetic expres-
> sion in Goethe's *Faust*. At the time Carus wrote, he certainly could
> not have guessed that he was building the philosophical bridge to
> an empirical psychology of the future.[11]

A few of the philosophical perspectives associated with Naturphilosophie (teleology, etc.) survived in the nineteenth-century biophysics movement that Freud and Jung both encountered as part of their medical training, Freud in the 1870s and
Jung in the 1890s. Although psychiatric historian Iago Galdston
has argued for a greater acknowledgment of the influence of the
vitalism of the romantic Naturphilosophen on Freud through
his influential friend Wilhelm Fliess and his vitalistic theories
based on ideas of periodicity, polarity, and bisexuality—all familiar concepts in romantic Naturphilosophie—other scholars
such as Frank Sulloway and Paul Cranefield have challenged
this.[12] Freud's first-degree intellectual ancestors were, in part,
the reductionistic scientific materialists, including his beloved
mentor, Ernst von Brücke.[13] However, the affinities between the
Naturphilosophen and Jung, as we have seen, were acknowledged repeatedly by Jung himself. It is tempting to speculate
that the eventual incompatibility of ideas between Jung and
Freud can be attributed to their very partisan participation in a
greater battle in the biological sciences between vitalistic Naturphilosophie and mechanistic *Naturwissenschaft*.

This idealism of Naturphilosophie was eventually challenged
and successfully replaced by the work of the Kantian "teleomechanists" or "vital materialists" such as Johann Blumenbach,

Karl Kielmeyer, Johann Christian Reil, and Karl Ernst von Baer;[14] by "scientific materialists" such as Karl Vogt, Jacob Moleschott, Ludwig Büchner, and Heinrich Czolbe;[15] and by the mechanism of evolutionists such as Darwin and German zoologist Ernst Haeckel. It was Haeckel who, along with Freud (but in a different vein), took scientific renown one step further and designed secular paths of cultural renewal or regeneration that were greatly influenced by evolutionary biological training.[16]

FREUD AND PSYCHOANALYSIS

It may seem outrageous to write a book on Jung without devoting considerable space to his relationship with Freud, but that relationship has been discussed in so many other volumes, and at such great length, that it would be impossible to do justice to yet another retelling of the Freud/Jung myth here. Perhaps the best such exposition is John Kerr's *A Most Dangerous Method: The Story of Jung, Freud, and Sabina Spielrein.*[17] It is time to step out of this important—but limiting—intellectual context. Instead, I would like to briefly draw attention to some alternative perspectives on Jung's involvement with Freud and psychoanalysis that, to my knowledge, have not been adequately addressed. In particular, I am interested in the historical role of psychoanalysis as a type of Lebensphilosophie and revitalization movement in a fin-de-siècle world of degeneration and decay.

In his autobiographical statements, seminars, and filmed interviews, Jung always acknowledges that Freud was a great man and his master. It would not be unreasonable to say that Freud was Jung's first experience of someone he considered a true living genius. In this regard, their relationship was analogous to Nietzsche's relationship with Richard Wagner, "the Master." In the presence of genius, both Nietzsche and Jung wisely observed, absorbed, and imitated. After repeated exposure to the genius and his ever-changing ideas (so true to the inconstant, mercurial nature of a genius!), however, the luster of divinity began to wear. In Jung's case, it was the seven weeks he spent with Freud on ships and in America in autumn 1909, each of them analyzing the other's dreams daily; for Nietzsche, it was the repeated personal contact with Wagner and especially

43

the cult-like atmosphere the *Meister* himself encouraged at the first Bayreuth festival in 1876. Nietzsche's rupture with Wagner and Jung's dissociation from Freud are played out according to nineteenth-century scripts of "genius": once one recognizes the spark of genius in oneself, there is no longer any need for discipleship.[18]

What attracted Jung to Freud and his ideas for so many years (1905–1912) and with such devotion? Volumes have been written trying to understand this relationship. In addition to Freud's charisma as a living exemplum of "genius," I propose that Jung was attracted to the practical aspects of Freudian psycho-analysis:

> 1. as a way to overcome the onus of hereditary degeneration in his institutionalized patients (and perhaps in himself)
> 2. by its later role as an agent of cultural revitalization through its core Nietzschean themes of uncovering, bond-breaking, and of irrationality and sexuality.

Psychoanalysis was originally a supposedly medical and then a cultural movement that promised a better existence (freedom from symptoms, self-knowledge) for the successfully analyzed. Full access to memory was the key to revitalization. These memories were sexual, infantile, and above all *personal*. This was indeed the basic message of the work that drew the world's attention to Freud and his mentor Josef Breuer, *Studies on Hysteria* (1895).[19]

It has been persuasively argued that Freud's conceptualization of psychoanalysis as a cultural movement was a "scientific" path (unlike political paths such as Marxism) to achieve liberal political revolution for marginalized groups such as Jews in an increasingly conservative and anti-Semitic Vienna.[20] Yet we must remember that psychoanalysis was absolutely unknown to the common citizen of Austria-Hungary at the time. It is often still forgotten that although he named and began practicing what he called psychoanalysis in his Viennese office in the mid-1890s, until 1900 or so Freud, working in his "splendid isolation," *was* the psychoanalytic movement. By 1902 Freud found four Jewish physicians (primarily internists)—Alfred Adler, Max Kahane, Rudolph Reitler, and Wilhelm Stekel—who were interested enough in his ideas to meet with him weekly at 19

Bergasse at meetings dominated by his intellect. This was the famous Psychological Wednesday Evening Circle, which grew to seventeen members by 1906 (the year that Freud and Jung began their correspondence; they first met in early 1907). In 1908 the First International Congress was held in Salzburg, Austria, attended by forty participants from six countries and in that same year Freud's Wednesday group was renamed the Vienna Psychoanalytic Society. In 1910 the International Psychoanalytic Association was founded, with Jung as its first president. By 1910 there were two official psychoanalytic journals.

The Viennese psychoanalytic movement grew rapidly in professional circles in Europe and America only after 1911 or so, but its first fateful success was the relative conversion of a group of eminent Swiss alienists (Bleuler, Jung, and their colleagues) at the Burghölzli by 1904 or so.[21] Bleuler (1857–1939), as chief of the Burghölzli, also held the prestigious Chair in Psychiatry at the University of Zurich, which, along with the other such Chairs in Vienna and Berlin, made him and his clinic one of the top three centers of modern psychiatry in Europe—indeed, in the whole world. When Bleuler and the Swiss took Freud seriously, others in Europe and elsewhere began to do so as well.

An often unacknowledged advantage of Freud's psychoanalytic theory was its shift of etiological significance from biological hereditarian factors (degeneration) to psychodynamic ones (repressed traumatic memories, etc.) in its earliest theoretical formations. Thus one was not doomed by the fate of one's "bad blood" and indeed, one could be renewed through psychoanalytic treatment. This made psychoanalysis especially attractive to the "tainted," including those tainted in Central European culture by their ethnicity, such as Jews.[22] According to psychiatric historian Sander Gilman, Freud "repudiated the model of degeneracy" despite the other dominant nineteenth-century biological assumptions of his theories.[23]

The introduction of a method of treatment that seemed to bypass the biological fate of degeneration and perhaps even reverse its symptoms must have seemed particularly attractive to those—like Jung—who were toiling in institutions where hopeless cases seemed to be the rule and not the exception. Other than ordering and perhaps administering the usual somatic treatments (baths, electrotherapy, work therapy, opiates and barbiturates, muffs, camisoles, and other physical restraints), psychiatrists in such institutions engaged in typical medical examination and the diagnostic classification of patients. The claims that Freud was making about psychoanalysis circa 1905 would seem like a ray of hope to the psychiatrist confined with his patients in the back wards of asylums, which were storerooms of human degeneration. Dementia praecox, as Kraepelin first defined it in his famous textbook in 1893, was a degenerative psychotic disorder. Jung, despite his obvious philosophical nature, was always interested in the practical application of ideas in the form of therapeutic methods. Although in his writings at this time (1904–1905) Freud actually said very little about how one should perform psychoanalysis, Jung and his fellow physicians at the Burghölzli attempted to read between the lines of Freud's writings and practice psychoanalysis on their patients. It was the first step towards liberation from hereditary taint that Jung would complete with his own unique formulations in 1916.

The evolution of the psychoanalytic movement from one based on primarily clinical concerns to a totalizing cultural revitalization has been documented by Kerr.[24] Conspicuously few scholars have dared to examine the psychoanalytic movement from the perspective of the sociology of religion even though, as Sulloway notes, "the discipline of psychoanalysis, which has always tapped considerable religious fervor among its adherents, has increasingly come to resemble a religion in its social organization" with its "secular priesthood of soul doctors."[25]

No single study of Freud's branch of the psychoanalytic movement as a charismatic group has been conducted, although, indeed, during the rise of psychoanalysis that was precisely how many viewed the energetic efforts and genius-cult of the "secret committee" circle surrounding Freud and the worldwide movement they promoted. As many other charismatic groups did, following the urgings of the Lebensphilosophen, Freudians appealed to "experience." They believed and violently argued that one could only understand Freud or psychoanalysis after being analyzed by a Freudian psychoanalyst. This reliance upon a specialist elite—initiated into secret, "occult" knowledge—who proceeded by an essentially "intuitive" method, illustrates the basis of psychoanalysis in an "aristocratic epistomology." Ironically, given Freud's alliance with reductionist materialism and atheism, in the twentieth century the psychoanalytic movement took on a more than passing resemblance to the nineteenth-century German vitalistic or Lebensphilosophie traditions that left the confines of academia and became social and cultural movements of Lebensreform.[26] The proselytizing Freudians did give Weber, the German "father of sociology," some serious concern, for in private correspondence as early as 1907 he singled out Freud's movement as a quasi-mystical charismatic group based on the personality and ideas of a charismatic leader who was considered to have almost divine qualities.[27]

Others noted the cult-like nature of the psychoanalytic movement as well. Starting in 1909, after the Clark Conference, Freud and psychoanalysis took the American psychiatric community by storm.[28] An apocryphal story about the 1909 ocean voyage to America has Freud turning to Jung and saying, as they arrive in New York harbor, "Don't they know that we're bringing them the plague?" History cannot deny that Freudianism began to infect the North American psychiatric community after this visit, but some critics were immune to the virus. The eminent Columbia University experimental psychologist Robert S. Woodworth charged Freudian psychoanalysis was an "uncanny religion."[29] Another prominent American psychologist, Knight Dunlap, asserted in his early polemical work, *Mysticism, Freudianism, and Scientific Psychology*, that "psychoanalysis attempts to creep in wearing the uniform of science, and to strangle it from the inside."[30] Many others also rejected psychoanalysis as an atheistic and materialistic cult.[31]

HAECKEL, OSTWALD, AND THE MONISTIC RELIGION

Another European movement explicitly designed to be an "anti-Christian" path of Lebensreform was the "Monistic Religion" of Ernst Haeckel (1834–1919). From his post as professor of zoology at the University of Jena, Haeckel dominated German evolutionary biology in the second half of the nineteenth century and was the most prominent proponent of the social implications of Darwinian theory. Over the years Haeckel made many creative departures from Darwin, so many in fact that the tenets

47

of Darwinism were occluded by the renovations of Haeckelism. Since he was a prolific author, and wrote books and articles for both the scholarly and popular presses, it has been said that he dominated the discussion of evolutionary theory in German Europe by providing "the most comprehensive surveys of the Darwinist position authored by a German."[32]

Haeckel published his views on human evolution in 1868, before Darwin did so in 1871 with *The Descent of Man*.[33] Darwin himself acknowledged Haeckel's priority by several years in formulating the theory of the descent of humans from simian ancestors. Historian of science and evolutionary biologist Ernst Mayr credits Haeckel for being "perhaps the first biologist to object vigorously to the notion that all science had to be like the physical sciences or to be based on mathematics."[34] Mayr says Haeckel was the first to insist that evolutionary biology was a *historical* science involving the historical methodologies of embryology, paleontology, and especially phylogeny.

In particular it was Haeckel's influential "Biogenetic Law"— "ontogeny recapitulates phylogeny"—based on the evidence of these historical methods in biology that eventually had profound implications not only for evolutionary biology, but for psychiatry and psychoanalysis, especially Jung's analytical psychology. Haeckel considered this law as a universal truth— indeed, for much of his early career, perhaps the *only* universal truth. That the stages of individual development (ontogeny) could be shown to replicate, in order, the states of the development of the human race (phylogeny) was a compelling theory. Each adult human being, then, in both development and structure, was a living museum of the entire history of the species.

Taking this principle as a starting point, as early as 1866 Haeckel proposed a new "natural religion" based on the natural sciences, since "God reveals himself in all natural phenomena."[35] In many later publications he promoted his pantheistic natural religion based on scientific principles—a philosophy he called "Monism"—as a way of linking science and religion. Haeckel was interested in theorizing about the driving natural force of life and evolution, which he insisted Darwin left out of his (therefore) incomplete theories. His somewhat quasi-vitalistic descriptions of monism provided that. However, his first specific recommendations for a monistic religion came in 1892 in a speech in Altenburg. He argued fervently for a monism as a new faith founded on a "scientific *Weltanschauung*," thus going beyond a mere substitution of atheistic materialism for Christianity (as he was generally perceived as doing by his contemporaries and even by many historians today).

As the 1890s in Central Europe were marked by the rise of völkisch utopianism based on a rejection of the Christian myth and an emphasis on the worship of nature (particularly the sun), many took Haeckel's call for the establishment of a monistic religion in his best-selling book of 1899, *Die Welträtsel* (*The Riddle of the Universe*), to heart as a way of winning the *Kulturkampf* ("the struggle for civilization").[36] Haeckel himself exhibited a messianic zeal in promoting his logical, new pantheistic "nature religion" through lectures during which he would display his own beautiful hand-colored drawings and etchings of cells, embryos, and other natural phenomena that appealed on an emotional level to those seeking a greater meaning in life through the study of its apparent rationality, organization, beauty, and essential *unity*. It was visual material that had a striking "shock of the new" quality about it in an age without cinema or television.[37] Haeckel's bizarrely beautiful drawings of radiolarians may have been the source images for a dream Jung had as a teenager that convinced him to study the natural sciences instead of becoming a philologist or archaeologist.[38]

"In the sincere cult of 'the true, the good, and the beautiful,' which is the heart of our new monistic religion, we find ample compensation for the anthropistic ideals of 'God, freedom, and immortality' which we have lost," writes Haeckel, echoing Winckelmann's Apollonianism.[39] In a secular rite of passage, the monist is thus reborn through the rejection of the tenets of organized religion (separation), an initiation into the proof of the essential unity of matter and spirit (a period of liminality), and then participation in local societies promoting monistic ideas (reincorporation).

By 1904 groups all over Central Europe had formed and were known as the *Monistenbund* (the Monistic Alliance), with some trying out rituals based on this new scientific religion. In Jena in 1906, under the guiding hand of Haeckel himself, they were formally organized under a single administrative umbrella, like cells united within the individual identity of a larger body. The

49

ground in German Europe has long been fertile for such ideas to take root, especially among German Darwinians, for "a large number of them had abandoned the Christian religion" and, like Haeckel, spoke out against organized religion.[40] The Monistenbund attracted many prominent cultural, occultist, and scientific celebrities as members, including physicist Ernst Mach and sociologist Ferdinand Tönnies. It also attracted such luminaries as the dancer Isadora Duncan,[41] then-Theosophist Rudolph Steiner,[42] and psychiatrist August Forel (1848–1931).[43] Forel was a former director of the Burghölzli and a dominant figure in Switzerland and in the French clinical tradition at the turn of the century. Although he is best remembered for his contributions to psychiatry (and his influence on other prominent figures, such as Bleuler, Adolph Meyer, and Jung), his Monistic League affiliation and his active promotion of eugenics and Social Darwinism are rarely discussed in the historical literature of psychiatry.[44]

Although Haeckel himself was not advocating an atheistic and materialistic philosophy at this time—he preferred the label "monistic"—this was the professed emphasis of many of his fanatical cultists. Monism was the unity of matter and spirit (*Geist*). Haeckel's Apollonian ideals soon disintegrated into Dionysian excess in his view, and he soon distanced himself from his own movement. In 1911 Nobel-laureate Wilhelm Ostwald of Leipzig University, a physical chemist, became president of the Monistenbund and founded a "monistic cloister" devoted to initiating Social Darwinian cultural reforms in the areas of eugenics, euthanasia, and economics. An elite devoted to the preservation of the Monistic Religion clustered around the charismatic Ostwald and his völkisch metaphysical works.[45] Indeed, it is these works of speculative philosophy (Ostwald even embraced the term *Naturphilosophie* for this exercise) that made him an international figure long before his 1909 Nobel Prize, and many considered him a prophet of the modern age.[46]

We know that Ostwald was a significant influence on Jung in the formation of his theory of psychological types. Jung mentions Ostwald's division of men of genius into "classics" and "romantics" in his very first public presentation on psychological types at the Psychoanalytical Congress in Munich in September 1913 (published in a French translation in December of that year in *Archives de Psychologie*).[47] The classics and romantics correspond, according to Jung, to the "introverted type" and the "extraverted type" respectively. Long quotations from Ostwald appear in other of Jung's works between 1913 and 1921—precisely the period of Ostwald's most outspoken advocacy of eugenics, nature worship, and German imperialism through the Monistenbund. An entire chapter of Jung's *Psychological Types* is devoted favorably to these same ideas of Ostwald.[48] Except for a one-sentence comment that "the concept of energy in Ostwald's monism" is "an example of the superstitious overvaluation of facts," Ostwald is often cited at length and frequently favorably.[49] We have evidence that Jung read the *Annalen der Naturphilosophie* that Ostwald founded in 1901 and that contains some of his essays on his vitalistic "modern theory of energetics," which may have influenced Jung's own later theoretical work on "psychic energy."[50]

World War I and Haeckel's death in 1919 reduced the size of the movement's membership. Before his death Haeckel himself was briefly a member of the Thule Society, the secret organization of prominent nationalists that included prominent members of the National Socialist movement of the 1920s, such as Rudolph Hess. However, due to its exaltation of science over religion and the human over the divine, some early members of the German Communist Party (KDP) in places such as Leipzig were also members of the Monistenbund. East German scholars have tended to focus on Haeckel's similarities to Marxism rather than his many fundamental disagreements with it.[51] During the communist reign in East Germany Haeckel was promoted as a great hero and his home, library, and artistic productions were carefully maintained by the communist regime in a museum in Jena.[52]

Jung's "Haeckelian Unconscious" (1909–1912)

Jung read Haeckel copiously during his medical-school years: "I interested myself primarily in evolutionary theory and comparative anatomy, and I also became acquainted with neo-vitalistic doctrines," Jung reveals.[53] Haeckel dominated these sciences. Jung discusses him in his Zofingia lectures, and, given Haeckel's great fame, Jung was certain to know of the promotional efforts of Haeckel and his Monistenbund. Jung read *Die Welträtsel* in 1899 and based his own later phylogenetic theories of the unconscious on Haeckel's recommendations for a "phylogeny of the soul." Haeckel proposes a "phylogenetic psychology" as a science of evolutionary research alongside embryology, paleontology, and biological phylogeny. Jung's own comparative method for compiling historical evidence for his hypothesis of the collective unconscious (which he began in October 1909) seems to have been based closely on the methodological suggestions of Haeckel. Haeckel wrote:

> The theory of descent, combined with anthropological research, has convinced us of the descent of our human organism from a long series of animal ancestors by a slow and gradual transformation occupying many millions of years. Since, then, we cannot dissever man's psychic life from the rest of his vital functions—we are rather forced to a conviction of the natural evolution of our whole body and mind—it becomes one of the main tasks of modern monistic psychology to trace the stages of the historical development of the soul of man from the soul of the brute. Our "phylogeny of the soul" seeks to attain this object; it may also, as a branch of general psychology, be called *phylogenetic* psychology; or, in contradistinction to *biontic* (individual), *phyletic psychogeny*. And, although this new science has scarcely been taken up in earnest yet, and most of the "professional" psychologists deny its very right to exist, we must claim for it the utmost importance and the deepest interest. For, in our opinion, it is its special province to solve for us the great enigma of the nature and origin of the human soul.[54]

Just as Haeckel is responsible for introducing historical methodology to evolutionary biology, Jung introduced an analogous historical approach to the study of the evolution of the human mind and the phylogeny of its unconscious roots in the first part of his *Wandlungen und Symbole der Libido* (1911).[55] When both parts—which had originally appeared in the psychoanalytic *Jahrbuch*—were published in book form in 1912, while the main title refers to Freud's influence on Jung, the second subtitle added to the volume, "Contributions to the History of the Evolution of Thought," may be an *homage à Haeckel*. It is somewhat suspect that Jung never mentions Haeckel by name in this seminal volume although he borrows significantly from him. Jung seems to have been put off by Haeckel's scientism and his perception of Haeckel as a strict mechanist.

This is how Jung introduces his "Haeckelian unconscious":

All this experience suggests to us that we draw a parallel between the phantastical, mythological thinking of antiquity and the similar thinking of children, between the lower races and the dreams. This train of thought is not a strange one for us, but quite familiar through our knowledge of comparative anatomy and the history of development, which show us how the structure and function of the human body are the results of a series of embryonic changes which correspond to similar changes in the history of the race. Therefore, the supposition is justified that ontogenesis corresponds in psychology to phylogenesis. Consequently, it would be true, as well, that the state of infantile thinking in the child's psychic life, as well as in dreams, is nothing but a re-echo of the prehistoric and the ancient.[56]

Two pages of digression later, Jung resumes:

We spoke of the ontogenetic re-echo of the phylogenetic psychology among children, we saw that phantastic thinking is characteristic of antiquity, of the child, and of the lower races; but now we know also that our modern and adult man is given over in large part to this same phantastic thinking, which enters as soon as the directed thinking ceases. A lessening of the interest, a slight fatigue, is sufficient to put an end to the directed thinking, the exact psychological adaptation to the real world, and to replace it with phantasies. We digress from the theme and give way to our own trains of thought; if the slackening of the attention increases, then we lose by degrees the consciousness of the present, and the phantasy enters into the possession of the field.[57]

And again, in summary:

Our foregoing explanations show wherein the products arising from the unconscious are related to the mythical. From all these signs it may be concluded that the soul possesses in some degree historical strata, the oldest stratum of which would correspond to the unconscious.[58]

Haeckel thus becomes the key to understanding the biological ideas underlying Jung's hypothesis of a phylogenetic layer of the unconscious mind circa 1909. In his first published theory to this effect, in 1911, Jung introduces the idea that his phylogenetic layer contains the mythological images and thinking of pagan antiquity: therefore, when Jung's use of language is analyzed to reveal his intent, it is a decidedly pre-Christian layer that has been covered up by centuries of Judeo-Christian sediment. Although initially viewed as, perhaps, "psychosis" or "incipient psychosis" in 1909, by 1916—after repudiating the relevance of the Christian myth in his own life in 1912—Jung instead advocates *deliberately* cutting through centuries of strangling Judeo-Christian underbrush to reach the promised land of the "impersonal psyche," a pre-Christian, pagan "land of the Dead," and to thereby be *revitalized*. The völkisch implications of this will be discussed at length in chapter 5.

BUILDING THE MARXIST GOD

A third movement of secular regeneration with mystery-cult aspects, which I will mention only very briefly here, can be found in the "god-building" movement in fin-de-siècle atheistic Russian Marxism. In the 1890s, a group of Bolsheviks led by Maxim Gorky (1838–1936), a friend and disciple of V. I. Lenin (1870–1924), and Anatoly Lunacharsky (1875–1933) carried on a search in Russia for spiritual renewal through the promotion of what they called the "god-building movement" (*bogostroitel'stvo*). The god-building movement was a call for "scientific socialism" to be a religion with a god at its center who was human. Sacred cult sites devoted to a chosen atheistic genius of socialism would be established to remind the populace of the immortal, god-like achievements of a true socialist man and thereby renew the pilgrim's hopes of a better life through socialism. The god-building movement was to be a true deification of mankind and of human potential. Lunacharsky, the primary theorist of god-building, laid out the details of his ideas in 1908 and 1911 in a two-volume work, *Religiia i sotsializm* (*Religion and Socialism*). Lunacharsky's model seems to have been the cult of genius surrounding Wagner at Bayreuth (see below), as Lunacharsky was the most important promoter of Wagnerism in Russia at the turn of the century.[59]

Lenin detested the Bolshevik god-building movement, and in a 14 November 1913 letter to his friend and disciple Gorky he argues that the belief in any human god constructed by such a movement would be nothing more than necrophilia. For Lunacharsky, this new human god was to be a Marxist version of Nietzsche's übermensch, who would be "a co-participator in the life of mankind, a link in the chain which stretches towards the overman, towards a beautiful creature, a perfected organism."[60] This human god could be a political genius such as Lenin, or a scientific one, such as developed somewhat around the figure of T. D. Lysenko. Ironically, Lenin was made the first socialist deity in the years immediately following his death in 1924, as has been documented by historian Nina Tumarkin.[61]

The Nietzschean Fantasy and Spiritual Elitism

The logical extension of the hypothetical success of these secular programs for the renewal or rebirth of the individual through ostensibly secular philosophies and methodologies would be the production of a new elite that would revolutionize human culture and lead it to a new utopia. In *Also Sprach Zarathustra*, Nietzsche rhapsodized about this fantasy of a new nobility that would be "the adversary of all the rabble" and be godlike, self-creating "procreators and cultivators and sowers of the future."[62] Psychoanalysis would have its elite of analysts and enlightened analyzed patients; the Monistic Religion, especially under Ostwald, would have its eugenically pure race of scientifically minded natural philosophers; the Marxists of Russia would have their vanguard of the proletariat and Lenin as their first deity.

The Nietzschean fantasy of the creation of a "New Man," a "genius" in the New Order of a revitalized society, was therefore at the root of these and other fin-de-siècle reform movements. Historians Mosse, Jost Hermand, and others have demonstrated that this same fantasy is one of the many mystical or prefascist sources of National Socialism.

The fantasy of a new nobility took other cultural forms as well. As historian Walter Struve has amply documented in *Elites Against Democracy* (1973), the period between 1890 and 1933 in Germanic Central Europe echoed with calls for Lebensreform that entailed the institution of an "open-yet-authoritarian elite" that would lead the way.[63] This dominant fantasy of bourgeois political culture was conceived in different forms by different theorists, whether they were liberals in search of elites such as Weber or Walter Rathenau, or conservatives such as Spengler or Keyserling. Although racism and anti-Semitism apparently were not part of most elitist programs and philosophies, such a link was made by certain völkisch theorists, especially the National Socialists.

In his extensive review of elite theories, Struve discusses the phenomenon of the formation of cultural elites during this period. Cultural-elite theorists claimed that the ability to create or understand "high culture" in its many forms was a gift of an elect few who must then personify these heights of refinement for the rest of society. The political aims of such groups were often subordinate to the cultural or metaphysical training of a select few initiates who would then form the vanguard for a new cultural and spiritual reawakening of Germany and the world. Of his many examples, Struve cites the highly influential circle around German poet Stefan George (the *Georgekreis*) as perhaps the best-known group.[64] Keyserling and his School of Wisdom is also included among Struve's examples of cultural elites.

Rather than referring to this phenomenon as cultural elitism, perhaps for some of these philosophies and cults the term *spiritual elitism* is more appropriate. The cults of spiritual elitism that I discuss in this book went beyond just the development of an aesthetic appreciation of "high culture" that the George circle (after 1904), in particular, emphasized. These spiritual elites often began as (and often remained) small but influential groups that deliberately separated themselves from greater society in order to develop their own spirituality through metaphysical or neopagan practices. Contact with a transcendental or mystical realm is a central component of becoming a member of a spiritual elite.

In German Europe during the period 1890–1933 we find these as the most prominent of the spiritual elites: the Cosmic Circle circa 1900, which included George and Klages; Keyserling's Darmstadt circle at his Wisdom School; elements of the Bayreuth Circle surrounding Wagner; hierarchical occultist organizations such as the many spiritualist circles and the Theosophical and Anthroposophical Societies; elite members of the leadership of the Monistic Religion movement; certainly the völkisch and Asconan cults (to be discussed later); and even, arguably, the disciples of Gross (a Bohemian circle) and Freud (a bourgeois circle).

The psychoanalytic method is a highly subjective one based on the intuition (acquired through analysis and training) and the authority of the analyst to interpret a mysterious realm of human experience (the unconscious mind) in others. As such, as Lukács has shown, the social organizations around persons who claim intuitive abilities—which sets them apart from others—only developed through a defining "extraordinary experience" (the personal or training analysis) and quickly became aristocratic elites with primarily self-serving economic and political agendas.

As we shall see, Jung's later claims for individuation (rebirth) through analysis (initiation) may be rooted in the same fin-de-siècle fantasy, one of a society influenced by a few perpetually creative, individuated human beings. However, as a form of spiritual elitism, Jung's self-proclaimed "silent experiment" in group psychology would be based on *religious* elements explicitly borrowed from the ancient Hellenistic mysteries and their modern occult imitators.[65]

Fin-de-Siècle Occultism and
Promises of Rebirth

THE VAST MAJORITY of fin-de-siècle persons seeking spiritual renewal that they could not find in Judaism or Christianity, in millenarian political movements such as Marxism or anarchism or völkisch utopian movements (such as Pan-Germanism, Pan-Slavism, or Zionism), or in secular movements such as Haeckel's and Freud's, became involved in occultism.[1] Although one could be "magnetized" by a professional mesmerist or undergo diagnosis and treatment by one of the dwindling number of phrenologists still in clinical practice, be manipulated by an osteopath, aligned by a homeopath, or submit to the medical therapeutics of "nerve specialists" such as hydrotherapy, electrotherapy, or rest cures and a high-fat diet,[2] these methods were the result of a relationship between an *individual* patient and an *individual* professional healer and were largely dissociated from ongoing communities with totalizing philosophies of life and networks of reinforcing social support. The sense of belonging to a community with shared goals and shared iconographies of the transcendent was the key element drawing millions to occultism. Each occult group could be distinguished by its unique image of the great chain of being and each designed its social norms and guided its economic activities accordingly. Furthermore, except for a few noted occult elites (such as the Order of the Golden Dawn in England in the 1880s, etc.), the larger occult movements were egalitarian. One did not have to be an artist, a writer, an appreciator of Wagnerian opera, the holder of a college degree, one of the wealthy, or an Oscar Wilde–like "aesthete" of any type to participate in most widespread occult movements. All that one needed was faith in the occult doctrine.

Outside of politics (which was still largely the occupation of men, except for radical groups that had substantial female membership, such as the anarchists or Marxists or groups that comprised the proto–women's movement), occultism was the most readily available vehicle of self-transformation open to the average fin-de-siècle individual of either gender, but it was particularly valuable for women. Participation in occult organizations, often at the highest levels, was a way for women in particular to experience social status and power denied them in other religious contexts, and to express gender-related social concerns and thereby influence society as a whole.[3]

Interestingly, a similar sociological dynamic may have been instrumental in the rise of the Christ cult in the polytheistic Roman Empire, for both the pagan apologist Celsus and the Christian apologist Origen of the third century C.E. specifically cite the leading role of women of the upper classes in the development of Christianity.[4] Such intelligent, wealthy women were also instrumental in the development of the social organizations surrounding the cults of the saints, whose widely distributed cult sanctuaries were the object of pilgrimages throughout the Roman world of late antiquity. Tombs, shrines, and their sacred relics generated enormous income for early Church organizations and bishoprics from fee-paying pilgrims seeking transformative experiences while praying and fasting in the presence of the decaying body part or former personal possession of a Christian saint or martyr.[5] However, once the bureaucratic organs of Christian authority began to ossify in the fourth and fifth centuries, unlike their pagan predecessors, "only among Christians is women's religious leadership an issue. Only Christians both attempt, sometimes successfully, to exclude women from religious office and community authority and argue about it."[6]

Of the many occultist movements of the nineteenth century, the intimately connected spiritualist movement and one of its offshoots, the Theosophical Society, deserve special comment as both were influential in very different ways on the life and work of Jung. An additional movement with mystical or occultist elements, Wagnerism, also deserves some comment, as does the broader völkisch movement that sprang up in German Europe at the turn of the century. These, too, as we shall see, were significant influences on Jung.

The fin-de-siècle trend towards extra- or anti-Christian movements that advocated personal religion was commented on by sociologists other than Germans such as Tönnies and Weber. In

France, Emilie Durkheim (1858–1917) observed early in his seminal work, *The Elementary Forms of the Religious Life* (1912), that, "Not only are these individual religions very frequent in history, but nowadays many are asking if they are not destined to be the pre-eminent form of the religious life, and if the day will not come when there will be no other cult than that which each man will freely perform within himself."[7]

Addressing this same issue in a 1974 essay on "The Occult and the Modern World," the eminent historian of religion Mircea Eliade discusses the personal religious practices of the occult revival of the 1960s and 1970s with reference to its similarities to the occult revivals of the nineteenth century. At issue in both the nineteenth- and twentieth-century occult revivals is not just a rejection of the Christian myth, but a desire to return to the example provided by the ancient mystery cults of the Hellenistic world:

> What is more general is a rejection of Christian tradition in the name of a supposedly broader and more efficient method for achieving an individual and, by the same stroke, a collective *renovatio*. Even when these ideas are naively or even ludicrously expressed, there is always the tacit conviction that a way out of the chaos and meaninglessness of modern life and that this way out implies an *initiation* into, and consequentially the revelation of, old and venerable secrets. It is primarily the attraction of a *personal* initiation that explains the craze for the occult. As is well known, Christianity rejected the mystery-religion type of secret initiation. The Christian "mystery" was open to all; it was "proclaimed upon the housetops," and Gnostics were persecuted because of their secret rituals of initiation. In the contemporary occult explosion, the "initiation"—however the participant may understand this term—has a capital function: it confers a new status on the adept; he feels that he is somehow "elected," singled out from the anonymous and lonely crowd. Moreover, in most of the occult circles, initiation also has a superpersonal function, for every new adept is supposed to contribute to the *renovatio* of the world.[8]

The membership of these various groups overlapped considerably, as their common promise of *renovatio* (renewal or rebirth) was the main attraction. Many individuals had contemporaneous involvement in two or more occultist movements and would drift in and out as desired. What could not be found in one organization could perhaps be found in another. There were several fin-de-siècle movements of renovatio through secret initiation into "old and venerable secrets" that were well known to Jung and the classical scholars of his day.

Spiritualism

It appears that in all eras of human history, and at all levels of societal complexity, there have always been individuals who have been regarded as specialists in communicating with the gods—or, more prevalently, with the dead. These mediums between the sacred and the profane traditionally enter altered states of consciousness in which they engage in direct dialogue with extramundane entities or in which they seem to become possessed by such entities, thereby allowing the otherworldly being to speak through the body and voice of the medium. This form of religious activity is prevalent even today.[9]

In pagan antiquity, the average individual in the Greco-Roman world would be very familiar with the entranced female oracle of Delphi, the Pythia, and a teeming multitude of soothsayers, diviners, exorcists, and others who claimed to receive special messages from beyond, which—for a fee—could be imparted to those seeking counsel.[10] It has been argued that there is evidence that the pagan world primarily considered Jesus of Nazareth a magician (*magus*) with special powers to command spirits and heal others through exorcisms (much like shamans in traditional societies), but that these images of Jesus were deliberately destroyed by the early Christian Church.[11] Since most early Christians were converted from Greco-Roman paganism, there is evidence that the induction of altered states of consciousness ("trances"), so characteristic of some Hellenistic oracular traditions, also played a role among some early Christian prophets.[12] This occult underworld of mediumship, possession, and exorcism has always existed in Europe despite attempts in various epochs (primarily by orthodox Christian and Communist elites) to erradicate it.

The loosening of the bonds of orthodox ecclesiastical authority in Europe following the Enlightenment allowed for more implicit tolerance of ecstatic or charismatic Christian activity from this "occult underground"[13] as long as the authority of organized Christian churches was not directly threatened.[14] The belief in the Christian afterlife remained strong among the majority of nineteenth-century individuals, and with the vicissitudes of numerous wars, incurable diseases, and high infant, child, and maternal mortality rates, there was a great hunger to maintain relationships with the deceased despite the barrier of physical death.

Given the weakening of traditional ecclesiastical authority and the greater emphasis on personal decision making and individual action so typical of the Protestant ethic, it is no coincidence that the spiritualist movement arose in a largely Protestant America, a "Protestant Empire," to use historian Sydney Ahlstrom's metaphor, whose increasingly distant ties with the Old World made the spirit world seem so accessible—especially since it did not require clerical intercessors.[15]

The spiritualist movement traces its origins to the rappings and other phenomena attributed to spirits of the dead in the house of the Fox sisters of Hydesville (near Rochester), New York, in 1848. Once the Fox sisters determined that the rapping noises emanating from the walls and floors of their house were a kind of Morse code (the telegraph was a relatively new phenomenon at that time), they began what the early historian of modern American spiritualism Emma Hardinge referred to in 1869 as "the achievement of a telegraphic communication between the visible and invisible worlds."[16] Once word spread that there was an easy method of contacting the dead, others attempted the same telegraphic method used by the Fox sisters and subsequently developed innovations (automatic writing, crystal gazing, possession trances, etc.) that led to new social and economic elites. A new social role emerged—that of the medium—who could dissociate and allow the spirits to speak directly through their vocal apparatus (the "mental medium") or induce spirits of the dead to write on slates, move planchettes, levitate furniture, or play accordions in the presence of flabbergasted clients (the "physical medium"). The most charismatic of this new class of mediums could in many instances attract a large following and become quite wealthy. By 1850 there were spiritualist circles surrounding mediums throughout New England and in other parts of the United States. By the early 1860s, spiritualism had become prominent in the parlors and salons of Europe. The horrific casualties of the American Civil War (1861–1865) stimulated the spiritualist movement in the United States, so that by the fin de siècle perhaps millions of individuals had, at one time or another, participated in such circles.

The allure of spiritualism was its simplicity and egalitarianism: almost anyone could attempt, with some margin of success, direct communication with the dead, and spiritualist circles and (later) organizations and "churches" (with Christian-oriented services) were open to anyone with "the will to believe," to use the words of William James (1842–1910), a student and explorer of the phenomena of spiritualism.[17] Seances could be held right in your own home at any time. The bureaucracy of Christianity, with its layers upon layers of mediators and its official discouragement of direct mystical experience, could thus be circumvented. Christianity supplied the theory; spiritualism provided the praxis, with technical assistance from Mesmerism, which taught hypnotic-induction techniques that could be used by aspiring mediums for entering trances.[18] Jung, as is well known, had a very early interest in spiritualism and attended many seances throughout his life. Jung used such hypnotic induction procedures to place his cousin Hélène Preiswerk into mediumistic trances during the seances he attended with her in the 1890s.

Women rose to positions of significant influence in spiritualist circles. It was there that they could assume spiritual leadership roles denied them by the patriarchal structure of the Roman Catholic and Protestant churches. Women not only comprised the majority of the most gifted mental and physical mediums, but they provided the organizational and financial support of the movement as well. Perhaps the single most influential woman in occultist circles in the nineteenth century (and in many ways, arguably the most influential woman in Europe and America at the time), was a Russian emigré to the United States, Helena Petrovna Blavatsky (1831–1891), spiritualist medium and the founder of the Theosophical movement.

Blavatsky and Theosophy

Little is known of the first four decades of Blavatsky's life, although several biographers have attempted to fill in the gaps.[19] She arrived in New York in the summer of 1873, apparently penniless, traveling steerage from France. Blavatsky was, by all accounts, a highly intelligent and canny individual, and before long she had secured an apartment on Irving Place in New York where she conducted spiritualist seances as a source of income. She produced both physical and mental phenomena: levitation, materializations, and messages from the deceased. Like most mediums, she had a "control" or "spirit guide," whom she met while in her trances and who supplied her with information from the beyond. Her first control was named John King, and she often referred to him as her "Holy Guardian Angel." Later, whenever she entered trances she began to have more frequent contact with a collection of guru-like "ascended masters," known as the "brothers" who were spiritual beings that existed in their sanctuary in Tibet. She became their disciple, their *tulku*, and began to dispense their teachings to her clients.

By 1875, after a glowing report on her mediumistic powers in the *New York Daily Graphic* by investigative journalist Colonel Henry Steel Olcott, her circle grew enormously popular. In addition to her seances, her salon hosted lectures by experts on archaeology and on various world religions and mystical traditions (including the ancient Hellenistic mystery cults). Aided by Olcott (whom she had won over as a loyal disciple) and W. Q. Judge, Blavatsky decided to found an organization that would promote her ideas. She chose the name *theosophy* ("knowledge of God" or "divine wisdom") for her doctrine, which was based on the idea that all of the world religions and spiritual traditions down through history were derived from a long-lost "secret doctrine" that had been revealed to her by these divine beings. The secret doctrine included detailed explanations of the karmic rules of reincarnation, of the cosmic memory bank known as the "Akashic records" that could be consulted by those suitably trained to learn the history of an individual soul or the arcane history of the human race (the lost continents of Lemuria, Atlantis, and the "root races" of mankind, which prominently described the "Aryan race"). The organization developed into a densely hierarchical secret society that required initiations into mysteries that at each level provided the "keys" for understanding more and more of the essence of life: the secret doctrine itself. Initiates into Theosophy were trained to develop their powers of clairvoyance, telepathy, teleportation, mediumship, and other psychic powers. At the highest levels of initiation they were trained to enter visionary trances to commune with spiritual beings who acted as spirit guides or gurus.

In this same year—1875—in New York, Blavatsky formed the first of many branches of the Theosophical Society that by 1900, would be spread throughout North America, Europe, and especially India, where large ashrams housed thousands of Theosophists engaged in spiritual practices and served as a world headquarters for the Theosophical Society. Exact numbers are impossible to determine with accuracy, but it would be safe to say that at its height, during the period of Annie Besant's leadership following the death of Blavatsky in 1891, the Theosophical movement directly involved hundreds of thousands, if not peripherally millions, of individuals.[20] Prominent among these were poets Lord Tennyson and W. B. Yeats; the young Mahatma Gandhi; the Goethe scholar, spiritualist medium, and founder (in 1913) of the rival occultist tradition Anthroposophy, Rudolph Steiner; and Thomas Edison, who was busy in the 1890s trying to invent a phonograph-like device to speak to the spirit world. (The Theosophical Society continues to thrive today, but with nowhere near the widespread cultural influence it wielded circa 1900.)

After founding the Theosophical Society in 1875, Blavatsky began writing her first Theosophical work, *Isis Unveiled*, which was published in New York in 1877. This work is not strictly an outline of Theosophical doctrine, which was still in its formative stages, but instead a survey of the Western occult traditions of alchemy, astrology, ritual magic, and witchcraft, and also Eastern philosophies. In this work she first puts forth the core Theosophical concept that a secret spiritual science and doctrine was known to the ancients but largely lost to us except in its diluted form in the teachings of the world's great religions. However, a secret spiritual brotherhood of adepts would transmit this doctrine to select individuals to translate for the masses of their respective ages. Such enlightened initiates, according to Blavatsky, included Jesus, the Buddha, Confucius, Zoroaster, Mohammed, and, of course, Blavatsky herself. Blavatsky claimed to be in trance-communication with these ascended masters who, indeed, were kind enough to write whole pages of *Isis Unveiled* for her while she slept(!). Blavatsky was well aware of the ancient Hellenistic mystery cult of Isis, and with the help of one of her spiritual gurus, she was initiated into these mysteries through a trance that allows Isis to merge with her and inspire her automatic writing. Automatic writing was also implicated in her more mature work, the two-volume Theosophical masterpiece, *The Secret Doctrine* (1888), which is her contribution (as she states in her preface) to the occultist tradition of "the great Adepts of the Aryan Race." This is how Blavatsky describes her method for writing *Isis Unveiled*:

> I am solely occupied, not with writing *Isis*, but with Isis herself. I live in a kind of permanent enchantment, a life of visions and sights, with open eyes, and no chance whatever to deceive my senses! I sit and watch the fair good goddess constantly. And as she displays before me the secret meaning of her long-lost secrets, and the veil, becoming with every hour thinner and more transparent, gradually falls off before my eyes. I hold my breath and can hardly trust to my senses! . . . Night and day the images of the past are marshalled before my inner eyes. Slowly, and gliding silently like images in an enchanted panorama, centuries after centuries appear before me . . . I certainly refuse point-blank to attribute it to my own knowledge or memory. I tell you seriously I am helped. And he who helps me is my Guru.[21]

Blavatsky's refusal to attribute her "images of the past" to previously learned material in her personal memory is a pivotal issue that concerned Jung as well. Cryptomnesia—"hidden memories" that one is not even aware of—was a lifelong problem for his hypothesis of a collective unconscious. Like Blavatsky and her two "mahatmas" or spiritual masters, Jung, too, would undergo visionary time travel to antiquity and be assisted by a series of imaginal figures, most notably his spiritual guru Philemon. These issues will be discussed in detail below.

It is commonly suggested that Jung's assistant and intimate companion Antonia Wolff (1888–1953), who first entered Jung's life in 1911, was the one who introduced him to Eastern philosophies and astrology. Although this suggested influence may be overstated, her sources of information on these subjects probably came from these ubiquitous Theosophical publications.

Part of the story of Theosophy's rapid spread throughout the fin-de-siècle world is due to the technological advances in printing that began to bear fruit by the 1880s, just at the time that the Theosophical Society came together as an active, purposeful organization. In 1846 the rotary press was invented (and with it the linotype machine, automatic paper feeders and cutters, cheap newsprint and paper, and the halftone process for reproducing photographs). Publications such as daily newspapers that could only manage say, a 25,000-copy circulation in the 1850s found themselves with manageable circulations of more than a million by the 1890s.[22] Both popular science and occultist publications became especially common and readily available in all urban areas of Europe by the end of the century.

The Theosophical Society played a key role in the dissemination of occultist doctrines at the turn of the century through its numerous local societies in America, England, Germany, Austria (Vienna), Switzerland (Zurich), and even Russia.[23] These local groups sponsored lecture series, classes, and especially distributed the numerous publications of the Theosophical Publishing Society based in London and Benares, India. Starting in the 1880s (and continuing today), any clerk, waiter, businessman, high-society maven, domestic servant, housewife, university professor, politician, institutionalized mental patient, indeed anyone, could easily find the ubiquitous Theosophical publications that summarized in plain language (but with a Theosophical slant) the ideas of Hinduism, Jainism, Islam, Buddhism, Western European philosophy, astrology, Neoplatonism, Egyptian religion, vegetarianism, the New Testament gospels and apocrypha, astral projection, clairvoyance and telepathy, polytheistic Greco-Roman religions, the Greek magical papyri (including the "Mithraic Liturgy"), Gnosticism, alchemy, Hermeticism, and the various Hellenistic mystery cults—just to name a few of the many topics covered in these productions.

The great philosophies of the East were distilled and marketed en masse to Western civilization to a greater extent than had ever been possible at any previous time in history. The enormous Theosophical publishing machine thus set the stage for the familiar countercultural fascination with these topics, beginning in Ascona, Switzerland and Munich circa 1900, and continuing through the beatniks, hippies, Greens, and New Agers of more recent times.[24]

In German Europe, Theosophical books, pamphlets, and especially periodicals began to appear in abundance in the late 1880s in original German editions. *Die Sphinx* began publication as a monthly in Leipzig in 1886. *Theosophisches Leben*, a monthly periodical, was published in Berlin between 1898 and 1920. Other prominent Theosophical periodicals that were widely available were *Die Gnosis* (Vienna, 1903); *Der theosophische Wegweiser* (Leipzig, 1898); *Lotusbluthen* (Leipzig, 1892, under the editorship of Franz Hartmann); *Metaphysische Rundschau* (Gross-Lichterfelde, 1896); *Prana* (Leipzig, 1909); *Theosophie* (Leipzig, 1910); *Der Wanderer* (Leipzig, 1906); and *Zentralblatt für Okkultismus* (Leipzig, 1907).

Additionally, from 1896 to 1904, the "Eugen Diederichs Verlag: Publishing House for Modern Endeavors in Literature, Natural Science, and Theosophy" was in full operation in Leipzig under the direction of the völkisch pantheist Eugen Diederichs. After moving to Jena in 1904, Diederichs played an important role in the dissemination of occult, mythological, and völkisch literature as well as the finest examples of German "high culture." Diederichs will be discussed at length in a later chapter.

In 1910 the Theosophical Publishing Society began publishing an enormous number of books on astrology, making such works available to the German-speaking public on a mass scale that was unprecedented. Interestingly, Jung's first mention of his study of astrology is in a 12 June 1911 letter to Freud.[25] By 1916 Jung could remark, "The truth is that astrology flourishes as never before. There is a regular library of astrological books and magazines that sell for far better than the best scientific works."[26] Jung is perhaps refering here to these very Theosophical publications. A superb bibliography of these obscure Theosophical and other (especially völkisch) books, journals, and pamphlets that appeared in German during this period can be found in a recent book by Nicholas Goodrick-Clarke.[27]

Although much of the information in these Theosophical works was based on mere fluff, a more valuable portion of it had previously existed only in dry, obscure scholarly volumes weighted down with footnote apparatus containing untranslated citations in Latin, Greek, Hebrew, Arabic, and other forbidding languages. Besides the occultist mishmash of this more serious material in the journals, certain gifted Theosophical authors could produce scholarly works on archaeological, mythological, religious, or occultist subjects that were still accessible to the common individual without a university education who sought extra-Christian sources of spiritual inspiration. Such a talented scholar and writer was G.R.S. Mead (1863–1933).

Mead remains an enormous—but still unacknowledged—influence on Jung. Jung's personal library contains no fewer than eighteen different scholarly studies written by Mead, all published by the Theosophical Publishing Society.[28] Many of these were volumes in the Theosophical Society's *Echoes from the Gnosis* series, and thus Mead was Jung's "stepping-stone to higher things."[29] Mead was a true Theosophist and viewed his impressive scholarly work as a personal path to spiritual renewal and wisdom (gnosis). All of his writings are focused on bringing the reader closer to his or her own personal mystical experience of gnosis through the study of the ideas of the ancient adepts. For Mead, as for Jung, scholarship was holy work. Jung's post-Freudian work (after 1912), especially his theories of the collective unconscious and the archetypes, could not have been constructed without the works of Mead on Gnosticism, Hermeticism, and the Mithraic Liturgy. These works were primarily responsible for giving Jung the key to the importance of Gnosticism and Hermeticism for his historical study of the unconscious. Jung cites Mead regularly in his works starting in 1911, and continues to throughout his entire lifetime. Near the end of his life Mead made several trips to Küsnacht-Zurich to visit with Jung. However, documents concerning the nature of their personal relationship have not yet come to light.

WAGNER AND WAGNERISM

It is difficult for those of us living in the 1990s to understand the tremendous cultural, musical, political, and religious impact that Richard Wagner (1813–1883) had on the entire Western world in the late nineteenth century. The German composer's influence extended far beyond just the musical innovations in his various operas (most notably the Ring Cycle and *Parsifal*). Wagner was a learned man and was greatly influenced by the philosophical works of Schopenhauer, the ancient Greek trage-dists, and especially the nineteenth-century literature on Teu-tonic or Germanic myths and legends ("German antiquity," as he referred to it), which made up the bulk of the titles in his private library in Dresden early in his creative career, and which are now in the museum of his former house, Wahnfried, in Bayreuth.[30] His numerous essays and commentaries on a wide variety of social, political, cultural, philosophical, and racial is-sues are contained in a sixteen-volume collection that rivals the size and scope of Jung's *Collected Works* or Freud's *Standard Edi-tion*.[31] Generations of disciples and cultural historians have gen-erated an immense secondary literature of scholarship and pseudo-scholarship on the life and work of this remarkable man,[32] who may be said to rank with Darwin and Marx in terms of the pervasiveness of his contemporary influence on Western culture.[33]

Wagner deliberately lived out the Romantic fantasy of a "phi-losopher-genius." He envisioned the operatic spectacles of his later decades as great Teutonic mystery-plays, and he sought to unite the soul of the German peoples through his music and Germanic mythological themes. Thus, after the Prussian unifica-tion of Germany in 1871 under the iron fist of Bismarck, Wagner found a national climate fanatically supportive of his Pan-Ger-manic utopian dreams. For years he petitioned various prospec-tive patrons for the money to build a special *Festspielhaus* in which to exclusively produce his grand operas. A town between Bavaria and Prussia was decided upon, and after four years of construction Wagner's theater-temple of the German nation had its inaugural festival in the summer of 1876.

Bayreuth became the only place to witness "the Master" in performance. Like Eleusis in ancient Greece, which was the only place in the pagan world to experience the mysteries of the Two Goddesses (Demeter and Persephone) and therefore unlike all other mystery cults with their multiple initiation sites, Bay-reuth became *the* place—especially if you were of Germanic her-itage—to be reborn. Nowhere was this idea more clearly stated than in a book by an Indologist from Vienna University, Leopold von Schröder, entitled *Die Vollendung des arischen Mysteriums in Bayreuth* (*Fulfillment of the Aryan Mystery at Bayreuth*) published in Munich in 1911. As von Schröder exuberantly explains:

> After a separation of more than five thousand years, the Aryan tribes can meet together for the first time in a designated place to contemplate the ancient mysteries fulfilled in a new form. Thanks to Wagner, Bayreuth has become the center of all the Aryan peoples, and this very fact guarantees an astonishing supremacy to Germany and the Germans.[34]

The fantasy was that one could emerge from Wagner's *Festspielhaus* and feel totally transformed, indeed as if a stranger to oneself, and many persons could attest that this did indeed happen. Wagner and his theater-temple performances became the center of a mystery cult with mystical overtones. People from all over the Western world made pilgrimages to Bayreuth, and during the annual festivals when the Ring Cycle would be repeatedly performed, Bayreuth took on the aura of a sacred shrine. Mark Twain irreverently recounted his 1891 visit to "the shrine of St. Wagner," feeling at times "like a sane person in the community of the mad" in Bayreuth, but he was not immune to its transformative mystical effects. Twain described it as "one of the most extraordinary experiences of my life. . . . I have never seen anything so fine and real as this devotion."[35]

Wagner, and especially the small Bayreuth Circle of zealous disciples after his death, distinguished between mere Wagnerites who came to his performances just to be seen or to hear the music, and then true Bayreuthers who were informed listeners and who constantly strove for an intellectual and spiritual understanding of its underlying philosophical and artistic meaning. Wagnerism soon became a worldwide phenomenon with hundreds of local chapters and associations throughout Europe and the United States. At the turn of the century, all the major universities in German-speaking countries (including Basel University, where Jung was studying) maintained Wagner associations of students, many of which were based on Pan-Germanic sentiments and its increasing association with anti-Semitism. Periodicals appeared such as the esteemed *Bayreuther Blätter*, which Wagner himself contributed to, or England's *The Meister*, in which the social, political, and especially the hidden mystical meanings in Wagner's literary and musical works were analyzed. Theosophists read between the lines of libretto or bars of music for elements of the eternal secret doctrine, for was not Wagner one of the true initiates along with Jesus, the Buddha, and Blavatsky? Nationalistic Germans sought cleansing and transcendence through his Bayreuth festival mystery initiations and were inspired by Wagner's essays advocating Pan-Germanism and anti-Semitism. In his commentary on Wagner's Ring Cycle designed to raise the level of consciousness of the average Wagnerite, George Bernard Shaw spoke of Wagnerism in Theosophical or mystery-cult language that appeals to the vanity of spiritual elitism:

> It is generally understood, however, that there is an inner ring of superior persons to whom the whole work has a most urgent and searching philosophic and social significance. I profess to be such a superior person; and I write this pamphlet for the assistance of those who wish to be introduced to the work on equal terms with that inner circle of adepts.[36]

Wagnerism became an influential social and political movement and a modern mystery cult based on the idealized image of Wagner and his life, and on his home and sacred theater-temple site in Bayreuth. For many, Wagnerism became a form of personal religion with a totalizing worldview and promise of transformation.[37] Even Cosima Wagner, his long-time mistress and then wife could repeatedly feel the numinous element in Wagner, revealing in her diaries, "That it is his art which found the note for the mystery of faith which possesses me, and that the wordless fervor of my soul sings through him—oh, what bliss, what grace!"[38]

In the twentieth century the elite Bayreuth Circle led by Cosima Wagner had become so openly anti-Jewish and nationalistic that in the 1920s Adolf Hitler, then the leader of the National Socialists, would make several pilgrimages to Bayreuth and kiss the dying hand of Houston Stewart Chamberlin (1855–1927), next to Cosima Wagner the dominant figure in Bayreuth after Wagner's death. When Hitler came to power in January 1933 he elevated Bayreuth to the position of an officially funded sacred national shrine and attended the annual festivities.[39] In 1923, after viewing Wagner's grave, an emotionally overwhelmed Hitler vowed to Cosima, Siegfried Wagner (her son by Wagner), and Siegfried's wife, Winifred, "Out of *Parsifal* I will make a religion!"[40] Thus during the 1930s, the Bayreuth festivals had become the mysteries of the Nazi state.

We have no concrete evidence, but given his frequent travels to Germany from neighboring Switzerland, it is quite probable that Jung visited Bayreuth. What *is* certain is that Jung was a Wagnerite and was smitten with *Wagnerismus* early in his psychiatric career and perhaps throughout his life. In a 13 June 1909 entry in her diaries, Jung's former patient, psychiatric assistant, and intimate companion Sabina Spielrein describes an intimate moment with Jung in 1907 or 1908 in which Jung's eyes "fill with tears" of understanding as she excitedly describes the "psychological" nature of Wagner's music. She says that both she and Jung found that they liked the opera *Das Rheingold* the best, and that this common love for Wagner was evidence that their "souls were profoundly akin."[41] Trigant Burrow, an American psychiatrist who trained with Jung for a year (1909–1910) in Küsnacht-Zurich, delightedly "sitting at the feet of this Swiss Seer" as he puts it, reveals in an 11 December 1909 letter to his mother that he attended a performance of Wagner's *Der fliegende Holländer* (*The Flying Dutchman*) with Jung.[42] Jung's friend, colleague, and biographer Laurens van der Post speaks of "Wagner's equinoxial music, which Jung himself, insofar as he allowed himself music, preferred."[43]

Wagner's selective treatment of Germanic mythology in his later operas often focused on the heroic figure of Siegfried, a symbol that became dominant in Jung's personal and professional lives. During a critical period at the beginning of his "confrontation with the unconscious," Jung has dreams of the murder of Siegfried that parallel events in the last opera in Wagner's Ring Cycle, *Götterdämmerung*. Jung personalizes this Wagnerian material in the self-analysis of his dream.[44] Siegfried as a "sun hero," a reborn son/sun like the Egyptian Horus (represented by a solar disk) is analyzed in his 1912 book, *Wandlungen und Symbole der Libido*.[45] A more intimate connection is, again, to be found in the diaries of Spielrein, who is, on and off, deeply in love with Jung and fantasizes about giving birth to a male Germanic child named Siegfried. Jung and Spielrein discuss this Siegfried fantasy of a common love-child in letters to each other dated as late as January 1918, long after they parted company, in which Spielrein refers to "my Siegfried problem."[46] Although Wagner had sired two daughters with Cosima while they were both married to others, Siegfried Wagner (1869–1930) was also conceived during this extramarital affair. By 1907 or so, this was the sort of well-known "celebrity gossip" that the average person knew about Wagner, and such a fantasy of the eventual heroic triumph of the genius to win his mistress and sire a Siegfried seems to have been one of the scripts through which Jung and Spielrein enacted their relationship. After becoming famous for his own theories and his own movement after World War I, Jung's home in Küsnacht-Zurich very much became the Bayreuth of the Jungians, the only place to experience the master in performance. Such was the impact of Wagner on the mnemonic consciousness of his initiates that his dramatic brand of Germanic mythology could be played out in the lives, dreams, and souls of individuals such as Jung and especially Spielrein, who was of Jewish descent.

Wagnerism was only one of the paths to völkisch renovatio. Others are outlined in the chapter that follows.

Völkisch Utopianism and Sun Worship

NINETEENTH-CENTURY Europe witnessed a revival of what has been termed völkisch ("folkish") movements, nationalistic groups bonded together by a common ethnic and cultural identity (the idea of Volk) and seeking a political and cultural return to an idealized past or golden age. A new utopian golden age of the Volk could then be established. Heredity became infused with social and political aims, and supported by "scientific" medical and psychiatric theories of hereditary degeneration. Many völkisch groups—especially Pan-German and Pan-Slavic groups—elevated notions of racial purity to a quasi-scientific, quasi-mystical ideal. Although Zionism is essentially a völkisch movement, as historians such as Carl Schorske have pointed out, it is primarily the Pan-Germanic movement of the nineteenth century that is meant by the term *völkisch* or *Volkstumbewegung* ("völkisch movement").

On and off since the sixteenth century wistful reference has been made to "the old Teutons" that are the mythic ancestors of ethnic German peoples. As with most national myths, very little in fact is known about the beliefs and actions of the actual Teutonic or Germanic tribes of pagan Europe. Most of the information upon which such fantasies are based comes from an ancient Roman source: the *Germania* by Tacitus. Historian Ekkehard Hieronimus has summarized the interest in Germanic religion since the recording of Germanic sagas and myths by Snorri Sturulson (1179–1241) until what he claims is the "late" (nineteenth-century) interest of German scholars in the history, life, and thought of the German Volk due to the "strong fixation of historians on the Greco-Roman area as the only world of culture."[1] Such nineteenth-century research on the Germans, Hieronimus argues, was adopted by neopagan groups devoted to reexperiencing the Germanic mysteries. Indeed, a return to the golden age and "natural" life of the Teutons has frequently been invoked by German groups appealing to renewal or rebirth.

In Germany and Switzerland, the Pietist movement in the early eighteenth century used such völkisch appeals in its efforts to revive religion by fashioning a specifically German brand of Protestantism. By the mid-1700s, according to Hermand, it was "often difficult to distinguish between the concepts of an 'inner' and an 'outer' fatherland in Pietist writings."[2] Furthermore, "in these circles the secularization of a number of bourgeois/protestant concepts such as the family, the community, and the notion of a sacrificial death was characterized by an increasing patriotism which drew parallels between Christ's martyrdom and the martyrdom of national heroes like Siegfried or Arminius."[3] These very same themes of sacrificial death and the identification of the Christian god with the Teutonic god would resurface prominently two centuries later in a signal work by a descendant of German Protestant pietists—Jung's noted *Wandlungen und Symbole der Libido* (1912).[4]

In the 1800s, the idea of uniting the dozens of German principalities and other political units was based on an appeal to reunite and revive the ancient Volk. Pan-Germanism spread throughout all the traditionally German areas as well as throughout Austria-Hungary and even in Switzerland. Before Pan-Germanism developed into a predominantly anti-Semitic movement at the end of the century, many secular Jews seeking greater political influence through more thorough assimilation into Christian circles (rather than further segregation through Reform Judaism) participated in Pan-Germanic activities. The young Freud was such a person, briefly caught up in Pan-Germanism during his student years. However, his experience with anti-Semitism during this time "put an end forever to the phase of German nationalistic enthusiasm through which he passed in early years."[5]

By the fin de siècle, small German völkisch groups, influenced in no small part by the occult revival of the nineteenth century, began forming throughout Germany and Austria-Hungary, and especially in Switzerland. Germanic seekers of renewal and rebirth who had perhaps started out in spiritualism or Theosophy began to become attracted to philosophies based on more mundane nationalistic, hereditarian, or anti-Semitic principles of renovatio. Thus, as in the case of the prominent Viennese occultist Friedrich Eckstein (1861–1939), participation in a Wagnerian *Bund* led to further metamorphoses into spiritualism and Theosophy.[6] Eckstein was the founder of the prominent Vienna Theosophical Society in 1886 and was a close associate of composers Anton Bruckner and Gustav Mahler, Viktor Adler (leader of the Austrian socialists), Franz Hartmann (a prominent Theosophist), and Steiner.

It was not long before völkisch groups began to adopt the methods of spiritualism and Theosophy to seek rebirth. Such an evolution seemed natural:

> The uses of theosophy for political purposes consisted in its universal and non-Christian perspective upon the cosmos, against which the sources of Teutonic belief, customs and folk-identity could be located. Indeed the very structure of theosophical doctrine lent itself to *völkische* thought. The implicit elitism of the mahatmas with superhuman wisdom corresponded to the whimsies of a master race; the notion of an occult gnosis in theosophy, notably its obscuration by Christian orthodoxy, accorded with the attempts to ascribe a long pedigree to German *völkische* nationalism, especially in view of its really recent origins.[7]

Circa 1900 völkisch groups that promised direct initiations into the mysteries of the ancient Teutonic tribes began to appear. Admittedly, most of these neopagan groups were rather fluid and left little recorded history, but as Hermand notes, this period was clearly marked "by a veritable deluge of the most diverse groups, parties, fraternities, and lodges" in which it is apparent that "the politically immature bourgeoisie has become intoxicated with Teutonism."[8] The innumerable pamphlets and booklets of völkisch groups have been lost to us as the ephemera or "fragments of a faith forgotten," but some scholars have devoted attention to what little remains.[9]

Common characteristics across many of these groups seem to have included the following: a rejection of Christianity in favor of a mystical Volk connection with the ancient Aryan peoples (especially the Teutons); nature-worship, hiking, and nudism;[10] neopagan rituals (dancing around bonfires, magical ceremonies invoking the Norse—and sometimes Greek—gods); the study of the Aryan roots of occult symbolism (such as the swastika, popularized in the writings of Blavatsky, and the Norse runes, which the Nazis later used as symbols on their uniforms and to represent various Nazi associations); the idealization of the ancient Teutonic warrior (such as Siegfried); the exaltation of "the deed" (*die Tat*) over mere words; the preference of intuition over rational judgment; techniques for the direct experience of God without Christian intercessors; a fascination with the medieval Grail legends and Wagner's *Parsifal*, with the purity of Aryan blood depicted as the grail that must be sought and protected at all costs;[11] and, of course, anti-Semitism.

The best documented circle is the Guido von List Society, founded in Vienna in March 1908. Von List (1848–1919) was a Viennese mystic and magician who, among many other activities, participated in ancient German pagan rites in a Hungarian castle with his colleague Jorg Lanz von Liebenfels and playwright August Strindberg. As a youth List had an unusual experience in a cathedral that he later interpreted as his call to become an initiate into the mysteries of the ancient Teutons. He experienced a pagan mystery initiatory experience, he claimed, as a fourteen-year-old exploring the subterranean crypts of St. Stephen's Cathedral in Vienna. Through visionary experiences, the secret wisdom of the ages were passed down to him from the ancient Aryan brotherhood of spiritual beings known as the *Armanen*. The similarities between this idea and Blavatsky's secret doctrine and brotherhood are many, for indeed List and his closest followers had extensive connections with Eckstein's Vienna Theosophical Society and other Theosophical groups.

Among the important information imparted to List was the true occult interpretation of the Nordic runes. Also, since the "life-force" of the universe flowed from nature, List believed that being close to nature brought one closest to "truth." List trained his closest disciples to enter trances and attempt to listen to nature and "see with one's soul." The highest initiates in the hierarchical List society were said to possess the capacity to communicate directly with the spiritual Teutonic brotherhood of the Armanen. In "Ariosophist" organizations such as this, then, völkisch utopian theories are pursued with practical methodologies derived from spiritualism and Theosophy.

"We must read with our souls the landscape which archeology reconquers with the spade," List often said about his method of achieving "*Intuitionen*," according to his biographer Joseph Baltzli.[12] Such a methodology finds similarities with those of the Romantic Naturphilosophen, Blavatsky circa 1875 and, circa 1916, Jung and his technique of "active imagination."

During this time other Germanic neopagan groups appeared that also completely rejected Christianity and sought to replace it with a revival of old Germanic "Wotanism," or "Odinism," or new forms of Germanic paganism. These groups began to appear with great frequency after the death of theologian Paul de Lagarde (1827–1891), who called for the establishment of a neopagan "Germanic Religion" in his seminal völkisch text of 1878, *Deutsche Schriften*. His essay in this volume on "The Religion of the Future" (*"Die Religion der Zukunft"*), may be said to be the blueprint for all the neopagan religious Lebensreform groups that would appear in the early twentieth century (including perhaps, if indirectly, Jung's). Lagarde placed the doctrine of the promise of the rebirth (*Wiedergeburt*) of the individual at the center of his new natural religion. As Fritz Stern notes, Lagarde "regarded rebirth as an incontrovertible fact of all human experience, hence as a valid basis as his hope for a religious revival."[13]

Some of these groups limited their membership to those of "pure" Aryan stock, pledged to keep the blood of their children pure, and resurrected ancient Germanic pagan holidays to replace Christian holy days in which the sun and nature were worshiped and at which animal sacrifices were offered. Perhaps the oldest of these groups was the Germanic Faith Fellowship (*Germanische Glaubensgemeinschaft*) of Ludwig Fahrenkrog, a professor of art, which was founded in 1907. Fahrenkrog's group grew out of Haeckelian monism as it emphasized the worship of the "life-principle" in all matter. However, an additional feature was a belief in the immortality of the soul. As the Germanic Faith Fellowship completely repudiated Christianity, the Bible was replaced with the sacred texts of the Elder Edda and the writings of Goethe.

The most influential of these neopagan groups was the Tannenberg Foundation of General Erich Ludendorff and his wife, Mathilde von Kemnitz, a famous völkisch writer, who became Frau Ludendorff in September 1926. A widely used symbol by the Tannenberg Foundation (and by many others of these neopagan groups) was the sacred hammer of Thor. General Ludendorff was an early ally of Hitler's and assisted him in the planning of the botched 1923 Munich putsch. However, in the late 1920s and early 1930s Ludendorff became an opponent of Hitler, and therefore when the latter assumed power in January 1933 the Tannenberg Foundation was banned. Nonetheless, in the years following the Great War Ludendorff campaigned for a new pantheistic Aryan-Germanic faith based on the old Indo-Aryan *Urreligion*. As Paul Banwell Means describes it, "In line with the Tannenberg program for the restoration of the ancient Germanic religion, General Ludendorff, accompanied by a few young men, would from time to time retire to the forests near Munich, where a bonfire was lighted and a horse sacrificed in honor of Thor, the god of Thunder."[14] As Ludendorff knew, horse sacrifice seems to have played a central role in the ancient religion of the Indo-Europeans.[15]

Other neopagan groups that wanted to institute a new Germanic paganism were the Society of German Believers (*Deutsch-gläubige Gemeinschaft*, founded in 1911); the Nordic Faith Fellowship (founded in 1927); the All-Aryan federation; the German Church of God; the Thule Society (which counted Haeckel and Rudolph Hess among its many members); the Midgard Federation; and the Society of Native Religion (*Heimatreligion*). The Germanic Faith Movement of J. W. Hauer, founded in 1933, differed from these groups only in the extent to which Wotanism would replace Christianity: Hauer and many in his movement opted for keeping some elements of Christianity, but this primarily entailed recasting Jesus as the "Aryan Christ."

THE SCIENTIFIC JUSTIFICATION OF SUN WORSHIP: NINETEENTH-CENTURY COMPARATIVE PHILOLOGY AND MYTHOLOGY

Perhaps the most central neopagan element in German völkisch movements was sun worship.[16] The worship of the sun was extolled as true ancient Teutonic religion, and while it was primarily a literary device and a powerful rhetorical metaphor for the experience of God, actual solar-worship rituals did take place among some völkisch groups during the annual summer solstice, especially between the very early 1900s and the 1930s. As a direct consequence of this Germanic neopaganism, in the 1930s the Nazi government banned the celebration of traditional Christian holidays and instead substituted others more appropirate for the "New Germany." The summer solstice was designated as one of these holidays.[17]

From at least the Romantic era, sun worship was offered by prominent Germans as the most rational alternative to Christ worship. Sun worship was the image at the center of fantasies of a return to "natural" paganism. This was most clearly stated by Goethe:

What is genuine except everything excellent which stands in harmony with purest nature and reason, even today serving for our highest development! And what is counterfeit except everything absurd, empty, dumb, everything which bears no fruit, at least no fruit of value! If the genuineness of a biblical document is to be decided by the question whether everything it tells us is true, then in a few points the genuineness of even the Gospels could be doubted. . . . And yet I consider the Gospels, all four, to be genuine; for there works within them the reflection of a majesty which preceded from the person of Christ. It is of such a divinity as any the deity has ever assumed upon earth. If I am asked whether it accords with my nature to give him reverent worship, then I say, "Completely!" I bow before him as the divine revelation of the highest principle of morality. If I am asked whether it accords with my nature to worship the sun, then I say once again, "Completely!" For it, likewise, is a revelation of the most high, and in fact the mightiest which has ever been granted us mortals to perceive. I worship it in the light and creative power of God, whereby alone we live and move and have our being, and all plants and animals together with us.[18]

Hence we have the noble Goethe equating Christ with the sun and making an appeal to the rationality of pagan sun worship. These same pagan sentiments stayed very much alive in the underground of German society in the nineteenth century, never far below the surface of "the bourgeois-Christian world," and erupted openly during the fin de siècle with völkisch neopaganism.

These neopagan groups were influenced—indeed legitimized—by the solar interpretation of the roots of all myths

81

(especially hero myths) from their alleged ancient Aryan sources by the German Sanskrit scholar and comparative mythologist Friedrich Max Müller (1823–1900).[19] His famous essay, "Comparative Mythology" (1856), helped lead the way for the creation of the academic discipline of the history of religions. Indeed it was Müller who named this new discipline the "science of religions" or the "comparative study of religions."[20] In England he is often credited for single-handedly founding the academic disciplines of comparative philology, comparative mythology, and comparative religion in that country.[21]

The "Solar Mythologists" promoted a theory that dominated the study of the history of religion in Central Europe and that was hotly debated (especially by skeptical British scholars such as Andrew Lang) until Müller's death in 1900.[22] Müller argued, on philological and comparative mythological grounds, that the appearance and disappearance of the sun, its worship as a source of life, was the true basis of most, if not all, mythological systems, especially among the Aryan peoples. "Is everything the Dawn? Is everything the Sun? This question I had asked myself many times before it was addressed to me by others. . . . but I am bound to say that my own researches lead me again and again to the dawn and the sun as the chief burden of the myths of the Aryan race."[23] Müller could even say, "Why, every time we say 'Good Morning' we commit a solar myth."[24] All European religions, therefore, could be traced back to the worship of the sun of the ancient "Aryans," a term that Müller argued should be used instead of "Indo-Europeans" to distinguish what was, in his opinion, a dichotomous division in European culture of persons depending on their "Aryan" or "Semitic" language.[25]

As historian Léon Poliakov has argued in his magisterial work, *The Aryan Myth: A History of Racist and Nationalist Ideas in Europe* (1971), these essential cognitive categories were accepted by almost every cultivated European by 1860,[26]due to the influence of Müller (in England and Germany) and his friend Ernest Renan (in France).[27] Müller and Renan had many predecessors, such as Friedrich von Schlegel, who resurrected the term "Aryan" in 1819 from the works of Herodotus, Joseph von Görres, Friedrich von Schelling, Hegel, Jacob Grimm, and a favorite of Jung's, Friedrich Creuzer.

This familiar schematic distinction between Indo-European or Indo-Aryan and Semitic that formed the central cognitive categories of nineteenth-century European thought arose primarily from the work of linguists in the highly respected science of comparative philology. In the scientific search for the ultimate origins of the human race, it is often forgotten what a central role comparative philologists played in intellectual circles in the decades before Darwin shifted this "grail quest" to evolutionary biology and ethology. It was thought that by comparing and analyzing the similarities and differences between languages that the original families of humankind could be identified. In the eighteenth and early nineteenth centuries this was, of course, traced by many scholars to mythic Biblical genealogies. Although Sir William Jones, a Chief Justice of India and a founder of the Royal Asiatic Society was the first to remark, in 1796, on the possibility that Sanskrit was the root language of Latin, Greek, Persian, and the modern European languages, the term "Indo-European" was coined in 1813 by Thomas Young in a review of a multivolume work (*Mithradates*, by Adelung) that linguistically analyzed the Lord's Prayer in its various translations.

However, it was German comparative philologist August Schleicher (1821–1868) who systematically analyzed the linguistic history of each of the Indo-European languages and attempted to reconstruct the earliest Indo-European form of the words being compared. Schleicher's was the first attempt at a reconstruction of the original, proto–Indo-European language that is the concern of historical linguists today.[28] It was Schleicher who first drew the diagram of the "genetic tree" model to illustrate the differentiation of language in the Indo-European family. According to linguistic historian J. P. Mallory, Schleicher was inspired by his "profound interest in biology."[29] These diagrams were later widely adapted by Blavatsky and the Theosophists to give the appearance of seriousness and scholarly legitimacy to their genealogical trees of the "esoteric phylogeny" of the "five root races" of mankind. The "first sub-race" branch of the "fifth root race" was the "Aryan race" according to the spiritual "mahatmas" Koot Hoomi and Morya in their spiritualist communications from beyond to Blavatsky's colleague A. P. Sinnett, and it was the race that contained the highest spirituality of all mankind.[30]

The methodology of philological science began to be used for purposes other than tracing the structural and historical origins of language. Etymological analysis, for example, could unlock the secrets of mythology. An early example of this approach is the 1835 analysis used by Jakob Grimm to trace the hidden presence of Teutonic gods and spirits in Germanic folklore.[31]

Müller—a philologist and Sanskrit scholar himself—built on the work of Schleicher, Grimm, and others by using etymological analysis as a way to uncover details about the ancient religions of the Aryan, Semitic, and "Turanian" (Mongolian, Chinese, etc.) peoples. His hypothesis was that these three areas were not only great language centers but also important religious centers. Linguistic and religious experience were thus intertwined. Müller also firmly believed that one could set aside the world of rationality and think the thoughts and feel the feelings of the ancients by learning to read "childish fables . . . in their original child-like sense."[32] Müller often noted that to the rational mind of the average bourgeois-Christian scholar, the tales in the "sacred books of the East" would seem like nothing more than gibberish. Therefore, to some degree, the scholar must fantasize about the material he is studying and make it come to life in a playful, childlike way without allowing rational cognition to impede access to the living religious thoughts of the ancients.

Müller dominated the scholarship on comparative mythology of his age, and as a prime force behind establishing the scientific status of the Aryan myth, his many works were used as a source of inspiration for many educated Volk. Since the work of comparative philologists like Schleicher and Müller established linguistic and mythological differences between the Indo-European and Semitic peoples dating back thousands of years, after Darwinian evolution through natural selection entered the world in late 1859 it was only natural that these scientific findings would be integrated with new biological speculation about origins.[33] With the shift of focus to the problem of biological inheritance and evolution, it was a very short step to infer that the seemingly vast differences between the Indo-Aryan or Indo-European peoples and the Semitic peoples were due to essential biological differences between these groups. The actual geography or natural world one lived in could also shape heredity, for the "soft-inheritance" transmission of such experiential factors was advocated by Darwin under the name "pangenesis." Basic biological units of heredity independent of environmental influences ("hard inheritance") were not posited until 1883 (August Weismann's "germ-plasm") and beyond ("Mendelian units" in 1900, and "genes" in 1909).[34] This line of thought made perfect sense in the evolution-mad late nineteenth century and formed the central cognitive categories of thought of that era. As we shall see, thanks to the scientific stature of philologists like Müller and Renan, it also formed the essential basis of Jung's early work.

The grounding of mythological, religious, and linguistic differences in biology, therefore, became the raison d'être of völkisch mysticism. The scholarship on ancient Aryan origins provided the content for elaborate fantasies about ancient Teutonic origins and religion that served political, social, and spiritual Lebensreform goals in fin-de-siècle German Europe. Once the biological factor had entered into the discussion about "origins" in a meaningful way with Darwin and Haeckel (after 1860), völkisch individuals could claim that their anti-Semitism had a *scientific* basis. Additionally, some felt they could advocate a literal return to the rituals of sun worship and find additional scientific support to justify their behavior and beliefs.

Haeckel, in fact, did not hide his anti-Semitic bias, and therefore, given his tremendous international stature as a noted scientist at the turn of the century, he bears significant responsibility for adding the "biological inferiority" twist to the Jewish question. Like others in the "völkisch establishment," such as Lagarde and Chamberlain, Haeckel gave public support to the fantasy of an Aryan Christ. Although the primary goal of Haeckel and the Monistic League was to deny even the reality of the historical Jesus, a secondary goal was at least to revise the essential myth in Aryan terms for those völkisch persons who were too uncomfortable with the idea of completely repudiating the trappings of Christianity. In the best-selling *The Riddle of the Universe* (1899), Haeckel first attacks the "pseudo-Christianity" of the nineteenth century, then introduces a "more credible" story: that Jesus was only half-Jewish because he was the

85

bastard son of a Roman officer who seduced Mary, his mother. The full passage needs to be read to be believed:

> The statement of the apocryphal gospels, that the Roman officer Pandera, was the true father of Christ, seems all the more credible when we make a careful anthropological study of the personality of Christ. He is generally regarded as purely Jewish. Yet the characteristics which distinguish his high and noble personality, and which give a distinct impress to his religion, are certainly not Semitical; they are rather features of the higher Arian [sic] race, and especially of its noblest branch, the Hellenes.[35]

Here we see yet again the "tyranny of Greece over Germany." If despite the superior program of monism many still desired to embrace Christian symbols, then Haeckel's logic was to let them worship a Hellenic Christ, not a Semitic one.

Sun Worshipers in German Europe

Eugen Diederichs and the "Sera Circle"

The best documented neopagan cult devoted to sun worship was that of Eugen Diederichs (1867–1930) of Jena, a prominent publisher of völkisch material in books and his journal, *Die Tat* ("The Deed"), although apparently he was not politically attracted to anti-Semitism or Nazism.[36] Due to his keenly felt calling to resurrect German culture through publishing German mystics such as Meister Eckhardt, Angelus Silesius, and Jacob Böhme, works on Germanic folklore (including fairy tales and mythology), and a wide variety of theosophical, anthroposophical, and mystical "nature religion" or pantheistic tracts, after establishing the Eugen Diederichs Verlag in 1896 he became perhaps the most highly influential aristocratic patron of the neo-Romantic and völkisch pantheistic elements in Central Europe. To be published by the Eugen Diederichs Verlag was to be accepted in intellectual circles in a way that publishing perhaps the same occultist material by the Theosophical Society would not be, although the publications of the Theosophical Society were nonetheless also widely read. Although other neoconservative publishers also helped to legitimize the ideas that laid the groundwork for the rise of National Socialism in the 1920s, the

Eugen Diederichs Verlag was the highly respected voice of neo-paganism and the religious—not the political—arm of the great völkisch movement.[37]

Like any educated Germanic European from this era with interests in Lebensphilosophie in its manifold forms, Jung's personal library contains many volumes published by the Eugen Diederichs Verlag, including editons of the Eddas and books by one of the analysts of the Zurich School who defected with Jung in 1914, Adolph Keller.[38] Indeed, Diederichs was perhaps the most important disseminator of Lebensphilosophie in Central Europe from 1896 to 1930. Diederichs personally chose the types of volumes he wished to reprint and that he felt should be read by his contemporaries, and his agenda was to deliberately resurrect the vitalism of the Lebensphilosophen to "help [it] achieve a greater contemporary effect."[39] Not surprisingly, many of the topics converge remarkably with the sources of Jung's intellectual influences. For example, in 1901 Diederichs began printing a multivolume series under the title *Gott-Natur* (*God-Nature*) that reprinted the works of Giordano Bruno, Paracelsus, Lamarck, Goethe, Carus, and other early nineteenth-century proponents of speculative Naturphilosophie upon which Jung built his theory of the archetypes.

Like Jung, Diederichs believed, in his words, that "being truly religious means being irrational" and that his calling as a publisher was to "push the irrationalist character of religion into the foreground" and assist in creating "a new mythos" or "mystique" for the spiritual reawakening of the Germanic peoples.[40] According to historian Gary Stark, "Diederichs hoped to complete the process and create a new religion in Germany in which God would be replaced by the irrational, vital life-force of the cosmos" and that therefore "genuine religion must be grounded on a subjective, intuitive metaphysics."[41]

As Lukács argues in *The Destruction of Reason*, such Lebensphilosophie movements that appealed to the reliance upon intuition instead of reason inevitably also required an initiated elite that had developed such intuition to its highest and that therefore would be capable of leading the rest of society to redemption. Indeed, Diederichs called for just such a spiritual aristocracy to lead what he termed an "organic people's state" (*organischer Volksstaat*) after the Great War. Diederichs's brand of spiritual elitism was a familiar one and echoed that of Jung, Keyserling, the Monistenbund, the Tannenberg Foundation, and others (including, it may be argued, the Nazi SS). Using the seventeenth-century Rosicrucians, in part, as his model, Diederichs's metaphysically trained spiritual elite was to be, in his words, "a secret yet open *Bund* of those who have the *Geist*."[42] Here again is the fantasy so prevalent in Germany between 1890 and 1933 of an "open yet authoritarian elite." Jung, as we shall see, likewise envisioned an elite "few" who would develop their "function of intuition" and lead a utopian "analytical collectivity" from his base of operations in Küsnacht-Zurich after the war.

Also like Jung, Diederichs was virulently anti-Christian in his agenda and preferred a return to the nature religion of the ancient Teutons. Following his spiritual mentor Lagarde, whose works he reprinted, Diederichs wanted to see a new Germanic religion rise up in Central Europe based on the central experience of rebirth (*Wiedergeburt*). Other than his works on Germanic folklore and mythology, which gave his readers just such a view of the ancient Teutons, Diederichs fought orthodox Christianity by deliberately reprinting texts that the Church had long considered heretical. Although classical scholars such as Hermann Usener, Wilhelm Bousset, Albrecht Dieterich, and Richard Reitzenstein had all begun to publish densely inaccessible scholarly studies on Gnosticism starting in the late 1890s, Diederichs widened the distribution of these ideas (as did the Theosophical Society at this time) by publishing works for the lay public on Gnosticism between 1903 and 1910. Jung owned a later (1924) study of these early heretical groups by Arthur Drews.[43] Diederichs also commissioned works by prominent but unorthodox theologians with Monistenbund connections to deny the historical existence of Jesus. The two most controversial were Drews's *Die Christusmythe* (*The Christ Myth*) of 1909 and Albert Kalthoff's *Das Christusproblem* (*The Problem of Christ*) of 1903, but he published nine other such works which, in the words of Stark, he hoped "would eventually reduce the figure of Christ to a mere symbol for the cosmic life-force."[44] Jung cites these works in his own, especially in *Wandlungen und Symbole der Libido*, which, as I will argue in later chapters, was a work that repudiated orthodox Christianity and promoted the völkisch mysticism of sun worship.

By the 1890s many völkisch individuals believed the sun "the sole God of the true Germans."[45] There was much talk of the Germans finding their "place in the sun." The swastika, an ancient Indian symbol of the continual regeneration of life (at least according to völkisch scholars), was placed within a circle symbolizing the sun and depicted on a flag as early as 1908.[46] Diederichs expressed the beliefs of many during this time: "My view of God is this, that I regard the sun as a source of all life. . . . I only want to experience within me the growth of the *Geist*."[47]

To experience this life-giving spirit (*Geist*) within, neopagan sun-worshiping rituals were performed by the "Sera Circle" (founded in 1904 by the not-so-youthful thirty-seven-year-old Diederichs) and its "German Youth Movement" members beginning in 1906.[48] These were rituals that involved hiking (a staple of the famous *Wandervogel* movement, which was founded "officially" in 1901), German folk dances, and a modern re-creation of an ancient Germanic festival of the "changing sun" (*Sonnwendfest*). As Stark describes it, "Carrying banners depicting the ancient Germanic 'sun wheel,' the group sang Germanic ballads, recited pantheistic poems and 'fire prayers,' and ended their celebrations by leaping through a bonfire."[49] These same rituals were repeated during the celebrations of the summer solstice after the Nazi government made it a state holiday in the 1930s. As late as 1918, in a talk before the students of Munich University on "Science as a Vocation," Max Weber lauded the religious feeling behind the rituals of the German Youth Movement as "something very sincere and genuine."[50] Weber—like many others, including, it may be argued, Jung—was impressed by the depth of spiritual fervor of the neopagan movement and its potential for a revitalization of Germanic culture even if fault could be found with its other aspects.

The merger of two ancient Indo-Aryan symbols—the Germanic sun wheel and the swastika—formed the basis of the symbolism of the National Socialist movement starting circa 1920. The Nazi flag, of course, contained a red field that symbolized the purity of Aryan blood, at the center of which was a white solar disk representing the sun. The swastika in the center of this white disk symbolized the recurrent energies of life, and, in order for the initiate to experience the life-force radiating from the sun in the center of the flag, the swastika was to be visually imagined as actually spinning around in this solar disk. Due to the influence of prominent persons such as Diederichs and his noted authors, interest in the Indian mandala symbolism of the ancient Aryans began to spread in Germanic Europe. Jung, for example, drew his first mandala in 1916 and then later expounded upon its significance as a symbol of the self or the "god-image within."[51] Mandala-like solar-disk symbols appeared on posters, arm bands, banners (such as that of the Sera Circle), the covers of publications, and elsewhere throughout Central Europe during these years. The circle as sun was *the* symbol of God to many intoxicated by völkisch utopianism and Naturreligion.

Haeckel, Ostwald, and the Monistenbund

In addition to the contributions of comparative philology and comparative mythology, which were true sciences in the early nineteenth century sense of the word, völkisch mysticism found further scientific backing in the ideas of Haeckel, when, by the late nineteenth century, German notions of science had come to mean the methodologies of the natural sciences, such as biology and comparative anatomy. It was Haeckel who reaffirmed, in his esteemed scientific opinion, that "a spirit [*Geist*] lives in all things."[52] It must be emphasized that Haeckel himself was *not* advocating a materialistic monism (unlike, for example, his eminent scientific critics such as Ludwig Büchner): "An immaterial living spirit is just as unthinkable as a dead, spiritless material; the two are inseparably combined in every atom."[53] Diederichs published many monist authors and invited them to his sun-worshiping rituals with his youthful disciples. Diederichs's journal, *Die Tat*, which he took over in 1911, was originally founded in 1909 as a monist publication.

Not surprisingly, Haeckelian monism, the "scientific religion," and völkisch nature worship were fused in the minds of many at this time.[54] In his important study, *The Scientific Origins of National Socialism*, Gasman calls Haeckel "the Volkish Prophet" and persuasively documents his thesis that "proto-Nazi Volkism did not invariably originate in opposition to science and modernism." Gasman argues that "one of the earliest, if not the earliest comprehensive program embodying National

VÖLKISCH UTOPIANISM

Socialist principles in Germany" was Haeckel and Ostwald's Monistic League, and therefore National Socialism arose "in the context of a movement which prided itself on its scientific ideology and modern view of the world."[55]

Part of this "scientific" monistic program was the view that if one was to insist on having a religion, sun worship was the most rational choice of all other alternatives (especially Christianity). In *The Riddle of the Universe*, Haeckel makes the following argument, additionally adopting the scientific doctrine of geological *vulcanism* or *plutonism* (the theory of the igneous origin of the Earth) to justify sun worship, and sounding, indeed, very much like Goethe:

> The sun, the deity of light and warmth, on whose influence all organic life insensibly and directly depends, was taken to be such a phenomenon [of naturalistic monotheism] many thousands of years ago. Sun-worship (solarism, or heliotheism), seem to the modern scientist to be the best of all forms of theism, and the one which may be most easily reconciled with modern Monism. For modern astrophysics and geogeny have taught us that the earth is a fragment detached from the sun, and that it will eventually return to the bosom of its parent. Modern physiology teaches us that the first source of organic life on the earth is the formation of protoplasm, and that this synthesis of simple inorganic substances, water, carbonic acid, and ammonia, only takes place under the influence of sunlight. . . . Indeed, the whole of our bodily and mental life depends, in the last resort, like all other organic life, on the light and heat rays of the sun. Hence in the light of pure reason, sun-worship, as a form of naturalistic monotheism, seems to have a much better foundation than the anthropistic worship of Christians and other monotheists who conceive of their god in human form. As a matter of fact, the sun-worshippers attained, thousands of years ago, a higher intellectual and moral standard than most of the other theists. When I was in Bombay, in 1881, I watched with the greatest sympathy the elevating rites of the pious Parsees, who, standing on the sea-shore, or kneeling on their prayer-rugs, offered their devotion to the sun at its rise and setting.[56]

Solar worship was also an obsession of the Nobel-laureate Ostwald, who mentioned it in many publications of his between

1910 and 1920. "The sun is the mother of us all, and we must be grateful to it for everything that we are and do," Ostwald says in an article published in *Die Sonne* (*The Sun*), the publication for the Monistenbund's youth movement.[57] Like the other monists who published in the many journals of the Monistenbund, Ostwald, too, blended solar symbolism and völkisch neopagan sentiments with prophesies of the rebirth or regeneration of Germany.

Following Haeckel's suggestions, the Monistenbund cosponsored with Diederichs sun-worshiping festivals based on their romantic concept of the ancient Teutonic "changing of the sun" ritual on the biannual solstices (21 June and 22 December). The journal *Der Monismus* (*Monism*) published the text of the reputed liturgy of the sun worshipers in an issue that appeared in 1910. The reference to the "children of the sun" (*Sonnenkinder*) comes directly from the work of the matriarchical cultural theorist Johann Jakob Bachofen (to be discussed in a later chapter) and the vulcanist or plutonist geophysical theory of Buffon and others (see below) that the earth was originally a fireball that had been flung off the sun:

> We are all children of the sun. Out of its womb our planet was born. An eternal law of nature compels us to be within its sphere and influence. The immensity of space is cold, still and lifeless— our luminous mother sun, warming and ripening our fruit, appears as the simple, true element of life. Our ancestors knew this in ancient times. Thus their justifiable joy when the sun made its slow victorious spiral across the sky. They then remembered that all those trees, which concealed their greenness in the wintertime, were consecrated to the god, Wotan.[58]

Keyserling and the School of Wisdom

Those Germanic souls for whom sun worship struck a deep chord and who may not have been comfortable in the growing fusion between the Monistenbund and the politics of German nationalism between 1914 and 1920, or those who perhaps no longer found Theosophy or Anthroposophy attractive, could find a home in Darmstadt after the Great War, with the circle gathered around Keyserling (1880–1947), who has been called "the most influential guru of Central Europe between 1918 and 1933."[59] After almost dying from a dueling wound in 1900, Keyserling began to explore philosophy and metaphysics, and also developed close connections with Wagnerism and the Bayreuth Circle. Houston Stewart Chamberlain, who was to emerge as one of the most dominant figures in Bayreuth, dedicated a book to Keyserling on Kantian philosophy that was published in 1905.[60] This book, and many others written and published around this time, contained Chamberlain's racial theories of the Aryan Christ and the superiority of Aryan biology and culture.[61] Keyserling, in turn, dedicated his own first philosophical work to Chamberlain.[62]

Keyserling maintained a friendship with Chamberlain until the latter's death in 1927 and sought his financial support (unsuccessfully) for establishing his School of Wisdom in 1920. Chamberlain was perhaps the leading racial theorist and internationally perhaps the best-known anti-Semite at the turn of the century, and so with the change in the political climate after the start of World War II Keyserling denied he had shared these views with Chamberlain, "somewhat implausibly," in the view of historian Geoffrey Field.[63]

Whether or not Keyserling was anti-Semitic, it is certainly clear that he was unabashedly a völkisch German in his metaphysical outlook. The work that won him international fame, *Das Reisetagebuch eines Philosophen* of 1918 (first English translation: *The Travel Diary of a Philosopher*, 1925), is an esoteric biography of his travels around the world in 1911. He wrote the work on his estate in Estonia between 1912 and 1918 where he waited out the war. It is primarily a völkisch exposition on how geography shapes the souls of the inhabitants of each of the lands he visits. Keyserling's work is thus very much an exaltation of the mid-nineteenth-century concept of *Bodenbeschaffenheit*, the "formative forces of the soil." The places he visits give him the necessary stimuli to expound on his philosophy, and India reminds him of the religious practice closest to his heart: sun worship. He writes:

> The more I advance in recognition, the more do I profess sun-worship myself. . . . Metaphysical recognition is nothing else but this becoming-conscious of the profoundest elements of being. . . .

93

Thus, all sun-worshippers are right before God. For the man who believes in myths, there are no facts in our sense; he knows nothing of the sun of the physicist. He prays before what he feels as the immediate source of his life. The man of later days, whose emancipated intellect raises the question of correctness in the first instance, must, of course, deny sun-worship; for him there is only the fact of astronomy, and this is undoubtedly no divinity. The spiritualized being does justice once more to the ancient faith. He recognizes in it a beautiful form of expression of a true consciousness of God. He knows that all truth is ultimately symbolic, and that the sun expresses the nature of divinity more appropriately than the best conceptual expression.[64]

The School of Wisdom was a forum for the teaching of yoga and other esoteric doctrines, as well as a place where once or twice a year conferences were held where Keyserling and noted scholars could lecture.[65] The School opened in 1920 and was in operation annually until only 1927 when in-house organizational tensions between strong personalities halted the programs. After this, Keyserling devoted much of his time to traveling. A final special tenth anniversary meeting in 1930 drew approximately three hundred people. When the Eranos Conferences began in Ascona, Switzerland, in 1933, many of these same lecturers began to appear in this new venue. Jung was the most prominent of them.

The School of Wisdom was to be the vehicle through which Keyserling trained his metaphysically superior elite to lead the spiritual reawakening of the world. His goal was "to develop sages from fragments of men" and to develop "the true leader of the future."[66] In the late 1920s he sought funding for a new "church of the intellect" that would be organized "aristocratically and hierarchically."[67] By 1929 Keyserling could express great confidence in the eventual success of the few who were the metaphysically "chosen" agents of cultural change in the modern world:

The spiritually minded minorities are more spiritual today all over the world, and that in a deeper sense than ever before. . . . In the eighteenth century, the masses believed in everything, the *élite* in nothing; today, even those of the *élite* who twenty years ago were at best indifferent to spiritual questions are either grasping the reality of the spirit or groping for it. And from the point of view of the future, the spiritually minded minorities count more than any minorities have ever counted in the past.[68]

Among the most prominent lecturers at Keyserling's *Schule der Weisheit* were Richard Wilhelm (1873–1930), the famous German expert on Chinese religion and the translator of the *I Ching* (published by the Eugen Diederichs Verlag), and Jung, who became a close personal friend of Wilhelm's.[69] In an appendix to *MDR* on Richard Wilhelm, Jung says, "I first met Richard Wilhelm at Count Keyserling's during a meeting of the 'School of Wisdom' in Darmstadt. That was in the early twenties. In 1923 we invited him to Zurich and he spoke on the *I Ching* at the Psychology Club."[70] Jung, Keyserling, and Wilhelm knew each other well, and the bulk of Jung's missives between 1927 and 1930 in his collected *Letters* are to these two men.[71] The letters to Keyserling are filled with solicited interpretations of Keyserling's dreams and indicate that Keyserling looked up to Jung as a quasi-guru. Jung's letters to Wilhelm are warmly collegial and ever-encouraging.[72]

During the late 1920s and early 1930s Jung wrote three very positive reviews of volumes of metaphysical social criticism published by Keyserling.[73] In the final review, from 1934, Jung even goes so far as to tell the world that Keyserling "is, in the truest sense, the mouthpiece of the *Zeitgeist*, or, to be more accurate, the *Zeitgeist* of the spiritual man. . . . Keyserling's mediumistic gifts have gathered together the loose, fluttering, fragmentary thoughts of a whole epoch."[74]

BODENBESCHAFFENHEIT:

VÖLKISCH LANDSCAPE MYSTICISM

In a symbolic gesture of the völkisch sympathy between Jung and Keyserling, Jung wrote an essay on how the "earthly environment" shapes the human soul specifically for a book that Keyserling edited, *Mensch und Erde* (1927). By this point Jung had already moved away from a purely biological or racial model of the unconscious mind (in fact, he had done so by 1916 when he proposed a collective unconscious) and instead embraced the more transcendental claims of mysticism and old Romantic Naturphilosophie. However, as we saw, the völkisch movement, with the prominent backing of Haeckel, continued to embrace quasi-Lamarckian notions of Darwinian pangenesis that gave scientific justification for such environmental influences.

The idea of Bodenbeschaffenheit gained further scientific credibility in an age of increasing materialism through a volume by the German natural scientist Bernhard von Cotta, *Deutschlands Boden: Sein Bau und dessen Einwirkung auf das Leben der Menschen* (*Germany's Soil: Its Construction and Effect on the Life of Humans*), published in 1853.[75] Cotta's thesis was to demonstrate "what influence the geological structures of countries have on their peoples."[76] The union of Volk with landscape, of *Blut und Boden*, was supported by Cotta's vision of "ideal natural regions" that were interpreted by other völkisch commentators as justification for the idea of a German nation-state as an organic, natural body. Such "soft inheritance" was still a credible idea in some German scientific circles at the turn of the century. Sounding very much like Keyserling in his *Travel Diary*, Jung makes the following claims of pangenesis:

> Just as, in the process of evolution, the mind has been molded by earthly conditions, so the same process repeats itself under our eyes today. Imagine a large section of some European nation transplanted to a strange soil and another climate. We can confidently expect this human group to undergo certain psychic and perhaps also physical changes in the course of a few generations, even without the admixture of foreign blood.[77]

As evidence, Jung cites the "marked differences" between Spanish, North African, German, and various Russian "varieties of Jews." He then goes on to predict the "Indianization of the American people," who were originally a "predominantly Germanic people." As evidence, Jung recalls watching "a stream of workers coming out of a factory" in 1912 in Buffalo and remarking to a friend that "I should never have thought there was such a high percentage of Indian blood." His American friend laughingly told Jung there wasn't a drop of Indian blood in any of them. Backpedaling, Jung deduced that it must have been the geography that shaped their phenotypic expression, not "Mendelian units" (genes). In an effort to further back up this typically völkisch logic, Jung cites the anthropometric work of the noted American anthropologist Franz Boas, whom Jung claims "has shown that anatomical changes begin already in the second generation of immigrants, chiefly in the measurements of the skull."[78]

The first indication of Jung's fascination with the idea of Bodenbeschaffenheit that was used so extensively by members of the *Volkstumbewegung* (especially by its most racist and anti-Semitic elements) is a report in a letter to Freud dated 6 April 1910 that he is reading a book by Maurice Low, *The American People: A Study in National Psychology* (1909), that "holds the climate largely responsible for the frequency of neurosis in America." Although the effect of climate in causing psychopathology is an idea dating to the ancient Greeks, Jung then gives it a decided völkisch twist by surmising, "Perhaps a harshly continental climate really is ill-suited to a race sprung from the sea."[79] Such logic could be reversed to argue that Jews whose ancestors were Semites from an arid, dry desert land do not fit in in Europe. Although Freud does not respond to Jung's comment, he was acutely aware that such logic was a major element in anti-Semitic rhetoric at this time.

Other than the "Mind and Earth" essay in Keyserling's 1927 book, perhaps the most nakedly völkisch essay Jung ever wrote was "*Über den Unbewusste*" (translated as "The Role of the Unconscious" in the *Collected Works*), which appeared in a popular Swiss monthly in two parts in 1918.[80] This essay is important not only because of its völkisch theories, but also because it is the first major new piece to be published by Jung after his 1916 proposal of a collective unconscious, which he refers to in this 1918 essay as the "suprapersonal unconscious" as well. According to Jung, "Christianity split the Germanic barbarian into an upper and a lower half, and enabled him, by repressing the dark side, to domesticate the brighter half and fit it for civilization." This is, of course, the familiar distinction that runs throughout Germanic culture since the time of Goethe between the natural man and his contemporary, imprisoned civilized counterpart. In völkisch contexts, speaking of the Germanic barbarian is not necessarily an insult but may be an idealization of the purely instinctual man. "But," Jung adds, "the lower darker half still awaits redemption and a second spell of domestication."[81] This lower half of the Germanic soul is rooted to the earth (its "chthonic quality," Jung terms it) and "is found in dangerous concentrations in the Germanic peoples."[82]

However, Jung says that "in my opinion this problem does not exist for Jews," because Jews are not "rooted" to the land as the Germanic peoples are. The Jew "is domesticated to a higher degree than we are, but he is badly at a loss for that quality in man which roots him to the earth and draws new strength from below." Furthermore, "The Jew has too little of this quality— where has he his own earth underfoot? The mystery of the earth is no joke and no paradox."[83] Jung's use of the concept of rootedness to explain psychological differences between Aryans and Jews places him squarely within the völkisch tradition of his day, for as Mosse explains:

> The term rooted was constantly invoked by Volkish thinkers— and with good reason. Such rootedness conveyed the sense of man's correspondence with the landscape through his soul and thus with the Volk, which embodied the life spirit of the cosmos. It provided the essential link in the Volkish chain of being. Moreover, rural rootedness served as a contrast to urban dislocation, or what was termed "uprootedness." It also furnished a convenient criterion for excluding foreigners from the Volk and the virtues of rootedness. In addition, the concept of rootedness provided a standard for measuring man's completeness and his inner worth. Accordingly, having no roots stigmatized a person as being deprived of the life force and thus lacking a properly functioning soul. Rootlessness condemned the whole man, whereas rootedness signified membership in the Volk which rendered man his humanity.[84]

Jung additionally says in this 1918 essay, "The soil of every country holds some such mystery. We have an unconscious reflection of this in the psyche; just as there is a relationship of mind to body, so there is a relationship of body to earth."[85] Therefore, since the relationship of Jews to the earth is different than that of the Germanic peoples, the psychoanalytic theories of Freud and Adler could only apply to Jews. "But these specifically Jewish doctrines are thoroughly unsatisfying to the Germanic mentality; we still have a genuine barbarian in us who is not to be trifled with."[86] This Germanic barbarian within is, according to Jung, an "anti-Christian" one, and although Jung warns it can "turn against us" (that is, against Germans like Jung), "it is a still untouched fortune, an uncorrupted treasure, a sign of youthfulness, an earnest of rebirth."[87] Reaching this hidden pagan layer of the collective unconscious within not only redeems the individual, but can lead to the birth of a new world, for as Jung says, "in reality only a change in the attitude of the individual can bring about a renewal in the spirit of the nations. Everything begins with the individual."[88]

As is clear from his 1918 and 1927 essays, Jung openly held this common idea of völkisch mysticism during the 1920s, and found it so important that he taught it to American and British disciples who most likely would not have a contextual understanding of the Germanic cultural heritage of this philosophy. Perhaps most importantly, they would not have fully understood its political use by the anti-Semitic elements in the völkisch movement to establish the superiority of the Aryan peoples of verdant Northern Europe over those Semitic peoples whose inferior souls were shaped by millennia in the dry, arid lands of the Middle East. On 13 January 1925, during a trip to the United States, Jung gave a talk to a group of American disciples in the apartment of Kristine Mann (1873–1945), a physician and one of the first Jungian analysts in America. According to the notes in the diary of another major disciple, Esther Harding (1888–1971), Jung "spoke on racial psychology and said many interesting things about the ancestors, how they seem to be in the land. As evidence of this, he spoke about the morphological changes in the skulls of people here in the U.S.A. and in Australia."[89]

Jung's 1925 seminar on analytical psychology contains more evidence of his reliance upon nineteenth-century geographical and geological metaphors to express the forces at work in his psychological theory. His 6 July 1925 lecture contains a diagram of the human personality in the form of a geological chart, which Jung calls his "'geology' of the personality."[90] It is a useful example of how Jung utilized well-known concepts and images from evolutionary biology and the earth sciences to make his more metaphysical ideas comprehensible to his students.

This is how Jung describes the relationship of the individual to the collective unconscious according to this diagram:

> I have often been asked about the "Geology" of a personality, and so I have tried to picture this after a fashion. Diagram 10 shows individuals coming out of a certain common level, like the summits of mountains coming out of a sea. The first connection between certain individuals is that of the family, then comes the clan which unites a number of families, then the nation which unites a still bigger group. After that we could take a large number of connected nations such as would be included under the heading "European man." Going further down, we would come to what we call the monkey group, or that of the primate ancestors, and after that would come the animal layer in general, and finally the central fire, with which, as the diagram shows, we are still in connection.[91]

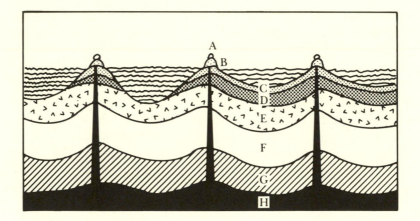

A = Individuals.
B = Families.
C = Clans.
D = Nations.
E = Large Group (European man, for example).
F = Primate Ancestors.
G = Animal Ancestors in general.
H = "Central Fire."

Figure 1. Jung's diagram of the geology of the human personality (from *Analytical Psychology*, p. 133).

Jung's use of the geological metaphor of the fiery magma of the earth's core as the central fire that connects all life, human and nonhuman, is related to an image that Jung invokes frequently during this period: that of the sun as the core of the human personality. This image of the psyche is represented in Jung's very first mandala drawing of 1916.[92] Indeed, geographical diagrams depicting a cross-sectioning of the earth and its magma core can indeed be seen as representing a fiery sun or star embedded at the center of the earth. If one accepts the theory that the earth was originally jettisoned from the sun, then indeed the hot core of the Earth is truly "sun." In a sense Jung owes this metaphor of the human personality, in part, to the Naturphilosophen for whom the earth was an anthropomorphized entity with its own soul or, indeed, psyche.[93] Psychotherapy could thus be imagined as a mining expedition or geographical exploration to reach the central source of life at the "core." As we shall see in a later chapter, this was indeed the case in the analysis of Hermann Hesse by one of Jung's disciples.

Both scientists and occultists have proposed a dynamic hot core similar to a sun deep within the planet. The French naturalist and philosopher the Comte de Buffon (1707–1788) believed that the earth had once been a fireball flung off from the sun, and that the crust was therefore the cooling exterior of a still volatile and extremely hot core of star matter. The material of the human body, it could thus be claimed, was made of star matter, making us all *Sonnenkinder*, "children of the sun." The often-cited maxim of the alchemists that was so dear to Jung, "as above, so below," thus takes on new meaning, as does another of Jung's favorite images—the account of Apuleius (through the character Lucius) in *Metamorphoses* (Book 11) who claims "I saw the sun in the middle of the night" (*"nocte media vidi solem"*) during a subterranean Isaic mystery-cult rite of initiation. Naturalists since the eighteenth century cited the worldwide prevalence of volcanoes and their lava flows as compelling scientific evidence of a hot molten core beneath the earth's crust, and the hypothesis of central heat or a central fire was a primary assumption of the vulcanist or plutonist school of geologists in the eighteenth and nineteenth centuries.[94] Geophysics and Naturphilosophie commonly overlapped at many junctures.

Thus, cross-sectional images of the planet since that time show a mandala-like sequence of concentric circles, indicating the Earth's various geological strata, with a central glowing spherical core of intense heat at its center. Such illustrations were common in the German popular-science journals that began to appear in the 1850s and would have been familiar images to the adolescent Jung. Jung's "geology of the personality" is hence based on a vulcanist or plutonist geophysical vision borrowed from his training in the natural sciences.

Also significant in Jung's 1925 lecture is his clear statement that he does not consider the collective unconscious to be solely inside the brain and nervous system. Since it can be located outside the brain, Jung says that "on this basis the main body of the collective unconscious cannot be strictly said to be psychological, but psychical."[95] This is an early appearance of a theoretical distinction Jung would make later in his career (in 1946) about the transcendental, quasi-physical, quasi-psychological, "psychoid" nature of the archetypes. Jung borrowed the term "psychoid" (as an adjective, not a noun) from the twentieth-century version of speculative Naturphilosophie and vitalism expounded by Bleuler, on "the natural history of the soul."[96] Both Bleuler and Jung attempted to distinguish themselves from the more nakedly vitalistic use of the term "die Psychoide" by Hans Driesch (1867–1941).[97] Jung's own full return to Naturphilosophie is never so clear as when he remarks,

> We cannot repeat this distinction too often, for when I have referred to the collective unconscious as "outside" our brains, it has been assumed that I meant hanging somewhere in mid-air. After this explanation it will become clear to you that the collective unconscious is always working upon you through trans-subjective facts which are probably inside as well as outside yourselves.[98]

With these examples of his mystical geological vision of the human personality, and from his relationship to Keyserling and others who shared this vision, we can see how deeply connected Jung remained to individuals and ideas in the völkisch movement and its occult establishment. Jung's vocal connection to the Volk was not fully understood by his predominantly American and British disciples of the 1920s, nor especially those who entered Jung's Küsnacht-Zurich orbit in the 1930s and who, in the aftermath of Hitler, could only see these ideas as belonging to the heritage of *another* völkisch movement of this era: National Socialism.

Perhaps most of the continuing controversy over whether Jung (or Keyserling, for that matter) was or was not a Nazi, or was anti-Semitic,—an argument that is often framed in unenlightening black or white dualistic terms—can be resolved by offering a *third* way: the larger context of pre-Nazi era völkisch philosophy that both *was* and *was not* used by Nazis and anti-Semites for their own ends. Perhaps what many critics are sensing in Jung is his essential völkisch identity, of which there is much evidence. Jung's is not merely a folk-psychology, but a "Volk-psychology." The claimed evidence of the active, open espousal of anti-Semitism or Nazism by Jung is, in my opinion, less directly compelling (hence the greater controversy over it), and is perhaps more fruitfully framed—from the historian's point of view—in its deeper völkisch context. As historians such as Mosse have continually stressed, anti-Semitism and National Socialism, while derivatives of this völkisch tradition, are not to be regarded as completely identical with it and its multiple offshoots, of which Jung and his analytical psychology is only one of many. It would make sense from a historical point of view to see overlaps between those in Jung's circle (himself included) with those in National Socialist circles during the 1930s, as indeed has been documented.[99]

Neopagans in Switzerland

Switzerland has a many-centuries-old tradition of being a land of heresy and unconventional sects. During the Middle Ages the Free Spirits, Waldensians, and even the Cathars made inroads into the lives of many in this region.[100] Southern Germany and Switzerland were primary centers of the Reformation of the sixteenth century, and the splintering of Protestantism into insular "sects" continued in Switzerland until the present century. The official Swiss census of 1 December 1888 counted 10,697 persons living in sects but only 8,384 Jews in a total population of 2.9 million, dominated by 1.7 million Protestants and 1.2 million Roman Catholics.[101] Although most of these sects were somehow connected with Christian ideas, there were some that operated as charismatic cults with bizarre belief systems that promoted intergenerational incest, the ingestion of urine and sperm, and other unconventional spiritual practices that led to their separate category in the Swiss census. The Swiss psychiatrist Hermann Rorschach (1884–1922) became fascinated with such sects near the end of his life and produced four publications of psychoanalytic ethnography that focused on two charismatic leaders of one such Swiss sect.[102]

Between 1900 and 1920 a Munich to Ascona countercultural axis seemed to be in full operation, making this circuit somewhat similar in spirit if not in size to the California of the 1960s. Switzerland and southern Germany became the home of these neopagan, sun-worshiping, nudist, vegetarian, spiritualist, sometimes anarchist, sexually liberated groups experimenting with new life-styles or a new experience-based philosophy of life.[103] Aschheim refers to these groups as "varieties of Nietzschean religion."[104] Taking their inspirational cue from Nietzsche's proclamation that "god is dead" in *Also Sprach Zarathustra*, they created their own forms of personal religion. When describing her impressions of the materially impoverished but spiritually adventurous life-style of these Bohemian colonies in Switzerland, Marianne Weber uses the same word that her husband Max employed to describe the essence of charisma: *ausseralltägliches* ("extraordinary," or "out of the everyday routine of life").[105] Swiss authorities were considered relatively benign compared to the more heavy-handed Austrian or Bavarian police. The groups operating in this Swiss version of the fin-desiècle New Age—some of them with völkisch concerns but most probably not—have been documented in Green's extraordinary work.[106]

Some neopagan groups took their sun-worshiping ideas from ancient Persian sources. At the turn of the century there was a resurgence of both scholarly and Theosophical interest in Persian mythology (primarily Zoroastrianism or Mazdeanism and Mithraism). The proximate cause of some of this interest in the 1890s was no doubt due to Nietzsche, as "Zarathustra" was the name used in Greek writings for Zoroaster (circa 600 B.C.E.), the prophet who converted the early (probably shamanistic) Indo-Iranian peoples to his religion based on the supreme deity

Ahura Mazda. Zoroastrian religion went through many revisions over one thousand years and in its latter forms is especially noted for its dualism and hierarchies of demons and angels. Classical scholars such as Franz Cumont (1868–1947) from Belgium traced the Hellenistic mystery cult of Mithras (100–400 C.E.) to ancient Persian roots, and Richard Reitzenstein (1861–1931) from Germany founded an entire school in the history of religions devoted to tracing the Iranian roots of Gnosticism, although this monomaniacal fascination with Iranian origins in the work of these two scholars has been rejected in recent years.[107]

The fascination of the Germans with Persian (Aryan) origins began during the Romantic Era of the early 1800s. Although Gustav Fechner (1801–1887), at first a professor of physics and later one of philosophy at the University of Leipzig, is best known for his *Elemente der Psychophysik* of 1860 (a work that is regarded as the first textbook in modern experimental psychology), he wrote many metaphysical works as well.[108] One of these, the *Zend-Avesta* (1851), a work of Romantic natural philosophy, takes its name from the title of the sacred books of the ancient Iranian Zoroastrians.[109] Zoroastrian solar mythology was extensively discussed by Müller in many of his publications. Jung himself cites Müller in this regard in his *Wandlungen und Symbole der Libido*. These, too, had found their way into occultist literature and in the earliest writings of Blavatsky in the 1870s.

By 1900 enough of the scholarly information had begun to seep into Theosophical publications and other occult literature, making such mythology available to neopagan cults. Around 1900 a "Cult of Mazdaznan" was founded in the United States by a German immigrant from Poznan, Otto Hanisch (1854–1936). Hanisch, who used an Iranian-sounding alias (Ottoman Zar-Adusht Ha'nish), alleged that he was born in Tehran and that his cult was a remnant of the Zoroastrianism of ancient Iran. The cult was based on vegetarianism, solar mysticism, and other practices derived from Hanisch's idiosyncratic interpretations of the *Zend-Avesta*. By 1910 the cult had spread to Europe and appears to have been based in Herrliberg, Switzerland (ten miles from Zurich) under the leadership of Karl Heise, a Zurich bookshop assistant, and a former student of Guido von List.

105

Near Zurich, Heise was the charismatic leader of a commune ("university," as the cult described it) called "Aryana" that practiced solar worship and vegetarianism. As James Webb notes, "The university was known as 'Aryana'" because "only the fair-skinned 'Aryan' races were permitted to become bearers of the new ideal."[110] Heise was a dominant figure on the Zurich occultist scene around 1910 and wrote many books on topics such as sun worship, reincarnation, and the astral body that were published between 1907 and 1919.[111] It has been suggested that the Mazdaznans included several influential members of the Bauhaus movement and thus influenced German aesthetics, but by 1916 the group had moved its headquarters to California.[112] Today the group seems to be most alive in France, and some occult bookshops in Paris have their own Mazdaznan sections for the group's more recent metaphysical and vegetarian literature.

It is not known if Jung knew of Heise or if he read any of Heise's occult works (none are listed in Jung's posthumous *Bibliothek* catalog), but it is interesting to note that it is precisely during this time (late 1909–1910) that Jung becomes fascinated with the literature on Zoroastrianism and Mithraism—and their basis in ancient Iranian solar worship.[113] We do, however, have solid evidence from a late period that Jung was aware of this solar-worshiping cult so near to his base of operations, as he mentions, in an essay published in 1928, the Mazdaznan in the same sentence with "Christian Science, theosophy, [and] anthroposophy" as examples of extra-Christian "individual symbol-formation" cults.[114] Jung appears not to have known Hanisch, for in remarks made during his "Zarathustra Seminar" in May 1934, Jung discounts the rumor that Nietzsche met Hanisch or his cult members in Leipzig as a student and hence got his idea for *Zarathustra* from them. Jung is also unaware that the cult originated in a later period. Jung is incorrect in his statement that "He [Hanisch] is certainly not the originator of the Mazdaznan sect; it is of older origin," thus also appearing not to have known Hanisch but *did* know of Hanisch's claims of an ancient origin for the Mazdaznans.[115]

Yet it is interesting that the first issue Jung chooses to clarify for his audience in his Zarathustra seminar is a critical denial of the role of the cult of the Mazdaznans as an influence on Nietzsche and therefore, by extension, on Jung himself. Given the fact that Jung was well aware of the Mazdaznans, and especially considering the prominent place Jung gave this cult among the other well-known occult traditions in his 1928 statement, it is probable that he did at least know of Heise and the sun worship of the Mazdaznans but did not want a public association with the cult or its philosophy with his own ideas.

NEOPAGANS IN ASCONA AND AT
THE BURGHÖLZLI

Thus this thriving neopagan movement was operating within Jung's Switzerland and could not have escaped his attention. In addition to the countercultural, antipolitical neopagans were the many highly nationalistic members of the German Youth Movement who could be seen hiking through Germany, Austria, and Switzerland during these years, some of whom were fully imbued with the sun-worshiping rituals and pantheistic literature of Diederichs and his publishing company. Many of the casualties of these groups would inevitably end up at the Burghölzli. The most prominent casualty with Asconan neopagan beliefs—the renegade psychoanalyst and anarchist Otto Gross (to be discussed later)—was admitted and treated by Jung in 1908. He was no doubt one among several.

The Burghölzli was the largest psychiatric-treatment facility in Switzerland and was therefore easily accessible on the countercultural route between the Bohemian districts of Schwabing in Munich and the village of Ascona. Absinthe, cocaine, morphine, opium, and other substances sometimes went along with the Nietzschean "new ethic" with tragic results, and spiritual purification rituals involving fasting, unusual diets, excessive hiking, and so on, could sometimes induce a brief psychotic reaction. An analogous influx of similar patients appeared in psychiatric hospitals and clinics during the "Psychedelic Era" of the 1960s, and continues even today. The hallucinations and delusions of these spiritual explorers could indeed contain the components of the mystical ideas and symbolism they had studied in their search for pagan regeneration. Such was the nature of a small portion of the institutionalized patient population of

107

the Burghölzli from which Jung made his clinical observations and from which he and his assistants (starting in 1909) collected data for the "phylogenetic" layer of the unconscious from which he derived his later (1916) theories. It was hardly a patient population free of exposure to occult or mythological material, whether through Theosophical or scholarly publications (especially those published by either the Eugen Diederichs Verlag or Verlag B. G. Teubner, or through direct participation in neopagan cult rituals.

Ascona, as Green has documented, grew into a spiritual center of sorts and was frequented by such gifted creative individuals as Hesse, D. H. Lawrence, Gross, Duncan, Mary Wigman, Rudolf von Laban, Keyserling, Franz Kafka, Max Brod, Paul Tillich, Weber (ironically, in 1913 and 1914), and in later years, Jung. Ascona, the countercultural mecca with its own circumambulated *qa'ba* (Monte Verita) and bearded and long-locked *Naturmenschen* in Tannhäuser-like sandals, became the site of the famous Eranos Conferences that Jung so dominated and which started in 1933.[116] Indeed, Carl and Emma Jung annually stayed in a villa on the "Mountain of Truth" (Monte Verita) itself.[117] By the time of the Eranos Conferences, however, the Naturmenschen were becoming scarce, for Ascona had begun to take on the air of a resort for the wealthy and "artistic" communities that it maintains today.

Laurens van der Post, a close friend and disciple of Jung's who is noted for his many books on his experiences exploring Africa, reports inviting Jung many times to join him on yet another voyage to the "dark continent" after Jung's fieldwork in Kenya in 1925. According to van der Post, Jung replied that before he could allow himself to return to Africa, "I found so much witchcraft in Switzerland I felt that I had to deal with all this witchcraft first." Perhaps we may now have a little clearer understanding of Jung's remark by understanding his Switzerland, which apparently did indeed have its share of neopagans and others participating in an occult underground—and, indeed, noted persons such as himself at play in the network of the occult establishment.

☒ CHAPTER SIX ☒

Wandlungen und Symbole der Libido
SOLAR MYSTICISM AS SCIENCE

ALTHOUGH A DISCUSSION of Jung's *Wandlungen und Symbole der Libido* (1912) at this point removes it from the chronological development of Jung's life and thought that I will construct in part 2 of this volume, it is perhaps more important to include this section here where it follows discussion of the long Germanic tradition of völkisch sun worship that Jung was so much a part of.

It is true, as so many commentators have said, that *Wandlungen* is only a partially intelligible book. Although there is more cohesion in the much shorter first part than the enormous second part, Jung piles layers upon layers of mythological references into almost every paragraph in this four-hundred-page book. The connection between one thought and the next is not clear, and as Kerr has pointed out, there are many internal contradictions in the proposed revisions of the libido theory of psychoanalysis that made the work practically unintelligible to even the psychoanalytic community of Jung's day.

For Jung, the writing of the book mirrored a personal transformation process in himself. He began work on it early in 1910, and part 1 of the work formed the basis of his very first public lecture devoted to the psychological interpretation of mythological material. He delivered the lecture on 16 May 1910 to a group of Swiss psychiatrists in Herisau, Switzerland, and sent a copy of it to Freud for comments. Although this early manuscript has not survived, we have Freud's comments and criticisms in an undated letter from late June or early July of 1910: "Despite all its beauty, I think, the essay lacks ultimate clarity."[1] Whether Jung's essay ever developed any clarity is disputable.

Jung's self-professed haste in producing *Wandlungen* was due, in part, to his desire to be in print with his own unique interpretation of comparative world mythology. His associate from the Burghölzli, Franz Riklin, had been the first to do so with a

109

psychoanalytic interpretation of fairy tales published in 1908. Between October 1909 and 1912 Jung and his associates read mythological works and then collected evidence of mythological content in the dreams, fantasies, hallucinations, and delusions of the patients of the Burghölzli. Jung had also by this time found a small publication by an American woman he never met, Miss Frank Miller, which contained many of her poetic reveries and visions.[2] Using this as a starting point, Jung wrote the massive two-part *Wandlungen*, published as a one-volume book in late 1912.

SYNCRETISM

The unintelligibility of *Wandlungen* has often been attributed by Jung and his disciples to his haste, and by his detractors to his "encounter with narcissism"[3] or perhaps even psychosis. Peter Homans captures the flavor of the reader's first impression of Jung's text when he concludes, "It is, in short, a record of Jung's own fantasies, not an interpretation of the myths and symbols of the past."[4] Kerr—who probably understands *Wandlungen* from a psychoanalytic perspective better than anyone ever has— "second[s] Homans's view, the longest of these essays is nothing more or less than the record of Jung's own fantasy life, recklessly projected onto ancient symbols and myths."[5] However, both Homans and Kerr have tried to understand *Wandlungen* from a purely psychoanalytic perspective. Perhaps we can discern a different meaning in this baffling text.

It may be argued that the confusing combination of "several different essays hurriedly stitched together at the last moment"[6] that comprise *Wandlungen* are due to its essential nature as a work of syncretism. Syncretism is usually defined as an attempted blending of irreconcilable principles or tenets, as in philosophy or religion. Or else it is the attempted blending of groups of individuals who adhere to seemingly irreconcilable religious or philosophical principles. Syncretic literature is almost always unintelligible at first to those not in the original melting pot that inspired the work in the first place, whether this is in a purely intellectual or a primarily social world. Trying to understand the Hellenistic Christianity of the various groups of two thousand years ago we call the Gnostics, for example, presents problems today for the devout Christian and occultist alike.

I propose that *Wandlungen und Symbole der Libido* is a syncretic work on several levels. It is, first and foremost, Jung's attempt at scientific syncretism in the nineteenth-century sense of Wissenschaft. Following Freud, Jung too claimed psychoanalysis was a science. *Wandlungen* was an attempt to prove this by blending the methodology of psychoanalysis with the esteemed *Wissenschaften* of comparative philology, comparative mythology, and evolutionary biology. It was an attempt to integrate the science of psychoanalysis with the other *Geisteswissenschaften* and *Naturwissenschaften*, indeed with the greater scientific body of knowledge of Jung's day.

A second syncretic agenda is perhaps a mystical one. It is a blending of different philosophies of personal religion based on notions of regeneration or rebirth. Psychoanalysis becomes not only a science but a way of cultural and individual revitalization—and by this time a personal religion for Jung. In *Wandlungen* Jung cannot help but rely on the ideas of the völkisch movement, as around 1910 the most intelligent and accepted blend of the scholarly literature on comparative philology, comparative mythology, and evolutionary biology in German could be found in the various literatures of this movement on the differences between Aryan peoples and Semitic peoples. Völkisch ideas permeate scholarly publications from the eminent Müller and Haeckel on down to the esoteric books and pamphlets of Theosophists and other occultists, and many were used (and some cited) by Jung in *Wandlungen*. This is, perhaps, most apparent in the relentless syncretism of solar mythology and psychoanalysis that begins in the last section of part 1—"The Song of the Moth"—and continues throughout the enormous part 2, thus making the second part of *Wandlungen* as bulky and unintelligible as the second part of *Faust*. It is especially in these sections that Jung's text becomes a liturgy of sun worship and völkisch Aryanism.

Here, perhaps, we can discern clues from Jung's personal life and letters. By 1911 and early 1912 Jung's growing estrangement from Freud was marked by a greater fascination with the symbolism of ancient mystery cults from the Hellenistic world

111

than with traditional Freudian sexual symbolism and its application, a practice that William James, in a letter to Flournoy, called "a most dangerous method." It was the symbolism of the mystery cult of Mithras in particular that seemed to rival the sexual symbolism of psychoanalysis in Jung's own personal symbolic system during this period.[7] By 1912, Jung reenvisioned psychoanalysis as a way to achieve both personal and cultural renewal and rebirth, as is evident in some statements in *Wandlungen*, but which is most apparent in an article on "New Paths in Psychology" that also appeared in 1912.[8] Upon the completion and publication of this work Jung realized he could no longer live in the "Christian myth":

> When I finished [*Wandlungen*], I had a peculiarly lucid moment in which I surveyed my path as far as I had come. I thought: "Now you have the key to mythology and you have the power to unlock all doors." And then I found myself asking what I had done after all. I had written a book about the hero, I had explained the myths of past peoples, but what about my own myth? I had to admit I had none; I knew theirs but none of my own, nor did anyone else have one today. Moreover, we were without an understanding of the unconscious.[9]

WANDLUNGEN AS SCIENCE

Jung opens *Wandlungen und Symbole der Libido* by suggesting that Freud and psychoanalysis can reveal something new and powerful about the ancient Greek culture so idealized by nineteenth-century Germanic Europeans. Winckelmann's serene and composed Hellas was already gone forever after the appearance of Heine, Nietzsche, and Wagner. Further, Jung implies in his introduction that ancient Greece, too, like the modern age, was the garden of sexuality. Jung reminds his reader that Freud's uncovering of the "Incest Phantasy" deep in the soul of every fin-de-siècle man, woman, and—most shockingly—every *child*, is the root of "the Oedipus legend." Even in ancient Greece, "similar passions moved mankind, and man was likewise convinced of the uniqueness of his existence."

With Freud's insights, "suddenly there is opened a revelation of the simple greatness of the Oedipus tragedy," and a pulse of life originating in ancient Greece is thus found still alive in the souls of modern individuals.[10]

Jung says it is a "vain illusion" that modern individuals are more moral than the ancients, and he argues that our common bond with the people of antiquity has been forgotten. Yet this reminder by psychoanalysis has profound implications:

> With this truth a path is opened to the understanding of the ancient mind; an understanding which so far has not existed, and, on one side, leads to an inner sympathy, and on the other side, to an intellectual comprehension. Through buried strata of the individual soul we come indirectly into possession of the living mind of ancient culture, and, just precisely through that, do we win that stable point of view outside our own culture, from which, for the first time, an objective understanding of their mechanisms would be possible. At least that is the hope we get from the rediscovery of the Oedipus problem.[11]

Let us examine this important statement more closely in its historical context. Winckelmann's beloved ancient Greece, so catalogued and institutionalized in museums by the twentieth century, had become banalized, reduced to pieces of statuary and mere literary references in the poetry and prose of a century of Germans. The rediscovery of the Greeks by Winckelmann, which had succeeded in awakening *Kultur* among the German peoples, had also revivified the Greeks and their pagan gods. Jung is arguing that modern individuals need to find the thought, passions, and especially the gods of ancient Greece that are still alive in each individual soul of today. This finding can be accomplished with the techniques of psychoanalysis, which are in Jung's pages allied with the uncovering methodologies of archaeology, philology, and comparative mythology.

Psychoanalysis literally becomes the archaeology of the soul for the first time in Jung's seminal work. It promises not only an understanding of the souls of individuals, but of modern culture as well. Perhaps most attractively, it is a way of objectively learning something new ("for the first time," Jung says) about ancient Greece and other ancient cultures. In the second part of

Wandlungen, the title of the third chapter explicitly holds out such a promise: "The Transformation of the Libido: A Possible Source of Primitive Human Discoveries."

Psychoanalysis therefore can increase the knowledge of other sciences: it becomes a way to revive archaeology and philology, which had been longing for breakthroughs since the days of Schliemann and Schleicher. Schliemann used Homer as his guide to finding and uncovering the past, discovering the gold of Troy in 1873 and the graves of Mycenae in 1876. Schleicher used the language of Homer (and others) as his guide to finding and uncovering the original language of all Aryans (Indo-Europeans).[12] Psychoanalysis was the new science for adding to our knowledge of these same ancient origins by tracing the historical development of the libido in individuals (ontogeny) and in the species (phylogeny). Psychoanalysis may thus take its place among the other revered *Wissenschaften*. Who knows what it may uncover?

In the first formal chapter of *Wandlungen*, entitled "Concerning the Two Kinds of Thinking," Jung uses the literature of philosophy, psychology, and psychoanalysis to distinguish between (1) directed, rational, focused thinking whose medium is *words* and (2) symbolic, alogical, fantastical thought that is irrational and expressed in *images*. The former is the hallmark and indeed the pride of the nineteenth-century bourgeois European; the latter is found in dreams, in children, in primitives, and in the mythological thought of pagan, pre-Christian antiquity. It is also found especially in persons with serious psychotic disorders, such as dementia praecox. Our personal sediment of infantile memories shades into the archaic levels of the mythological cognition of the ancients and of primitives. These two kinds of thinking comprise the main strata of the individual psyche. If the top layer of the individual psyche is disturbed, mythological material from the ancestry of humankind reemerges in the form of delusions and hallucinations.

The symbolic method of psychoanalysis as practiced in the literature of Freud, therefore, becomes a new Rosetta Stone. It is, however, a Rosetta Stone that translates the hieroglyphs of the second type of thinking into the psychoanalytic language of the first. Until the very last chapter of *Wandlungen*—"The Sacrifice," about which more will be said later—the dynamic energy or libido in humans as biological organisms was sexual energy *only* in all previous psychoanalytic works. In language that obscures his intent, Jung posits a theoretical revision that he develops more fully in later works, redefining libido as a more general term for psychic energy rather than strictly for sexuality. This incompatibility of ideas is, of course, the intellectual excuse for the break between Jung and Freud.

By confirming that psychoanalysis is a science that employs a historical method of uncovering the origins not only of the development of the individual, but also of the species, Jung implies that it is ultimately grounded in biological processes. As noted earlier, Haeckel's evidence that "ontogeny recapitulates phylogeny" is the result of the successful application of the historical method to biology. Jung likewise in *Wandlungen* sets out to document the evolution of thought in the style of Haeckelian evolutionary biology. In Jung's case, patterns of human experience are categorized and analyzed to chart lines of development and typical patterns of strata. The basic schema, however, comes from psychoanalysis. Given Jung's attempted innovations and their internal contradictions in *Wandlungen*, other than the basic distinction of strata between "the two kinds of thinking," the psychoanalytic schema makes almost no sense to the reader after the first chapter.

Yet, since on a gross physical level each adult individual was once a fetus with reptilian features at one point in life, analogously, why could the thoughts and feeling, indeed echoes of libido, of the noble ancient Greeks not be evident somewhere in the soul of every European? Jung's deliberate use of Haeckelian evolutionary biology in *Wandlungen* implies the possibility that one day, through the historical science of psychoanalysis, biology and psychology would converge via the principle that ontogeny recapitulates phylogeny. This echoes Haeckel's similar proposal in 1899 for a "phylogenetic psychology" to study the "phylogeny of the soul." If typical stages in the development of human thought (as observable derivatives of transformations in libido) could be schematized, and then found to dovetail with the stages of biological development in humans, psychoanalysis could make a tremendous contribution to knowledge in a way unparalleled by any other science.

Again, the biological basis of his argument is implied by Jung in the first chapter of *Wandlungen* by invoking Haeckel's "Bio-genetic Law," but not his name. Although in various places he offhandedly refers to biology, he does not develop a biological argument.[13] It is central, however, to the entire book. Biology is very much in Jung's mind when he says early in *Wandlungen* that: *"Thus, there must be typical myths which are really the instruments of a folk-psychological complex treatment."*[14]

Jung spends great effort attempting to blend the psychoanalytic method with those of comparative mythology and comparative philology. From the comparative mythology of Müller, Jung follows the method of piling example upon example of myths from different ancient cultures and those contemporary primitive cultures found in ethnographic literature. Three primary categories emerge, all interrelated: the comparative mythology of the hero, of self-sacrifice (usually in connection with the hero), and of solar myths and their predominance in all cultures and in the fantastical layer of thought in all human beings.

If examined outside of the context of the psychoanalytic literature, *Wandlungen* might very well be regarded as an eccentric work of Müllerian solar mythology. Jung's assumptions about the historical development of consciousness match Müller's ideas, and not surprisingly: Müller dominated European thought on the subject of comparative mythology for almost fifty years and Müllerian assumptions had seeped into the cognitive categories of nineteenth-century thought.[15] Over the course of his career, Müller developed what can only be called a cognitive theory of cultural evolution.[16] Müller argued that there was a period of human history that predated even the earliest Aryan civilizations in which human beings did not have adequate language for abstract thoughts and inexplicable experiences. This was, as Müller called it, the "mythopoetic age" in which the first Aryan gods were born.[17] The gods represented perhaps the most powerful and inexplicable forces that humans can encounter: the forces of nature, and in particular the dominant role of the sun in the natural world. As humans had a limited verbal capacity in these early days and could not process information efficiently, single words had to take on multiple meanings, both concrete and abstract. There were two primary cognitive processes at work here according to Müller, which served as heuristics: polyonymy, where one word had to carry many meanings, and homonymy, where one essential idea could become attached to several different words.

In this early mythopoetic age, many words could signify the sun, with multiple webs of associations attached to them, which would then overlap with other such webs. Thus, the ancient Vedic supreme god Dyanus could be associated with words for light, fire, brightness, clarity of thought, power, air, and dawn, among others. Müller hypothesized that as migrations separated the original Aryan peoples and as civilization developed, bringing about an increase in language and an increase in the ability to process greater and more complex loads of information, humans eventually forgot the seminal core complexes (usually Vedic gods) at the center of these webs of associations. Thus, through the decay or "disease of language," new stories were made up to account for the forgotten Vedic origins. Out of these stories Persian, Indian, Greek, Roman, Germanic, and other mythologies arose. This philological method allowed one to trace the development of the Aryan peoples step by step, back to an Edenic time before history was recorded.

Müller's excitement over peering into the dawn of human history is evident in much of his work. After arguing that the names of the "highest god" in Sanskrit (Dyaus), Greek (Zeus), Latin (Jove), and ancient German (Tiu) were essentially the same, he relates:

> but I hardly dwelt with sufficient strength on the startling nature of this discovery. These names are not mere names; they are historical facts, aye, facts more immediate, more trustworthy, than many facts of medieval history. These words are not mere words, but they bring before us, with all the vividness of an event which we witnessed ourselves just yesterday, the ancestors of the whole Aryan race, thousands of years it may be before Homer and the Veda, worshipping an unseen Being, under the selfsame name, the best, the most exalted name, they could find in their vocabulary,—under the name of Light and Sky.[18]

The symbolic method of psychoanalysis that Jung employs in *Wandlungen* is based on just such assumptions of the polyonymy and homonymy of the words used to describe the everyday experiences of fantasies and dreams. Often it is one idea—sexuality—attached to several different words that points to their ultimate origin. Jung takes this essential psychoanalytic premise and applies it to the content of world mythology ad infinitum in *Wandlungen*. The following digressive paragraph is only one of many such examples that fill the volume:

The symbolism of the instrument of coitus was an inexhaustible material for ancient phantasy. It furnished a widespread cult that was designated phallic, the object of reverence of which was the phallus. The companion of Dionysus was Phales, a personification of the phallus proceeding from the phallic Herme of Dionysus. The phallic symbols were countless. Among the Sabines, the custom existed for the bridegroom to part the bride's hair with a lance. The bird, the fish, and the snake were phallic symbols. In addition, there existed in enormous quantities theriomorphic representations of the sexual instinct, in connection with which the bull, the he-goat, the ram, the boar and the ass were frequently used. An undercurrent to this choice of symbol was furnished by the sodomitic inclination of humanity. When in the dream phantasy of modern man, the feared man is replaced by an animal, there is recurring in the ontogenetic re-echo the same thing which was openly represented by the ancients countless times.[19]

If Müller could be monomaniacal about tracing the origins of all human thought and culture to the sun, Jung as psychoanalyst could trace all human origins back to the genitals and their sexual functions. Jung even borrowed from the methodologies of philology and comparative mythology to do it. However, throughout this book, Jung is highly selective about the types of myths he chooses. He prefers solar myths and indeed draws his material disproportionately from Aryan cultural roots (India, Iran, and Hellenistic world, with a smattering of Wagnerian Teutonic mythology). Indeed, on the rare occasions on which Jung approaches the Semitic cultures (Jews, Arabs, etc.), it is generally with reference to Job or to Jesus and the Christian myth. He could have chosen to write, for example, a book interpreting African myths or North American Indian myths, but even in the places where, for example, Miller herself (who is quite lost in this book) provides a fantasy about an Amerindian (Chiwantopel), Jung turns to Aryan mythologies for amplification.[20] Jung's father was an Orientalist and knew Arabic and Hebrew and his maternal grandfather (whose poetry is cited in *Wandlungen*) was a professor of Hebraic Studies, and so sources of information about the Semitic cultures were not alien to Jung.

Hence, *Wandlungen* is an attempted syncretism of psychoanalysis and the German sciences most devoted to the study of Aryan culture. It is therefore a syncretic blend of sexual mythology and solar mythology as two major theories of the true ancient origins of the human soul and of human culture.

It is primarily in part 2 of *Wandlungen* that we find Jung also attempting to blend the historical method of psychoanalysis with the methods of comparative philology. Endless etymological digressions are inserted into the text. For the reader's sake I will not repeat any of them here.[21] When Jung was writing part 2 in late 1911 and early 1912, he apparently assigned Emma Jung to do this etymological research that appears in the book and lends it its scientific persona, at least by nineteenth-century German standards.[22]

WANDLUNGEN AS SOLAR MYSTICISM

It is not difficult to see how Jung's book would have been recommended reading among völkisch cultists or Asconan sun worshipers: almost every page contains references to solar mythology and its connection with world mythology and sexuality. Mixing sun worship with the new ethic of sexual freedom was a potent brew for Asconans thirsty for validation by established medical or scholarly authorities that they claimed so much to despise. These solar references increase in frequency starting in the chapter "The Song of the Moth" in part 1, in which Jung interprets a romantic poem by Miller entitled "The Moth to the Sun."[23] Jung says that in this poem *"Her longing for God resembles the longing of the moth for the 'star.'"*[24] In a manner resembling the methodology of Müller's solar mythology, Jung then reminds the reader that "in the preceding chapter the following chain of associations was adduced: the singer—God of sound— singing morning star—creator—God of Light—sun—fire—God of Love."[25]

119

Jung's further analysis of the content of this poem makes it clear that the sun or star Miller is talking about is not an external one, but an inner one. Indeed, it is the god within. The resonance with the völkisch neopaganism of this time is accomplished by way of using psychoanalytic terminology. Thus:

> In the second poem where the longing is clearly exposed it is by no means the terrestrial sun. Since the longing has been turned away from the real object, its object has become, first of all, a subjective one, namely, God. Psychologically, however, God is the name of a representation-complex that is grouped around a strong feeling (the sum of libido). Properly, the feeling is what gives character and reality to the complex. *The attributes and symbols of divinity must belong in a consistent manner to the feeling (longing, love, libido, and so on).* If one honors God, the sun or the fire, then one honors one's own vital force, the libido. It is as Seneca says: "God is near you, he is with you, in you."[26]

Here Jung offers the psychoanalytic term "libido" as a mystical substitute for "vital force" or even "God." Just as we feel the surge of vital power within us as living biological beings, so then are we also experiencing the god within.

As we shall see, the experience of the god within was always a key promise of Jung and his method of psychotherapy, as Homans astutely noted, and it is indeed a central part of Jung's repudiation of traditional Christianity that offered a God that was distant, transcendent, and absolute.[27] In the pages of *Wandlungen* we see the first liturgical exegesis of these core Jungian concepts.

Having a god within could lead to the experience of becoming one with God, or merging with this God-force in some way. It is clear from his many statements in *Wandlungen* that Jung felt that the central experience of transformation in the ancient mystery cults of the Hellenistic world involved just such a process or experience of self-deification. Jung mentions the mysteries of Isis and of Mithras especially in this regard. Jung relates the following observations:

> To bear a God within one's self signifies just as much as to be God one's self. . . . There are even plainer traces, to be sure, in the "becoming-one-with-God" in those mysteries closely related to the

Christian, where the mystic himself is lifted up to divine adoration through initiatory rites. . . . These representations of "becoming-one-with-God" are very ancient. The old belief removed the becoming-one-with-God until the time after death; the mysteries, however, suggest this as taking place already in this world.[28]

Bringing the experience of becoming one with God into the familiar present, Jung explains: "The identification with God necessarily has as a result the enhancing of the meaning and power of the individual." However, this is in fact a defense against the individual's "all too great weakness and insecurity in real life. This great megalomania thus has a genuinely pitiable background."[29]

Throughout "The Song of the Moth," and indeed throughout the rest of the book Jung dizzyingly unites the following in an associative chain of equivalences: the sun—the phallus—brightness—god—father—fire—libido—fructifying strength and heat—hero. To conclusively back up this argument, Jung mentions the famous case of the "Solar Phallus Man"—a contemporary individual, institutionalized in the Burghölzli, who has a hallucination (or perhaps a delusion) that the sun has a phallic tube hanging from it that produces the wind.[30] This case found by Jung's assistant, J. J. Honegger, is the perfect exemplum of Jung's whole argument in this book and is a symbol of Jung's attempted union of sexual psychoanalysis and solar mythology.

Inwardly perceived, "divine vision is often merely sun or light,"[31] as it is the "inner light, the sun of the other world."[32] Again: "The comparison of the libido with the sun and fire is in reality analogous."[33] Like Müller's concept of the "disease of language" through which the initial core concepts of associative webs lost their meaning as civilization forgot the "mythopoetic age" Jung argues, in a comparison of the Book of Revelation with the Mithraic Liturgy that:

> The visionary images of both texts are developed from a source, not limited to one place, but found in the soul of many diverse people, because the symbols which arise from it are too typical for it to belong to one individual only. I put these images here to show how the primitive symbolism of light gradually developed, with the increasing depth of the vision, into the idea of the "sun-hero," the "well-beloved."[34]

Echoing the words of Goethe, Haeckel, and so many others, in this chapter Jung also cites a very similar remark by Renan in his *Dialogues et fragments philosophiques* (1876), justifying the rationality of sun worship: "Before religion had reached the stage of proclaiming that God must be put into the absolute and ideal, that is to say, beyond this world, one worship alone was reasonable and scientific: that was worship of the sun."[35]

It is with this final burst of solar mythology that Jung mercifully ends part 1. Part 2, however, picks up right where he left off and the entire first paragraph of part 2 is Jung's appeal to the rationality of sun worship:

> The sun is, as Renan remarked, really the only rational representation of God, whether we take the point of view of the barbarians of other ages or that of the modern physical sciences. . . . the sun is adapted as nothing else to represent the visible God of this world. That is to say, that driving strength of our own soul, which we call libido. . . . That this comparison is no mere play of words is taught to us by the mystics. When by looking inwards (introversion) and going down into the depths of their own being they find "in their heart" the image of the Sun, they find their own love or libido, which with reason, I might say with physical reason, is called the Sun: for our source of energy and life is the Sun. Thus our life substance, as an energic process, is entirely Sun.[36]

After this opening exposition on sun worship as experiencing God as the sun within, Jung cites long passages from Vedic literature to back up his assertions. He finds it important to use these Vedic texts to "join it to the idea most important for us, that God is also contained in the individual creature."[37] Jung interprets these Vedic texts with statements such as: "Whoever has in himself, God, the sun, is immortal, like the sun."[38]

The remainder of part 2 of *Wandlungen* is primarily an exposition on the hero and themes of sacrifice. It is this part of the book that Jung sees as containing the book's central message, for as he said during a seminar in 1925 about *Wandlungen*: "The problem it brought to focus in my mind was that of the hero myth in relation to our own times."[39] Typical mystery-cult scenarios such as going down into Mother Earth to receive one's initiation (usually a battle or struggle of some sort), which is translated into psychoanalysis as finding the wellsprings of one's own libido through a process of introversion. In part 2 Jung introduces his interpretation of Wagnerian opera, with Siegfried equated with Christ as sun heroes, "reborn sons," and as self-sacrificing gods.[40] They are also equated with Mithras, a solar deity from an ancient Hellenistic mystery cult.

Homans was perhaps the first to fully realize the anti-Christian implications of *Wandlungen und Symbole der Libido*. In his view:

> the intellectual heart of this book is not the revised libido theory, or Jung's interpretation of the Miller fantasies, or even his analyses of the mythologies of the world. It is the fate of Christianity in the light of modernity and in particular the new science of psychoanalysis. Jung's libido theory may have been a departure from Freud's, but it still added up to a secular, non-Christian view of the present.[41]

How does Jung repudiate orthodox Christianity in *Wandlungen*? The key may be found in his ideas on Mithraism, which are found throughout the book.

MITHRAISM VS. CHRISTIANITY AS ARYANS VS. SEMITES

Although these mystery cults had been extensively commented upon by previous generations of scholars, the fin de siècle was a time when the irrational elements of antiquity could finally be explored, and this included a new look at the mystery cults. Also, for the very first time, classical scholars finally felt comfortable analyzing the rise of Christianity in its pagan context.[42] Jung's information about Mithraism came primarily from Cumont and Dieterich who, along with German classicists, led this renaissance of scholarly interest in the Hellenistic mystery cults.

Cumont was the very first to gather all of the primary evidence of Mithraism in his magisterial two-volume *Textes et monuments figurés relatifs aux mystères de Mithra*.[43] It is a comprehensive, descriptive, and interpretive collection of all of the archaeological monuments, inscriptions, texts, and references relating to Mithraism from antiquity. A more popular edition of the "Conclusions" of the first volume of Cumont's magnum opus was published in French in 1900 and later in German as *Die Mysterien des Mithra*.[44] Jung's library contains the 1911 German edition of the latter book as well as Cumont's two-volume set.

Jung's view of Mithraism was largely Cumont's, which in turn was a Christianized one: Mithras was an ancient Iranian solar god (like Helios) and a god of correct order and behavior (like Apollo). He is referred to in inscriptions as *Sol Invictus*, the "invincible sun." Mithraism was a survival of the old dualist Mazdean (Zoroastrian) religion of ancient Persia, dating back to at least 600 B.C., but continuing to live underground, only to be adapted to the Roman world of late antiquity (100–400 C.E.). The all-male cult (primarily Roman soldiers and merchants) was based on a masonic lodge–type model of grades of initiations, of which (at least in Rome) there were seven. Cumont insisted that Mithraic mystery initiations involved sacramental feasts at which bread and water were consecrated and at which blood was offered as a sacrifice in ceremonies involving robed priests who offered prayers, sang hymns, and rang bells—as in the Roman Catholic Church—at the holiest moment of the ritual: the unveiling of the ubiquitous image of Mithras killing a bull, the famous *tauroctony* that Jung reproduces in his *Wandlungen*. Indeed, practically all of these basic elements of Cumontian Mithraism—which Jung refers to repeatedly throughout *Wandlungen* and, indeed, throughout his life—can be found in a single chapter of Cumont's book on *The Mysteries of Mithras* entitled, "The Mithraic Liturgy, Clergy and Devotees."

The problem today (and ultimately for Jung's argument in *Wandlungen*) is that recent scholars have called into question almost all of Cumont's basic assumptions about the ancient Iranian origins of the Roman Mithraic mysteries and about the Christian-like sacramental ceremonies. Using the same archaeological and textual evidence that Cumont was the first to compile, and hunting down new evidence and deducing new theories, Mithraic scholars now offer a very different interpretation of the mysteries. The main difficulty is simple: although there is a wealth of archaeological material that is well preserved because the Mithraeums were built underground, there is not one single recorded account of the central myth (*hieros logos*) of Mithraism. Nor does Mithraic iconography provide us

Figure 2. Tauroctony with two trees (from M. J. Vermaseren,
Corpus Inscriptionem et Monumentorum Religionis Mithriacae;
reprinted by permission of the heirs of M. J. Vermaseren
and of Kluwer Academic Publishers).

with the story.[45] Any attempted interpretation of the myth of
Mithras, then, is an imagining, a reconstruction, a fantasy.

The other Mithraic scholar who was approvingly and repeatedly mentioned by Jung in *Wandlungen* and later works is Albrecht Dieterich (1856–1908). Dieterich was a professor of classical philology and religion at the University of Heidelberg from
1903 until his death. Along with Weber and other prominent
scholars from many disciplines, Dieterich participated for many
years in a discussion group on religion (which they called the
"Eranos" circle), started in 1904 by theologian Gustav Adolf
Deissmann, where he undoubtedly presented summaries of
his research on Mithraism and the Greek Magical Papyri.[46] Dieterich's *Eine Mithrasliturgie* of 1903 posited that certain key pas-

sages from the famous Greek Magical Papyri were parts of an authentic Mithraic Liturgy."[47] This particular section of the Greek Magical Papyri begins with an announcement that it is a revelation from "the great god Helios Mithras." It then goes on to describe the celestial ascent of the initiate and a series of prayers of invocation that result in the appearance of, among other entities, Mithras: "a god immensely great, having a bright appearance, youthful, golden-haired, with a white-tunic and golden crown and trousers, and holding in his right hand a golden shoulder of a young bull."[48] Given these characteristics, it is not difficult to see how Jung could easily equate Mithras with the golden-haired Teutonic hero of Wagnerian opera, Siegfried.

The Mithraic Liturgy ends with some advice from Zeus, which Jung scribbled in the upper margin of a famous letter to Freud of 31 August 1910, suggesting it should be adopted as a "motto for psychoanalysis: Give what thou hast, then thou shalt receive."[49] Jung's playful appeal to Freud for a Mithraic credo for psychoanalysis indicates his increasingly strong identification with the Mithraic mysteries. The Mithraic Liturgy is also important in the development of Jung's later psychology for another reason: it is the source of the mythological material regarding a sun phallus. Although Jung used this example throughout his entire life as proof of the collective unconscious, there are serious problems with Jung's story. The story of the Solar Phallus Man will be told in a later section.

In several places in *Wandlungen*, Jung juxtaposes Mithraism with Christianity as "the two great antagonistic religions, Christianity on the one side, and Mithracism on the other,"[50] especially since both rose in prominence in the Roman empire at about the same time (100–400 C.E.). Here Jung is following Cumont (and before him, Renan) in arguing that, if historical events had gone a little differently, the Western world would be Mithraic and not Judeo-Christian today.[51] Jung repeated this line (somewhat wistfully, perhaps) in *Wandlungen* and in his 1925 seminars on analytical psychology.[52] It was clearly an idea that stuck with him for decades.

Although Jung points out the similarities between the two religions (as having a sacrifice as the central image, of being social systems for the restraint of animal impulses, etc.), there are some fundamental differences that Jung does not point out but that become apparent in light of the discussion above. Mithraism, as a survival of Zoroastrianism, is a far more ancient form of worship than Christianity, which only dates to the first century C.E. Mithraism is therefore an ancient Aryan religion, and Christianity originally a Semitic one. The rivalry between Mithraism and Christianity is the rivalry between an ancient Aryan sun god and a Semitic god. Here Jung follows Cumont, who refers to Mithras as "the old Aryan deity."[53] Indeed, the very first line of Cumont's *The Mysteries of Mithra* tells us that, "In that unknown epoch when the ancestors of the Persians were still united with those of the Hindus, they were already worshippers of Mithra."[54] This "unknown epoch" is, of course, the Müllerian "mythopoetic" Aryan epoch of tribal prehistory so often addressed in nineteenth-century scholarship.

Jung imagines Mithraism to be a form of nature worship and not a form of religion forged in the iron cage of civilization, as Christianity had been during the Roman empire. Jung says that Mithraic worship is "nature worship in the best sense of the word; while the primitive Christians exhibited throughout an antagonistic attitude to the beauties of this world."[55] Jung further charges:

> In the past two thousand years Christianity has done its work and has erected barriers of repression, which protect us from the sight of our own "sinfulness." The elementary emotions of the libido have come to be unknown to us, for they are carried on in the unconscious; therefore, the belief which combats them has become hollow and empty. Let whoever believes that a mask covers our religion, obtain an impression for himself from the appearance of our modern churches, from which style and art have long since fled.[56]

The natural Urreligion of the prehistoric Aryans was Jung's idea of the true source of all the Hellenistic mystery cults (e.g., the Great Mother, Isis, Osiris, Dionysus), but this was especially true of Mithraism. Mithraism was a direct survival of the Urreligion from the primordial homeland or *Urheimat* of the ancient Aryans, the Indo-Iranian region. In Jung's view, based on the scholarship of his day, the ancient Greco-Roman mystery cults were all based on the experience of rebirth for their initi-

127

ates through special secret rites of initiation that focused on the transformative experience of becoming one with god. In the Mithraic cult, therefore, this would mean becoming one with an ancient Aryan god. The Aryan peoples—unlike the Semites— held onto their natural religion longer than any other group and were thus closer to the *Urreligion* of the sun and sky of all original humans.

In light of the historical method of psychoanalysis offered by Jung for uncovering evidence for the phylogeny of the human soul, his geophysically informed vision is plain: in the individual psyche there are strata that comprise the sediment of two thousand years of Christianity. Two thousand years of Christianity makes us strangers to ourselves. In the individual, the internalization of bourgeois-Christian civilization is a mask that covers the true Aryan god within, a natural god, a sun god, perhaps even Mithras himself. This is as true as the scientific fact that within the earth is glowing sun-matter that is hidden by thousands of years of sediment as well. In society, too, Christianity is an alien mask that covers our biologically true religion, a natural religion of the sun and the sky. The scientific proof are the cases of patients with dementia praecox documented by Jung and his Zurich School assistants (Honegger, Nelken, and Spielrein) that demonstrate that there is a pre-Christian, mythological layer of the unconscious mind. It is archaic and corresponds to the thought and especially to the souls of our ancestors. It does not produce purely Christian symbols, but instead it offers images of the sun as god.

By documenting this phylogenetic layer of the unconscious mind one also learns about the earliest origins of the human race. Therefore, we learn something new about not only archaeology, but evolutionary biology. What Jung doesn't explicitly say—but it is fundamental to his project to demonstrate the utility of psychoanalysis as the new Wissenschaft—is that we also learn about the origins of the very planet we live on, and that this method can add to our knowledge of the earth sciences. The strong implication by Jung, especially after a brief flirtation with the cultural stages of Bachofenian theory circa 1912–1913, is that (1) the universality of solar symbolism in material from the phylogenetic unconscious and (2) evidence of still-existing sun worship in primitive societies around the world (which Jung would one day see for himself in Africa and in the American South-west) are expressions of prephylogenetic memories from our in-animate history. As the earth sprang from the sun and took many millions of years to cool off before life emerged from non-life and began the process of evolution, these memories of being torn from the sun must somehow be in the very matter that comprise our physical bodies. This is one of the areas in which Jung's line of thought parallels Henri Bergson's ideas and in-deed may have been informed by them, for Bergson's hypothe-sis of a biological unconscious in which humans can intuit the memories of their evolutionary past was put forth in his books *Mattière et Mémoire* (*Matter and Memory*) in 1896 and *L'Evolution Créatrice* in 1907. Libido, Bergsonian *élan vital*, *Lebenskraft* (the old term of the Naturphilosophen and the vitalists for the "force of life"), and the sun are therefore indeed one.[57]

This form of holism, as historian Anne Harrington terms it, was not limited to Jung but became the response of many Ger-man researchers (such as the Gestalt psychologists) to the exis-tential crisis of science in the period between the wars.[58]

"THE JEWS DO NOT HAVE THIS IMAGE"

The presence of solar symbolism in Semitic cultures (ancient Egypt, for example) was indisputable, but many scholars felt that evidence of other similarities with the religions of the an-cient Aryans was lacking. Semitic cultures were not regarded by Jung as based as directly on the same natural sources or Ur-religion as the ancient Aryans and therefore did not have "mys-teries" in the sense of a direct experience of the divine through initiation rituals. This opinion was also found in the bulk of the work of nineteenth-century scholars concerned with Aryan and Semitic differences. In *Eine Mithrasliturgie*, Dieterich notes in a discussion of the motif of rebirth in ancient India, in the Helle-nistic mysteries of Isis, and in other Aryan cultural contexts that, "the Jews do not have this image" (*die Juden haben das Bild nicht*).[59] The so-called mysteries mentioned in the literature of Hellenistic Judaism and early Christianity (especially in the first three centuries C.E.) were not considered to be from original Semitic sources (as was the original "Christ cult" and "Jesus

129

movement") but instead were a syncretic result of contact with the Hellenistic world and its Aryan mysteries. The metaphors of *mysteria* and initiation were borrowed from the pagans, but their initiatory rituals were not.[60]

In nineteenth-century German scholarship Christianity was more often than not portrayed as a Semitic religion alien to the Aryan cultures of Greece and Rome. This was also very much the view of those German Protestant theologians known as the Tübingen School whose iconoclastic ideas gained ascendancy in the 1860s. Jung shared these views of vast spiritual and psychological differences between Aryan and Semitic ancestries, and they are reflected frequently in much of his work until the late 1930s.

Hence, for the educated völkisch neopagan circa 1911 or 1912 who may have stumbled across this work, it would seem that *Wandlungen und Symbole der Libido* was the scientific confirmation of everything that one would believe about the necessity for the repudiation of Christianity and the practice of sun worship. Jung's volume is indeed the "völkisch Liturgy."

Jung's Völkisch Sources for

Wandlungen

It is clear from an analysis of the intellectual sources of Jung's ideas, and the literature he cites, that he approves of the work of prominent völkisch scientists and scholars, many of them Monists. The cultural, linguistic, and especially biological differences between Aryans and Semites—which, again, made sense in the scientific world of the fin de siècle without the Hitlerian taint such ideas have today—are used pejoratively in the works of völkisch writers to promote the superiority of Aryans over Semitic peoples. Jung was well aware of the biases in the works he was citing. He, too, was very much concerned with the problem of differences in the psychologies of Aryans and Semites and openly discussed these nineteenth-century *scientific* issues with Freud, who also adhered to such a model of ethnic terminology.[61]

Freud himself uses the term "Aryan" to distinguish the non-Jews in the psychoanalytic movement in his correspondence to fellow Jewish psychoanalysts such as Karl Abraham and Sandor Ferenczi, as Peter Gay has documented in his biography of Freud. In letters to Ferenczi in May and June 1913, following Jung's formal break with Freud in January of that year, Freud tells him that psychoanalysis must remain independent of all "Aryan patronage." He also insists that because of fundamental cognitive differences between Aryans and Jews, psychoanalysis as a science should look only a little different depending on whether it is in the hands of the almost exclusively Jewish Viennese or the largely Christian Swiss. Freud tells Ferenczi: "Certainly there are great differences with the Aryan spirit. . . . Hence there would surely be different Weltanschauungs here and there. [But] there should be no distinct Aryan or Jewish science. Their results should be identical; only their presentation may vary."[62]

We have already discussed at length the influence of Haeckel in *Wandlungen*, and his anti-Semitic views that go beyond mere thinking in terms of Aryans and Jews have also been mentioned. The work of Ostwald was also known and admired by Jung and must be taken into account as part of the uncited völkisch background to *Wandlungen*. We have also discussed Jung's selective attention to the literature of comparative philology and comparative mythology concerning the Aryan peoples and his relative neglect of extant sources of such information (admittedly much less developed) on Semitic or other peoples.

One very brief but very significant citation by Jung needs special attention. In the first part of *Wandlungen* Jung cites with approval the immensely influential 1899 work of historical speculation by Chamberlain, *Die Grundlagen des Neunzehnten Jahrhunderts (Foundations of the Nineteenth Century)*.[63] Jung briefly mentions Chamberlain's odd view of Christian asceticism as "biologic suicide because of the enormous amount of illegitimacy among Mediterranean peoples at the time."[64] The ease with which Jung cites Chamberlain demonstrates how acceptable völkisch racial philosophy had become among the educated elites of German Europe by this time. Mosse says that *Grundlagen* "had a deep impact on Volkish thought," for "culminating in [its] message of imminent victory for the German race, Chamberlain's book became a favorite book in the Volkish movement. In many ways it attained the stature of being the

Bible of racial truth, thought and victory."[65] Field best sums up the seminal message of this sizable two-volume work:

> All the major elements of German racism converge in Chamberlain's writing: Aryan supremacy, anti-Semitism, messianic and mystical notions of race, Social Darwinism, and recently developed doctrines of eugenics and anthroposociology. Above all he joined the Teutonic myth, German nationalism, and cultural idealism. For him—unlike Gobineau—race, nation and *Volk* were almost identical. Admittedly, he was careful to include Slavs and Celts along with the Germanic peoples in the Teutonic race, but his description made it clear that the purest and least corrupted specimens inhabited the German Reich. The vitality of Britain, Russia and France had been exhausted by racial degeneration and their growing adherence to foreign, particularly Semitic, ideals.[66]

Besides this notable but brief citation of Chamberlain, Jung also cites the völkisch work of Drews, who, in *The Christ Myth* (1910) and other works, "worked together with many Monists to spread the idea that Christ was not an historical figure, but a myth."[67] In the same footnote in which Jung mentions Drews he also cites with approval the work of the radical Protestant theologian Dr. Albert Kalthoff, the pastor of St. Martin in Bremen, who was the first working president of the Monistic League. Mosse says that Drews was the chief adviser to the Eugen Diederichs Verlag, which was the publisher of Drews and Kalthoff.[68] It is clear that by 1911–1912 Jung was reading extensively in the literature of monism and völkisch racism.

This fact could not have been lost on Freud and the Viennese. Chamberlain was a known anti-Semite and his *Grundlagen*, published twelve years before Jung's citation of it, was well known for its racism. This reference must have jumped off the page at Freud. The most strained letters between Freud and Jung really begin after Freud's reading of part 1 of *Wandlungen*, and the open break in intimate relations between the two men is well under way by November 1912, when we have the first evidence that Freud has read part 2. As a Jewish intellectual in Austria-Hungary Freud could not have missed Jung's fascination with Aryan origins and his citation of monist and völkisch literature.

Jung was *never* openly anti-Semitic; the evidence for this seems clear. But given the estrangement from Freud and his Viennese Jews, and the citation of such threatening material in *Wandlungen*, it is no wonder that our first evidence of Freud's view of Jung as an anti-Semite comes in an exchange of letters with Ernest Jones in December 1912. "Jung is going to save the world, another Christ (with certainly anti-semitism combined)," Jones complains to Freud on 5 December 1912. Freud concurs in his 8 December response: "I thank you for your very just remarks about Jung. . . . In fact he behaves like a perfect fool, he seems to be Christ himself, and in the particular things he says there is always something of the *Lausbub* [rascal]."[69] In an 8 July 1915 letter to his American supporter, James Jackson Putnam, Freud could say that he liked Jung until he was taken over "by a religious-ethical 'crisis'" imbued "with higher morality, rebirth" and that Jung demonstrated "lies, brutality and anti-Semitic condescension toward me."[70]

"A Foreign Growth"

Perhaps a brief review of some of my conclusions in this chapter will clarify any potential misinterpretation of my argument.

Jung's *Wandlungen und Symbole der Libido* of 1912 may very well be interpreted (and *was* by some) as a modern mystical contribution to the solar mythology of Müller, and in that sense it was an Asconan work of sun worship. However, a more defensible argument is that it is most assuredly a representative völkisch work of its era, although Jung's völkisch interests were not political ones.[71]

The compilation of mythological material in *Wandlungen* contains central völkisch themes that were regularly discussed in conversation and in the journals of the time, such as *Die Tat* and the many journals of the Theosophical Society and the Monistenbund: the hero as sun; the sun as God; the god as self-sacrificing deity; Siegfried, Christ, Mithras, and other pagans identified as related personifications of the same self-sacrificing Aryan god (hence Jung's implicit adoption of the "Aryan Christ"); mythic interpretations of Wagnerian opera and its Teutonic mythology (the Ring Cycle) and redemptive Holy Grail (*Parsifal*) imagery; the association of blood with the sun and with the hero; the presence of a pre-Christian ancestral layer (or racial or phylogenetic layer) of the unconscious mind within each of us that can be contacted and whose pagan ancestral images can be immediate and directly experienced;[72] and, especially, a fascination with the climax of ancient Greco-Roman mystery initiations resulting in the self-deification of the initiate (realizing the god within, the life-giving sun or star within, was a dominant völkisch catchphrase).[73] All of these themes, familiar to völkisch neopagans and Asconan *Naturmenschen* alike, are repeated over and over again in *Wandlungen* and in Jung's later writings.

Jung clearly identifies himself with the spirit of German Volkstumbewegung throughout this period and well into the 1920s and 1930s, until the horrors of Nazism finally compelled him to reframe these neopagan metaphors in a negative light in his 1936 essay on Wotan.[74] However, it must be pointed out that while he warns against the possible excesses and dangers of the return of Wotan in this essay, he seems nonetheless to hold the view that Wotan (and by implication not the Judeo-Christian god) is indeed the true god of the Germanic peoples, who therefore must make this knowledge conscious or risk "possession" by this ancient Aryan deity.

Jung's own consciousness of his German völkisch identity—lost through decades of obfuscation of the historical Jung by a world blinded by Hitler and Nazism and by generations of his disciples who are more interested in the promotion of the eternal values of his ideas rather than the specifics of his life—is boldly revealed in a letter of 26 May 1923 to Oskar Schmitz (1873–1931), a writer and a pupil of Jung's who introduced Keyserling to Jung's work in 1922 and who arranged for Jung to speak at Keyserling's School of Wisdom. In this letter Jung clearly identifies himself as a descendant of the pagan Germanic tribes who had the "foreign growth" of Christianity grafted onto them and argues against having any other alien philosophies from the Orient taught to those of Germanic heredity:

> These antecedents do not apply to us. The Germanic tribes, when
> they collided only the day before yesterday with Roman Chris-

134

tianity, were still in the initial state of a polydemonism with polytheistic buds. There was as yet no proper priesthood and no
proper ritual. Like Wotan's oaks, the gods were felled and a
wholly incongruous Christianity, born of monotheism on a much
higher cultural level, was grafted onto the stumps. The Germanic
man is still suffering from this mutilation. I have good reasons for
thinking that every step beyond the existing situation has to
begin down there among the truncated nature-demons. In other
words, there is a whole lot of primitivity in us to be made good.

It therefore seems a grave error if we graft yet another foreign
growth onto our already mutilated condition. This craving for
things foreign and faraway is a morbid sign. Also, we cannot get
beyond our present level of culture unless we receive a powerful
impetus from our roots. But we shall receive it only if we go back
behind our cultural level, thus giving the suppressed primitive
man in ourselves a chance to develop. How this is to be done is a
problem I have been trying to solve for years. . . . We must dig
down to the primitive in us, for only out of the conflict between
civilized man and the Germanic barbarian will there come what
we need: a new experience of God. I do not think this goal can be
reached by means of artificial exercises.[75]

A 1916 document included later in this volume demonstrates
how Jung sought to solve this problem practically by developing his own method of giving individuals—through analysis—
a "new experience of God," and uses symbols of völkisch mysticism such as *Parsifal*, Goethe and even the "World Tree," a very
common symbol invoked at this time by völkisch Germans as a
reference to Wotan and his sacred groves as an alternative to the
Semitic Christian "tree" (crucifix) of Jesus.

Again, to repeat: it would not be fair to characterize Jung
or his work during this early period as "prefascist" or "pre–
National Socialist." Not all völkisch neopagan groups pursued
political aims. The best that can be said is that the evidence is
compelling that Jung's work arose from the same Central European cauldron of neopagan, Nietzschean, mystical, hereditarian,
völkisch utopianism out of which National Socialism arose. Like
Jung and his small Psychological Club and later international
movement, the leaders of National Socialism conducted their
movement as if it were a mystery cult and made great use of the

symbolism (runes, swastikas) of the occult. And, perhaps, like Hitler, who immersed himself in völkisch mythology, occultism, and even the Monistic Religion books of Haeckel during his lean years in Vienna between 1908 and 1913, it may be said that Jung, too, made "a religion out of *Parsifal*."

JUNGIAN PSYCHOLOGY AS SUN WORSHIP

Jung's earliest psychological theories and method can be interpreted as perhaps nothing more than an anti-Christian return to solar mythology and sun worship based on Romantic beliefs about the natural religion of the ancient Aryan peoples. What Jung eventually offered to völkisch believers in sun worship circa 1916 was a practical method—active imagination—through which one could contact ancestors and also have a direct experience of God as a star or sun within.

Jung's aim, in one form or another, was always religion. By 1921, after forming his cult and publishing his theories on the collective unconscious and the archetypes, Jung could have very well included himself within the heritage of the "German genius" when he says, "The solution of the problem in *Faust*, in Wagner's *Parsifal*, in Schopenhauer, and even in Nietzsche's *Zarathustra* is *religious*."[76] The solution of the problem in Jung is religious, too. It was also the preferred solution of many other neopagan groups in Central Europe at this time who also did not pursue political answers to the questions of existence. Jung knew the leaders of many of the more "establishment" neopagan movements, such as the German Faith Movement of Hauer, with whom Jung co-led seminars in the 1930s. It was in these religious movements of the völkisch world that Jung found kindred spirits. As one contemporary observer would remark in 1935, "In fact, one might almost say that the National Socialist party represented the political aspect and the Germanic Faith Movement the religious aspect of a common folk-movement."[77]

The original Jung cult in Küsnacht-Zurich did not become like the other vegetarian and Theosophical neopagan groups because these were too countercultural for the essentially bourgeois Jung to emulate. Many (but certainly not all) of them tended to be apolitical, anarchistic, or sexually libertine, and did not fuse their spirituality or sexuality with racial or political agendas. Jung was more comfortable with the völkisch mysticism that had penetrated the bourgeois educated classes of Central Europe, from which National Socialism disproportionately found its membership in the 1920s. As Mosse reminds us in *The Crisis of German Ideology*, "It was the literate bourgeoisie that was saturated with the [völkisch] ideology. This class came to comprise the largest single bloc in the movement, and at the turn of the century the anti-Semitic stereotype and the Aryan ideal came close to being commonplace bourgeois notions."[78]

The similarity between Jungian psychology and National Socialism is that both movements promoted Weltanschauungs based on (1) the traditional Germanic symbolism of völkisch mysticism and (2) "Nietzscheanism" in the elitist and pseudo-liberational sense astutely identified by Tönnies. They both, in their unique ways, offered what Stern calls "the promise of miracle, mystery and authority" to those of predominantly Aryan heredity.[79] I therefore argue that the Jung cult and its present day movement is in fact a "Nietzschean religion," with all of the internal contradictions between the words and deeds of its disciples implied by this oxymoron. It was founded on Nietzschean principles by Jung himself and promotes a Nietzschean philosophy using seductive Dionysian metaphors from Nietzsche.[80] I make this argument in the sections that follow in part 2 of this volume. It may seem quite disturbing to many that Jung's earliest ideas and cult (circa 1916) are based primarily on the völkisch mysticism of sun worship. The most blatant survival is the central place of the concept of the self in Jung's later psychology, which most commonly presents itself as an image of God or as an experience of the god within in the form of a circle or an Indian (Aryan) *mandala*. God, of course, has many thousands of faces, but out of all of the possibilities it is this central metaphor that Jung invokes time and time again. Sun worship is perhaps the key to fully understanding Jung and the story I tell in this book.

PART TWO

PRELUDE TO A CULT

Chronology and Biography

Spirits, Memory Images,
and the Longing for Mystery

1895–1907

Earlier I noted that Jung's prime years of maturation were during a period of an unusually potent convergence of familial and cultural preoccupations with the spirituality of antiquity, heredity, evolution, memory, and the dead. Through the long historical excursion above I have attempted to sketch only those cultural elements of this matrix that greatly influenced Jung but which have rarely been discussed by Jung scholars. Those who are longtime readers of the works of Jung will understand the relevance of the preceding historical introduction, and it is hoped that those new to Jung will better understand the argument I make in the remainder of this volume.

Given the cultural matrix outlined in part 1, we shall see below that it is arguable that Jung set out to design a cult of redemption or renewal in the period beginning as early as 1912. This was a mystery cult that promised the initiate revitalization through contact with the pagan, pre-Christian layer of the unconscious mind. By doing so, one would have a direct experience of God, which was experienced as an inner sun or star that was the fiery core of one's being. One could also thereby learn to enter the "Land of the Dead" and contact one's ancestors. Thus, as I shall argue, by 1916 Jung had successfully integrated the core nineteenth-century concerns of the spirituality of antiquity, memory, heredity, evolution, and the dead into his psychological theories and methods and in the foundation of the Psychology Club in 1916—the true formalization of the Jung cult.

This section is concerned with the evidence from Jung's life and work that presage the formal founding of his cult of redemption in 1916. Although the discussion has primarily been historical up to now, a brief chronological summary of Jung's life and work during these years is provided in the following chapters to assist the reader in understanding the sequence of events that served as a prelude to cult building. The history of the development of many of Jung's later ideas is also evident here. Therefore, we must first return to his medical-school days, where Jung's first experiences in cults with elitist or transcendental concerns are evident.

1895–1900

Jung entered the medical school at Basel University on 18 May 1895 and completed his studies there in the winter semester of 1900–1901. During his first year, Jung's father died, on 28 January 1896. On 11 December 1900, Jung took up his position as an assistant staff psychiatrist at the Burghölzli.

Jung's participation in the Zofingia fraternity during these years has fortunately been preserved for us in *The Zofingia Lectures*. The transcripts of these five lectures (given between November 1896 and January 1899) reveal Jung's early interest in the literature of spiritualism (Sir William Crookes, Johann Karl Friedrich Zöllner, as well as David Friedrich Strauss on the "Seeress of Prevorst"), philosophy (Kant, Schopenhauer, von Hartmann, and Nietzsche), and in theology (especially Albrecht Ritschl).

We can also learn a great deal about the education he was receiving in evolutionary biology from these lectures. He refers to Darwin's theory of natural selection as the mechanism that produces variation in evolution but that, Jung insists in May 1897 (following the opinion of most Germans of that time), "cannot adequately explain evolution."[1] Instead Jung argues, "In the field of phylogeny, more than in any other, it is necessary to postulate the existence of a vital principle," which Jung refers to as "soul. . . . an intelligence independent of time and space" and as such possibly immortal.[2]

This vital principle and talk of an immaterial soul approaches the metaphors used openly by von Hartmann and even Haeckel during the 1890s, although in a later lecture (January 1899) Jung seems to equate Haeckel with mechanistic science and not with his beloved vitalists.[3] Although Jung read Haeckel, he instead allies himself with philosophers such as von Hartmann and his *Philosophie des Unbewussten* (*Philosophy of the Unconscious*) of 1868, despite the fact that by the 1890s a combination of vitalistic and volitional factors made the works of these two men very similar.[4] Jung's early identification with the vitalistic school of evolutionary biology and his rejection of the mechanists can be seen in the following rhetorical flourish that also betrays a hint of Jung's elitism:

> One day people will laugh and weep at the same time over the disgraceful way in which highly praised German scholars have gone astray. They will build monuments to Schopenhauer, who linked that materialism with bestiality through the conjunction "and." But they will curse Carl Vogt, Ludwig Büchner, Moleschott, DuBois-Reymond, and many others for having stuffed a passel of materialistic rubbish into the gaping mouths of those guttersnipes, the educated proletariat.[5]

Jung never deviated from vitalism throughout the remainder of his career. It was with the vitalistic school of evolutionary biology and it origins in the Naturphilosophie of the Romantics that Jung was always to remain—even when new discoveries in genetics and other areas seemed to legitimize the predominant scientific worldview in the twentieth century that includes a biology based only on mechanistic materialism. As we shall see, Jung was most modern in his scientific worldview during these student years, after which his ideas slowly retreated further back into a philosophy that more closely resembled early nineteenth-century biological science and its Romantic idealism.

Mystery

In the Zofingia lecture of January 1899, "Some Thoughts on the Interpretation of Christianity, with Reference to the Theory of Albrecht Ritschl," we find the first evidence that Jung has opted for the direct experience of mystery over the sterile Christian religion of his day and its absolute, distant, transcendent God. Lauding Ritschl (1822–1889) for the philosophical basis of his theology, Jung nonetheless uses the Protestant theologian's denial of the mystical element in religion to make the point that such approaches are doomed to fail, for as Jung argues "the mystery will remain in the human heart until the end of time."[6]

This lecture is significant, too, because in it Jung reveals he has digested Nietzsche by the age of twenty-three, making many references to *Zarathustra*. It is also significant because in his opening remarks Jung describes Jesus as a "god-man" with the unmistakable characteristics of Schopenhauer's description of genius.[7]

These references to Schopenhauer, Nietzsche, and von Hartmann abound because, after searching the spiritualist literature in vain, Jung took up the study of philosophy (not the psychiatric literature) to understand the trances of his mediumistic first cousin, Hélène Preiswerk, during seances that Jung himself may have initiated as early as June 1895. Jung later claimed the seances only took place from July 1899 to the fall of 1900 and were not organized by him.[8] In any event, Jung used hypnotic techniques to place his fifteen-year-old cousin Helly into "somnambulistic" trances in which alternate "spirit" personalities would emerge and speak through her, including dead ancestors such as his maternal grandfather (and common relative of Jung and the Preiswerk women in the circle), Samuel Preiswerk (1799–1871). Through her "control" spirit personality "Ivenes," Helly even impersonated the legendary woman whom Goethe seduced to allegedly become the mother of Jung the Elder. The Jung family legend of Goethe as ancestor was thus impressive even to Hélène, who by this time had additionally fallen in love with the budding genius Jung.

Jung took copious notes and eventually based his doctoral dissertation on Helly (in which she is called "S. W."), which was published in 1902 under the title, "On the Psychology and Pathology of So-Called Occult Phenomena."[9] He analyzed her hysteria and somnambulistic symptoms according to the German and French psychiatric literature of his day. He based its style on the acclaimed book by Flournoy, *From India to the Planet Mars* (1899), who during the same period in Geneva sat in on the seances of a "Hélène Smith." Flournoy traced all the fantastic content of her spiritualistic trances (previous lives on Mars and in ancient India), to previous experiences in her life or to previously read published sources, even though she herself apparently had no conscious memory of exposure. Such hidden memories that seemed like new experiences when resurfacing in conscious awareness was evidence of a function of human memory called cryptomnesia. In later years, especially during the process of his break with Freud, Jung made many trips to visit his "fatherly friend" Flournoy in Geneva.[10]

While the publication of his doctoral dissertation on "S. W." did much for furthering his career as a physician and university professor, it upset the Preiswerk family and further stigmatized Helly as a hysteric and therefore a hereditary degenerate. Basel was still a relatively small city in the 1890s, especially for those of the Pfarrerstand caste, and it was relatively easy to see through Jung's pseudonyms and scant fictionalizations. Based on the interviews that he conducted with family members, Ellenberger explains that, "In those days considerable stress was put on heredity, and the whole maternal side of the family appeared to be tainted with insanity. Rumors circulated that the younger Preiswerk daughters could not find husbands because of Jung's dissertation and that Hélène had died from a broken heart. Actually, she died from tuberculosis at the age of thirty."[11]

Jung's concern over the fateful degeneracy latent in his own blood may have influenced his sudden decision to specialize in psychiatry, for by the standards of the dominant medical philosophy of his day, Jung was a prime candidate for eventually exhibiting and suffering the stigma of hereditary degeneration: besides Helly's hysteria, Jung's mother had bouts of mental illness, and Jung himself may have been a "bad seed," suffering from hysterical fainting fits as a child that were diagnosed as degenerative "epileptic fits" by one doctor.[12] Later, as a man, he must have feared that his confrontation with the unconscious may have been the prodromal phase of a lifelong degenerative psychosis. The theory of hereditary degeneration has been called, and rightly so, "the Christian notion of original sin embodied in the nervous system,"[13] and it obsessed persons at all levels of society at the turn of the century.[14]

Spiritualism and evolutionary biology, then, formed the earliest basis of Jung's later psychological theories and methods. Jung read widely in the literature of psychical research, which was a field taken much more seriously in Germany at the time and was the original experimental psychology there in the nineteenth century. The first German Society for Experimental Psychology was not devoted to the more mundane subject matter of

Wundt, who was known as the founder of modern experimental psychology, but instead was devoted to psychical research.[15] Jung's interest in spiritualism remained throughout his years of psychiatric activity at the Burghölzli (1900–1909) and his involvement with Freud, whose disdain for Jung's fascination with occultism is well known. Jung attended seances with Bleuler and others in the early 1920s and then again in the 1930s.[16] Communication with the dead resurfaced as a dominant concern during his confrontation with the unconscious (1912–1918 or so) and Jung often refers to the collective unconscious after 1916 as the land of the dead. The phenomena of spiritualism and the literature of psychical research were the primary topics of Jung's as-yet-unpublished seminar on modern psychology, which he gave from October 1933 to February 1934 at the Swiss Polytechnical School in Zurich, covering the work of Schopenhauer, Nietzsche, Carus, Flournoy, and especially Justinius Kerner and the Seeress of Prevorst.[17] Spiritualistic concerns were never very far away from either Jung's psychological theories or his psychotherapeutic techniques.[18]

1900–1909

Memory

During these years Jung achieved international fame as an experimental psychopathologist with the diagnostic word-association studies conducted by him and his colleagues at the Burghölzli (1902–1909).[19] These experimental studies are still an unacknowledged precursor to modern cognitive science, as they are concerned with the quantitative exploration of such contemporary foci of cognitive research as attention, differential processing of information, and implicit memory.[20] Jung was fascinated with the processes of human memory and the phenomena of memory disorders, as his earliest psychiatric publications attest.[21]

Jung's interest in the psychological processes of memory, however, is first in evidence in his Zofingia lectures referring to Christ, and it resurfaces in the seminal 1916 document concerning the forming of the Psychological Club. Ritschl used the

philosophical and psychological literature of his day to accentuate his theology, for which Jung admires him and yet attacks
him for using the language of Wissenschaft to remove the
mystery necessary for religious experience. According to Jung
(who, like Ritschl, had read the works of Fechner, Lotze, and
Wundt on mental images and contents) "the Christ present to
the Ritschlian Christian constitutes the sum of all the images in
memory handed down by tradition, that is, of all mental images
concerning the person of Christ, in conjunction with the feeling
of value that we confer on the totality of these images."[22] Ritschl
argues that "exact memory is the medium of personal relationships" and also of the relationship between "God or Christ and
ourselves."[23] Jung further chides Ritschl for condemning mystics who claim a direct relationship, a *unio mystica*, between man
and God, as Ritschl claims this experience is always mediated
by the personal and cultural contents of one's individual memory images. In January 1899, when this talk was given, Jung
could reject the mediatory role of memory, but he later reveals
his adoption of a similar idea in his 1916 manifesto by claiming
that with Christ's death, his "Imago" (memory image) arose in
the "collective soul of mankind" (our transpersonal long-term
memory-storage bank) and itself became a personified symbol
of the collective soul. Memory (images in the collective soul)
mediates the relationship between the historical Jesus and the
modern individual. The motivating force of an ideal comes from
its affective tone in one's memory.

Memory is the essential problem of consciousness, for if we
understand memory, we understand our individual experience
of the continuity of the self. The early experimental psychologists understood this, and this is why memory was such a focus
of interest to these researchers.[24] Memory is also the essential
problem of heredity and evolutionary biology. Why do children look like their parents? And yet, why are they also somewhat different from them? Biologically, what is "remembered"
from one generation to the next? Hence, the problem of evolution soon became the problem of distortion in biological memory. Most importantly, it became Jung's "problem." Jung's early
interests in the problem of memory posed by evolutionary biology, Ritschlian theology, and *Parapsychologie* (psychical re-

search) are at first explored spiritualistically, then experimentally, then psychoanalytically, and then united in his theories of the collective unconscious (1916) and the archetypes (1919).

Embourgeoisement and Its Unraveling

Fresh from medical school, Jung began his psychiatric career in December 1900 at the Burghölzli under Bleuler. The Burghölzli was not only the insane asylum of Canton Zurich, but also the Psychiatric Clinic of Zurich University where its medical students were trained. Jung's first position was as Assistant Staff Physician (1900), then Senior Assistant Staff Physician (1902), then Senior Staff Physician (1905), making him second-in-command to Bleuler until Jung left the Burghölzli in the spring of 1909 to move into his new house in Küsnacht and to devote his full energies to his private practice, writing, teaching, and involvement with the psychoanalytic movement. From 1905 to 1913 Jung taught at Zurich University under the title of *Privatdozent* (lecturer). We therefore see in the life of Jung his successful pursuit of a bourgeois life as a physician and a university professor that was very much in the tradition of his forefathers.

On 14 February 1903 Jung married Emma Rauschenbach of Schaffhausen, Switzerland, the daughter of a wealthy German industrialist. Under Swiss law at this time, the husband had complete access to his wife's assets and could use them at his disposal without her consent. The financial resources that Emma Jung brought to her marriage, while not specifically known, are regarded as considerable and maintained the stability of a bourgeois lifestyle in Switzerland that allowed Jung to risk the many changes in his occupational life between 1909 and 1914, by which time he had severed all ties with institutions or his primary professional associations. This was one major sign that Jung was rejecting many of the external trophies of the bourgeoisie and was evolving into a less conventional, more modern lifestyle.

Cracks in the foundation of Jung's Christian-bourgeois character began to appear very shortly after he took up residence at the Burghölzli in December 1900. An erotic attachment to a Jewish patient sent shock waves through his psyche. Early evidence of Jung's inner conflict survives in the form of his own word-association test protocol, which is thinly disguised in the very first publications (in 1904–1905) of the results of this research.[25]

In this report, it is Jung who is "Subject 19," a "Physician, 25 years old." The entire "complex-constellation" relating to Jung's erotic attachment to this Jewish patient is highlighted and analyzed in a special section introduced with the following remarks:

> The subject had, during the time of the experiments, formed an attachment to a young woman. To make the experiments understandable it must also be mentioned that the young man had also not yet outgrown adolescent internal conflict, and as he had a strict Christian upbringing, his inclination for a Jewish girl worried him a great deal. Let us call her Alice Stern; we shall be keeping as near the truth as is necessary for the experiment.[26]

Jung was further challenged in 1904 after the arrival of yet another "Jewish girl" at the Burghölzli, the eighteen-year-old Sabina Spielrein (1885–1941). Spielrein was admitted as a patient at the Burghölzli with a diagnosis of "psychotic hysteria" on 17 August 1904 and remained as a patient there until 1 June 1905. It was during this time, on 28 April 1905, that she registered as a medical student at Zurich University.[27] Spielrein was Jung's first case of hysteria to be treated with psychoanalytic techniques. After some therapeutic success, Spielrein assisted Jung, Riklin, and their colleagues in conducting the word-association experiments. Jung developed an erotic attachment to Spielrein at about this time, and their mutual erotic attraction and relationship has been documented elsewhere.[28] Their "closer erotic relationship" probably began at some point in 1907.[29]

In January and February 1907 Jung participated as a subject in Ludwig Binswanger's association experiments at the Burghölzli. As Kerr has noted, Jung's erotic attachment to Spielrein and its similarity to that revealed in his earlier protocol of 1901–1902 are extensively revealed in this second protocol in the form of Jung's "star complex." As Binswanger notes, Jung used the word "star" as a response several times and it seemed to be associated with a complex of feelings related to Spielrein.[30]

Thus, even in Jung's word-association protocols early in his career we have evidence of the first eruptions of the problems of

Aryan/Semitic differences and the use of the word "star" (or sun) as a metaphor of significant meaning for Jung. During these early years, as the foci of his fantasies and secret erotic desires, first the unknown Jewish girl and then Spielrein were each, in turn, the "star within" for Jung.

Freud and Psychoanalysis

These years in Jung's life also mark the beginnings of his involvement with Freud and psychoanalysis. As I noted earlier, these years of association with Freud and psychoanalysis are the best documented period in the biography of the historical Jung and need not undergo further examination here. The important point to remember, however, is that during these years with Freud, Jung never gave up his interests in evolutionary vitalism, in spiritualism, in the dissociational psychology of Janet and the French clinical tradition, or in the spirituality of antiquity—all of which would resurrect and converge in the psychology he developed after his break with Freud.

Otto Gross, Nietzscheanism, and Matriarchal Neopaganism

1908

THE RETREAT FROM DEGENERACY THEORY

THE YEAR 1908 marked a turning point in the history of psychiatry and in the history of the psychoanalytic movement. It is also the year in which we have the first evidence that the neopagan Bohemian netherworld of Ascona invaded the bourgeois-Christian sanctuary of Jung's soul.

Bleuler published a paper in this year in which the term *schizophrenia* was used for the first time.[1] Bleuler coined the term as an alternative to dementia praecox, coined by Kraepelin in 1893 to refer to a group of psychotic disorders that were all progressively degenerative in course and that seemed to lead to death. Bleuler, while recognizing that such hopelessly degenerative cases did indeed exist, documented that there were a large number of chronically ill patients whose symptoms seemed to plateau or even, in rare cases, remit. Not all cases of persons with dementia praecox degenerated to the point of death. Hence, Bleuler's new concept was a major step away from the dominance of theories of hereditary degeneration in psychiatry.

Jung presented a paper on "The Content of the Psychoses" in the Zurich town hall on 16 January 1908 and repeated essentially the same ideas at the very first psychoanalytic congress, held in Salzburg, Austria, on 26–27 April 1908.[2] Following the antihereditarian basis of psychoanalysis, Jung, too, denied that dementia praecox was due totally to hereditary degenerative factors and cited the role of childhood trauma in producing psychological complexes that may then only secondarily stimulate the production of a "toxin" in the brain.[3] As his Freudian colleagues (such as Karl Abraham, who argued viciously with Jung over this issue) realized, Jung's theory was not the total rejection

151

of degeneracy theory that they would have preferred and upon which psychoanalysis staked its claim as a science and healing art.

It was also in this year that Jung's associate, Riklin, presented and published the first psychoanalytic treatment of fairy tales.[4] This set the entire psychoanalytic movement off in a different direction, for until this time it was a clinical movement that relied on observations of patients who could talk back and give associations to their dreams and fantasies. This was the basis of the argument that psychoanalysis was a science. Myths and fairy tales, however, do not talk back. Hence, as Kerr argues in *A Most Dangerous Method*, 1908 was the year that psychoanalysis became a Weltanschauung with a mission to transform the culture at large and revise its history. In 1908 the psychoanalytic movement was a physicians-only club and Freud wanted it to remain such: "We are physicians, and wish to remain physicians," Freud told Otto Gross at the 1908 Salzburg conference after Gross spoke on the "cultural perspectives of science."[5] Despite Freud's wishes, very soon after this time, the psychoanalytic literature began to tackle European culture as a whole (its literature, fairy tales, myths, Wagnerian opera, etc.). Because of this, it began to attract the broader attention of luminaries in the arts and in academia.

Gross Arrives at the Burghölzli

1908 is also important because it marked the fateful encounter between the Nietzschean physician, psychoanalyst, and later anarchist Gross (1877–1920) and Jung. By many accounts, including Freud's, Gross was a brilliant, creative, and charismatic individual.[6] According to Jones, Freud "expressed the opinion that Jung and Otto Gross were the only true original minds among his followers."[7] Gross had written many insightful psychiatric and psychoanalytic works and had worked under Kraepelin in Munich. He was also trouble. His morphine and cocaine addictions necessitated numerous psychiatric hospitalizations (starting in 1902) at the Burghölzli and elsewhere, beyond this May 1908 institutionalization under the care of Jung. He was the most radical prophet of the new ethic of eroticism and had an enormous effect on many famous people of his era. He appeared as a character in many novels written by people who knew him.[8] Gross was a valuable addition to the psychoanalytic movement not only because of his genius, but also because he was not of Jewish descent and was, perhaps most importantly, the son of Hanns Gross, a professor at Graz in Austria and the father of modern scientific criminology.[9]

Gross developed an interest in Freud at least as early as 1904 and was a respected participant in the psychoanalytic movement during its first years of true international recognition (which started in earnest in 1906 or so). However, also during this time Gross had sunk deeper into chronic morphinism and, using Nietzsche as his theoretical basis, became interested in practical methods of changing Germanic society. Gross used psychoanalysis as the practical technology of Nietzscheanism, but pushed it to extremes not advocated by Freud, Jung, or other psychoanalysts. Gross could give impromptu all-night psychoanalytic sessions in the cafés in Schwabing and convince those who were spellbound by his personality to act out their sexual desires without shame or guilt.

He naturally found his way from Schwabing to Ascona by 1905, and lived there on and off until 1913. This was a counter-cultural sphere of social intercourse that Gross dominated, but it should be remembered that this world was one that was totally distasteful and very foreign to the bourgeois universe of Freud and Jung in 1908. Gross's domain was, in fact, the familiar nineteenth-century world of "Bohemia"—that fluid realm of art, youth, ambition, addiction, ingenuity, and criminality that was so antithetical to bourgeois life. According to its innovative cartographer, Henry Murger, Bohemia maintained the following boundaries: "Bohemia, bordered on the-North by hope, work and gaiety, on the South by necessity and courage; on the West and the East by slander and the hospital."[10] There is no more apt description of the contours of the Bohemian world in which Gross lived, loved, and died.

By 1909 it was clear that Gross was more of a liability than an asset, and so Freud declared him persona non grata and his works were rarely cited thereafter in the literature of psychoanalysis—a leading reason why Gross's works have only relatively recently been collected and reprinted.[11]

Gross is perhaps most famous for his associations with persons who were to become major literary figures, or with persons who would, in later years, spread Gross's Nietzschean gospel to such figures. Gross's famous sexual liaisons with both of the von Richthofen sisters (Else Jaffe and Frieda Weekly, who both, like Gross himself, were married), and the influence of Gross that these sisters then transmitted to their later lovers (Frieda to her later husband, D. H. Lawrence, and Else to her mentors and lovers, Max Weber and "mini-Max," his brother Alfred, also a famous sociologist) have been documented by Martin Green.[12] Both Gross's wife, Frieda Gross (a longtime friend of the von Richthofen sisters), and Else Jaffe gave birth to sons he sired in 1907, and both mothers named these children Peter. Max Weber was the godfather of Gross's son by Jaffe.[13] Since Jaffe was a student and intimate member of Max and Marianne Weber's circle in Heidelberg, an Apollonian world of intellectual discourse and patriarchal bourgeois-Christianity, Gross quickly became identified as the charismatic but dangerous Nietzschean prophet of immorality.

In 1906 and 1907 Gross stayed with Jaffe and her husband Edgar for short periods in their home in Heidelberg, eventually converting the latter, too, who was a close associate of Weber, to his new sexual ethic. During these visits the Webers met Gross, to whom Max "attributed an almost charismatic power" in a letter to Jaffe dated 13 September 1907.[14] This letter is also important because it contains Weber's reasons for rejecting an article submitted by Gross to the *Archiv für Sozialwissenschaft* in the summer of 1907. The article (which has not survived) was entitled, "Über psychologischen Herrschaftsordnung. I. Der Psychologismus seit Nietzsche und Freud." Weber sent the manuscript to Jaffe for her to return to Gross, claiming that the paper was not a work of scholarship but filled with "metaphysical speculations" about a psychiatric ethics of societal reform. Weber tells Jaffe, therefore, "it seems to me that it is not necessary to wash these apparently inescapable diapers in our *Archiv*."[15]

Around this time, Weber had read the few major works of Freud in existence, concluding that there is no doubt that Freud's thought *can* become a very significant source for the interpretation of whole series of phenomena in cultural history, particularly in the history of *religion* and of manners and morals—although from the viewpoint of a cultural historian its significance is by no means as universal as assumed by Freud and his disciples in their very understandable zeal and joy of discovery.[16]

Beginning in 1908, this was indeed the direction that the psychoanalytic movement took. However, even as early as 1907, Weber had observed that Freud's circle had taken on the appearance of a charismatic cult centered on Freud's genius and person, and that psychoanalysts such as Gross (and even Jung at this time) vigorously proselytized their doctrine as if it were a religion by making the appeal to experience. Weber discussed this in his critique of Gross's manuscript:

> The categorical imperative which reads, "Go to Freud or come to us, his pupils, in order to learn the historical *truth* about yourself and your actions; otherwise you are a *coward*," not only betrays a somewhat naive "departmental patriotism" [*Ressort-Patriotismus*] on the part of a psychiatrist and professional *directeur de l'âme* [spiritual advisor], but, owing to its unfortunate amalgamation with "hygienic" motives, deprives itself of any ethical value. But, as I have indicated, from this essay, which is moralizing from beginning to end, I cannot derive any other practical postulate but this "duty to know oneself" with psychiatric help. *Where* is there the slightest indication of the *substance* of those new relativistic *and yet ideal* (*nota bene!*) values that are to serve as the basis of the critique of the "old," "dubious" values?[17]

Weber's critique of the Nietzschean, "pseudoliberational" philosophy underlying psychoanalytic technique as practiced by Gross is equally applicable to Jung's early circle and its survival in the present-day Jungian movement. If open-ended transformation and reform are offered as the promise of individuation, then where, indeed, are the substantive values underlying this new state of being? Belief in such open-ended perpetual evolution then renders the individual susceptible to influence from elites who claim to be "in the know" about the vague course of such a "process" and who make their livelihood by selling the promise of rendering such knowledge to their clients. This was a danger that Weber identified early and warned against.

Jaffe's pregnancy and Gross's arrival in Heidelberg in 1907 disturbed the Webers and ignited an open debate on the role of passion in a bourgeois life guided by ethical idealism. The Webers confronted Gross and his followers, and Marianne Weber says in her third-person biographer's voice that "they had endless discussions with the adherents of the 'psychiatric ethos.'"[18] The Webers were shocked by Gross's disciples, but to their credit they did not launch a campaign to condemn them, attempting instead to understand these young sexual revolutionaries. "Indeed, [the Webers] had to admire the courage of those who risked themselves by sinning and then overcame the sin."[19]

This is how Marianne Weber describes Gross and his ideas in her biography of her husband:

A young psychiatrist, a disciple of S. Freud with the magic of a brilliant mind and heart, had gained considerable influence. He interpreted the new insights of the master in his own fashion, drew radical conclusions from them, and proclaimed a sexual communism compared with which the so-called "new-ethics" appeared quite harmless. In outline his doctrine went something like this: The life-enhancing value of eroticism is so great that it must remain free from extraneous considerations and laws, and, above all, from any integration into everyday life. If, for the time being, marriage continues to exist as a provision for women and children, love ought to celebrate its ecstasies outside this realm. Husbands and wives should not begrudge each other whatever erotic stimuli may present themselves. Jealousy is something mean. Just as one has several people as friends, one can also have sexual union with several people at any given period and be "faithful" to each one. But any belief in the permanence of feeling for a single human being is an illusion, and therefore exclusiveness of sexual community is a lie. The power of love is necessarily weakened by being constantly directed to the same person. The sexuality on which it is founded requires many-sided satisfaction. Its monogamous limitation "represses" the natural drives and endangers emotional health. Therefore, away with the fetters that prevent a person from fulfilling himself in new experiences; free love will save the world.[20]

Yet, as the Webers found, "it was a delusion to build up certain psychiatric insights into a world-redeeming prophecy."[21] Indeed, Max Weber could sharply conclude, "since the 'psychiatric ethic' only demands, 'Admit to yourself what you are like and what you desire,' it really makes no new demands of an ethical nature."[22] Gross's version of a Nietzschean psychoanalytic ethic that promoted perhaps nothing more than a form of permanent Dionysian revolution as individuation was distasteful and indeed dangerous in the eyes of the Webers. However, they had great difficulty convincing certain of their friends that this new ethic was a delusion, and they could only watch from the sidelines as marriages bent and broke around them.

Marianne Weber says that, "The Freudian was successful and his message found believers. Under his influence both men and women dared to risk their own and their companions' spiritual well-being." One such person who underwent a tremendous personal conversion experience to this sexual Nietzscheanism through direct contact with Gross was none other than Jung.

"My Twin Brother"

At Freud's suggestion, shortly following the Salzburg conference (which was also attended by Gross), Jung began an intensive psychoanalytic treatment to save Gross from his addictions. In May, Gross was admitted as a patient to the Burghölzli. Despite certain erotic temptations, and despite his interest in psychoanalysis and its sexual obsessions, in 1908 Jung was still very much a nineteenth-century bourgeois-Christian physician. Although philosophically a Nietzschean himself, he detested everything that Gross enacted in the name of Nietzsche (drug abuse, sexual licentiousness, and even orgies). After meeting Gross at a conference in 1907 at which Jung made his first public defense of Freud, Jung writes a letter to Freud in which he first admits he envies psychoanalyst Max Eitington's "uninhibited abreaction of the polygamous instinct," and then launches into a condemnation of the very similar ideas of Gross:

> Dr. Gross tells me that he puts a quick stop to the transference by turning people into sexual immoralists. He says the transference to the analyst and its persistent fixation are mere monogamy

157

symbols and as such symptomatic of repression. The truly healthy state for the neurotic is sexual immorality. Hence he associated you with Nietzsche. It seems to me, however, that sexual repression is a very important and indispensable civilizing factor, even if pathogenic for many inferior people. Still, there must always be a few flies in the world's ointment. What else is civilization but the fruit of adversity? I feel Gross is going along too far with the vogue for the sexual short-circuit, which is neither intelligent, nor in good taste, but merely convenient, and therefore anything but a civilizing factor.[23]

Thus it is not surprising that we find in a 13 May 1908 letter of Jones to Freud the following statement, written after Gross had agreed to submit himself to treatment: "I hear that Jung is going to treat him psychically, and naturally feel a little uneasy about that for Jung does not find it easy to conceal his feelings and he has a pretty strong dislike to Gross; in addition, there are some fundamental differences of opinion between them on moral questions. However, we must hope for the best."[24]

But it was Jung, not Gross, who was most transformed by the experience. An amazing reversal in Jung's attitude occurred. Jung and Gross spent exhausting analytic sessions of twelve hours or more together, with Jung telling Freud, "Whenever I got stuck, he analyzed me. In this way my own psychic health has benefitted."[25] By the end of it, even after Gross suddenly escaped by jumping over a garden wall to seek a return to his source of drugs, the disappointed Jung could still say, "In spite of everything he is my friend, for at bottom he is a very good and fine man with an unusual mind. . . . for in Gross I discovered many aspects of my true nature, so that he often seemed like my twin brother—except for the Dementia praecox."[26]

What did Jung discover about himself in Gross? Based on his behavior and interests after this encounter, Jung discovered he was more modern, irrational, and passionate and had much less Hellenic composure or fewer bourgeois-Christian attitudes than he had been previously willing to allow. Jung began to view himself—and his life—with new, modern eyes. Gross helped Jung to begin making the difficult transition from bourgeois-Christian to modern consciousness. Perhaps the natural state of humans who were civilized only in the last few thousand years after a million or so of evolution was indeed the primal polygamy of our ancestors. If the complex adaptations of a species come about only gradually and over very long periods of time, as Darwin suggested, then perhaps the human species could not have had sufficient time to develop complex new adaptations to the demands of the civilized world. Civilized urban life and its moral and social constraints would thus be a crushing pathologizing impediment to a form of life whose complex adaptations—such as the brain and the human mind or soul—were only suited for tribal life in a small *Gemeinschaft* of hunters and gatherers. Just such a view of the powerful determining forces of our ancestral biology on present behavior was widely held by fin-de-siècle figures such as Gross and Jung, if not in these precise terms. If they were still alive today they would indeed be intrigued to find specifically this notion of biologically based polygamous impulses from an ancestral past as a major determinant of human social behavior gaining scientific ascendancy in the work of sociobiologists and "evolutionary personality psychologists" in the 1990s.[27]

Jung's relationship with Spielrein took a sudden erotic turn due to the encounter with Gross. Whether Jung and Spielrein had engaged in a sexual relationship prior to this time is unknown, but the conditions for such a possibility blossomed after Gross converted Jung to his philosophy. Sometime in late 1908 or 1909 Spielrein writes in her diary:

> I sat there waiting in deep depression. Now he arrives, beaming with pleasure, and tells me with strong emotion about Gross, about the great insight he has just received (i.e., about polygamy); he no longer wants to suppress his feeling for me, he admitted that I was his first, dearest woman friend, etc., etc., (his wife of course excepted), and that he wanted to tell me everything about himself.[28]

In later letters to Freud in 1909 and 1910 we have Jung's confessions of his "polygamous components" that got him into a scandal with Spielrein,[29] and later Jung's cryptic assertion that, "The prerequisite for a good marriage, it seems to me, is the license to be unfaithful. I in my turn have learnt a great deal."[30] Jung has clearly adopted the language and philosophy of Gross by this time. He also by this time had begun his intense study of mythology and would have been reminded of the central role of polygamy in the prehistorical matriarchal society envisioned by Bachofen (1815–1887), the famous eccentric private scholar from Basel who was a local celebrity of sorts due to his challenge to the Judeo-Christian conception of a society based on the patriarchal family. Bachofen had a certain notoriety in academic circles, and although regarded as an outsider, nonetheless entertained university professors, including Nietzsche, in his home. Jung reports seeing his scholarly heroes Burckhardt and Bachofen walking the streets of Basel and he—like most educated persons—certainly knew the scandalous implications of Bachofen's theories.[31] So did Gross. Gross, however, was very interested in putting such theories into practice.

"The Mothers! The Mothers! It Sounds So Strangely Weird!"

J. J. BACHOFEN, OTTO GROSS, STEFAN GEORGE, AND JUNG

"Die Mütter! Mütter!—'s klingt so wunderlich!"
Goethe, Faust, *part 2, act 1*

MATRIARCHY AND POLYGAMY

DURING those long hours with Gross, Jung must have learned of Gross's confrontation with Weber and his circle, his sexual liaisons and illegitimate children, and his deep involvement in the Schwabing-Ascona countercultural axis that Jung would have been too bourgeois and too afraid of ruining his career to explore himself. Included in this analysis was no doubt a heavy dose of Gross's own Weltanschauung, a Lebensphilosophie of sexual liberation and Nietzschean spirituality, which must have included a discussion of his exploits at Ascona among the neopagans. Perhaps most importantly for our discussion, Jung probably heard Gross expound upon his adoption of the Asconan nature philosophy (if not the practice) of sun worship. Jung also no doubt heard Gross explain Bachofen's theory of the matriarchal origins of human society that Gross and other Asconans were attempting to reintroduce into European—especially patriarchal German—society through their own communal social experimentation. Gross's immersion in these areas has been amply documented in Green's fascinating works.

According to Green, "Otto Gross was familiar with every kind of heresy" and that "his teachings attacked not just Christianity but the whole complex of secular faiths that had grown

161

up around Christianity in the West, and had largely stifled and supplanted it."[1] Like many attracted to the Schwabing-Ascona counterculture, Gross was smitten with ideas of a return to pre-Christian forms of society and pagan spirituality—which in his mind included the freedom to engage in sacred group sexual practices as he envisioned our ancestors doing. In his last years Gross even promoted a form of psychotherapy based on the practice of sexual orgies that he referred to as the "cult of Astarte."[2] By 1911, after giving Gross's philosophy and orgiastic practices serious consideration, Jung could then write with Gross perhaps very much in mind, "The existence of a phallic or orgiastic cult does not indicate *eo ipso* a particularly lascivious life any more than the ascetic symbolism of Christianity means an especially moral life."[3]

By the time he had met the von Richthofen sisters in 1906 and Jung in 1907, Gross had gone beyond his psychiatric, philosophical, and psychoanalytic training and began developing a Lebensphilosophie that additionally incorporated Bachofen's theories of ancestral human polygamy and matriarchy.

BACHOFEN

Ellenberger has performed a useful service by devoting attention to the considerable (but often uncited) influence of Bachofen on Nietzsche, Freud, and Jung.[4] Indeed, Ellenberger states: "The influence of Bachofen's ideas reached psychiatric circles through various channels, and his influence on dynamic psychiatry has been immense."[5] Gross, with his influence on Jung, is arguably one of the most potent sources of Bachofen's influence on Western culture through its dissemination in the Jungian movement of the twentieth century. Bachofen's ideas were also taken quite seriously among many other prominent scholars, such as Jung's friend and colleague, the Indologist Heinrich Zimmer.[6]

Bachofen spent considerable time in the 1850s analyzing the remnants of Greco-Roman culture, whether in museums or on trips to Italy. In his attempts to decipher the hidden meanings of the symbols of antiquity, he began to believe that he was finding traces of a lost period of human experience that was literally prehistorical. In his view, he was finding evidence of a matriarchal world that had been deliberately obliterated by the patriarchy that eventually overthrew it. Although the first formations of his ideas can be found in an earlier book on mortuary symbolism, his main theory was outlined in the 1861 book, *Das Mutterrecht* (*The Law of Mothers*).[7] It reflects certain dominant leitmotifs of nineteenth-century German intellectual history, especially those of an earthly paradise and of the fascination with the powers of the "chthonic."[8] Jung's personal library contains the 1897 edition of *Das Mutterrecht*, plus several other volumes of works by Bachofen.[9]

Bachofen hypothesized that the human race passed through three stages, the first being one of polygamy and equality, the second being matriarchical, and the third and present stage patriarchal. It must be noted that while some modern feminist theorists support the idea of a prehistoric matriarchy, there is no historical precedent for matriarchy nor any uncontroversial prehistoric evidence for such a society, although some anthropologists and sociobiologists see evidence of a polygamous prehistory in which women shared equal power with men.[10]

Bachofen's stages of human development were as follows:

1. The stage of "hetairism," in which polygamy (meaning both polyandry and polygyny) was the norm in this wild, instinctual, nomadic, communistic, and liberated society. Both sexes lived instinctually and freely, but also cruelly and savagely by nineteenth-century bourgeois standards. There was no agriculture, and no marriage, for women were free and promiscuous and did not know or care to know the fathers of their children. The goddess of this "tellurian" phase marked by its earth symbolism was an ancient form of Aphrodite.

2. The second phase of history was the true phase of mother right (*Das Mutterrecht*), which Bachofen said was a lunar phase in which agriculture became the economic and social basis of a society identified with Mother Earth. The first laws that promoted the continuation of a society based on egalitarian values came into being. The most serious crime in this society was matricide. The body and the earth were glorified and the intellect or *Geist* (spirit)

were not. The night and the darkness of subterranean caves were exalted as sacred, and so nocturnal and subterranean initiations into mysteries began in this era. There was also a fascination with the dead and contact with their spirits. Bachofen thought that the Eleusinian mysteries of the Hellenistic world had their origins in this period of matriarchy. Indeed, the great goddess of this era was none other than Demeter, the mother-goddess of Eleusis. This was fitting as Demeter was a goddess of the grain, and Bachofen believed women invented agriculture.

3. A relatively brief transitional phase in which Dionysus is the most prominent deity follows this second stage and leads to our present stage of patriarchy, symbolized by the sun, the glorification of the intellectual sphere, and rule by men. The god of this era was Apollo. Once patriarchy was established, all signs of matriarchy were systematically wiped out, although Bachofen sees it everywhere in the same way that Blavatsky claimed to see evidence of the "secret doctrine" hidden away in the world's great religions and philosophies.

In a very patriarchal Germanic Europe, Bachofen's ideas were either ignored or condemned by scholars and cultural critics in the greater Fatherland. So prevalent did Bachofen's ideas become during the fin de siècle (however embarrassingly for the academic world) that in 1900, when Marianne Weber began writing her first book on *Wife and Mother in Legal Development*, she devoted considerable space to attacking the matriarchical theories of Bachofen and Friedrich Engels before constructing her own argument against patriarchal marriages.[11] It has been said by Guenther Roth that in this volume, "Marianne Weber waxed most eloquent in passages that can be read as a general indictment of German law and German husbands."[12] Yet, the condemnation of patriarchal power structures did not necessarily mean an advocacy of Bachofen and a return to matriarchy. Indeed, to cite Bachofen with approval (tacit or otherwise) in a scholarly work could ruin one's academic career and credibility. To use a modern analogy, Bachofen was the Erik von Däniken of his age. Therefore, despite his admiration for the man, Jung only cites Bachofen once in all twenty volumes of his *Collected Works*, and only in an essay written much later in his career.

The case was different with Gross. His four 1913 essays in

the anarchistic/communistic/sexual liberationist journal *Aktion* that he wrote in Berlin after fleeing Ascona in that year give full expression to his syncretic amalgam of Nietzscheanism, psychoanalysis, anarchism, utopianism, and Bachofenian theory that he had been espousing for years in professional meetings, cafés, publications, and even in his analytic sessions with Jung. In *"Zur Überwindung der kultirellen Krise"* ("On Overcoming the Cultural Crisis"), which appeared in *Aktion* in April 1913, Gross makes the following argument in revolutionary language that is also used by Jung in his 1912 "New Paths in Psychology" essay and in some of his writings during the Great War.[13]

Gross begins by stating that, "The psychology of the unconscious is the philosophy of revolution" (*"Die Psychologie des Unbewussten ist die Philosophie der Revolution"*). Psychoanalysis is called upon to ferment revolt within the psyche and thereby liberate one's own unconsciously bound individuality. The revaluation of all values that will be fulfilled in the coming age begins with Nietzsche's thought and Freudian technique. Freud's is a practical method through which we can liberate the unconscious for empirical knowledge so that we can know ourselves. With this a new ethic is born that is based on the moral imperative to really know oneself and one's neighbors. Gross then expounds upon the idea that we will subsequently realize that we are only fragments of our true potential selves and that this fragmentation results, in part, from the conflicts of our sexual lives. Sexuality is the motive for an eternity of inner conflicts. These conflicts, however, are the result of impositions of the outside world tragically introduced on the individual in childhood and are due to the conflict between individuality and one's own introjected authority. Previous revolutions succeeded because these revolutionaries carried their introjected authority within their own psyches, and this therefore resulted in the establishment of further patriarchal states. We must be aware that it is in the family that this authority originates, and that the fusion of sexuality and authority that results from patriarchal family structures imprisons each person's individuality. The time of crisis in high culture is due to the imprisonment of the wife and family unit in slavery. The revolutionary of today, with the help of the psychology of the unconscious, fights oppression in its most basic form: the father and patriarchy (*"gegen den Vater und gegen das Vaterrecht"*). The coming revolution is the revolution for matriarchy (*"Die kommenden Revolution ist die Revolution fürs Mutterrecht"*), concludes Gross.

Bachofen's influence is obviously evident in this essay. Nicolaus Sombart, reviewing Green's *The von Richthofen Sisters*, agrees that, "Otto Gross participated intellectually here in the myth of matriarchy that took place in Schwabing at the turn of the century as the spiritual counterpoint to its antithesis, the authoritarian male society."[14] Bachofen's matriarchy was linked not only with the new ethic of sexuality (hence the emphasis on polygamy by Gross, and its later acceptance and practice by Jung), but with political and social aims as well. Sombart colorfully describes the circumstances under which Bachofen's theory blossomed in countercultural circles:

> Culled from various sources—the offshoots of German romanticism, religious philosophy and mythology, Marian heresies, irrational protest movements, occult eastern sect-theologies—a notion developed in the nocturnal discussion groups of a society of outsiders (writers, artists, homosexuals, flipped-out Contessas, Professors' daughters and Jews with an identity crisis), the notion of an archaic, prehistoric, ideal social order which was wonderful and wondrous, the ideal of a golden age in which mankind was happy because men had not yet snatched away power for themselves, because private property was not yet the basis of power and the state not yet an instrument of repression, an age in which war had not yet become "a regular form of communication" among nations, an age in which women—or to be more accurate, the Female principle—decided the forms of socialization and cultural life.[15]

Perhaps the most important of these "nocturnal discussions" were held in the Schwabing-Munich group known as the *kosmische Runde* (the "Cosmic Circle") between 1897 and 1903.[16] The main members were independent scholar Alfred Schuler (1865–1923), philosopher and graphologist Ludwig Klages (1872–1956)—both of whom would become prominent in the völkisch movement—Karl Wolfskehl, a Jewish poet and professor of literature from the University of Munich, and, intermittently, the noted poet Stefan George (1868–1933). After 1903

George later had his own cult-like circle known as the *George-kreis* and although he himself disdained politics, his völkisch metaphors in his poetry inspired many prominent members of the political völkisch movement. George formed an artistic mystery cult complete with recitals of prophetic poetry, ceremonial talismans and gowns, the wearing of bishops' miters, etc.[17] This sort of formal costume ceremonialism had long been associated with various occult circles in Europe and underwent a revival with the decadent "satanist" movement in France and later in England in the 1880s among the culturally elite members (including W. B. Yeats) of the Hermetic Order of the Golden Dawn.[18] The group of young men (Schuler was thirty-two, the rest in their twenties) met to read and discuss mythology, cultural history, and literature. Among their favorite authors were three of Jung's most powerful influences: Nietzsche, Carus, and Bachofen.[19]

In 1899 Klages introduced Bachofen's *Mutterrecht* to the group, which collectively began an intense period of study to understand the implications of Bachofen's research.[20] Soon the Cosmic Circle conducted elaborate ceremonial invocations and rites of worship to the Great Mother Earth (*Erdmutter*) and glorified in theory and practice Bachofen's initial stage of hetairism (*das Hetärentum*).[21] The cult promoted open opposition to Judeo-Christian culture and the bourgeoisie. After the growing anti-Semitism of Klages and Schuler led to a break with George and Wolfskehl in 1903, Klages and Schuler combined their ideas of an Earth Mother cult and hetairism with the vitalism of evolutionary biology and promoted a völkisch paganism based on the mystical sacralization of "blood" (*die Blutleuchte*). They eventually joined forces with Diederichs and his Sera Circle and the German Youth Movement to participate in sun worship rituals and other forms of völkisch neopagan spirituality.[22] Echoing opinions expressed in 1936 by Marianne Weber, Green agrees that "the prewar Schwabingites were the richest source of all those anti-Christian and antibourgeois tendencies which Germany had to deal with in the late thirties."[23]

A more extensive study of Jung's connections with members of these circles still needs to be written, since we have indications that he had direct contact with individuals who were part of George's circle at one time or another. For example, Jung's German colleague Gustav Heyer, who was a frequent lecturer at the Eranos Conferences in the mid-1930s and an associate as well of Hauer, had connections with the George circle in Munich and was himself a devotee of Klages's völkisch Lebensphilosophie.[24] Although Jung does indeed refer to Klages during his seminars on Nietzsche's *Zarathustra* in the 1930s, these references are not very revealing as to their personal relationship. In the 1920s Klages lived in Kilchberg, Switzerland, not far from Jung. Alongside his other völkisch pursuits, Klages had pioneered handwriting analysis as a way to discern personality traits and had set up a Graphological Institute in Munich as early as 1897. Although primarily an author of philosophical works, his brand name for his practical psychology was "characterology."[25] So-called "expression analysis" and characterology formed the core of German psychology during the Nazi era and into the late 1950s. These techniques were used most prominently for the selection of German military officers during the Nazi era.[26] Evidence concerning the relationship between Klages and Jung has not yet come to light. Given the sanitizing of Jung's biography and image by his disciples, this is not surprising, for Klages was and is still viewed by many as a precursor to German fascism and Nazism.[27] What we do know is that in 1925 Jung published a paper on psychological types in the very first issue of a Munich journal on characterology edited by Klages, which indicates a closer association between these two men than has previously been realized.[28]

As the members of these Schwabing and Ascona circles overlapped considerably, Gross was connected to the Cosmic Circle through his relationship (probably quite intimate) with the lover of Klages and Schuler (among others, including Rainer Maria Rilke), the Contessa Franziska ("Fanny") zu Reventlow (1871–1918).[29] Klages described her as a "pagan saint," and like Lou Andreas-Salomé, who also intersects these circles, she was acknowledged by many for her intellect and spirit and as a major inspiration for the work of many of her friends and lovers. In her 1913 autobiography she described the circle of Schwabing as "a spiritual movement, a *niveau*, a direction, a protest, a new cult, or rather an attempt to use old cults to achieve new religious possibilities."[30] This Schwabing-hatched ideal proved to be the core passion of not only Klages, George, and their circles, but also that of Gross and especially Jung.

The Hero, the Descent to the Mothers, and Rebirth

By 1911, Bachofen's theories of the evolution of human culture begin to appear in a recognizable form in Jung's thought. Jung's Haeckelian unconscious was, as we shall see, briefly a Bachofenian unconscious as well. Like Klages, Jung combined biological vitalism with the Earth Mother cult and Bachofenian matriarchy to create a völkisch movement of his own.[31]

Bachofen is evident in Jung's very first theory of a phylogenetic unconscious, as described in his *Wandlungen und Symbole der Libido* in 1911 and 1912. Indeed, it is in the letters and publications of Jung in 1912 that we find the height of Bachofenian ideas in his thought before declining in importance after this specific year. Let us now examine the implications of Jung's "Bachofenian Unconscious."

Jung, well aware of the negative reception of Bachofen by scholars in the primary centers of science in German Europe, the universities, does not dare to cite the eccentric Bachofen's works. However, beginning with the chapter entitled "The Unconscious Origin of the Hero" in part 2 of *Wandlungen*, it is Bachofen's theory of human development that Jung uses as his basis for identifying the strata of transformations of the libido that he has excavated in his study of the phylogenetic unconscious. Indeed, this chapter in particular is pure Bachofen and sets the stage for Jung's discussion of hero myths and their relation to the mother complex in the remainder of the book.

Jung begins this very important chapter by once again reviewing his phylogenetic hypothesis of part 1: "The unconscious is generally diffused, which not only binds the individuals among themselves to the race, but also unites them backwards with the peoples of the past and their psychology. Thus the unconscious, surpassing the individual in generality, is, in the first place, the object of a true psychology, which claims not to be psychophysical."[32] Jung then also reviews his syncretic discussion of solar myths and psychoanalysis of this previous section:

> Comparison with the sun teaches us over and over again that the gods are libido. It is that part of us which is immortal, since it represents that bond through which we feel that in the race we are never extinguished. It is life from the life of mankind. Its springs, which well up from the depths of the unconscious, come, as does our life in general, from the root of the whole of humanity, since we are indeed only a twig broken off from the mother and transplanted.[33]

Jung then introduces Bachofen through a discussion of his own archaeological observations. Jung tells his readers that, "In the antique collection at Verona I discovered a late Roman mystic inscription in which are the following representations."[34] Jung then reproduces these four symbols, beginning with an obvious representation of the sun. Jung says: "These symbols are easily read: Sun-Phallus, Moon-Vagina (Uterus)." What is remarkable is that these four images represent exactly, and in the correct temporal order, the stages of human cultural evolution identified by Bachofen. Patriarchy is the Apollonian stage represented by the Sun; the phallus represents the transitional Dionysian phase; the moon is the stage of matriarchy and the vagina (uterus) is the stage of undifferentiated hetairism. Ellenberger has diagrammed how this exact sequence of stages in Bachofen corresponds to Freud's stages of psychosexual development: the ancient hetairic period corresponds to the infantile period of "polymorphous perversity"; matriarchy resembles the pre-oedipal, incestuous period of strong attachment to the

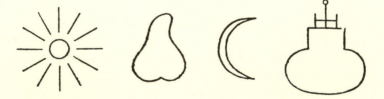

Figure 3. Jung's four images of cultural evolution, as derived from Bachofen (from *Psychology of the Unconscious*, p. 198).

170

mother; the transitional Dionysian period is represented by the phallic stage; and patriarchy by the genital stage.[35]

In Freud, Bachofen is perhaps the (unacknowledged) basis of psychoanalytic ontogeny; in Jung, Bachofen is the key to psychoanalytic phylogeny. Haeckel provides the unifying key from evolutionary biology: "ontogeny recapitulates phylogeny." This, in a nutshell, is the basic structure of the theory of the mind that Jung develops in *Wandlungen und Symbole der Libido*.

We can point to evidence in the correspondence between Freud and Jung to confirm this. In a letter to Freud dated 8 May 1912, and written at least two months after finishing part 2 of *Wandlungen*, Jung attempts to explain his new ideas on incest to Freud with a direct and obvious indication that he has accepted Bachofen's ideas as a basis for rejecting Freud and his Oedipus-complex theory of incest with its patriarchical bias. The Oedipal theory of cultural development only holds true in a patriarchical model. Jung tells Freud, in part:

> A far more genuine incest tendency is to be conjectured for the early, cultureless period of matriarchy, i.e., in the matrilineal family. There the father was purely fortuitous and counted for nothing, so he would not have had the slightest interest (considering the general promiscuity) in enacting laws against the son (In fact, there was no such thing as a father's son!).[36]

Freud's curt response of 14 May 1912 first informs Jung that, "It will surely come as no surprise to you that your conception of incest is still unclear to me." Furthermore, Freud's letter not only contains an explicit statement favoring Darwin's "hypothesis in regard to the primordial period" over Bachofen's, but contains a jab at Jung's own polygamous behavior, which became known by this point. Freud lets Jung know that he is aware that Jung may be hiding behind Bachofen's theory to justify his own actions when he tells Jung: "Mother-right should not be confused with gynaecocracy. There is little to be said for the latter. Mother-right is perfectly compatible with the polygamous abasement of women."[37]

Thanks to the astute scholarship of Ellenberger, we can point to an even earlier indication that Freud found the revision of psychoanalysis along Bachofenian lines by Jung (and before

171

him, Gross) absolutely repugnant. In February of 1912 a condensed summary of a book by the French art historian Sartiaux written by Freud appeared in the *Zentralblatt für Psychoanalyse* and was a direct slap at Jung (the disciple "John" in the following excerpt) and his fascination with Bachofen and matriarchy (mother-goddesses such as Diana and Mary) in opposition to Freud ("St. Paul"):

> Twenty centuries ago, in the town of Ephesus, the temple of Diana attracted numerous pilgrims, as Lourdes does today. In 54 A.D. the Apostle Saint Paul preached and made converts there for several years. Being persecuted, he founded his own community. This proved to be detrimental to the goldsmiths' commerce, and they organized an uprising against Saint Paul with the cry "Great is the Diana of the Ephesians!" Saint Paul's community did not remain loyal to him, it fell under the influence of a man named John, who had come with Mary, and promoted the cult of the Mother of God. Again pilgrims flocked, and the goldsmiths found work again.[38]

As Ellenberger wryly observes, "One need not be well versed in hermeneutics to guess its allegorical meaning."[39]

Let us return to *Wandlungen*. Using these four Bachofenian symbols as the basis of his evidence, Jung argues:

> Let this suggestion suffice—that from different directions the analysis of the libido symbolism always leads back again to the mother incest. Therefore, we may surmise that the longing of the libido raised to God (repressed into the unconscious) is a primitive incestuous one which concerns the mother.[40]

Jung then digresses from this point, comparing the travels of the sun in the sky to the typical wanderings of the hero in hero myths. Dying and resurrected "redeemers" such as Gilgamesh, Dionysus, Hercules, Christ, and Mithras, are cited by Jung as examples of wandering heroes. Heroes wander because they are like the sun, which "seeks the lost mother." The sun rises from and goes back to a mysterious realm in its wanderings each day, the Goethean "realm of the mothers." Therefore, hero myths are solar myths. Furthermore, Jung concludes: "But the myth of the hero, however, is, as it appears to me, the myth of our own suffering unconscious, which has an unquenchable longing for all the deepest sources of our own being; for the body of the mother, and through it for communion with infinite life in the countless forms of existence."[41]

Jung then ends this chapter with a long reproduction from *Faust*, part 2, in which Faust makes his initiatory descent into the eerie realm of the mothers. What is of note is that when writing this scene in late 1829 and early 1830, as we know from his comments to Eckermann and from other sources, Goethe had in mind the ritual descent of the initiate of the Hellenistic mysteries of the "Two Goddesses" of Eleusis, the mother-goddess Demeter and her daughter, the maiden (*Kore*) Persephone.[42] Although no firm evidence exists of what the initiatory experience entailed for the initiate into the Eleusinian mysteries, it is generally assumed that the initiate saw some representation or had a vision of Persephone in the underworld, which then gave the initiate "better hopes" for his or her position in the afterlife. In other words, the mysteries revitalized and redeemed the initiate through the ritualized descent to the underworld of the mothers. Goethe knew the descriptions of the Eleusinian mysteries from his reading of Plutarch, and of course both he and Jung would have known Cicero's statement that at Eleusis the initiate is shown "how to live in joy, and how to die with better hopes."[43] That is about all that we know about the actual experience of the initiate. The extraordinary experience of the Eleusinian mysteries—which were formally conducted for more than one thousand years—is one of the greatest kept secrets of antiquity.

Goethe, too, kept possession of this secret. When Eckermann asked Goethe during an interview held on 10 January 1830 to explain more fully Faust's experiences in the underworld, Eckermann reports Goethe's response: "He, however, in his usual manner enveloped himself in mystery, looking at me wide-eyed and repeating the words: 'The Mothers! Mothers! It sounds so strangely weird!'"[44]

The remainder of *Wandlungen* is subsequently predicated on Bachofen's theory of prehistoric hetairism and matriarchy and how hero myths reveal that a return to the mother is somehow revitalizing—just as the initiate in the Eleusinian mysteries experienced *renovatio* through contact with the transcendent realm of gods. The sun hero descends to the realm of the mothers (or

173

into Mother Earth) where he typically does battle and reemerges reborn. This is a classic scenario ritually enacted in the Hellenistic mysteries. The star, therefore, is another expression of the sun in the night sky of the Motherworld or as the sun descended into the subterranean depths of Mother Earth. However, in *Wandlungen*, Jung is claiming that there is ontogenetic and phylogenetic evidence that through a return to the realm of the mothers (the deepest strata of the unconscious) within each of us, we are reborn. The first step to this new life is through introversion, when one's "libido sinks into its 'own depths'" into what Jung refers to, significantly, as *"the world of memories."*[45] Yet rebirth occurs only if this process of introversion is then reversed and one returns to the abandoned "upperworld": "But if the libido succeeds in tearing itself loose and pushing up into the world above, then a miracle appears. This journey to the underworld has been a fountain of youth, and new fertility springs from this apparent death."[46]

Given this theory, it was logically a very short step for the ever practical-minded Jung to eventually develop psychotherapeutic techniques of introversion—active imagination—in order to allow individuals direct access to this revitalizing realm of the mothers, or the underworld of the ancestors or of the dead. But as his discussion of the "Terrible Mother" in his chapter on the "Symbolism of the Mother and of Rebirth" suggests, this descent is not necessarily a pleasant experience. Indeed, although it may be revitalizing for some, "annihilation" may ensue from the hero's "battle of deliverance from the mother." As a work that uses published fantasy material from Frank Miller and especially clinical material (delusions and hallucinations) from the inpatient population of the Burghölzli, in *Wandlungen* Jung is much more interested in demonstrating that such fantasy material is the product of psychotic regression of dementia praecox.

The implication of Jung's theory is that the most regressed psychotics would exhibit the most pre-Christian, "tellurian" symbols in their delusions and hallucinations, as these formed the basis of the earliest societies of human beings, as Bachofen suggested. In the deepest tellurian stratum, earth symbols would be mixed with both solar and lunar symbols, both sun and star, which would be found fused together, especially in bisexual forms. In Bachofenian prehistory, the currents of libido these symbols represent would function in their natural state and present no problem to our ancestors. As humans evolved into lunar matriarchy and solar patriarchy, these stages and their representative symbols point to graduated differentiation and individuation from the earlier polymorphous and diffuse consciousness of hetairism. In the modern psychotic patient, whose psyche, biologically and psychologically, is no longer covered so tightly by many millennia of patriarchal consciousness (only the last two thousand years of which were Judeo-Christian), the emergence of these tellurian streams of libido in particular present major difficulties and incapacitate the individual. However, theoretically, by analyzing psychotic symbolism it might be possible to tell how regressed a patient is.

As we know, by the time he had published the second part of *Wandlungen* in 1912 Jung realized he was no longer a believer in the Christian myth and essentially realized his pagan spiritual roots and identity. That he chose the matriarchal theories of Bachofen and the Germanic scholarship on the Aryan peoples to give form to his new pagan identity is certain. What I argue here is that it was Gross that unlocked these mysteries for Jung and paved the way for the formation of Jung's own mystery cult of redemption by 1916, which Jung deliberately operated outside the bounds of the conventional academic and medical worlds. In this sense the Jung cult very much belongs to the Schwabing-Asconan tradition that also looked to Bachofen for clues to individual and cultural rebirth. As Sombart observes about these fin-de-siècle cults:

> The myth of matriarchy was tied to the past, esoteric and elitist, and mixed with the most exceptional sun, blood and death cults. It was consciously aimed against an established academic science (and the academic business too). It had the character of a secret doctrine, whose proponents did not think about being enlightened or politically effective but trusted the personal magnetism of the "initiated" and "knowing."[47]

It is especially in this latter form, of a cult of individuals seeking guidance from a charismatic prophet, that the Jung cult existed from the very start and has attempted to preserve through its present-day caste of Jungian analysts who claim charismatic authority as true initiates of the Jungian mysteries within the larger Jungian movement. More will be said about this in the last chapter.

In his 1909 *Jahrbuch* essay on "The Significance of the Father in the Destiny of the Individual," which contains material from his mutual analysis with Gross, Jung ends his remarks with a cryptic Latin passage from Horace that may very well refer to the influence of his "twin brother" Gross on his life, both for better and for worse: "[Why this should be so] only the Genius knows—that companion who rules the star of our birth, the god of human nature, mortal though he be in each single life, and changeful of countenance, white and black."[48]

Gross is only the most prominent and best recorded of the unknown number of unknown patients admitted to the Burghölzli with Asconan connections and a significant knowledge of mythology, occultism, and the Hellenistic mystery cults. Jung reports that, from 1904 to 1907, 1,325 patients were admitted to the Burghölzli, and we may conjecture that this number was probably not too different for the next four-year period of 1908 to 1911.[49] How many of these were Asconan casualties, or Theosophists, or others with mythological knowledge about sun worship and Bachofenian matriarchal symbolism we cannot say for certain. However, there is evidence that other patients there also may have had this specialized knowledge: in 1908 Jung mentions the case history of "a man between 30 and 40 years of age" (like Jung), "a foreign archeologist of great learning and extraordinary intelligence" who "published several outstanding works."[50] Who was this scholar? Was it someone whose monographs Jung cites in his own works? This special nature of the patient population of the Burghölzli should be kept in mind as we further examine Jung's claims for evidence for a phylogenetic and later collective unconscious.

Visionary Excavations of the Collective Unconscious

1909–1915

1909–1910

AT SOME POINT following his return from the September 1909 Clark Conference in the United States with Freud, Ferenczi, and others, Jung had his now-famous dream of descending temporally and spatially in an old house that he claims gave him his first ideas of a collective unconscious. In actuality, it gave him the idea for his first formal model of the phylogenetic unconscious. There are many versions of this famous dream in the literature on Jung (especially a highly embellished one by Jaffé in *Memories, Dreams, Reflections*),[1] but perhaps the most direct information about it can be found in Jung's remarks made on 6 April 1925 during his English-language seminar on analytical psychology. After describing how he and Freud analyzed each other's dreams on the American voyage (Freud, of course, less ably than Jung as dream interpreter), Jung says the following:

> On my way back from America, I had a dream that was the origin of my book on the *Psychology of the Unconscious*. In those times I had no idea of the collective unconscious; I thought of the conscious as of a room above, with the unconscious as a cellar underneath and then the earth wellspring, that is, the body, sending up the instincts. These instincts tend to disagree with our conscious ideals and so we keep them down. That is the figure I had always used for myself, and then came this dream which I hope I can tell without being too personal.
>
> I dreamed I was in a medieval house, a big, complicated house with many rooms, passages, and stairways. I came in from the street and went down into a vaulted Gothic room, and from there into a cellar. I thought to myself that I was now at the bottom, but then I found a square hole. With a lantern in my hand I peeped

down into this hole, and saw stairs leading further down, and down these I climbed. They were dusty stairs, very much worn, and the air was sticky, the whole atmosphere very uncanny. I came to another cellar, this one of very ancient structure, perhaps Roman, and again there was a hole through which I could look down into a tomb filled with prehistoric pottery, bones, and skulls; as the dust was undisturbed, I thought I had made a great discovery. Then I woke up.[2]

Jung's "descent" temporally and spatially into the past in this dream reminded him of his previous career interest in archaeology and in prehistoric man. He told his audience in 1925 that he had "a strongly impersonal feeling about the dream"—hence, the feeling that the images were *not* from a personal source but from a phylogenetic or transcendent one. Freud, however, interpreted Jung's dream as a death wish against certain people associated with him that he "wanted dead, and buried under two cellars."[3] Freud's interpretation was personal and ontogenetic.

Jung was not satisfied with Freud's interpretation, and in order to get at the meaning of the dream, Jung began spontaneously using a procedure that he later cultivated as the basis of his psychotherapeutic technique: active imagination. Indeed, Jung's first recorded use of active imagination may be traced to his September–October 1909 attempts to divine the meaning of his dream. Here Jung tells his audience how he used his imagination to make excavations into the phylogeny of the soul:

> Involuntarily I began to make fantasies about it, though I did not know anything about the principle of fantasizing in order to bring up unconscious material. I said to myself: "Isn't it fine to make excavations. Where am I going to have a chance to do that?" And actually when I came home I looked up a place where excavations were being made, and went to it.[4]

Here we have Jung resorting to visionary practices already quite familiar to him from his involvement with spiritualism and from his knowledge of the claims of Blavatsky and the initiated Theosophists that the ancestral past could be contacted directly through the imagination. Jung, however, reframes the practice to make it seem less occultist and more scientific by making an analogy to archaeology—a style of translating or repackaging arcane or occultist ideas to make them congruent with the psychiatric and scientific terminology of his day. Jung was, after all, a famous scientist and physician and his disciples were disproportionately drawn from the bourgeoisie. Just as Guido von List told his followers, "We must read with our souls the landscape which archeology reconquers with the spade," Jung himself indulged in such a practice and taught it to generations of his own disciples. Such "visionary excavations" were very much au courant within the major occult traditions and the völkisch underside of Central European culture at this time.

Jung visited active archaeological sites and observed actual excavations into the prehistoric past. Immediately upon his return he began an intensive study of mythology and Hellenistic pagan spiritual practices in the classical scholarship of his day. "Archeology or rather mythology has got me in its grip," he writes to Freud on 14 October 1909.[5] On 8 November 1909 Jung additionally remarks, "All my delight in archeology (buried for years) has sprung into life again."[6]

He reports beginning his readings with the four-volume set by Heidelberg University professor Friedrich Creuzer (1771–1858), the *Symbolik und Mythologie der alten Völker besonders der Griechen*, originally published between 1810 and 1812.[7] If there can be said to be one single source of Jung's collective unconscious it is arguably to be found in Creuzer's highly influential works. This is true in two senses. First, Creuzer's work was the first truly comprehensive scholarly source in the German language for information about the spirituality of antiquity, especially about the ancient mystery cults of the Greco-Roman world. As a result, the information contained in it was widely disseminated in Germanic culture throughout the nineteenth century, and indeed the work went through several editions, making Creuzer perhaps the first source for any German scholar beginning a study of the mythology or the mystery cults. Creuzer was the foundation upon which successive generations of German scholars built their own ideas about Hellenic antiquity, whether they agreed with him or not.

As an example of what classicist Bruce Metzger has called the "precritical stage" of the study of the Hellenistic mystery cults, Creuzer (and others in the late eighteenth and early nineteenth centuries) "believed that by the Mysteries a constant succession of priests or hierophants transmitted from age to age an esoteric doctrine, better and nobler than that of the popular religion. Whether this recondite science had been derived originally from the hidden wisdom of India or Egypt, or from the Old Testament, or even from a primitive revelation to all mankind, was debated with characteristic disregard for historical methodology."[8] Therefore, when occultists mined this scholarly literature during the fin de siècle they found models upon which to base their secret doctrines and elitist, hierarchical cult structures and initiation ceremonies.

Creuzer's perspective on the ancient Hellenistic mysteries permeated Germanic culture through its influence on such individuals as Goethe and Wagner. Goethe's *Bibliothek* reveals that he owned both editions of Creuzer's work.[9] Whereas volume three is concerned with the themes of "heroes and daimons" in ancient Greek spirituality, the Dionysian mysteries, and Orphic cosmology, the entirety of volume four is devoted to the cult of the "Two Goddesses" (the Greek Demeter and Persephone, or the Roman Ceres and Proserpina) at Eleusis and the Eleusinian mysteries. When Goethe wrote the famous descent to the mothers scene in the second part of *Faust* that so captivated Jung, he used the original descriptions of the Eleusinian mysteries of Pausanias and Plutarch cited by Creuzer as well as Creuzer's own contemporary descriptions.

Wagner also digested Creuzer as preparation for writing the operas that Jung so admired.[10] Wagner's library at Bayreuth contains the original edition of Creuzer, and he admired Creuzer's intuition about the place of the irrational in the Hellenistic mysteries, although Winckelmann's Apollonian idealization of the ancient Greeks is quite apparent in Creuzer's work. In an entry in her diary for 1 December 1880, Cosima Wagner reports:

> Friends in the evening.—R. talks once more about Schelling and C. Frantz, and when somebody mentions the former's philosophy of mythology and recalls Creuzer, R. says: "All these people like Creuzer saw something, they made mistakes but they saw something. Their successors see nothing, just think they ought to say something, too."[11]

Through his pervasive cultural influence in the ongoing "tyranny of Greece over Germany," Creuzer's work is the headwaters of the long, flowing intellectual current that extends from Goethe to Wagner to Jung.

The second sense in which Creuzer's work is the true foundation of Jung's collective unconscious is in the use of it as an encyclopedic guide for identifying mythological clinical material by Jung and his colleagues. In early 1909 Jung had left his position at the Burghölzli to go into private practice in Küsnacht, so in the winter of 1909 he assigned his three psychiatrist assistants who were still at the Burghölzli—Spielrein, Jan Nelken, and Honegger—to read the works of Creuzer and others on mythology and archaeology and to collect data from the institutionalized patients there as evidence for a phylogenetic layer of the unconscious mind. Creuzer's particular slant on mythology and especially the mysteries thus frames, indeed biases, the data that Jung and his assistants claimed as pure and scientific. Nowhere is this more evident than in the strange case of the patient at the Burghölzli known now to us as the Solar Phallus Man.

The Problematic Tale of the Solar Phallus Man

Jung told the story of the Solar Phallus Man time and time again throughout his life as conclusive evidence of a collective unconscious.[12] As Shamdasani has correctly observed, the Solar Phallus Man "carried on his shoulders the weight and burden of proof of the Collective Unconscious."[13] The Solar Phallus Man, Jung and his disciples claimed, had hallucinations and delusions with content that resembled an ancient Hellenistic magical text from the second century C.E., and therefore this was convincing proof of a phylogenetic or (later) collective unconscious. As late as 1959, in the famous televised "Face to Face" interviews of Jung by John Freeman, when Freeman asks, "Is there any one case that you can now look back on and feel perhaps it was the turning point of your thought?" it is the case of the Solar Phallus Man that Jung refers to.[14] What, then, are the circumstances surrounding the important case of the Solar Phallus Man?

The first fact, and one deliberately hidden, it appears, by Jung himself, is that the Solar Phallus Man was a patient of Honegger's, whose first clinical experience with institutionalized psychiatric patients began only in the winter of 1909 at the Burghölzli under Bleuler. In *Wandlungen und Symbole der Libido* there are two explicit references to Honegger that were removed by Jung in his extensive 1952 revision of this work, *Symbols of Transformation*. In these later works, Jung claims the Solar Phallus Man was *his* patient and makes no mention of any role by Honegger. In part 1 of *Wandlungen*, published in 1911, the case of the Solar Phallus Man is introduced as follows:

> Honegger discovered the following hallucination in an insane man (paranoid dement): The patient sees in the sun an 'upright tail' similar to an erected penis. When he moves his head back and forth, then, too, the sun's penis sways back and forth in a like manner, and out of that the wind arises. This strange hallucination remained unintelligible to us for a long time until I became acquainted with the Mithraic Liturgy and its visions.[15]

Jung then cites a translation of a passage from the Mithraic Liturgy in a 1907 Theosophical publication by G.R.S. Mead.[16] In *Wandlungen* Jung also repeatedly cites the work that probably first drew his attention to the Mithraic Liturgy contained in the Greek Magical Papyri, the small book by Dieterich entitled *Eine Mithrasliturgie*.[17] Jung owned and used the second edition of this book (1910). Jung's claim throughout his life is that this institutionalized patient could not have had prior access to such mythological ideas and that therefore this was indisputable evidence of the collective unconscious. Jung's response to Freeman in the 1959 interview is typical of the many published references to the Solar Phallus Man Jung made when bolstering his arguments in print for a collective unconscious:

> [Freeman] *But how could you be sure that your patient wasn't unconsciously recalling something that somebody once told him?*
> [Jung] Oh, no. Quite out of the question, because that thing was not known. It was in a magic papyrus in Paris, and it wasn't even published. It was only published four years later, after I had observed it with my patient.[18]

It is clear that by the 1930s, long after Honegger's suicide in March 1911 and therefore long after he was forgotten except by only a very few intimates, the story of the Solar Phallus Man took on the following new shape:

1. The patient was Jung's and Honegger disappears from the history of analytical psychology.

2. Jung later claimed the patient's delusions were observed in 1906, although Honegger's clinical work began only in 1909, which would have been the only time Honegger could have "discovered" the Solar Phallus Man's hallucination.

3. The text of the Mithraic Liturgy was published in 1910, four years after Jung claims he discovered the Solar Phallus Man.

This latter story was maintained firmly by Jung and has been repeated by generations of uncritical disciples, many of whom were close to Jung in his later years and who knew the true story.[19]

Jung first took credit for the case of the Solar Phallus Man in the essay "Die Struktur der Seele" in 1930, which is the date of the foreword to the collection of his essays in which it appears, *Seelenproblem der Gegenwart*, but which was published in 1931.[20] However, although Jung most certainly knew the patient, we now know for certain that he was indeed Honegger's special case. Honegger's personal papers, which disappeared in 1911 after his suicide, reappeared in November 1993 in photocopies deposited by William McGuire at the Library of Congress in Washington, D.C., and contain a written case history of the Solar Phallus Man. His name was "E. Schwyzer," and he was born in 1862.[21]

The contradictions in the story over priority and date of discovery are disturbing enough. However, perhaps most disturbing is that Jung later found out that a 1903 edition of Dieterich's work existed, but he still stuck with his story. This is indicated by a footnote added by the editors of the *Collected Works*: "As [Jung] subsequently learned, the 1910 edition was actually the second, there having been a first edition in 1903. The patient had, however, been committed some years before 1903."[22] Why, then, did he continue in print and in person (as in the 1959 BBC interviews) to stick to the false story?

If, as the London editors of the *Collected Works* claim, this patient was admitted years before 1903, this does not rule out the Solar Phallus Man's contact with such material through the widely available Theosophical literature in German or, perhaps, even through the work of Creuzer or Bachofen. As Ellenberger was the first to notice, Creuzer contains a brief discussion of the motif of a solar phallus (*Sonnenphallus*) in the third volume of his *Symbolik und Mythologie der alten Völker*.[23] In the introduction to *Das Mutterrecht*, Bachofen makes the statement that "the phallic sun, forever fluctuating between rising and setting, coming into being and passing away, is transformed into the immutable source of light."[24] Thus, the Solar Phallus Man, locked away in a Swiss institution, may have also had access to Bachofen's work either during or prior to his incarceration.

There are further contradictions. Indeed, in *Wandlungen und Symbole der Libido*, Jung himself cites the 1907 Theosophical work by Mead that contains a translation of the Mithraic Liturgy (with Theosophical commentary), and which Mead clearly indicates on the first page (the contents page) is based on Dieterich's *Eine Mithrasliturgie*. Mead's work came out a full three years before Dieterich's second edition. Furthermore, Jung's own copy of the second edition of *Eine Mithrasliturgie* is clearly labeled on the title page, right under the author's name and in the center of the page, *"Zweite Auflage"* (second edition). The case of the Solar Phallus Man, therefore, may most optimistically be regarded as one of biased cognition; at its worst, it may be regarded as evidence of deliberate distortion by Jung and his colleagues to keep the magical story of the Solar Phallus Man alive to bolster the belief of others in the collective unconscious.

The Zurich School Excavates the Phylogenetic Unconscious

Given the fact that Honegger, Nelken, and Spielrein were primed to look for certain mythological information consistent with the phylogenetic hypothesis, they obviously would tend to ignore other information that would be considered irrelevant to it. And given the century of Hellenic mythological education in German countries; the wide distribution of Theosophical materials; the equally available and more highly regarded folkloric, Gnostic, mythological, and solar-worshiping pantheistic publications of Diederichs Verlag; and the nearby neopagan movement between Schwabing-Munich and Ascona, such mythological material was not hard to find among the inpatients of the Burghölzli. It was from these patients that the scientific proof was allegedly found for an archaic, impersonal strata of the psyche.

In late January 1910—after three months of study, according to McGuire—Jung "gave a lecture in Zurich to an audience of student scientists, in which he aimed to show that 'in the individual fantasy the *primum movens* . . . is mythologically typical."[25] This may be the first tentative public presentation by Jung of a psychological interpretation of mythological material for which he is so well known today.

On 30 and 31 March 1910, the Second Psychoanalytic Meeting was held in Nuremberg, Germany. On the first of these two days Honegger presented a talk entitled "On Paranoid Delusions," of which only an abstract published in the *Jahrbuch* in 1910 has survived.[26] In it, Honegger analyzes the delusional system of a case of paranoid dementia according to the mythological material he has learned from the books that Jung had assigned him over the past six months (since October 1909 at the earliest—hardly enough time for the busy young institutional psychiatrist to master the literature on archaeology and mythology). The patient has delusions with themes containing "ancient mythological and philosophical ideas." Since the patient is a "store clerk, without higher education," Honegger claims he "could not have had an inkling of these myths and philosophies."

Honegger's abstract is important for two reasons: first, here we have the first recorded claim in print, so often repeated by Jung and his disciples, of the absolute certainty of the purity of the material collected from an individual and the absolute certainty of its phylogenetic source. Second, as is also the case with Jung and generations of his disciples, there is no indication that any effort was made to follow in the tradition of Flournoy (and Jung himself in his own doctoral dissertation of 1902) to first determine if these persons had somewhere, at some time, previously been exposed to mythological material but then had forgotten the source, i.e., the phenomenon known today as source amnesia, or in Jung's day, cryptomnesia. The only criteria for controlling the purity of the material (often cited as if they are independent variables in the experimental sense) are (1) the occupational level of the individual and (2) his or her educational level. It is astounding how often Jung himself uses these criteria throughout his life to validate his claims of the transcendental source of mythological contents in dreams and fantasies of everyday people. He assumes that only classical scholars, archaeologists, or perhaps university-educated persons were exposed to Hellenistic themes. This assumption is a major leap of faith and is unconvincing. Indeed, it is epistemologically and historically unsound. As I have established, such mythological knowledge was probably to be expected in the Central European populations that inhabited the back wards of the Burghölzli and the consulting rooms of psychoanalysts like Freud and Jung.[27]

A third reason that Honegger's abstract is important is that it is the first indication of the method of collecting evidence for a phylogenetic unconscious: the study of a single individual. In the evidence presented by Jung and his disciples in the decades since 1910, most of the case studies are devoid of much personal history and instead focus on the mythological interpretation of fantasies dissociated from the real-life circumstances of the subject. Assumptions about the collective or universal nature of mankind are based on information gathered from a very small number of single case studies in Jung's corpus. For example, Jung used the single case-study method to document the spontaneous appearance of mandalas and alchemical ideas in the paintings and drawings of a female American patient he treated in the late 1920s, his famous "A Study in the Process of Individuation" (1950). Jung assures his readers in his usual style that "all these ideas and inferences were naturally unknown to my patient" and that "there could be no question of my having unintentionally infected her with alchemical ideas."[28] This patient, as we now know, was the prominent Jungian Kristine Mann, who came to Jung only after an extensive interest and active participation in Swedenborgian circles and who had exposure to occult literature and ideas—including alchemical symbolism—long before her involvement with Jung.[29]

Honegger's abstract is also important as the first evidence establishing the Haeckelian basis of Jungian theory. Honegger claims, "The autochthonous revival of ancient myths, philosophical ideas and theories of the world, represents a regression that goes back not only to an individual's childhood but also to that of the whole human race. It can be compared in the sphere of anatomy to malformations representing ontogenetic throwbacks to early stages of phylogenesis." This is Haeckel's biogenetic law in Jung's own phylogenetic psychology, stated by Jung through his disciple Honegger.

In opening remarks to his first published essay on what was to later become *Totem and Taboo* (remarks that do not appear in his *Standard Edition*), and that appear in the inaugural issue of *Imago* (March 1912), Freud likewise makes this same leap of faith:

> For everyone involved in the development of psychoanalysis, it was a memorable moment when C.G. Jung, at a private scientific gathering, reported through one of his students that the fantasies of certain mental patients (dementia praecox) coincided strikingly with the mythological cosmogonies of ancient peoples of whom these uneducated patients could not possibly have had any scholarly knowledge.[30]

On 16 May 1910 Jung himself presented his first extensively detailed psychological analysis of mythological material, particularly material relating to the Mithraic mysteries, to a group of Swiss psychiatrists in Herisau. The Herisau talk has been shown by Kerr to be the basis of part 1 of *Wandlungen und Symbole der Libido*, which appeared in autumn 1911.[31] Jung during this time is experiencing dreams with mythological content, including a dream he associates with the cult of Mithraism in which herds of cattle break through the walls of a Gothic cathedral.[32] Jung tells Freud in a letter dated 20 February 1910 that "my dreams revel in symbols that speak volumes."[33] The dreams with vivid mythological content that was seemingly derived from his intense reading in comparative religion and mythology continued on and off for the rest of his life.

Jung's Vision of a
Golden Age of Psychoanalysis

It is in 1910, while Jung was steeped in his researches of mythology, in particular the ancient mysteries, that we find our first direct evidence that he began to openly acknowledge his desire to form a religious sect of psychoanalysis.[34] In a letter to Freud dated 11 February 1910, Jung says that he, too, like Freud, has received an invitation from a "Bern apothecary" by the name of Alfred Knapp to join a new organization, the *Internationaler Orden für Ethik und Kultur* (the International Order for Ethics and Culture), which was a forum for the practical change of society. In an earlier letter to Jung (13 January 1910), Freud seems to think such an association for psychoanalysis may be a good idea and asks Jung's opinion.[35]

Jung responds that the project appalls him. Jung feels the association will be an "artificial one," since "religion can only be replaced by religion."[36] Jung asks, rhetorically: "Is there a new savior in the I.F.? What sort of new myth does it hand out for us to live by? Only the wise are ethical from sheer intellectual presumption, the rest of us need the eternal truth of myth."[37]

Jung then seems to reveal to Freud his concept of psychoanalysis as a replacement for Christianity, and indeed as a movement of redemption and rebirth. The language is Nietzschean, indeed Dionysian, and would fit well with the mythologically based philosophies of cultural and individual *renovatio* of Gross, or of the members of the Cosmic Circle, or of any number of Asconan groups. Jung says that, "The ethical problem of sexual freedom really is enormous and worth the sweat of all noble souls. But 2000 years of Christianity can only be replaced by something equivalent," an "irresistible mass movement."[38] This would, of course, be the new religion of modernity: psychoanalysis. Jung writes:

> I imagine a far finer and more comprehensive task for [psychoanalysis] than alliance with an ethical fraternity. I think we must give it time to infiltrate into people from many centers, to revivify among intellectuals a feeling for symbol and myth, ever so gently to transform Christ back into the soothsaying god of the vine, which he was, and in this way absorb those ecstatic instinctual forces of Christianity for the *one* purpose of making the cult and the sacred myth what they once were—a drunken feast of joy where man regained the ethos and holiness of an animal. That was the beauty and purpose of classical religion, and from which God knows what temporary biological needs has turned into a Misery Institute. Yet what infinite rapture and wantonness lie dormant in our religion, waiting to be led back to their true destination! A genuine and proper ethical development cannot aban-

don Christianity but must grow up within it, must bring to frui-
tion its hymn of love, the agony and ecstasy over the dying and
resurgent god, the mystic power of the wine, the awesome an-
thropophagy of the Last Supper—only *this* ethical development
can serve the vital forces of religion.[39]

Jung then concludes this passage by telling Freud that "[psy-
choanalysis] makes me proud and discontent" and that he
would "like to affiliate it with everything that is dynamic and
alive. One can only let this kind of thing grow."

Freud's response to all this was a reprimand: "But you
mustn't regard me as the founder of a religion. My intentions
are not so far-reaching. . . . I am not thinking of a substitute for
religion: this need must be sublimated."[40] Freud was clearly put
off by Jung's zealotry and his blend of Christian and Dionysian
imagery that spoke to Aryans but not Jews. In Jung's follow-up
letter (20 February 1910), Jung apologizes for "another of those
rampages of fantasy I indulge in from time to time."[41] He tells
Freud by way of explanation that, "All sorts of things are cook-
ing in me, mythology in particular."[42] By 17 April 1910, Jung is
so lost in his mythological studies that he tells Freud,

> At present I am pursuing my mythological dreams with almost
> autoerotic pleasure, dropping only meager hints to my friends.
> . . . I often feel I am wandering alone through a strange country,
> seeing wonderful things that no one else has seen before and no
> one needs to see. . . . I don't yet know what will come of it. I must
> just let myself be carried along, trusting to God that in the end I
> shall make a landfall somewhere.[43]

Yet, by August 1910 Jung returns to the theme of a millenarian religion of psychoanalysis. He reveals in a letter to Freud
that the adversaries of psychoanalysis "are saying some very remarkable things which ought to open our eyes in several ways."
In particular, "All these mutterings about sectarianism, mysticism, arcane jargon, initiation, etc., mean something." Indeed,
such outrage can only be aimed at something "that has all the
trappings of a religion." Jung does not refute this charge of a
religion-like nature to the psychoanalytic movement. Instead,
Jung then suggests to Freud that psychoanalysis should create
an elite (in essence a Nietzschean new nobility), to protect itself
against its critics and then to finally usher in a golden age on

earth. Jung is, of course, engaging in one of his rampages of hyperbole and his remarks are made partially in jest. What is interesting in this letter is that instead of denying the charges of cultism, Jung instead offers his admittedly excessive "apocalyptic vision" that seems to express his desires to promote such a secret society:

> And finally, [psychoanalysis] thrives only in a very tight enclave of minds. Seclusion is like a warm rain. One should therefore barricade this territory against the ambitions of the public for a long time to come. . . . Moreover [psychoanalysis] is too great a truth to be publicly acknowledged as yet. Generously adulterated extracts and thin dilutions of it should first be handed around. Also the necessary proof has not yet been furnished that it wasn't you who discovered [psychoanalysis] but Plato, Thomas Aquinas and Kant, with Kuno Fischer and Wundt thrown in. Then Hoche will be called to a chair of [psychoanalysis] in Berlin and Aschaffenburg to one in Munich. Thereupon the Golden Age will dawn.[44]

What this letter establishes is that, even before Jung broke away and founded his own group, his fantasy of the psychoanalytic movement was one very much like Creuzer's (and others') of the ancient mystery cults of the Greco-Roman world: a hierarchical organization led by a select few hierophants or adepts who are privy to esoteric knowledge by rising in the ranks, initiation by initiation, until gaining entry into the governing elite. Such a sacred organization was to operate outside the usual conventions of society, offering an extraordinary experience of revitalization or rebirth to those brave enough to seek the challenge. By 1916, having long grown weary of Freud's reticence, Jung was well on the way to establishing such a sacred organization himself.

1911–1912

In the early part of 1911, Honegger committed suicide through a lethal injection of morphine. His scientific papers validating Jung's phylogenetic hypothesis were never published and instead vanished until recently. In 1912, papers validating the mythological content of Jung's hypothesized phylogenetic layer of the unconscious in psychotic patients are published by Nelken and Spielrein. Spielrein's paper, written in close collaboration with Jung, is highly supportive of the phylogenetic hypothesis. Nelken admits, however, that although he agrees with the hypothesis, his patient had a "more than superficial" exposure to mythological knowledge.[45] It is interesting to note that neither Jung nor anyone else has ever commented on Nelken's final revelation, which negates the validity of the entire thrust of Jung's theory and, in many respects, Nelken's own paper.

By mid-year Antonia Wolff has entered Jung's life as his assistant. Wolff, Jung's ex-patient, apparently introduces him to Eastern philosophies and astrology (most probably through the Theosophical literature). By June 1911 Jung is casting astrological horoscopes and, given the state of tension between the two men, Jung probably casts Freud's chart as well.[46] However, such a horoscope of Freud in Jung's hand has not yet been made public from his posthumous personal papers, nor have the raw horoscopic calculations Jung made of his patients and others that he knew. In autumn, the first part of *Wandlungen und Symbole der Libido* is published in the *Jahrbuch*. Freud, at this point, is still cautiously supportive.

Wandlungen is, as bears repeating, an extensive amplification of the psychoanalytic and mythological implications of a small group of published reveries of a remarkable woman Jung never met.[47] Although it is difficult to say precisely when Jung found the published fantasies of Frank Miller (Kerr suggests late 1910),[48] his attention to them made him aware of his own irrational, mythopoetic fantasy life for the very first time. This shocked his bourgeois image of himself as a rational, organized, sensible *Herr Doktor* with a keenly focused and directed mind and a strong will. To willingly fantasize, to welcome one's own irrationality, was a dangerous and degenerative lapse into modernity.

In writing *Wandlungen und Symbole der Libido*, as we now know from his personal statements, Jung even used for his scientific method of psychoanalysis one very similar to that suggested to scholars by Müller for understanding the myths: suspend one's own rational bourgeois-Christian thought processes and read these fables with the eyes and mind of a child. Jung had begun using a similar technique as early as 1909 to gain ac-

cess to unconscious knowledge, but apparently not to the extent
of these later years. In doing so while working on Miller's fantasies, Jung realized for the first time that he had an autonomous
fantasy life in his own mind.

> I was in my consciousness an active thinker accustomed to sub-
> jecting my thoughts to the most rigorous sort of direction, and
> therefore fantasizing was a mental process that was directly re-
> pellant to me. As a form of thinking I held it to be altogether im-
> pure, a sort of incestuous intercourse, thoroughly immoral from
> an intellectual viewpoint. . . . It shocked me . . . to think of the
> possibility of a fantasy life in my own mind; it was against all
> the intellectual ideals I had developed for myself, and so great
> was my resistance to it, that I could only admit the fact in my-
> self through the process of projecting my material onto Miss
> Miller's.[49]

Also during this autumn 1911 period Emma Jung began psychoanalytic treatment with Leonhard Seif, who breached medical confidentiality and briefed Ernest Jones, a rival of Jung's, on
the intimate details she revealed in her sessions. Jones passed
this private information on to Freud and it was no doubt later
liberally shared among the members of Freud's "secret committee." This seems to have been a political maneuver to discretely
coerce Jung into remaining under Freud's authority through his
fear of the potential blackmail value of the personal details revealed by Emma. By autumn 1912, when Jung's defection seems
certain, Jones remarks to Freud, "I am hoping that her influence
over him will be of value to us."[50]

The Prototype of the Jung Cult

In January and early February 1912 the psychoanalytic movement came under attack from several directions in a debate published in a Zurich newspaper. The debate started when the *Neue
Zürcher Zeitung* published a summary of a meeting held by the
Zurich branch of the *Kepler-Bund*, an association with chapters
in several localities in German Europe named after the famous
astronomer and devoted to fighting "pseudoscience" in its manifold forms. The Kepler-Bund originally arose in opposition to
Haeckel's Monistenbund, as many scientists considered Hae-

ckel's works pseudoscientific and dangerous to society. The Kepler-Bund was, then, essentially an association of skeptics and debunkers. In early January 1912, the Zurich Kepler-Bund devoted an evening to debunking psychoanalysis.

In the *Neue Zürcher Zeitung*, psychoanalysis was attacked as being a pseudoscience along with hypnosis and other mind cures.[51] Jung's newly published essay on "New Paths in Psychology" (see below) was attacked for its obvious revolutionary rhetoric, and Jung wrote in to defend himself. A critic responded that one did not need to be a physician to see that psychoanalysis was a pseudoscience that had unleashed an unhealthy psychic epidemic. Jung and Riklin eventually sent in an imperious statement of protest under the guise of their official roles in the Zurich Psychoanalytic Association, still hiding behind the *persona medici* (the "mask of the physician") in their stated obligation to "energetically reject the insulting and severely disparaging accusations formulated by laymen against medical specialists."[52]

The critic ("F. M.," or Franz Marti) further accused the psychoanalytic movement of unscientifically extending their efforts to analyzing not only the living but the dead as well in the psychoanalytic assault on folklore, religion, and art. These are areas in which psychoanalysts are laymen, so how can they justify entering these areas?

Finally, even the distinguished retired director of the Burghölzli, August Forel, who was hardly a layman in medical or scientific areas, entered the debate. However, Forel was more interested in objecting to the critic's polemical association of hypnosis and other psychotherapies with Freudian psychoanalysis, which Forel himself despised. "I must definitely declare that lucid researchers fully agree with Mr. F.M. with his condemnation of the one-sidedness of the Freudian school, its sanctifying sexual church, its infant sexuality, its Talmudic-exegetic-theological interpretations."[53] Forel's parting shot at Jung and Freud in the 1 February 1912 issue thus ended the published debate.

However, the response to this assault on Jung and psychoanalysis by his circle in Zurich proved to have historical repercussions that are still with us today. With attacks coming from respected physicians such as Forel (who was also no doubt perceived as representing elements within the highly organized *Monistenbund*) and the scientists and physicians of the Kepler-Bund, the need for a formal group of loyalists who were not psychoanalysts and that was not led by Jung became apparent. Such a formal group of loyalists could themselves repel future attacks on psychoanalysis and thereby lend support to the Zurich Psychoanalytic Association, which was all too alone when defending itself against its critics.

In mid-February 1912, indeed almost exactly two weeks after the published debate had ended, the prototype of Jung's later cult was established in Zurich with Jung's close associate Riklin as the chairman. The public attack had served to more tightly bind Jung's disciples into a common identity and thereby greatly enhance the social cohesiveness of this group of outsiders. Indeed, it became the vehicle from which Jung culled the members of his elite Psychological Club in 1916. The group was called the *Gesellschaft für psychoanalytische Bestrebungen* (the Society for Psychoanalytic Endeavors). Jung announces the founding of this group in a letter to Freud dated 25 February 1912, and refers to it (as he did to his later Psychological Club) as an experiment:

> A more noteworthy news item is the founding of a lay organization for [psychoanalysis]. It has about 20 members and only analyzed persons are accepted. The organization was founded at the request of former patients. The rapport among its members is loudly acclaimed. I myself have not yet attended a meeting. The chairman is a member of the [psychoanalytic] society. The experiment seems to me interesting from the standpoint of the social application of [psychoanalysis] to education.[54]

Several aspects of this organization make it highly significant. First, these events in Zurich marked just one of the indications that psychoanalysis had truly become a cultural movement with its own Weltanschauung. No such formal organization of ex- and current patients who were not also psychoanalysts had ever been created within the various centers of the psychoanalytic movement. Lay organizations were outside the stated goals of Freud's view of psychoanalysis as they existed in February 1912. The only organized psychoanalytic groups were professional ones made up of psychoanalysts who were also physicians.

Although not accepted as members of the official psychoanalytic community, preapproved lay persons could attend lectures or psychoanalytic discussion groups led by official psychoanalysts. For example, Lou Andreas-Salomé attended psychoanalytic discussion groups in Berlin (with Karl Abraham) and Vienna (with Alfred Adler) and was later accepted into Freud's Wednesday night meeting of his inner circle (in late 1912), but until her official acceptance as an analyst she was still considered very much an outsider. No one other than a physician and an approved member of the psychoanalytic association had published in a psychoanalytic journal when in January 1912 "Frau Lou" sent Jung, as editor of the *Jahrbuch*, a query about the possibility of a submission for publication. Jung's quandary over this precedent-setting decision is over how exclusive the psychoanalytic elite should remain. In a 2 January 1912 letter to Freud, Jung writes:

> Frau Lou Andreas-Salomé, of Weimar fame, wants to send me a paper on "sublimation." This, if it amounts to anything, would be a step towards the "secularization" of the *Jahrbuch*, a step to be taken with great caution but one which would widen the readership and mobilize the intellectual forces in Germany, where Frau Lou enjoys a considerable literary reputation because of her relations with Nietzsche. I would like to hear your views.[55]

Freud, to his credit, replied to Jung that "the 'secularization' of [psychoanalysis] is of no great moment now that we are bringing *Imago* into existence, and there is no need for the *Jahrbuch* to be 'stiff and proud.'"[56] Her paper was later published in the second volume of *Imago* in 1913, and by October 1913 when she saw her first patient in psychoanalysis, Andreas-Salomé had gained significant influence in the psychoanalytic movement through her close relationship with Freud.[57] Thus, it appears that January–February 1912 marked the time when psychoanalysis fully became a cultural movement in practice after many years (since 1908) of preparatory theoretical innovations that indicated the movement would turn in such a direction.

However, the new group in Zurich went very far very fast in bringing about this transition. Indeed, it went much faster than any group associated directly with Freud or any of his close associates. Lectures applying psychoanalytic theory to the aesthetics of art, music, and other nonclinical cultural areas were part of the programs of the Society for Psychoanalytic Endeavors in 1912 and 1913.[58] The goal of the members of this Society was to extend the psychoanalytic Weltanschauung to the broadest reaches of world culture. The membership of this group probably comprised the majority of the students in the private seminars Jung began to give in 1912 and 1913 on his own theories and methods of psychoanalysis and the related material and presentations by Jung and others on mythology and comparative religion.[59]

A further important point to remember is just who these persons were who founded this organization. Although Riklin, as an officially approved psychoanalyst, lent legitimacy to the organization through his chairmanship, the actual members were those still rare Europeans who had sought out the modern and controversial treatment of psychoanalysis for their problems and had found great meaning in its view of human nature. These were individuals who had willingly submitted themselves to a form of treatment in which intimate sexual details of their lives were freely handed over to others. Such intimate self-disclosure proved to be a powerful act of liberation, while facilitating one's bonding to a new group of like-minded people. The most intimate sexual activities were then discussed in graphic terminology with other patients. It was only natural that they would seek each other out after meeting informally at lectures, in the waiting rooms of their analysts, or elsewhere, for who else in bourgeois-Christian society circa 1912 could they communicate with? How many of their friends, or members of their families, could really understand the keen insights into the world that psychoanalysis had given them? Each member of this group had undergone the experience and had been convinced of its value. Their conversion, as they soon realized, made them outsiders from conventional society.

A final point that must be emphasized is that it was Jung who was the true leader of this group. Jung's position as the president of the International Psychoanalytic Association, as editor of the *Jahrbuch*, and especially as Freud's hand-picked successor who nominally ran the psychoanalytic movement from Zurich (it was not run from Freud's Vienna), made Jung the crowning representation of a psychoanalyst—and therefore the specialist who truly knew the secrets of psychoanalytic treatment. Coupled with Jung's vibrant personality and scintillating intelligence, these facts endowed Jung with considerable charisma among the psychoanalytic laity of Zurich, many of whom were patients of his at one time or another. Included in this latter category in February 1912 would be Wolff and Emma Jung, who both later became analysts.

Here, then, with the Society for Psychoanalytic Endeavors, we have our first evidence for a charismatic group centered on the work and personality of Jung, which became the basis of the Jung cult. Jung's circle in Zurich thus now could be said to be characterized by

1. A *shared belief* in the psychoanalytic view of human nature and in the liberating or healing or revitalizing effects of psychoanalytic treatment.

2. A high level of *social cohesion* through their shared identity as analyzed individuals set them apart from their previous bourgeois-Christian lives.

3. The influence of the members by the group's *behavioral norms*, such as acknowledging the authority of the psychoanalyst as an expert and therefore as someone with knowledge and power, and the use of the special charismatic language of psychoanalysis ("libido," "sublimation," "complex," "penis substitute," etc.) in everyday conversation with fellow group members.

4. The attribution of charismatic power to the psychoanalytic movement as a whole, and to Jung and the psychoanalysts as particular individuals.

Widening the Gap from Freud

In February 1912, Jung finished his famous chapter, "The Sacrifice," for his second part of *Wandlungen und Symbole der Libido*. In later years he often remarked how it signaled his final separation from Freud. However, it is not published until September of that year when Jung is a safe distance away in New York City giving the famous Fordham University lectures on the "Theory of Psychoanalysis."[60] The chapter on "The Sacrifice" does indeed explicitly reject Freud and his libido theory and contains thinly veiled Mithraic allusions to this effect.[61]

During this period of tension between Freud and Jung it

seems clear that both men attempted to work out a solution to their differences.[62] Although tensions were building throughout 1911, by early 1912 in his letters Jung is openly questioning Freud's authority on matters psychoanalytic. Freud fights back in less direct but obvious ways, such as the February 1912 *Zentralblatt* piece comparing Jung to the apostates who formed the matriarchical cult of the Great Mothers (Diana, Mary). After finishing the "Sacrifice" chapter of *Wandlungen*, Jung bluntly challenges Freud in a letter to him dated 3 March 1912:

> Of course I have opinions which are not yours about the ultimate truths of [psychoanalysis]—though even this is not certain, for one cannot discuss everything under the sun by letter—but you won't, I suppose, take umbrage on that account. I am ready at any time to adapt my opinions to the judgement of anyone who knows better, and always have been. I would never have sided with you in the first place had not heresy run in my blood. Since I have no professorial ambitions I can afford to admit mistakes. Let Zarathustra speak for me:
> "One repays a teacher badly if one remains only a pupil."[63]

However, by the fall of 1912, with the publication of *Wandlungen* and its obvious rejection of Freud and use of symbols associated with Germanic völkisch groups and Jung's uncritical citation of major völkisch figures known for their outspoken racial theories and anti-Semitism, Freud not only viewed Jung's split as a difference of opinion but as one based on anti-Semitism as well (see earlier discussion).[64] By January 1913 the relationship was over, and the rest was silence.

Not everyone in the Society in Zurich could understand Jung's apostasy, and local opposition to Jung led him to reconsider his plan of action. By the autumn of 1912, Jung began to withdraw from social contact with many of his followers, leading to speculation about his mental health and his intentions. By December Jung not only realizes he is not an orthodox Freudian psychoanalyst but that he is also no longer an orthodox Christian.[65] The seeds of this rejection of the Christian myth could be discerned as early as his medical-student days and it is not surprising given the cultural and familial influences that led many (including Jung) to question either the divinity of Jesus or his status as the only savior of humanity. Salvation could come from many men and from many movements of the new twentieth century. For Jung, by 1912, it was clear to him that psychoanalysis as he interpreted it was the new path of redemption, and he began to speak out in public quite forcefully that this was so—but not without some fierce opposition.

Jung Joins Gross in a Call for Revolution: "New Paths in Psychology"

It was in very late 1911 or very early January 1912 that Jung's remarkable essay, "New Paths in Psychology," appeared in a Swiss popular culture journal, *Rachers Jahrbuch für Schweitzer Art und Kunst*.[66] This essay is the first public evidence we have from Jung that he is not only interested in breaking with the cult surrounding Freud (which by autumn 1912, unknown to Jung, had formed a secret committee to protect the image and purity of the ideas of Freud)[67] but in specifically forming his own psychoanalytic movement based on Nietzschean metaphors of liberation and self-sacrifice. The "New Paths" essay is a fin-de-siècle manifesto of a new cultural movement. In places Jung is bombastic and writes in the "style of decadence." It was this piece that, in part, fanned the flames of discontent among the Zurich members of the Kepler-Bund who now saw psychoanalysis as an additional enemy in their war against the monist religion of Haeckel, Ostwald, and their disciples.

In the history of the Jungian movement, the "New Paths" essay is Jung's equivalent of Lenin's 1902 *What Is to Be Done?* In it, Jung's Nietzscheanism prevails. He calls for an intrapsychic overthrow of custom, a revolution in the internalized European traditions that enslave the individual personality: "The hypnotic power of tradition still holds us in thrall, and out of the cowardice and thoughtlessness the herd goes trudging along the same old path."[68]

European civilization (and its Judeo-Christian values and organized religions) makes humankind ill: "Neurosis, therefore, is intimately bound up with the problem of our time and really represents an unsuccessful attempt on the part of the individual to solve the general problem in his own person."[69] The prob-

lem is the conflict between staying on the old paths of nineteenth century bourgeois-Christian culture or giving in to the
exploration of new ones that initiate the individual into modernity. How can one be brought into the twentieth century and be
renewed or reborn in a degenerating world? For the answer
Jung refers to a famous line from the Mithraic Liturgy that he
once suggested to Freud as a motto for psychoanalysis: "Give
up what thou hast, then thou shalt receive!" Those who wish
renewal and rebirth through the new agent of cultural and
personal transformation—psychoanalysis—"are called upon to
abandon all their cherished illusions in order that something
deeper, fairer, and more embracing may arise within them."
And, most significantly for the mystery-cult hypothesis ad-
vanced here: "Only through the mystery of self-sacrifice can a
man find himself anew."[70]

The internal conflict of the modern individual "is connected
with the great problems of society." Therefore, Jung asserts,
"when the analysis is pushed to this point, the apparently individual conflict of the patient is revealed as a universal conflict of
his environment and epoch. Neurosis is thus nothing less than
an individual attempt, however unsuccessful, to solve a universal problem."[71] This problem is "the problem of present-day
sexual morality." Sounding very much like Gross, Jung's Nietzscheanism comes out in Dionysian metaphors of liberation and
greater creativity through sexual freedom:

> His increased demand for life and the joy of life, for glowing real-
> ity, can stand the necessary limitations that reality itself imposes,
> but not the arbitrary, ill-supported prohibitions of present-day
> morality, which would curb too much the creative spirit rising up
> from the depths of the animal darkness.[72]

Psychoanalysis therefore becomes the path of redemption, of
revitalization, of rebirth. Indeed, in passages in this essay removed by Jung in later editions, psychoanalysis becomes a totalizing worldview or Weltanschauung: "The funnelling of the
individual conflict into the general moral problem puts psychoanalysis far outside the confines of a merely medical therapy. It
gives the patient a working philosophy of life based on empirical insights, which, besides affording him a knowledge of his

own nature, also make it possible for him to fit himself into the scheme of things." Jung has wide-ranging cultural concerns here that go far beyond the clinic.

In a prophetic voice, Jung concludes his essay with the prediction that "great is the power of the [psychoanalytic] truth and it will prevail":

> All these weird and wonderful phenomena that congregate round psychoanalysis allow us to conjecture—in accordance with psychoanalytic principles—that something extremely significant is going on here, which the learned public will (as usual) first combat by displays of the liveliest affect. But *magna est vis veritatis et praevalebit*.[73]

In subsequent years, once the break with Freud was certain and he had secured his own stable circle of disciples, Jung revised and enlarged this "New Paths" essay extensively and even retitled it several times, specifically in 1917, 1926, and in 1943. In its first revision it was translated into English and became the essay, "The Psychology of Unconscious Processes," and appeared in the seminal introduction of Jung's work to the English-speaking world, *Collected Papers on Analytical Psychology*, edited by Constance Long and published in 1917. In the introduction (written in December 1916) to the 1917 German edition of this essay, Jung discusses the relevance of his ideas by stating that, "The great problems of humanity were never yet solved by general laws, but only through a regeneration of the attitudes of individuals."[74] In the second German edition of this work, which appeared in 1918, Jung's preface contains a statement that resembles the language of Gross's *Aktion* essays of 1913:

> Every individual needs revolution, inner division, overthrow of the existing order, and renewal, but not by forcing them upon his neighbors under the hypocritical cloak of Christian love or the sense of social responsibility or any of the other beautiful euphemisms for unconscious urges to personal power. Individual self-reflection, return of the individual to the ground of human nature, to his own deepest being with its individual and social destiny—here is the beginning of a cure for that blindness which reigns at the present hour.[75]

Thus, by the end of 1912 Jung knew he had repudiated the Christian myth and its promises of redemption and salvation. The seeds planted by Gross in 1908 finally bore fruit in abundance by 1912: psychoanalysis was the method by which humankind could be liberated. Psychoanalysis became the new salvation of the world, with Jung as the prophet who understood the religious nature of such a movement. Religion, after all, could only be replaced by religion.

In addition, by this time, through his intensive study of the classical scholarship of his day on the ancient mystery cults, he clearly began to form his brand of psychoanalysis around the metaphors of *mysteria*. A letter to Freud dated 3 December 1912 seems to indicate that Jung viewed neurotic symptoms as a form of initiation that could lead to the inner mysteries of the human personality. But what were these deeper mysteries that would arise from within? Jung had to experience them himself first before imparting his vision of them to his tribe of disciples in Küsnacht-Zurich.

The Anima and Bachofen

Jung's interest in spiritualism gave him ample experience of how one may deliberately enter a dissociative state, or trance, that allowed such automatisms as automatic writing or even alternate personalities to emerge. Jung had observed this at seances, and indeed, his entire mother's side of the family (including Jung's maternal grandfather, Samuel Preiswerk) seemed to have regularly engaged in discourse with spirits. Jung's first encounter with the feminine entity he later called the anima seems to have begun with his use of such mediumistic techniques.

In October 1913 Jung began having repeated visions of Europe being destroyed in a sea of blood. Jung thought this was perhaps a sign of "a great social revolution, but curiously enough never a war."[76] Jung decided the best therapy for the distress these visions of blood were causing him was to write them down. His conviction that what he was up to at this stage in his life was no longer science is evident in the story of what happened next: "While I was writing once I said to myself, 'What is this I am doing, it certainly is not science, what is it?'

202

Then a voice said to me 'That is art.' "[77] The voice turned out to be that of a woman Jung knew.[78]

Jung then wondered if his unconscious was forming an alternate personality, such as is found in cases of multiple personality. He decided to interact with the voice, insisting in his own spoken voice that what he was doing was not art. To further engage the voice, Jung used a technique used by the spiritualist mediums: "I thought, well, she has not the speech centers I have, so I told her to use mine, and she did, and came through with a long statement. This is the origin of the technique I developed for dealing directly with the unconscious contents."[79] Jung is therefore admitting here that his psychotherapeutic technique of active imagination is based on the techniques of spiritualism. In this sense, too, Jung's method is akin to that of the völkisch groups who also borrowed the techniques of spiritualism in order to contact nature spirits, Teutonic ancestors, and the Germanic gods.

Rather than simply regarding the feminine voice as a "spirit control" like Blavatsky's mahatmas, Jung looked to his scientific theory of the phylogenetic unconscious to solve the difficulty. At this time (October 1913) Jung still adhered to the model of the phylogenetic unconscious described in earlier chapters. It had a basis in Haeckelian biology and the strata of the phylogenetic unconscious matched the stages of human cultural evolution proposed by Bachofen. Therefore, the voice was of an archaic goddess who ruled during the early matriarchal stages of human existence. Thus Jung says he "thought for a time that the anima figure was the deity. I said to myself that perhaps men had had a female God originally, but, growing tired of being governed by women, they had overthrown this God."[80]

This is pure Bachofen. Jung also seems to have derived his theory of the psychological-type differences in women from Bachofen as well. As Jung remarks earlier in the 1925 seminar, "As you know I think of women as belonging in general to two types, the mother and the hetaira."[81]

Jung later abandoned this Bachofenian idea of an archaic feminine god within and later referred to this feminine entity in men as the anima. However, for a time, Jung used this technique of speaking out loud first in his own voice, and then in a feminized voice, as psychotherapy, but then later conducted the dialogue in the form of automatic writing. Thus during November 1913 Jung felt, as he put it, as if "I was in analysis with a ghost and a woman."[82] The following month was when Jung had his deification experience and initiation into the ancient Aryan/Mithraic mysteries.

1913–1914

January 1913 marks the break in formal relations between Freud and Jung. Jung's apostasy was complete. Prominent among those clinical colleagues remaining with him are Riklin, Jozef Lang (later Hermann Hesse's analyst), Alphonse Maeder, Mary Molzer, Wolff, Hans Schmid-Guisan, Martha Boddinghaus (Sigg), J. Vodoz, C. Schneiter, Adolf Keller, Nelken, Hinkle, and Long. This core group of analysts comprised the Zurich School of psychoanalysis, which was later named complex psychology or analytical psychology.[83]

The God Complex

In this same year Jones published a thinly disguised attack on Jung, depicting him as manifesting a "colossal narcissism" and a belief that he is god.[84] Following suit, in 1914 Freud publishes his famous paper "On Narcissism," which is indirectly concerned with his experience with Jung. Jung does not respond to these attacks until 1916.

Jung's fascination with the experience of becoming a god, or becoming one with the god within, which was so energetically discussed in *Wandlungen und Symbole der Libido*, coupled with his zeal to turn psychoanalysis into a religion of revitalization, were very evident to his estranged Freudian colleagues. Rumors of Jung's belief in his own deification were seemingly everywhere in psychoanalytic circles at this time. In 1913 Jones published a paper in the *Internationale Zeitschrift für ärztliche Psychoanalyse* exposing the gossip about Jung. "This week," Jones writes, "I hope to finish my paper on God-men, in which there is the opportunity of saying some sweet things, quite indirectly, to Jung; it is very enjoyable."[85]

The "typical" case example in Jones's paper, "The God Complex: The Belief That One is God, and the Resulting Character Traits," is unmistakably Jung, with not-so-subtle jabs at Gross and Klages:

> To revert to our typical man: he takes a particular interest in any methods that promise a "short-cut" to the knowledge of other people's minds, and is apt to apply such methods as the Binet-Simon scale, and the psycho-galvanic phenomenon, word-association reactions, or graphology in a mechanical and literal manner, always hoping to find one that will give automatic results. The more unusual the method the more it attracts him, giving him the feeling of possessing a key that is accessible only to the elect. For this reason he is apt to display great interest in the various forms of thought-reading, chiromancy, divination, and even astrology, as well as in occultism and mysticism in all their branches.[86]

The derogatory mention of the "god-man's" interest in a short-cut method is in reference to a conclusion offered by Jung in 1906 (prior to his meeting and probably prior to his corresponding with Freud) at the end of his paper on "Psychoanalysis and the Association Experiments" that, "The associations may therefore be a valuable aid in finding the pathogenic complex, and may thus be useful for facilitating and shortening Freud's psychoanalysis."[87] By 1913, when decent relations between Jung and Freud had ceased, this was perceived as an insult by Freudians.

What produces an egomaniacal man with a God complex? "In my opinion," says Jones, "the main foundation of the complex is to be discovered in a colossal *narcissism*, and this I regard as the most typical feature of the personalities in question."[88] Jones asserts a primary manifestation is "narcissistic exhibitionism" through which a person regards himself as irresistible to others. When Jones says that, "this power . . . is the same ascribed to the tabu king or to the sun and lion symbols of mythology," he is slyly tying Jung's fascination with Mithraism and its solar symbolism and lion-headed deity to his alleged pathological narcissism.[89] These personality characteristics are also very similar to Weber's definition of charisma. Other characteristics include aloofness, surrounding one's personality with "a cloud of mystery," an "interest in psychology," "omnipotence phantasies," "omniscience," and "an attitude of disinclination toward the acceptance of new knowledge." Also:

> The subject of *religion* is usually of the greatest interest to such men, both from the theological and the historical side and from the psychological; this sometimes degenerates into an interest in mysticism. As a rule they are atheists, and naturally so because they cannot suffer the existence of any other God.[90]

Jung's enemies mocked his (and his "twin brother" Gross's) all-too-obvious zeal for being an agent of cultural rebirth. Jones stabs here as well:

> Like all other human beings, they are convinced in their unconscious of their own *immortality*, whether this be ensured through direct continuity or through an eternal series of rebirths; they have thus neither beginning nor end. The belief in their *creative power*, as was mentioned above, is more subordinate, at all events in comparison with other ones, than might have been expected, yet it is often pronounced enough. The belief in self-creation, and rebirth phantasies, are practically constant features. It is further revealed in such phantasies as visions of a vastly improved or altogether ideal world, naturally created by the person in question, or even of the birth of a new planet where everything is "remolded nearer to the heart's desire"; far-reaching schemes of social reform also belong here. In general there is in such men a vein of romantic idealism, often covered by a show of either materialism or realism.[91]

Jones probably could not keep from chuckling as he wrote these lines, and reading this piece in the *Zeitschrift* in 1913 must have wrought irrepressible guffaws from the analysts who knew Jung personally. Despite the obvious hatchet job, Jones's piece is important because it gives us a picture (albeit a diabolically caricatured one) of how Jung was perceived at that time and of the gossip about what he was trying to do in Zurich: namely, set up a religious cult with himself as the totem.

Jung Recognizes His Charisma and Becomes a Prophet

Throughout the winter of 1912 and throughout 1913 and 1914 Jung reported having vivid bad dreams, fantasies, and extreme inner tension. "In 1913 I felt the activity of the unconscious most disagreeably," Jung told his audience during his 1925 seminar on analytical psychology.[92] At times he was apparently close to suicide and kept a revolver next to his bed in case he felt he had passed beyond the point of no return. The tension stopped with the outbreak of the First World War, thus giving Jung the impression that his keenly felt distress was mostly due to a precognitive prophetic sensitivity to the forthcoming war and not only to his own personal psychological issues. "I had the feeling that I was an over-compensated psychosis, and from this feeling I was not released until August 1st, 1914."[93] By reframing his experience as a way of suffering for the good of humanity rather than just over, as Jung put it, "the debris of my former relationships,"[94] indeed by seeing the universal in the particular, Jung healed himself.

Jung's image of himself as a prophet who could receive from his unconscious information about the collective situation of humankind has been amply documented by scholars such as John Gedo and Peter Homans, although from a Freudian/Kohutian psychoanalytic perspective that lapses into pathography.[95] Perhaps less baldly pathological and more objectively psychological hypotheses based on individual cognitive differences between people can be made to account for Jung's charisma.

As Jones hinted when he said that the man with a god complex considered himself irresistible, Jung had no doubt noticed very early in his life that he had the capacity to intellectually dominate and indeed fascinate others who were perhaps less intelligent and less animated in temperament than he. The dominance by persons of high intelligence over those with lower intelligence is an often-observed phenomenon in social psychology, and Jung was clearly extremely intelligent. Jung's self-admitted loss of interest in friends and acquaintances after a while may be a factor of the discrepancy between his extraordinary mental acuity and that of those of lower intelligence who would make up the majority of persons he would meet in usual social circumstances. They would not stimulate him after a while. In these early years it appears only Gross and Freud (and later Flournoy) could do so. Jung's capacity to quickly absorb information and then reorganize it into novel combinations as needed is clearly documented throughout his *Collected Works*. Furthermore, his ability to rise to dominant positions in whatever social organization he participated in is compelling evidence of this, as are the numerous testimonials from others who knew him, confirming his commanding presence. Just to cite one example, when speculating on why Freud was so captivated by Jung, Jones says, "What, I think, most attracted him to Jung was Jung's vitality, liveliness and, above all, his unrestrained imagination."[96]

Certainly by 1914, and no doubt earlier, Jung had begun to associate his charismatic effect on others with his self-perceived intuition or extrasensory ability. *MDR* is filled with such paranormal stories. Indeed, *MDR* even contains a dream Jung apparently had in June or July 1914 in which Jung as a redeemer in the guise of a Dionysian Christ, the "soothsaying god of the vine," fed the multitudes by picking "sweet grapes full of healing juices" off a frozen and otherwise barren tree "and gave them to a large waiting crowd."[97] This places him in the role of a prophet, of which he was well aware, and seems to have consciously and deliberately sought. Fin-de-siècle Europe and the first decades of the new century especially were an age in which scientific or medical or artistic "geniuses" brought their considerable intellects to bear on the greater problems of humanity and stepped easily into the role of the social critic or prophet. We need only to point to Wagner, Haeckel, Ostwald, Max Nordau, George, and Freud for such examples of role models. Combined with his spiritualistic experiences and his fascination with occultism, Jung was a natural to step into a deliberately "spiritualized" prophetic role in which his charisma could, like that of the *theos aner* of late antiquity, be attributed to his intimate contact with extramundane energies. In a comment made to his disciples on 27 April 1925, Jung not only presages his "mana personality" concept of 1928 but also seems to be talking about himself, even alluding to his relationship with Spielrein and their fantasized love-child "Siegfried," when he says:

> When the unconscious produces such a fantasy the personal contents are given an impersonal aspect, there being in the unconscious a tendency to produce collective pictures that make the connection with mankind in general. One sees this process going on in dementia praecox and in paranoia perfectly clearly. It is precisely because these people often have fantasies and dreams that are collectively valid that they get followers. First they make a break with the world through their morbidity, then comes the

revelation of a special mission, and then they begin to preach. People think them thrilling personalities, and women feel it a tremendous honor to have children by them. By primitives they are imagined to be full of gods and ghosts.[98]

Starting in 1912, of course, Jung had made his "break with the world" and entered a period that has been romanticized by himself and his followers as his "confrontation with the unconscious." Jung first publicly disclosed these details of his inner development during the 1925 seminar on analytical psychology, and Jaffé tells us she used this material to write the chapter on the "Confrontation with the Unconscious" in *MDR*.[99] What has not generally been known until recently is that Jaffé only told part of the story, and the full story in the transcript of the 1925 seminar had only been allowed to be read by Jungian analysts and approved patients of such analysts. Until it was published in 1989, the story of Jung's visionary experiences were kept secret. Generations of Jungians, including Jaffé, were no doubt trying to protect the idealized image of Jung from his detractors, and for a good reason: for in 1925 Jung told the story of his own deification.

Jung Becomes a God

Jung spent 1913 reanalyzing his childhood memories and dreams and recorded them for posterity in his "Black Book" and later "Red Book" diaries. As these supposedly childhood experiences were being reremembered by the thirty-eight-year-old mythologically and psychoanalytically sophisticated Jung, their content must be considered to have undergone considerable distortion and their claim to be pure childhood memories must be disputed. A century of experimental research in psychology has demonstrated time and time again how autobiographical memories undergo distortion and reconstruction every time we reremember them. Thus, the account of his "First Years" Jung wrote in his own hand in *MDR* when in his eighties must be taken as yet another example of how his life story was an exemplum of his transcendental theory of the archetypes and the collective unconscious.

It was in December 1913 that he begins the deliberately induced visionary experiences that he later named "active imagination." From this time forward, Jung engages in these visions with the attitude that they are real in every sense of the word. In these visions he descends and meets autonomous mythological figures with whom he interacts. Over the years (certainly by 1916) a wise old man figure named Philemon emerges who becomes Jung's spiritual guru, much like the ascended "masters" or "brothers" engaged by Blavatsky or the Teutonic Brotherhood of the Armanen met by List. Philemon and other visionary figures insist upon their reality and reveal to Jung the foundation of his life and work. He refers on many occasions to the place where these beings live as "the land of the Dead." These visionary experiences—Jung's mythic confrontation with the unconscious—form the basis of the psychological theory and method he would develop in 1916. The account first given in the 1925 seminars differs markedly in many respects from the well-known version in *MDR*, and so reference to both must be made.

In the spring of 1925, when Jung "spoke for the first time of his inner development"[100] he was forty-nine years old, awaiting the completion of the first half-century of life on 26 July. When the year began he was in the United States and had visited with the sun-worshiping Taos Pueblo Indians of New Mexico. On 23 March of that year he began a weekly seminar in Zurich—apparently his first in English—on the broad topic of his analytical psychology.

Jaffé's version of Jung's story in *MDR*[101] is taken largely from the brief remarks made at the end of his lectures on 11 May and 1 June 1925.[102] (A middle lecture given on 25 May dealt primarily with the problem of opposites and his theory of psychological types.) In this familiar version, Jung uses the techniques of active imagination to make a descent into the unconscious, the land of the dead, where he meets an old man with a white beard and a beautiful young girl, who is blind. The old man introduces himself as "Elijah" and Jung is then "shocked" to learn the girl is "Salome." Elijah assures him that this couple "had been together since eternity." With them was a large black snake, which had an affinity for Jung. "I stuck close to Elijah because he seemed to be the most reasonable of the three, and to have a clear intelligence. Of Salome I was distinctly suspicious."[103]

In the 1925 seminars Jung then amplifies these figures with references to motifs in mythology and symbolism.[104] He explains that the snake is associated with hero myths. Salome is "an anima figure, blind because, though connecting the conscious and unconscious, she does not see the operation of the unconscious."[105] In *MDR*, Salome is blind because "she does not see the meaning of things."[106] Elijah represents "the wise old prophet," a "factor of intelligence and knowledge." Here we have Jung associating the role of the prophet with wisdom. Elijah and Salome are, furthermore, personifications of logos and eros, says Jung, but, he adds, "it is very much better to leave these experiences as they are, namely as events, experiences."[107]

One point on which these two versions depart is the depiction of Philemon, Jung's "imaginal guru." In *MDR*, Jung reveals that this figure, "a pagan" with "an Egypto-Hellenistic atmosphere with a Gnostic coloration," developed out of the Elijah figure in subsequent fantasies and dreams.[108] Philemon is not mentioned in the 1925 seminars.

During the lecture Jung delivered on 8 June 1925 (which contains the material not in *MDR*), he further amplifies these figures according to his own typology: "As I am an introverted intellectual my anima contains feeling [that is] quite blind. In my case, the anima contains not only Salome, but some of the serpent, which is sensation as well." He describes Salome as an evil figure, and confesses: "When Elijah told me he was always with Salome, I thought it was almost blasphemous for him to say this. I had the feeling of diving into an atmosphere that was cruel and full of blood."[109]

The initial *katabasis*, or descent into the underworld, was followed by a second: the long-suppressed story of Jung's self-deification experience. As was pointed out in the discussion of *Wandlungen* in chapter 6, Jung thought the climax of the initiatory rites of passage in the ancient Teutonic and Hellenistic mysteries involved a self-deification, a becoming one with god. In these visionary experiences of 1913, Jung himself undergoes such an initiation.

Jung tells his 8 June audience that, "a few evenings later, I felt I should continue. So again I tried to follow the same procedure, but *it* would not descend. I remained on the surface."[110] He felt it was an inner conflict that prevented him from going down into the underworld. He imagines "a mountain ridge, a knife edge, on one side a sunny desert country, on the other side darkness." He then sees a white snake on the light side and a black snake on the dark side, and a fight ensues that Jung feels is a fight between "two dark principles." When the head of the black snake turned white and was defeated, Jung felt he could go on.

He then sees Elijah on a rocky ridge, a ring of boulders, which he interprets as a "Druidic sacred place." Although such ancient rings of megaliths were well known to Jung, it is interesting to note that just such an image appears on the title page of what is often included as the sixth volume in Creuzer's *Symbolik und Mythologie der alten Völker*, the second volume of Franz Joseph Mone's *Geschichte des Heidenthums* (*History of Paganism*) of 1825, which concerns "the religions of the southern Germans and the Celtic peoples."[111] It is not clear from Jung's *Bibliothek* if he owned the Mone volumes that appeared under Creuzer's name. Perhaps they were lost over the years and did not accompany Jung through his final days. But if so, Jung may have used these images from Mone/Creuzer as initial stimuli for active imagination—which is how Jung describes the technique in later writings, although one may use a dream image or other fantasy material to animate one's imagination.

Inside, the old man climbs up on a mounded Druidic altar, and then both Elijah and the altar begin to shrink in size while the stone walls get larger. He sees a tiny woman, "like a doll," who turns out to be Salome. A miniature snake and a house are also seen. Jung then realizes, as the walls keep growing, "I was in the underworld." When they all reach bottom, Elijah smiles at him and says, " Why, it is just the same, above or below."[112]

The possibility that the haunting images from Creuzer and Mone may have provided the initial images for Jung to bring alive with his technique of active imagination is further supported by the fact that volume 2 of Creuzer's work contains an image of two very small figures in white robes surrounded on two sides by stone boulder walls. These tiny figures additionally stand at the stone foyer of a cave that appears to go into a mountain, thus being an entrance into the underworld such as those found at mystery-cult sites, particularly sites of the Mithraic mysteries.

Jung then completes the tale of the second descent into the unconscious with the following remarkable statement:

Then a most disagreeable thing happened. Salome became very interested in me, and she assumed I could cure her blindness. She began to worship me. I said, "Why do you worship me?" She replied, "You are Christ." In spite of my objections she maintained this. I said, "This is madness," and became filled with skeptical resistance. Then I saw the snake approach me. She came close and began to circle me and press me in her coils. The coils reached up to my heart. I realized as I struggled that I had assumed the attitude of the Crucifixion. In the agony and the struggle, I sweated so profusely that the water flowed down on all sides of me. Then Salome rose, and she could see. While the snake was pressing me, I felt that my face had taken on the face of an animal of prey, a lion or a tiger.[113]

In a meaningful shift of focus that must have taken only a few minutes during the spoken lecture, Jung then compares his experience with that of the initiates in the Hellenistic mysteries: "You cannot get conscious of these unconscious facts without giving yourself to them. . . . these images have so much reality that they recommend themselves, and such extraordinary meaning that one is caught. They form part of the ancient mysteries; in fact it is such figures that made the mysteries."[114]

It is now clear that Jung believed he had undergone a direct initiation into the ancient Hellenistic mysteries and had even experienced deification in doing so. This "mystery of deification" gave him "certainty of immortality." This is a remarkable statement. He then interprets his experience for the audience, without, interestingly, ever addressing his *imitatio christi*:

Awe surrounds the mysteries, particularly the mystery of deification. This was one of the most important of the mysteries; it gave the immortal value to the individual—it gave certainty of immortality. One gets a peculiar feeling from being put through such an initiation. The important part that led up to the deification was the snake's encoiling of me. Salome's performance was deification. The animal face which I felt mine transformed into was the famous [Deus] *Leontocephalus* of the Mithraic mysteries, the figure which is represented with a snake coiled around the man, the snake's head resting on the man's head, and the face of the man that of a lion. This statue has only been found in the mystery grottoes (the underchurches, the last remnants of the catacombs). The catacombs were not originally places of concealment, but were chosen as symbolical of a descent to the underworld.[115]

After presenting his audience with a few historical details concerning Mithraism as he knew it from the scholarship of his day, Jung says: "It is almost certain that the symbolical rite of deification played a part in these mysteries." He then proceeds to identify the *Deus Leontocephalus* as "Aion, the eternal being," who is derived from a Persian (Zoroastrian) deity whose name means "the infinitely long duration."[116] In closing this astounding lecture, Jung once again returns to his theme of initiatory deification in the ancient mysteries: "In this deification mystery you make yourself the vessel, and are a vessel of creation in which the opposites reconcile."[117] An unidentified person then asks Jung the date of this dream, and he replies: "December 1913. All this is Mithraic symbolism from beginning to end."[118]

Several issues need to be addressed: first, it is clear that Jung believed he had experienced becoming one with a god," just as he had described it in *Wandlungen und Symbole der Libido*. Second, this deification was part of an initiation into the ancient mysteries of Mithras. The lion-headed god that scholars (rightly or wrongly) have called Aion is indeed a part of most Mithraic cult sites that archaeologists have studied. Speculation about the role of such a deity is abundant.[119] For Jung, the figure of Aion became his secret image of his god within, his *imago Dei*, and in later years he entitled a book *Aion: Researches in the Phenomenology of the Self* (1951). *Aion* contains a frontispiece photograph of a famous statue of this Mithraic deity that today stands in a hallway in the Vatican Museum through which one must exit when leaving the Sistine Chapel.[120]

Third, it must be remembered that according to the scholarship of Jung's day Mithraism was a survival of ancient Zoroastrianism, thus giving it a direct link with the earliest Aryan homeland (Urheimat) and peoples. An initiation into the Mithraic mysteries was most importantly an initiation into the most ancient of Aryan mysteries. This makes Jung's self-deification and travels in the ancestral lands of the dead directly akin to the völkisch visionary initiations into the Teutonic mysteries by List, his Armanen, and the other Ariosophist groups who were doing exactly the same sort of procedure at exactly the same time as Jung.

Figure 4. Mithraic Kronos (Aion)
found in Ostia (from Franz Cumont,
The Mysteries of Mithras).

By indulging in such highly personal self-disclosure about his
life in the 1925 seminars, Jung was modeling the way for his
disciples to follow if they, too, wanted to be redeemed by initiation into mysteries that would give them the "certainty of immortality." Jung had already been teaching his patients and disciples the technique of active imagination by 1916, and indeed it
became a practical method for contacting a transcendent realm
of the dead, ancestors, or gods. By contacting and merging with
the god within, true personality transformation would then follow. Jung had, then, by this time very much left the realm of
science (even in its nineteenth-century sense) and had founded
a mystery cult or personal religion. This was a mystery cult that
promised a direct experience of the transcendent and that ri-
valed the major occultist (Theosophy, Anthroposophy) and
mystical völkisch movements of his day in their common search
for *renovatio*.

215

Completing the Personal Transition

In 1913 and 1914, therefore, Jung withdrew even further from his former bourgeois life-style and ideals. He lived out a wild, intense, mad fantasy life. He had also become intimately involved with his former patient and assistant Wolff, in an extramarital relationship that would last forty years. The openness of this relationship confirms another aspect of his new modern identity: his adoption of the Asconan ethic of polygamy suggested to him by Gross and seemingly justified for its revitalizing effects by the theories of Bachofen and, in a pseudo-Nietzschean sense, Freud. We know that Jung recommended polygamy as an alternative to divorce as late as the 1920s to the American psychologist Henry A. Murray, who then carried on a three-way relationship with his wife and mistress (Christiana Morgan), acted out (with Morgan) a wide variety of sexual fantasies and sex-role reversals in order to develop contrasexual psychological components, and in later years even built his own tower in Massachusetts to mimic Jung's.[121]

Jung resigned from his lectureship (*Privatdozent*) at the University of Zurich in April 1914 and was not to have another formal teaching assignment until 1933, after his movement had been firmly established outside the scientific, academic, and medical worlds. Also in 1914, after his recent reelection (despite his break with Freud), Jung resigned as president of the International Psychoanalytic Association. Although his outside activities are limited and he does not publish much in 1913, 1914, and 1915 (the year in which the war was at its height), he gave private seminars on his own interpretation of psychoanalysis to a growing number of disciples who resided in Küsnacht-Zurich (including British and American students), and he encouraged his students to study mythology and the history of religion.[122]

Although it may well be argued in retrospect that Jung officially removed himself from the established academic, medical, and scientific discourse when he linked up with Freud and began publishing in psychoanalytic journals, Jung very much chose the path of the outsider during these post-Freudian years. Beginning with his publication of "New Paths in Psychology" in the annual yearbook published by Rauscher in Switzerland in January 1912, and especially after 1916, Jung mostly either published his own monographs separately (through Deutike or Rauscher) or chose to address a wider public audience through publishing essays in popular Swiss publications. This was true throughout the rest of his career. The only papers of his that seemed to end up in psychiatric or medical journals were usually the transcripts of lectures given at various congresses in Geneva, England, America, or Germany. For the rest of his life the bulk of Jung's work was published in such popular press magazines and newspapers as the *Neue Zürcher Zeitung, Schweitzerland, Wissen und Leben, Basler Nachrichten, Europäische Revue, Berliner Tageblatt, Allgemeine Neuste Nachrichten, Kölnische Zeitung, Neues Wiener Journal, Münchener Neuste Nachrichten, Du: schweitzerische Monatsschrift*, and the *Neue schweitzer Rundschau*.[123] It is from largely politically conservative Swiss and German periodicals like these that Jung's works were collected, not from scholarly or medical journals.[124] Like Freud and the Freudians, who published in their own psychoanalytic journals, Jung was also beyond any possible criticism from existing scientific traditions of peer review. Hence, by many standards, and by choice, what Jung created and promoted was a vitalistic Lebensphilosophie that extolled the irrational and the intuitive and a transcendental Weltanschauung that was closer to a religion than to twentieth-century science.

The Collective Unconscious,
the God Within, and Wotan's Runes

1916

THIS YEAR—1916—marks perhaps the most important period in Jung's life. From a historical perspective, 1916 is the time when Jung's core ideas shift radically and he becomes more comfortable in his role as a charismatic leader or prophet who has religious insights to impart to his disciples, many of whom have taken up permanent residence near him in the Küsnacht-Zurich area. In this year one published paper (in which he introduces the concepts of the collective psyche, primordial images, and individuation for the first time) and three unpublished papers form the core of his later theory of the collective unconscious and its archetypes and outline the blueprint that his movement was to follow.

It is clear from this material (which is confusingly scattered throughout several volumes of his *Collected Works* or in some cases is simply absent from them) that in 1916 Jung is obsessively concerned with the experience of self-deification or "god-likeness" and with the resulting positive and negative reactions to experiencing a merger with the god within. Jung believes at this point the transformative effect of the ancient Aryan (Indian, Iranian, Greco-Roman, Teutonic) mysteries comes from the initiate literally becoming one with god. From a reading of the material he produced in this important year, it may be argued that Jung believed at this time that for those of Indo-European descent, who were biologically closer to the natural Ur-religion of the first humans, such an inner god is not a Christian god but a solar deity, either in the form of an inner sun or an inner Aryan Christ who could be a regenerative symbol of a successful katabasis or descent to "the realm of the Mothers." In this realm one may have to do battle with the Terrible

218

Mother in order to fight back up to the light, to individuality or individuation.

Jung's familiar psychological theory and method, which are so widely promoted in our culture today, rests on this very early neopagan or völkisch formulation—a fact entirely unknown to the countless thousands of devout Christian or Jewish Jungians today who would, in all likelihood, find this fact repugnant if they fully understood the meaning behind the argument I make here. Let us now review the missing pieces of evidence from the mysterious year of 1916 and peer into the dark and ancient origins of Jung's psychology and movement.

"The Structure of the Unconscious"

As we now know, Jung was engaging in intensely dissociative and potentially dangerous psychological exercises in the years between 1913 and 1916. This self-exploration was accompanied by a withdrawal from the bourgeois-Christian world that anchored the first half of his life and by extreme tensions in his significant relationships, particularly with his wife and his mistresses (Spielrein and Wolff). We have only bits and pieces of information about what Jung actually said and did in private with his intimates and his core group of disciples from 1913 to 1919 or so. However, this scant information from this dark era, when war raged throughout Europe and disrupted the usual forms of intellectual and scientific discourse, is enough to let us know that what Jung published or said publicly in medical or other scientific forums was vastly different from what he was saying and doing in private. While minimally maintaining his credibility as a psychiatrist or psychologist in his contacts with the outside world, in Küsnacht-Zurich he was privately building his own religious movement based on ideas of redemption, regeneration, and rebirth through contact with a transcendent realm.

In an attempt to outline a scientific justification for his private actions, Jung finally published a theoretical article in French in the journal edited by his "fatherly friend," Flournoy, who was beginning to have physical and emotional problems of his own by this time and who would die in 1920. This was *"La Structure de l'inconscient,"* which appeared in the pages of the *Archives de Psychologie*.[1] According to the editors of the *Collected Works*, this paper evidently served as the basis of a public lecture given to the Zurich School for Analytical Psychology, which seems to indicate that the occasion was a formal and professional one.

Jung begins this seminal essay with a new distinction between what he now calls the personal and the impersonal unconscious. These are the new general terms that Jung introduces with this essay to identify the strata of the unconscious mind. This new model replaces the notion of a phylogenetic unconscious characterized by layers of Bachofenian cultural stages, as is implicitly suggested in *Wandlungen*. The contents of the personal unconscious are "of a personal nature in so far as they are acquired during the individual's lifetime."[2] In agreement so far with Freud and the other psychoanalysts with regard to analysis, Jung says, "Whoever progresses along this path of self-realization must inevitably bring into consciousness the contents of his personal unconscious, thus enlarging considerably the scope of his personality."[3]

Yet this old model of the unconscious is not the whole story, for Jung then says there are "primordial images" that he has documented in *Wandlungen und Symbole der Libido* that point to a deeper layer of the unconscious mind. He later referred to these primordial images as "dominants" in 1917 and as "archetypes" in 1919. The emergence of one such primordial idea is found in the phenomenon of "godlikeness." This psychological state occurs when the contents of the unconscious are "assimilated," and it leads to a grandiose distortion of consciousness that promotes delusions of omniscience. Jung says in this essay that he borrowed the term "godlikeness" from Adler.

What we find in this early 1916 version—and not in any version after 1917—is that the core of the remainder of this essay is Jung's relentless explanation of the psychological experience of godlikeness. Given his fascination with the self-deification experiences of the ancient mysteries, and his own secret experience of being deified and therefore initiated into the ancient Mithraic mysteries, this 1916 essay can no longer be read as simply an objective report of a clinical phenomenon. It is, in a sense, a scientific rationalization for Jung's own experiences. It is also a long overdue response to Jones's paper, "The God Complex" (1913), and Freud's "On Narcissism" (1914), both of which were aimed, in part, at Jung.

By using the experience of godlikeness as a starting point, Jung then leads the reader into his very first published mention of a collective psyche, which he later refers to as the collective unconscious.[4] This collective psyche is biologically based, according to Jung, who also seems to indicate that the collective psyche is inherited in some sense, without reference to the known modes of hereditary transmission posited by the science of 1916. He makes an analogy to the human brain and its innate ability to perform functions that are "neither developed ontogenetically nor acquired."[5] However, "in as much as human brains are uniformly differentiated, the mental functioning thereby made possible is collective and universal." Jung then says that this basic biological fact explains why "the unconscious processes of the most widely separate peoples and races show a quite remarkable correspondence . . . in the forms and motifs of autochthonous myths."[6]

In this early statement, however, Jung sticks closely to analogies that seem to indicate he is still advocating a biologically based notion of a phylogenetic unconscious with discernible (although non-Bachofenian) layers: "Inasmuch as there are differentiations corresponding to race, tribe, and even family, there is also a collective psyche limited to race, tribe and family over and above the 'universal' collective psyche."[7] For the average bourgeois-Christian Central European patient that made up the bulk of Jung's caseload at this time, the family would be one's own birth family, the tribe would be Germanic, and the race would be Aryan (or Indo-European).

In reviewing the structure of his sequential argument for the evidence he presents in this essay, let us be absolutely clear about what Jung is proposing: our ability to experience godlikeness is what Jung is offering to the world as compelling proof for the existence of the collective psyche. The experience—indeed Jung's own experience—of becoming one with God is therefore *not* derived from a psychopathological process of "colossal narcissism" as Jones would have it, but instead it is strong evidence of "a certain psychic function having a collective character supraordinate to the individual mentality."[8] It is,

indeed, only a potentially deranging, yet also a potentially re-
newing or "creative" supernormal experience akin to "the mo-
ments of inspiration in genius [that] often bear a decided resemblance to pathological states."[9]

Jung is here reframing for us—and especially for himself—an
experience that he and others have had that has generally been
regarded as degenerate or psychotic. Deification is not necessarily lunacy, he wishes us to believe, but direct experience of a
transcendental realm (transcendental, that is, from the point of
view of the individual ego): the impersonal unconscious. Attempts to "annex" contents of the unconscious, especially the
impersonal unconscious, enlarge and bloat the individual personality, leading to a state of subjective godlikeness. The term
Jung invented around this time for the method of seeing the
gods was "active imagination."[10] Therefore, analysis—that is,
psychotherapy in a Jungian style circa 1916 that employs dissociative active-imagination techniques—allowed patients to feel
they were gods by allowing them to constellate the god within.
This interior god is in all of us and we experience it through
techniques Jung devised and utilized. Thus Jung says:

> In a certain sense this feeling of "godlikeness" exists *a priori*, even
> before analysis, not only in the neurotic but also in the normal
> person, the only difference being that the normal individual is ef-
> fectively shielded from any perception of his unconscious, while
> the neurotic is less and less so. On account of his quite peculiar
> sensibility, the latter participates to a greater extent in the life of
> the unconscious than does the normal person. Consequently,
> "godlikeness" manifests itself more clearly in the neurotic and is
> heightened still further by the realization of unconscious contents
> through analysis.[11]

Furthermore, Jung says that, "That is why, in any analysis
that is pushed far enough, there comes a moment when the subject experiences that feeling of 'godlikeness' that I have spoken
of."[12] The patient is "pushed" in this sense by the dissociative
procedure of active imagination.

How does one initially experience the god within? Jung says
that, among other symptoms, it is felt through a dream in which
the dreamer is the "earth, the sun, or a star"[13]—precisely the

three central images of Bachofen's tellurian, solar, and lunar stages. Other initial signs and symptoms of the state of god-likeness are listed by Jung in this remarkable paragraph:

> This condition frequently announces itself by very peculiar symptoms, as for example dreams in which the dreamer is flying through space like a comet, or feels that he is the earth, the sun, or a star, or that he is of immense size, or dwarfishly small, or that he is dead, is in a strange place, is a stranger to himself, confused, mad, etc. He may also experience body sensations, such as being too large for his skin, or too fat; or hypnagogic sensations of falling or rising endlessly, of the body growing larger, or of vertigo. Psychologically this state is marked by a peculiar disorientation in regard to one's own personality; one no longer knows who one is, or one is absolutely certain that one actually is what one seems to have become. Intolerance, dogmatism, self-conceit, self-depreciation, and contempt for "people who have not been analyzed," and for their views and activities, are common symptoms.[14]

Several things need to be pointed out in this passage. First, Jung is no doubt reporting many of the things he himself had been experiencing since at least late 1913, as many of the dream images he lists were part of his reported dreams and fantasies during this period. Second, the certainty that "one actually is what one seems to have become" may very well point to Jung's own self-deification when he became Aion, the lion-headed god of the ancient Mithraic mysteries. Or, as many other bits of evidence suggest, at some point during this period Jung may have very well felt as if he himself were Christ, after recognizing and merging with the "Christ within."[15] The Mithraic Aion and the Christian image of the crucified Jesus are merged in Jung's December 1913 self-deification experience, making him, in essence, the Aryan Christ. Third, the attitude of contempt for people who have not been analyzed seems to confirm my charismatic-cult hypothesis, for the analyzed person in Jung's cult would have the psychological and especially the social status of an initiate, someone who is "one of us." This is the arrogance of an elite that feels it has found "the answer" and resents the larger body of society for not also seeing the light. Participation in such an intensely religious group (hidden as it may be behind the veneer of Jung's medical degree and scientific reputation) would quickly create an "us versus them" mentality of the Jungian new nobility versus the herd.

This phase of analysis is one of its "real dangers," according to Jung,[16] and to his credit he does devote considerable space in the remainder of this essay to describing the potential mishaps of willfully contacting the collective unconscious. Alternatively Jung also argues that, if one could stand it, one was rewarded with a direct experience of the spirituality of the ancients, for with this outburst of fantasy from the collective psyche, "all the treasures of mythological thinking and feeling are unlocked."[17]

Jung declares: "Access to the collective psyche means a renewal of life for the individual, no matter whether this renewal is felt as pleasant or unpleasant." This was an idea that finds its first expression in part 2 of *Wandlungen und Symbole der Libido*, for one could either be revitalized or "annihilated" by an experience of material from the phylogenetic unconscious.

Yet, for the world at large, with this essay Jung holds out the promise of something more tremendous, something that no other psychoanalyst, or psychotherapist or priest or minister or rabbi or especially any medical authority could offer them, something that could heal the festering fin-de-siècle neurosis produced by modernity: rebirth.

Jung's paper in the *Archives de Psychologie* was only the official public version of what Jung and his circle were up to as the Great War devastated Europe. A clearer picture of what Jung was doing and saying to his closest disciples can be found in the material that he presented to them in seminars, lectures, or private analytic sessions. The picture we begin to see is, again, that of a religious cult of redemption and not anything remotely resembling the standard practice of psychiatry or of any academic or medical professional society. Perhaps only the monistic religion movement and its advocacy of sun worship could claim to unite science and neopagan religion as self-assuredly as in the actions and pronouncements of its eminent scientific and culturally elite membership. Jung was waging war against Christianity and its distant, absolute, unreachable God and was training his disciples to listen to the voices of the dead and to become gods themselves.

"The Transcendent Function"

Many of Jung's earliest theoretical formulations prior to his final theory of the collective unconscious and its archetypes only appeared in print near the end of his life or were found among his personal papers after his death. Jung's famous paper on the transcendent function in which he describes in detail, and more extensively than in any of his other writings, the technique of active imagination was written in 1916, circulated privately among Jung's disciples, but only published in June 1957. This first appearance in print was in the form of an English translation by A. R. Pope and was "privately printed" by the Students Association of the C. G. Jung Institute in Zurich.[18] This translation was taken directly from the original German manuscript by Jung. The translation that appears in CW 8 with a 1958 introduction by Jung is, like so much of the material in the Collected Works, an expanded version of the original that has been revised to make the material fit Jung's final theories of the collective unconscious and its archetypes. The original version of "The Transcendent Function" contains important insights into the development of Jung's theories and the dissociative techniques he was teaching his pupils and patients in the course of psychotherapy.

Jung begins his argument with an observation that is rooted in his view of human evolutionary history, that "the definiteness and directedness of the conscious mind is a function which has been acquired relatively late in the history of the human race, and is for instance largely lacking among primitive peoples even today."[19] Such an adaptation, while necessary for survival in a civilized world, has been acquired by humanity "at a very heavy sacrifice."[20] Yet, "without it, neither science nor society could exist, for they both presuppose a reliable continuity of the psychic process."[21] Consciousness, as we experience it, is largely characterized by this directed process, and it has a certain "threshold intensity" that its contents must attain to remain in consciousness.

Yet from an evolutionary perspective, consciousness is a recent and therefore somewhat imperfect adaptation that "evolved" (in almost the original embryological sense of the term) and is still evolving from the "unconscious."[22] Consciousness is the progressive endpoint of a purposive process, and implicit within the polarity of consciousness and unconsciousness in Jung's model of the psyche is the tension between a relatively recent adaptation to a relatively current environment and the greater force of ancient and complex adaptations to an ancestral environment as inherited determinants of present behavior. "The conscious forms the momentary process of adaptation," Jung asserts, "while the unconscious contains not only all the forgotten material of the individual's own past, but also all inherited behavior traces of the human spirit."[23] Furthermore, "The unconscious contains all the fantasy combinations which have not yet attained the threshold intensity, but which in the course of time and under suitable conditions will enter the light of consciousness."[24]

Survival depends upon the continued adaptive "unfolding" (the original meaning of *evolutio*) of consciousness from unconsciousness. Maladaptive patterns occur in neurotics, in whom Jung says the "threshold between the conscious and the unconscious gets shifted more easily, or in other words the partition between the conscious and the unconscious is much more permeable," or in psychotics, where the person is "completely under the direct influence of the unconscious."[25] However, the directed processes of consciousness are "one-sided" according to Jung and can be "an advantage and a drawback at the same time."[26] Too much directedness of consciousness can instead threaten survival. As Jung warns:

> Life today demands concentrated directed functioning and with it the risk of considerable dissociation from the unconscious. The further we are able to detach ourselves from the unconscious through directed functioning, the more readily can a powerful counter-position be built up in the unconscious, and when this breaks loose it may have devastating consequences.[27]

The most adaptive and desirable state of being, therefore, is one that allows for the continuing unfolding of consciousness through the "union of *conscious* and *unconscious* contents," a process that Jung calls the psychological "transcendent function." It is, in perhaps a vitalistic sense, Jung's psychological reframing of Haeckel's teleological recapitulation theory, for successful ontogeny is predicated upon a natural passage through the stages of phylogenetic development and the individual is therefore dependent primarily upon ancient biological forces for present survival. The remainder of Jung's essay concerns techniques for how the transcendent function may be brought about through specific therapeutic techniques—namely, the synthetic or "constructive method of dream analysis" (as opposed to Freud's causal and reductive analytical method) and active imagination.

The völkisch obsessions of those in Jung's circle at this time are quite evident in an example of his constructive analysis of the dream of "an unmarried woman patient" in which "someone gives her a wonderful, richly ornamented, ancient sword dug up out of a tumulus.[28] Jung provided three columns that then give side-by-side descriptions of the patient's own associations, the Freudian (psychosexual and decidedly Oedipal) analytical interpretation (which is ontogenetic), and then Jung's own "constructive interpretation," which places more emphasis on a phylogenetic perspective.

The patient associates the sword with a dagger that her father owned that "he once flashed in the sun in front of her." She describes him as strong-willed and polygamous. The bulk of the associations that Jung selectively reports, however, concern the sword, its connection to the patient's racial heritage, and its magical properties (it is inscribed with runes). This is how Jung reports his patient's associations to the sword in the dream:

> A *Celtic* bronze sword: Patient is proud of her Celtic ancestry. The Celts are full of temperament, impetuous, passionate. The ornamentation has a mysterious look about it, ancient tradition, runes, sign of ancient wisdom, ancient civilizations, heritage of mankind, brought to light again out of the grave.[29]

Jung's constructive interpretation directs the patient's attention to the teleological, phylogenetic, and indeed spiritual message of the dream for the healthy development of her own psychological existence. Instead of an interpretation that is based on the circumstances of her early life, Jung essentially tells the patient that the symbol of her willful and polygamous father in the dream is in actuality a symbol of the actual nature of the unconscious, which Jung equates here with the Schopenhauerian concept of the will and with its natural polygamous impulses. In her dream, furthermore, Jung says her father also symbolizes her ancestral heritage "which is also in her"—an inner father-land, which also symbolically makes her "her father's daughter." Note the völkisch imagery and the references to archaeological metaphors in Jung's full interpretation below. Also note that, through the figure of the father, Jung may be describing not only himself but also his ideal image of an individuated human being who has learned to live adaptively through the transcendent function:

> It is as if the patient needed such a weapon. Her father had the weapon. He was energetic, lived accordingly, and also took upon himself the difficulties inherent in his temperament. Therefore, though living a passionate, exciting life he was not neurotic. This weapon is a very ancient heritage of mankind, which lay buried in the patient and was brought to light through excavation (analysis). The weapon has to do with insight, with wisdom. It is a means of attack and defense. Her father's weapon was a passionate, unbending will, with which he made his way through life. Up till now the patient has been the opposite in every respect. She is just on the point of realizing that a person can also will something and need not merely be driven, as she had always believed. The will based on a knowledge of life and insight is an ancient heritage of the human race, which also is in her, but till now lay buried, for she is in this respect, too, her father's daughter. But she had not appreciated this until now, because her character had been that of a perpetually whining, pampered, spoilt child. She was completely passive and completely given to sexual fantasies.[30]

The necessity of integrating the phylogenetic forces of instinct into the present as the key to a full life is described by Jung in a passage that he removed in his 1958 revision of the essay and that does not appear in the *Collected Works*. With this passage Jung speaks with the voice of a prophet who has had a vision of an ideal—if somewhat vague and paradoxical—state of human nature:

> The transcendent function lies between the conscious and the unconscious standpoint and is a living phenomenon, a way of

life, which partly conforms with the unconscious as well as the conscious and partly does not. It is an individual-collective phenomenon which in principle agrees with the direction of life anyone would follow, if he were to live in a completely unconscious, instinctive way. This explains why primitive man so often appears as the symbol for the transcendent function. Back to nature in Rousseau's sense is impossible and would only be a futile regression. One can, however, go forwards and through psychological development again reach nature, but this time consciously taking account of instinct.[31]

Jung notes, however, that from a psychotherapeutic standpoint, dream analysis alone is an imperfect method for facilitating the transcendent function. Jung then describes techniques for encouraging "the emergence of fantasies which are lying in readiness" in the unconscious.[32] Jung claims that patients can be trained to do this by "first of all in systematic practice to eliminate critical attention, whereby a vacuum is produced in consciousness."[33] In essence, the techniques Jung then recommends are those that actively promote the dissociation of consciousness and therefore disrupt the so-called normal sense of continuity of self, identity, volition, and the processes of memory.

According to Jung, for the transcendent function to operate the individual must learn to take the unconscious seriously. "By taking the unconscious seriously I acknowledge my readiness to accept the regulating effect of the unconscious and permit it to influence my actions."[34] Jung therefore suggests that "visual types" will have inner images that may also be drawn or painted and "auditory types" may hear inner words that may be transcribed. Spiritualistic practices such as automatic writing and the use of a planchette are recommended in some cases. Jung encourages those persons with artistic inclinations to draw, paint, or sculpt their inner visions and voices. Interestingly, given the proximity of Ascona and its importance as a center for the development of modern dance at about this time due to the continuing influence of Duncan, Laban, and Wigman, it is possible that Jung had Asconan patients in mind when he notes that there are "those who are able to express the contents of the unconscious by bodily movement" but they are "fairly rare."[35]

In this essay Jung very much concretizes and personifies the unconscious as an "other" that must be engaged in a dialogue. Nowhere does Jung's psychology seem so mediumistic, and it is indeed perhaps for this reason that this essay was privately circulated for more than forty years before being allowed publication. Given the nature of the unconscious as the realm of the ancestors or the inner fatherland, Jung's psychotherapeutic techniques for promoting the operation of the transcendent function are equivalent to the methods used by other spiritualist mediums for receiving messages from the deceased and perhaps even the wisdom of the ages. According to Jung, the ego must "have it out" with the unconscious by "taking the lead" in the following way:

> The way this can be done is best shown by those cases in which the "other" voice is more or less distinctly heard. For such people it is technically very simple to note down the "other" voice in writing and to answer its statements from the standpoint of the ego. It is exactly as if a dialogue were taking place between two human beings with equal rights, each of whom gives the other credit for a valid argument and considers it worthwhile to modify the conflicting standpoints by means of thorough discussion, and in this way to strike a balance or at least make a compromise.[36]

Because of Jung's "project for a mediumistic psychology," as Shamdasani puts it, it must be emphasized that from 1916 onwards, in practice, Jung probably had far more in common with figures such as Blavatsky, List, and Steiner than he did with Freud, Adler, or even Gross.

"Adaptation, Individuation, Collectivity"

Another unpublished manuscript was found in 1964 in the archives of the Psychological Club in Zurich and is signed and dated in Jung's handwriting "Oct. 1916." This paper, "Adaptation, Individuation, Collectivity," appears to have been an elaboration of the addendum that appeared in later published versions of "The Structure of the Unconscious," as it, too, is an organized, step-by-step presentation of Jung's psychological theory as he was developing it in that year. It does not appear in his *Collected Works* with any of the other materials from this chronological period, but instead is tucked away in a volume of miscellaneous writings that only appeared in 1976.[37]

It is clear from this document that in 1916 Jung was still trying—at least nominally—to ground his "official" psychological theory in evolutionary biology. Throughout this piece the key idea is "psychological adaptation" to outer and inner conditions, which means "adaptation to the unconscious." Jung is therefore positing here that human survival is dependent upon an adaptation to the forces of the unconscious. Neurosis then becomes a "disturbed or diminished process of adaptation" to these inner and outer realities.[38] In language resembling Ostwald more than Freud, Jung then offers a paragraph describing his theory of the "energetics of adaptation."[39]

It is in the following section, much longer, on "adaptation in analysis" that Jung introduces his program for Lebensreform not only for the individual, but for the analyzed elite of patients reentering society. Jung observes that in analysis some patients develop an intensely emotional dependence upon the analyst—the transference—which is an "over-compensation for a resistance to the analyst."[40] Jung says that "this resistance arises from the demand for individuation, which is *against* all adaptation to others."[41]

Using the language of Gross and Nietzscheanism, Jung admits that "individuation cuts one off from personal conformity and hence from collectivity." Since, also, "individuation is exclusive adaptation to inner reality and hence an allegedly 'mystical' process," one must consider cutting oneself off from one's former anchors in the world or in society (one's professed faith, political beliefs, morality, family) in the way prescribed by Jung and his disciples. The appeal to the healthful and revitalizing aspect of individuation through analysis with Jung, and the promise of "mystical experiences" in doing so, was an attractive hook for many seeking novel paths of unconventional spirituality.

By October 1916 the new path of spiritual liberation was called "individuality" by Jung (following the language of von Hartmann) or, following his masters Schopenhauer and Nietzsche, "individuation."[42] It demanded breaking bonds with one's family, one's society, even one's God, for "by cutting himself off from God" the individual becomes "wholly himself."[43]

Yet a stiff price is paid for this necessary apostasy: "Since the breaking of the patient's previous personal conformity would mean the destruction of an aesthetic and moral ideal, the first step in individuation is a tragic *guilt*. The accumulation of guilt demands *expiation*. . . . Every further step in individuation creates new guilt and necessitates new expiation."[44] Hence: individuation is continual rebirth through sinning (breaking bourgeois-Christian norms) and redemption (translating transcendental insights into social action). This is a notion straight from the Nietzschean doctrine as preached by Gross, for it combines spirituality and medicine with the anarchistic and Marxian fantasies of "perpetual revolution."

By being analyzed by Jung and his associates, patients would not only heroically suffer psychological crucifixions and heal themselves, but afterwards they could redeem society as well by becoming initiates of this new secret wisdom of the ages. In this essay Jung gives his disciples a dry theoretical explanation for the "contempt and hate that come from society" at those in the Jung cult who have separated themselves from a bourgeois-Christian world that could only frown on such neopaganism.[45] "But," Jung says, "inner adaptation leads to the conquest of inner realities, from which values are won for the reparation of the collective."[46] In a section on "Individuation and Collectivity" that follows, Jung proposes linking individual spiritual development with the fate of humankind, using such statements as, "The individual is obliged by the collective demands to purchase his individuation at the cost of equivalent work for the benefit of society."[47]

These latter statements bear closer examination as they are crucial to the philosophy behind the practice of Jung and his cult at this time. Through the techniques Jung taught his patients, which he expected them to practice well after therapy was over, they could access the religious wisdom of the ages. If they survived the initial ordeal without permanent damage, they could announce these insights from the ancestors and apply them to the rest of society, thereby redeeming humanity by leading it to a spiritual reawakening. As these initiates, the elite corps of the individuated, can receive information directly from the collective unconscious (the land of the ancestors or the dead), they have the advantage and, indeed, the obligation, to proselytize this new doctrine for the benefit of society. In practice this is, of course, how charismatic groups of all types have operated and even succeeded, from the Christ cult of two thousand years ago ("the kingdom of God is at hand") to even Alcoholics Anonymous today, which also uses peer pressure (sometimes not so subtle) to convince new members to rely upon their "God" or "higher power" within to cure their addiction and its roots in "spiritual bankruptcy."[48]

Hermann Hesse's Initiation into Wotan's Mysteries

How do we know that the ideals stated in this unpublished paper from October 1916 were really put into practice? Such a utopian occult doctrine was communicated by Josef Lang, a psychiatrist and an analyst trained by Jung and a member of his inner circle, to none other than Hermann Hesse. Hesse, a prominent figure in the Asconan counterculture in the decade preceding his contact with Lang, first underwent an analysis with Lang in 1916 and 1917 and then with Jung himself in 1920. We have independent confirmation of Lang's rather oracular statements to Hesse from Hugo Ball, a close friend of Hesse's and his first biographer. Ball was allowed to briefly quote some material from Lang's personal notes of four analytic sessions from late October 1917 in his *Hermann Hesse: Sein Leben und Werk*, which was first published in 1927.[49] These notes and all others kept by Lang were apparently destroyed by his daughter after his death in 1945.

Hesse's noted modern biographer, Ralph Freeman, summarized Ball's citations in his own examination of the life of Hesse but left out some important details. Here, first, is Freeman's summary of these passages from Ball's book:

> Biblical in tone, Dr. Lang wrote on October 23: "You will hear the voice that calls out from the primordial depths of the earth" to proclaim the "Laws of the Dead" who shall be the harbingers of

a New Era. Two days later, he rhetorically asked his patient: "Where are you today?" and then projected an image of himself, the therapist, as a laborer within Hesse's psyche, hammering to break the crust that prevents him from penetrating the ice of his patient's soul. "I seek to approach you in order to touch," ends this strange entry—a new means of breaking down the barriers between men. The third entry, of October 26, 1917, contains the most vivid and significant image. Dr. Lang refers to the psyche as a mine shaft: "I hammer within my mine shaft that encloses me and gives me no light that I do not radiate myself. You hear my hammering in the roaring within your ear. Your heartbeat is the hammering of my arms that long to be freed."[50]

In the original 1927 German edition of Ball's book, it is clear that in the passage from 23 October 1917 that Lang is very much Hesse's psychopomp or guide into the depths and is acting in almost a mediumistic role as well: "You will hear the voice that calls out from the primordial depths of the earth, and I will announce to you the Law of the Magma in whose springs I reign. You shall learn from me the Laws of the Dead which will become the Laws of a New Age."[51] As Jung's disciple, Lang is demonstrating a technique that he could have learned only from Jung: analyst as a director of imagery, as occult expert, as medium, and as millenarian prophet. Furthermore, in terms of Jung's "geology of the personality" it is a Jules Verne–like journey to the center of the earth and to the living sun within its nucleus.

The passage for 25 October is indeed the strangest and contains evidence of a deliberate blurring of psychological boundaries between the two men, for not only does Lang tell Hesse that he is working to break through the hard crust of ice that encases Hesse's soul, but he uses a German word for "penetrate" (*durchdringen*) that can also have sexual connotations. The passage also seems to contain some evidence that Lang may have been using a more formal hypnotic induction procedure with Hesse, and he suggests to him that he is always with him. "Go quietly to sleep," he tells Hesse, "for I am always near to you, [and] often during the day and during the night I am sending the rays of your thoughts into the dark well of your soul, where I seek to approach you in order to touch."[52] Lang is delib-

erately introducing himself into Hesse's psyche to become an
actor in the poet's inner drama and is involved in directing
Hesse's thought processes. What Lang is attempting to teach
Hesse is the introversion or "regression of libido" into the
depths of the collective psyche (the "dark well of your soul"),
or active imagination. No matter what time of day or night
Hesse begins to experience such active imagination outside of
the formal analytic sessions, Lang is suggesting to Hesse that he
will be safe because he will be there with him.

At the beginning of the 26 October session, Lang asks Hesse,
"What do you want to say to me today?" ("*Was willst Du mir
heute sagen?*") Freeman translates the full passage from this session. What is interesting is that Lang here introduces the image
of each man, deep within his own "mine shaft," but their shafts
are side by side, or indeed are one, for Lang is busy deep within
the collective unconscious (and is therefore *inside* Hesse) trying
to heroically redeem Hesse and thereby free himself ("Your
heartbeat is the hammering of my arms that long to be freed").

Freeman leaves some interesting material out of Lang's notes
from the last session reported by Ball, that of 28 October 1917.
After somewhat idiosyncratic references to the redemption of
sins, Lang tells Hesse, "I am hammering in your mine shaft, and
one day you will understand and read the Runes which I have
chiseled into the stones of your soul, the primordial Scripture of
men which you must teach them, the tablets of the Law of what
is to come."[53] Here Hesse is instructed to make his own descent
into Mother Earth (*Erdmutter*) and contact the dead, the ancestors who will teach him a new "Law of what is to come," which
it is then Hesse's duty to teach others. This example from
Hesse's analytic sessions with Lang is so very congruent with
Jung's public and private statements in 1916 that we must assume that this sort of procedure was de rigueur within Jung's
circle.

Another point needs comment here, and that is Lang's deliberate reference to the "Runes." This reference was left out of
Freeman's translation, and it is significant. Hesse is taught to
descend into the depths, the land of the ancestors, and to one
day read and understand the "Runes." Lang's use of this term is
of course understandable within Germanic culture, as the ancient Norse runes were not only used as an alphabet but for

magical divination, and hence would indeed be the perfect form for an esoteric prophecy to be transcribed. The runes and their mystifying symbols were familiar to most educated persons in Central Europe, as their images would appear from time to time in speculative articles in the popular press that attempted to decipher them. They were also the subject of many books and articles in Theosophical publications and in the Germanic folklore works of the Diederichs Verlag. Some of the basic runic symbols were certainly familiar to Jung, Lang, and Hesse. However, there are perhaps deeper layers to this seemingly innocuous remark by Lang.

Since Hesse is being trained in a technique in which he is meant to actively imagine a visionary experience, it is perhaps instructive for us to do the same if we want to fully see what is going on in this scenario. Lang says that he etched these runic symbols on the stone tablets of Hesse's soul, which hence is characterized by its mystical Germanic essence. Lang does not refer to "hieroglyphs," for example, which would entail the use of a metaphor from a Semitic culture. Once Hesse learns to read the runes, he, too, can then also be a prophet of the coming spiritual reawakening like Lang and Jung. The law of the new age is a "primordial Scripture" written on stone tablets in the runic symbols of the ancient Teutons. It is important to keep this image in mind of a Teutonic Ten Commandments. Thus, what Lang may be suggesting to Hesse on deeper levels is that he has a significant role to play in the coming völkisch spiritual revolution. Given his already prominent role as a poet, essayist, and novelist, and as an Asconan who also had relationships (however tenuous in reality) with völkisch figures such as Diederichs,[54] it would seem logical for Hesse to play a key role in such a cultural transformation of the German peoples and, like a Teutonic Moses, lead them to the promised land.

Hesse's first novel, *Peter Camenzind* (1903), was of a youth who loves nature and who would "obstinately go his own way," in Hesse's words, "mirroring nature and world in his own soul and experiencing them in new pictures."[55] This young Nietzschean and pantheistic nature-hero was idolized by many in the German Youth Movement of the time, although Hesse himself did not approve of such herd-like nature worship. Yet *Peter Camenzind* sparked the first Hesse cults among Asconan and völkisch neopagan youths, and by the time he began treatment with Lang in 1916 Hesse—whether he liked it or not—was viewed by many as yet another prominent voice of völkisch mysticism.

Interest in the esoteric meaning of the runes peaked around this time due to the work of Guido von List. In 1908 the famous volume *Die Geheimnis der Runen* (*The Secret of the Runes*) appeared as the first in the series of his occult texts and it sparked an intense interest in rune occultism.[56] List connected the well-known ancient runic symbols found by archaeologists (plus some he borrowed from other cultures and sources) with poems from the ancient Norse Elder Edda (republished by Diederichs with a new translation in 1912) concerning the god Wotan in his role as magician and necromancer. In one poem, the "Havamal," Wotan willingly undergoes nine days and nights of torture in order to gain secret mystical knowledge. This is Wotan's self-sacrifice. Wotan is lanced with a spear and is hung upside down from the cosmic tree Ygdrasil. At the height of his suffering he suddenly divines the cosmic meaning of the universe and, after descending from the tree, reveals that he has invented the runes in order to transmit this mystical knowledge. These runes, if read correctly, could give one secret knowledge of immortality, self-healing, success in battle, and success in love. In a sense, these were the same concerns of the initiates into the ancient Hellenistic mysteries, leading List and others to infer therefore that the ancient Teutons had their own mysteries, and that they had "practiced a gnostic religion emphasizing the initiation of man into natural mysteries."[57]

List referred to this ancient Teutonic religion as "Wotanism" and attempted to resurrect it with his own hierarchical secret society and its inner ring of initiates, the HAO (the *Hoher Armanen Orden*, or Higher Armanen Order), which was founded during a summer solstice period of ritual activity in Vienna at List's headquarters in 1911. As a secret society, it is difficult to determine for certain what List's esoteric rites entailed, but based on his statements in his publications it can be safely inferred that his initiates were trained to have visionary contacts with the spiritual brotherhood of the ancient Teutons, the *Armanenschaft*, and from them to learn occult knowledge—such as how to read the runes. As their cue came from the stories of

Wotan in the Eddas, such rituals may have also involved auster-
ities and a "descent" before learning the meaning of the runes.

The resemblance between the story of Wotan and the invention of the runes in the Eddas, the initiatory practices of List and
his Wotanists, and the visionary script that Lang is suggesting
Hesse follow and experience for himself is striking. Analysis is
Hesse's ordeal, but if he can survive it, he will undergo a descent and receive esoteric knowledge written in the language of
the ancient Germans that he must then use for prophetic purposes. Although we have no evidence of a direct link between
Jung and members of his cult with any of the known Wotanist
or Ariosophist occult groups, it seems quite arguable that Jung's
group used the same völkisch and even Wotanist imagery in its
own initiatory practices.

By promising his analyzed patients access to the collective unconscious, Jung's movement competes with Theosophy and anthroposophy as "modern gnostic systems" (as Jung referred to
them) or movements that also promise contact with the spirit
world or the ancestors. Jung's method and cult became a modern gnostic system through which one can contact an "interior
spiritual world whose existence we never suspected,"[58] perhaps
a world of the ancestors akin to the völkisch idea of an "inner
Fatherland" invoked by eighteenth-century German pietists.
Like Theosophy and anthroposophy, the Jung cult is a reaction
to the sterility of Christianity, for such "modern gnostic systems
meet the need for expressing and formulating the wordless oc-
currences going on within ourselves *better* than any of the existing forms of Christianity."[59]

THE VOYAGE TO THE CENTER OF THE EARTH

Perhaps, however, there was a single common source—whether
cryptomnesiac or deliberately conscious—of this particular cluster of runic and geological descent motifs for List, Jung, Lang,
and Hesse: the science fiction of Jules Verne (1828–1905). The
material in the first five chapters of Verne's *Voyage au Centre de
la Terre* of 1864 bears an uncanny resemblance to the imagery
used by Lang in his sessions with Hesse and match List's concern with visionary descents and runic symbols and Jung's ob-

session with subterranean mystery-cult initiations and his "geology of the personality." The works of Verne were the common heritage of most adolescents of the fin de siècle, and it would have been unusual for men such as Jung, List, Lang, and Hesse not to have read Verne's famous work during their youth. Indeed, it must be remembered that Jung grew up in Basel, a part of Switzerland that was greatly imbued by French language and culture, and may have even read Verne in the original French.

Verne's novel begins with young Henry Lawson visiting his German uncle, Professor Von Hardwigg, in "the fatherland." Hardwigg is "a professor of philosophy, chemistry, geology, mineralogy, and many other ologies."[60] Henry idolizes his uncle and aspires to be a learned man like the old professor. "Like him, I preferred mineralogy to all the other sciences. My anxiety was to gain *real knowledge of the earth*. Geology and mineralogy were to us the sole objects of life, and in connection with these studies many a fair specimen of stone, chalk, or metal did we break with our hammers."[61]

While visiting his uncle in his study, a scrap of parchment falls out of a leather-bound copy of Snorri Snurluson's *Heimskringla*, which contains the Eddas. The professor had never noticed this parchment before. Henry does not recognize the script in the book or on the parchment, but the professor explains, "It is the Runic manuscript, the language of the original population of Iceland, invented by Odin himself."[62] Verne then reproduces the inscription on the parchment in the form of three columns of runic symbols.

Figure 5. "Runes" (from Jules Verne, *Journey to the Center of the Earth*).

In the second chapter of the novel, Henry and the professor begin their philological analysis of the parchment. The first words that make any sense to them are the name of the parchment's author: Arne Saknussemm. Significantly, given the occult obsessions of List and Jung during adulthood, Hardwigg tells Henry that Saknussemm was "a learned professor of the sixteenth century, an alchemist," and he compares Saknussemm favorably with "Avicenna, Bacon, Lully, Paracelsus" as the "true, the only, learned men of their day." Since they made "surprising discoveries," the professor tells Henry he is convinced the parchment contains just such a secret that must have "profound meaning."[63]

By chapter three Henry and the professor have cracked the runic code and find that the alchemist makes the following astounding claim:

> *Descend into the crater of Yocul of Sneffels,*
> *which the shade of Scartaris caresses,*
> *before the kalends of July, audacious traveler,*
> *and you will reach the center of the earth. I did it.*
> ARNE SAKNUSSEMM[64]

With more than a passing resemblance to Faust, the professor immediately decides he must retrace Saknussemm's way and experience for himself the mysteries at the center of the earth. Although in chapter five Henry claims such a journey is impossible because of the "central heat" of the earth, the professor retorts, "I care nothing for theories. . . . Neither you nor anybody else know anything about the real state of the earth's interior. All modern experiments tend to explode the older theories. . . . and the only way to learn is, like Arne Saknussemm, to go and see."[65]

Although a fantastic world of giants and a great inner sea appear in Verne's fantasy of the interior of the earth, in Jung's geology of the personality the journey to the center of the earth leads to a very different discovery: an inner sun.

THE STAR OR THE SUN AS THE GOD WITHIN

Now the prophet of a new age, Jung promised a direct experience of God. As documented, as early as 1911 Jung had a belief in, and perhaps already an experience of, the god within in the form of a blazing sun or star. This primordial image from

Figure 6. Jung's solar mandala of his own psyche
(from *Mandala Symbolism*, p. ii).

the phylogenetic unconscious was discussed at length in *Wandlungen und Symbole der Libido*. This was a völkisch idea of the
god of the ancient Aryans and by 1916 was certainly an idea
well known to the educated bourgeoisie of Germanic Central
Europe. Völkisch mystical cults taught their initiates to contact
this solar god within. Jung did the same for his disciples.

The first evidence here is the signed and dated colored drawing of a mandala that Jung made in 1916. The word "mandala,"
which is Sanskrit for "circle," comes from the ancient Aryan
homelands of India. In the form of religious icons they are used

241

for a multitude of purposes, but their initial representation is thought to be of the sun. Jung's very first mandala drawing is reproduced in full color in the volume by Jaffé, *C. G. Jung: Word and Image*. Within its series of ever-smaller concentric circles, as Jung describes it, the core is a "larger sphere characterized by zigzag lines or rays" and "represents an inner sun."[66]

The inner core of the personality, representing the source of all life, is thus represented in this mandala as a sun. If individuation is adaptation to inner reality, it is a descent into the deepest regions of the psyche to seek closer contact with the source of all life, the inner sun as the god within.

A second compelling piece of evidence comes from Jung's *Septem Sermones ad Mortuos* or "Seven Sermons to the Dead," also written in 1916 under claimed paranormal circumstances in Jung's household. The account of its writing given in *MDR* is replete with psychokinetic events and ghostly Crusaders who have come to Jung for a consultation.[67] Jung had the long, oracular exposition privately printed in 1916 under his pseudonym of the famous heretical Gnostic "Basilides of Alexandria." It was again privately printed in 1925 in an English translation by H. G. Baynes. On 17 January 1917, Jung sent a copy of *Septem Sermones ad Mortuos* to a psychiatrist friend, Alphonse Maeder, with the following explanation:

> Allow me to give you personally the enclosed little present—a fragment with far-reaching associations. I deserve no credit for it, nor does it want or pretend to be anything, it just *is*—simply that. Hence I could not presume to put my name to it, but chose instead one of those great minds of the early Christian era which Christianity obliterated. It fell quite unexpectedly into my lap like a ripe fruit at a time of great stress and has kindled a light of hope and comfort for me in my bad hours. Of course it won't mean anything more to you than what I mean by it: a token of my joy over our wordless understanding yesterday evening.[68]

The "Seven Sermons to the Dead" is a spiritualistic work in the style of the Gnostics in which Jung, under his pseudonym, gives advice to the dead on how they might find ultimate redemption. Besides his admiration for the Gnostic doctrine of the real Basilides (and his god "Abraxas"), Jung is perhaps also hinting by this pseudonym that someone from Basel has written this piece.[69] The earliest recorded name of modern Basel dates from 334 C.E., during the Roman occupation, when the town was then called Basilea.

Jung (through his disciple Jaffé) acknowledges in *MDR* that it was written under the influence of his spiritual guru Philemon, who had become an integral part of his life at this time. In this sense Philemon became the counterpart to List's Armanen Brotherhood or Blavatsky's mahatmas and the spiritual Brotherhood. In *MDR*, Jung says: "I was compelled from within, to formulate and express what might have been said by Philemon. This was how the *Septem Sermones ad Mortuos* with its peculiar language came into being."[70]

The "Seven Sermons" can be summarized as follows:[71] The dead arrive at Jung's house claiming that they had gone to Jerusalem and "found not what we sought." "New Jerusalem" is, of course, an ancient Christian metaphor of the utopian promised land and as such has a long history in Western European Judeo-Christian culture. These dead are Christian Crusaders who found that even after death they did not experience the redemption that they had expected in life and that had been promised to them by Christianity. In other words, they felt cheated out of immortality, the victims of deception by representatives of Christ.

After outlining a new Gnostic cosmology for the disappointed Christian dead in the first six sermons, including an exposition on Abraxas, Jung/Basilides reveals the secret key to the mystery of redemption in the seventh sermon. They are not to seek salvation outside of themselves (e.g., traveling to Jerusalem), but instead the secret to rebirth is found in the "innermost infinity." By looking inwards, one can see, in the distance, a "single Star in the zenith" of this inner world, a Platonic hypercosmic sun: "The Star is the god and the goal of man." The inner Star is the "one guiding god" and the place where the soul travels after death. Approaching closer to the star on the zenith of one's inner world helps one realize that it too, is a sun. Thus, the star and God are sun and are one. With this knowledge of the pagan path of redemption, the grateful dead become silent and vanish up into the night sky to travel to seek their own inner stars.

CHAPTER ELEVEN

Jung and George as Kings of the "Secret Germany"

Most interpretations of the "Seven Sermons to the Dead" are from occultist, psychological, or parapsychological perspectives (mostly Theosophical and Jungian).[72] Yet, if we examine this work within the cultural matrix in which Jung lived, perhaps a different interpretation is possible. In many respects, *Septem Sermones ad Mortuos* resembles the poetry of Stefan George. As such, this work may have additionally been an exercise in poetic creativity for the supposedly autonomous genius or "daimon" of Jung—Philemon—who wrote the *Septem Sermones* seeking novel forms of expression. Jung, of course, knew of the poetry and cult of the *Georgekreis*, and would have been attracted to his sophisticated style, for as George's interpreters have noted:

> The affinity of Stefan George's poems to classical forms and themes and his esoteric allusion to mythic and poetic traditions appreciated fully only by the highly educated, created an enthusiastic response to his works among university students and young academics, particularly those interested in philology and philosophy as avocations. George's intellectually demanding idealism, his teaching that the world can be re-created through the spirit and the word, gave their pursuits, which had become ever more questionable in a materialistic age, an intense and urgent new meaning.[73]

George's vision was of a völkisch intellectual and spiritual elite, of an underground, "secret Germany," that would lead the way for the revitalization of the German peoples.[74] As George himself despised politics, this was to be a spiritual movement of the Volk. Many who would later become involved in National Socialism in the 1920s and 1930s read George with a passion, and even carried volumes of his poetry into battle with them during the First World War. George was so horrified by the Nazis and by the climate of anti-Semitism that he left Germany and died in exile in Switzerland in 1933.

The communal intellectual and spiritual elite that would bring about the rebirth of the German peoples was portrayed in his 1907 collection of poetry, *Die Siebente Ring* (*The Seventh*

244

Ring), as "guardians" or as heretical Crusaders from the mystical Order of the Knights Templar.[75] Such guardians are by no means Christians in the poetry of George, but are pagan Crusaders like those Christians Jung converts to the Gnostic heresy in *Septem Sermones ad Mortuos*.

However, although the overlapping imagery and themes between Jung and George are many, it is George's collection of one hundred short poems entitled *Der Stern des Bundes* (*The Star of the Covenant*) that most resembles Jung's *Septem Sermones*. This work appeared in print in January 1914, although many of the poems had been individually printed in various places between 1909 and 1913. Once again we have the star as a central völkisch symbol of divinity. It is also the uniting symbol of the covenant between the members of the utopian Bund, who are pledged to live out a Nietzschean "new life" of experience. George's *Der Stern des Bundes*, like Jung's piece, is told with the voice of a prophet or "vatic personality" who interacts with a chorus of followers. It is clear from the "Introit" that the prophet's God is experienced as an inner star or sun:

> Who is your god? All that my dreams avowed,
> Kin to my vision, beautiful and proud.
> He is the force the lap of darkness vented,
> The sum of every greatness we were granted,
> The deepest source, the inmost blaze,—he is
> Where I have found the purest form of these.
> He flooded every vein with richer teeming
> Who first for one was rescue and redeeming.
> He filled the gods of old with fresher breath,
> And all the words the world has done to death.
> The god is veiled in highest consecration,
> With rays around he manifests his station,
> Embodied in a son whom stars begot
> And a new center conjured out of thought.[76]

The reader is urged to compare this poem with "Seven Sermons to the Dead" for stylistic similarities and to make his or her own judgment. Although this particular poem may or may not have been a direct influence on Jung, it seems arguable that the "Seven Sermons" was indeed a contribution to this oracular stylistic tradition for which George was so noted. In their respective realms of poetry and of psychotherapy, George and Jung were the kings of "the secret Germany," who fashioned elites for leading the redemption and rebirth of Germanic Europe. The crusading members of Jung's Bund were also united by the image of an inner god as a sun or a star, as well as, in later years, their own "new center conjured out of thought"—the Aryan mandala as a symbol of the "self."[77]

PART THREE
THE JUNG CULT

"The Silent Experiment in Group Psychology"

1916

W<small>E HAVE SEEN</small> how the Society for Psychoanalytic Endeavors, which was created in Zurich in February 1912, formed the first foundation of a charismatic cult centered on the Lebensphilosophie of psychoanalysis and on the person of Jung. We have also seen how Jung grew into his role as a leader or prophet of a cultural revitalization movement that was anti-Christian in focus and that therefore sought to "replace religion with religion." Jung lost many disciples in Zurich after his 1913 break with Freud, but those that remained continued to seek psychoanalytic treatment from Jung and his associates, recommended this form of treatment to others, and attended his lectures and seminars during the years of the Great War.

Insulated from the storm that raged all around Switzerland, the small group of current and former patients of the analysts of the Zurich School formed interwoven social networks that extended far beyond the borders of Zurich. The sanctuary that Switzerland provided from the war probably served to intensify the feeling of social cohesion among the Jungians and no doubt convinced them that their program for a spiritual revitalization of a mad society was exactly what the world needed. When the war ended, *they* would provide the leadership for a new spiritual awakening, with a physician and noted man of science as their prophet and *pater pneumatikos* ("spiritual father"). The social upheaval that always follows such conflagrations would even perhaps provide an opening for the Jungians to step in and grab the world's attention, indeed to enact what the ancestors told them was "the Law of what is to come." As Jung was to say first in 1916 and then over and over again throughout his life, "only a few are capable of individuating," and it was those disciples in Jung's innermost circle who were therefore the vanguard of this new nobility or spiritual elite.[1]

The formal governing organ of this new spiritual elite was to be the group of current and former patients and their analysts who blurred the boundaries of their relationships by participating in the Psychological Club after its formation in 1916. Fortunately, we have what appears to be a summary transcript of a talk Jung gave in 1916 at the meeting at which the Psychological Club was founded. It has been found among the papers of Fanny Bowditch Katz, an American patient of Jung's and Jung's Dutch associate, Maria Moltzer, who underwent analysis with the two of them in 1912 and 1913. Moltzer, however, remained her primary analyst, and as is apparent from their mutual correspondence, they remained in touch long after Katz's return to America. The document concerning the Psychological Club is probably an original English transcript typed by Moltzer in Zurich and, it is assumed, mailed to Katz in America. In the upper right-hand corner of the document "Frl. Moltzer" is written in an unknown hand.

What follows, then, is the heretofore unpublished talk, thought to be by Jung. It will be obvious immediately to the reader that it is spiritual redemption that is the focus of interest among this group of people and that this is not—nor was it ever—a professional psychiatric or medical association of any sort. In 1959—with obvious reference to alchemy and the relationship of the medieval or renaissance alchemist or "adept" to his female assistant, the *soror mystica* ("mystical sister")—Jung would mention in his introduction to a posthumously published collections of the writings of Toni Wolff that "she also helped me to carry out, over a period of forty years, a 'silent experiment' in group psychology, an experiment which constitutes the life of the Psychological Club in Zurich."[2] Indeed, it may very well be argued that this document acknowledges that the "silent experiment" was the Jung cult of redemption and rebirth that was formalized on the day that Jung made the following remarks:

> In the symbol of Christ lies an identification of the personality with the progressive tendency of the collective soul. I purposely say the progressive tendency of the collective soul in order to indicate that the collective soul has various aspects. One is a tendency which is represented by the Terrible Mother, but there is

another which contains the symbols of redemption for suffering humanity. This side of the collective soul is symbolized by Christ.

In Christ the human and the divine in man are one—for which reason Christ is also the God-man.

Through the death of Christ, His personality and His Imago living in mankind became separated. Christ died, and His Imago arose among men—and the collective soul of mankind was accepted in the symbol of Christ. Thus a new ideal arose, an ideal so strong that its power still holds mankind today.

The identification with the progressive tendency of the collective soul is characterized by the intuitive type. This type cannot live in the existing functions, and is forced to maintain his intuition until he has found his adaptation to life. For this reason he follows mainly the progressive tendency of the libido. This identification of the personality with the collective unconscious manifests itself always in the phenomenon of self-deification—be it an identification with the function of intuition, with the function of extraversion, or with the function of introversion. It is a self-deification according to the function, but the phenomenon always remains the same. It is therefore a question of the overcoming of self-deification, which might also be compared with the Death of Christ, a death of the greatest agony.

Perhaps the freeing of the personality from the progressive tendency of the unconscious belongs to one of the most painful tasks to be accomplished on the road to development to full individuality. Through the freeing of the personality from the progressive tendency arises a chaos, a darkness and a doubt of all that exists, and of all that may be. The opposite tendency of the progressive is activated, and the whole Hell of the overcome past opens, and hurls itself upon the newly gained present demanding its rights, and threatens to overpower it.

This moment brings a feeling of great danger. One is quite conscious of standing before death. The directing line, so long given one by the identification with the progressive tendency, is suddenly wiped out—and not until one has found the continuity of the new functions created in the unconscious, can one get a feeling of the possibility to live.

The separating of the personality from the collective soul seems to disturb phylogenetically certain pictures or formations in the unconscious—a process which we still understand very little, but

251

which needs the greatest care in treatment. The struggle with the Dead is terrible, and I understand the instinct of mankind which protests against this great effort as long as it is possible to do so.

But we human beings have not only instinct, we have also intuition—an insight into the inexorable which life demands of us, and so the struggle goes on between instinct and intuition, until both have been harmoniously united.

Here too the parallel with Christ continues. The struggle with the Dead and the descent into Hell are unavoidable. The Dead need much patience and the greatest care. Some must be brought to eternal rest, others have a message to bring us, for which we must prepare ourselves. These Dead need time for their highest fulfillment, only after full duty has been done to the Dead can man return slowly to his newly created personality. This new individuality thus contains all vital elements in a new constellation.

In studying Christ's Descent into Hell I was surprised to find how closely the tradition coincides with human experience. This problem is therefore not new, it is a problem of general mankind, and for this reason probably too, symbolized through Christ.

I will not mention these parallels further here, as it would carry me too far from my subject, and I hope to elucidate this problem more fully in a work on the Transcendental Function. It was a problem of the past, and is a problem of our time. The night, the chaos and the despair which appear before the *Menschwerdung*, has been defined by artists of not long ago. So, Goethe's Faust is enveloped in night—he becomes blind, and dies—only then the transfiguration. [It is] the Transcendental Function which reveals the completed human being of our time.

In Wagner's *Parsifal* we find the same phenomenon, only nearer to life. On Good Friday Parsifal comes back to the Gralsburg. He is entirely in black, the symbol of death, and his visor is closed. The belief in being able to fulfill the work for which he has struggled for so long has deserted him, and it is Gurnemanz and Kundry, both very much changed, who free him from his madness and show him the way to the Gralsburg.

Only after one has freed oneself from the collective soul, only after one has passed through death and the soul has been realized, can the collective problem be really solved. The further conclusion is that this problem must in principle be our problem also—the essential element in the Collective being that it pertains to all. The Collective soul may be brought to constellation in a different way in every individual, but in principle all these manifestations are the same. When the Holy Ghost revealed Himself to the Apostles on Whitsuntide, the Apostles spoke in tongues, which means that each spoke in his own way, each had his own way of praising his own God, and yet all praised the same God.

Only after the overcoming of self-deification, only after the human being has been revealed to himself, and man recognizes the human being in mankind, can we speak of a real analytical collectivity—a collectivity which reaches out (extends) beyond type and sex.

But we have not yet come so far, we are on the way to the *Menschwerdung*. The recognition that each has to fulfill his especial task, and to go his own especial way, leads to the respect for the individual and his especial path. Only those who have been forced through their own individual laws to go their own ways, and thereby have come in conflict with the prevailing traditions, come to Analysis.

An analytical collectivity can therefore only be founded on a respect for the individual and the individual path. The difficulties which arise along the individual path in relation to collectivity can only be solved analytically, and it must follow that for those who wish to build up an analytical collectivity, it must be an inevitable duty to solve such conflicts according to the principles of Analysis.

That which those who subject themselves to Analysis have in common is their striving to solve individual problems. This mutual interest suffices for a Club. A Club can be based on any one collective element, for which reason I approve of the Club. In a Club those persons can join together who have a common road to go, and wherein they thus feel themselves strengthened in their efforts. So, small Clubs will grow up in the main Club, the so-called original groups, which again will have their own development to pass through, will be dissolved, or in time be changed into other groups. For this reason there must be an analytical Club that has perfect freedom to build an endless number of small groups, and each must respect the other. Thus the individual principle will be carried over to the collective principle, for a Club, or a small group, is, as long as it forms a unit in itself, identical with an individuality.

From which follows that I should like to have the following principles introduced into the statutes of an analytical Club:

1. Purpose of the Club: analytical collectivity.
2. Respect for the Club as a whole.
3. Respect for the small group, as such.
4. Respect for the individual and his individual purpose.
5. Where difficulties arise in the Club, in the small groups or among individuals, they must be solved according to analytical principles.
6. Where insolvable difficulties arise they must be brought before an analytical tribunal.

Nothing is new under the sun. That which I see ahead of us as an ideal analytical collectivity Goethe saw and speaks of in his "*Geheimnisse.*" If it were not so long, I should be glad to read it to you now—it may not be familiar to you all.

The poem was written in 1816 and no doubt was far ahead of its time. It describes a collectivity founded on the principle of the religious acceptance of the individual path, and the *Mensch-werdung.* As a symbol this Cloister has a Cross wound with roses, symbol of the resurrected life—the Tannhäuser motif of the budding staff, the Chider, or the Tree of Life.

The ancients say of the Tree of Life, "A Noble Tree planted with rare skill grows in a garden. Its roots reach down to the bottom of Hell—its crown touches the Throne of God, its wide spreading branches surround the Earth. The Tree stands in fullest beauty and is glorious in its foliage."

This Tree is the expression of a collective function, created by Analysis and life.

The Jung Cult and Redemption

As is immediately evident to any reader of this remarkable document, it is the manifesto of a religious movement whose goal is not only the salvation of the individual, but also of the world, and it is founded on a vague utopian ideal of an "analytical collectivity." Let us examine the meaning of this text in light of the discussion that has been presented thus far.

Jung here is still incorporating themes from *Wandlungen und*

Symbole der Libido. In doing so, he outlines a sequence of psychological experiences, a phenomenology of personal transformation, which we now know he himself underwent and then presented to his disciples as a universal pattern to be emulated by them.

Jung's phenomenological exposition goes like this: within the unconscious there is a *progressive* flow of libido, which if the individual personality (the ego) "identifies" with it, he or she undergoes the experience of self-deification and becomes (symbolically) Christ. As we have shown, Jung himself underwent such a deification experience in which he merged with Aion and Christ. If the individual (ego) identifies with the *regressive* flow of the libido, he or she suffers the pain of dismemberment and annihilation in the "realm of the Mothers" and becomes (symbolically) a victim of the Terrible Mother. If one does not heroically resurface from these depths, one then becomes permanently damaged and will then probably develop dementia praecox.

As a symbol of a successful self-deification process, Christ is exemplary for he is both divine and human. After the death of the historical Jesus, his memory image nonetheless continued to live in the collective soul and, over many generations, actually came to symbolize the collective soul of humankind. Jung differs from his old theological nemesis Ritschl in this regard, for Jung's memory image of Christ is lodged in a transcendental sphere of human nature and is not merely transmitted by cultural traditions and institutions, as Ritschl argued.[3] Jung's invocation of Christ as a symbol of the collective soul also resonates with the völkisch thought originating in the late nineteenth century with figures such as Julius Langbehn (among many others) that Mosse identifies as "another tendency in Volkish thought—namely, to substitute the image of the Volk for the person and function of Christ."[4]

When the modern individual (ego) undergoes a transformation and begins to identify with the collective unconscious, he or she therefore becomes Christ (self-deification). Whether one is an extraverted, introverted, or intuitive type (Jung later changed this prototheory of psychological types markedly), one always becomes, in a sense, Christ. The issue then becomes how to overcome, in a Nietzschean sense, one's experience as a god.

However, if one becomes Christ, he or she must then reenact the story of Christ. After experiencing the agony of psychological death (as Christ did on the cross) and then, after fully experiencing both humanity and divinity through being a dying and suffering god, one must also reenact Christ's katabasis or descent to Hell (the "realm of the Mothers," or the collective unconscious). After the initial deification experience, and after successfully overcoming it (through analysis, as implied here by Jung), the "whole Hell of the overcome past opens" and one begins a confrontation with the collective unconscious.

Here Jung is still holding on to his phylogenetic hypothesis (if tenuously), for "the separating of the personality from the collective soul seems to disturb phylogenetically certain pictures or formations in the unconscious." Yet this is about as scientific as Jung allows himself to get, for the process he describes is more akin to the mediumistic techniques of spiritualism than anything else. Jung equates disturbing these images with disturbing the dead. While in the collective unconscious—which then is equivalent to a transcendent land of the dead—one has a "terrible struggle" with the dead.

It is clear that Jung views the role of the individual as a redeemer of the dead as well as of oneself and of society. Like Hermes the psychopomp, the individual has the responsibility to lead some of the dead to eternal rest. Other members of the dead have an important message of salvation to bring to humankind. Thus, the individual who undergoes Jung's brand of analysis must also become a spiritualist medium who can receive messages from the deceased for the benefit of humankind. Indeed, one *must* have contact with the dead before one can achieve individuality, a process that Jung here calls the *Menschwerdung* (the process of "becoming a human being").

After comparing the process of individuation to the death, descent, and rebirth of Christ the god-man, Jung then makes a reference to Wagner's *Parsifal* and its paganized Christian theme of redemption. This reference, and the cluster of references at the end of his talk to Goethe and his poem of a secret (*Geheimnis*) religious cloister like the Templars, to Wagner again and his *Tannhäuser*, and to the Tree that is a symbol of Wotan and Wotanism, all point to Jung's merger of the image of Christ with dominant symbols of the völkisch movement. The deliberate

reference to these Germanic symbols, which would resonate especially with his Germanic disciples, is very telling. One may
very well argue, therefore, that—based on the convergence of
evidence we have from 1916—the Jung cult began as a völkisch
movement devoted specifically to the spiritual revitalization of
the Germanic Volk.

PSEUDOLIBERATIONAL NIETZSCHEANISM

Jung is telling us with this document that his movement is one
based on the metaphors of Nietzscheanism. Jung wants those
who have already had the experience of being "forced through
their own individual laws to go their own ways, and thereby
have come in conflict with the prevailing traditions." These prevailing traditions are, of course, the organized Judeo-Christian
faiths. There is no place with him, therefore, for those who still
adhere to such ideals. Jung instead welcomes these spiritually
disaffected persons in particular to analysis, through which they
then can form their own personal religion and thereby, echoing
Nietzsche's own words, obey only their own law.

Yet we see here the contradictions that Tönnies noticed in the
Nietzsche cult of the 1890s. Jung offers the promise of truly becoming an individual after becoming a god, or rather, after
learning to directly experience the god within. This is a process
of self-sacrifice and struggle during which one must give up
one's former image of god, indeed most effectively smashing
the Judeo-Christian idol with the "hammer" of questions that
is analysis. Jung's analysis helps to destroy the hold that the
Judeo-Christian god has over the individual. The promise here,
then, is Jung's promise of liberation, of freedom, of becoming a
continually self–re-creating individual in a state of constant becoming, a perpetual revolution of the soul.

With the vital, scintillatingly intelligent, and sensitive Jung as
their living model, it is no wonder that Jung's disciples could
believe—with Jung's own promises—that they, too, could one
day be as charismatic as he. This is the first contradiction that
becomes apparent in Jung's Nietzschean cult doctrine, for what
Jung offers to his disciples (and through them, to the world) as
a process of individuation is simply his own pattern of experi-

ence. Analysis becomes, then, a ritualized reenactment of Jung's *own* experience as a suffering and dying god, just as Roman Catholic communion is a ritualized reenactment of the Last Supper. Paradoxically, Jung offers his own unique path as the one for his disciples to mimic. He has found the way and is imparting this vision to his tribe. Despite his urgings and promises to the contrary, Jung is offering himself as the imago of individuation.[5] And given his personal charisma, in the eyes of these earliest disciples (and of those in the Jungian movement today who are enamored by the manufactured pseudocharisma of the deceased Jung), the way to be a unique individual is to imitate Jung.

A second contradiction in Jung's pseudoliberational Nietzschean doctrine is his paradoxical argument that a small group of individuals is "identical with an individuality" and is therefore not contrary to one's own individuality. Here is the appeal to spiritual elitism and the justification for forming a Nietzschean new nobility of the individuated. With this appeal, and the blueprint for a blossoming number of groups to spread all over the world from Zurich, Jung is in essence directly challenging the organs of Christianity and is setting up his own hierarchical religious cult with its own "analytical tribunal." Jung thus becomes the heresiarch who, through the arbitrary powers of his charismatic authority (as with *all* charismatic leaders, as Weber has demonstrated), can personally determine the new ethical standards and social policies of his new heresy. It is ironic that by doing so Jung simply repeats those aspects of organized religion that he and his fellow iconoclasts found so repugnant in the first place.

In 1928 Jung would again emphasize the need for an enlightened elite of the few individuated persons who are chosen to lead the rest of humanity by vocation, literally a call to follow an "inner necessity." After a discussion of the self, which Jung says "might equally well be called the 'God within us,'"[6] and then of the importance of things we may consider evil and therefore purposely ignore to our own detriment, Jung says the following:

> Here I am alluding to a problem that is far more significant than these few simple words would seem to suggest: mankind is, in essentials, psychologically still in a state of childhood—a stage that cannot be skipped. The vast majority needs authority, guid-

ance, law. This fact cannot be overlooked. The Pauline over-coming of the law falls only to the man who knows how to put his soul in the place of conscience. Very few are capable of this ("Many are called, few are chosen."). And these few tread this path only from inner necessity, not to say suffering, for it is sharp as the edge of a razor.[7]

Thus, to be among the few individuated members of the Jung cult means one is no longer infantile and that one has a higher purpose or calling to lead those unfortunate multitudes who cannot or will not see the light. This is Jung once again appealing to the spiritual elitism that so many have found seductive.

The Analytical Collectivity as Völkisch Utopianism

Jung deliberately fused the symbol of Christ with potent Germanic cultural symbols because it spoke to the völkisch mystical elements within his circle and indicated his intention to redeem those of Aryan heredity. We know from his own statements that, during at least his first sixty years, Jung felt European individuals should follow European paths of spiritual development that their distant ancestors followed and not alien ones such as Buddhism, Hinduism, or, it may be argued, the "alien" faith of Christianity—with its Semitic origins—that was imposed as a "foreign growth" on the pagan Germanic peoples.[8] Jung toned down his rhetoric considerably after 1936 or so when he began to realize the impending disaster for humanity that Hitler and the Nazis could bring about through their racial policies. However, based on his essentially völkisch view of human nature in 1916, it is clear that Jung's proposed path of spiritual redemption could only work for those of Indo-European ancestry, or for those few extraordinary secular Jews who had lived on European soil and who therefore had souls that were imbued with the combined pagan and Christian influences that literally arose from the blood soaked into the land itself. Aryans could experience the sacrament of rebirth. Semites did not have this "image" and therefore were excluded from redemption.

This essentially Aryans-only path to redemption that Jung envisioned in 1916 is supported by a "secret appendix" to the by-laws of the Analytical Psychology Club of Zurich. According to these secret rules, Jewish membership in the club was limited to ten percent and Jewish "guest membership" to twenty-five percent of the total. This fact—which only came to light in 1989—is confirmation of Jung's long-standing covert anti-Semitism, as he removed the Jewish quota only in 1950.[9]

Jung's proposal of an analytical collectivity is essentially the utopian vision that he and his cult sought to bring about. This explicit utopianism in Jung—like most visions of utopia—is somewhat vague, but it is very much within a long tradition of Germanic utopianism that became especially prominent in Central Europe after 1870, throughout Jung's developmental years. In order to fully understand what Jung is proposing with his "analytical collectivity," these contemporary utopian ideas that permeated the fin de siècle and beyond must be explored.

German utopianism in the nineteenth and early twentieth centuries almost always meant a return to pre-Christian, pagan spirituality in some form. We have seen how Goethe exemplified this trend in the Romantic movement by suggesting replacing the fairy tale of Christ-worship with sun worship. The Romantic revival of the Greek gods in Germany also led to utopian visions of a Hellenic Germany based on the best, most rational, and most aesthetically superior Apollonian aspects of ancient Greek culture.

In the 1870s, Nietzsche and Wagner unleashed a stream of utopian fantasies that reversed these notions with their appeal to a return to an irrational, organic, Dionysian community of oneness of will and expression. Nietzsche's *The Birth of Tragedy* argued that Bismarckian Germany should be reborn, but *not* on its Apollonian or arid, rational (hence patriarchical) values, but on a return to the ideals of the earliest Greek communitarian society, a prerational, pre-Socratic world of instinct and harmony with the forces of nature and its inherent tragedy. With Wagnerian opera in mind, the unifying Dionysian element was to be music. Nietzsche implores, "Let no one try to blight our faith in a yet-impending rebirth of Hellenic antiquity; for this alone gives us hope for a renovation and purification of the German spirit through the fire magic of music."[10] Nietzsche's appeal to a return to a pre-Christian utopia in which the creative forces of nature would be unleashed was a seductive one:

Yes, my friends, believe with me in Dionysian life and the rebirth of tragedy. The age of the Socratic man is over; put on
wreaths of ivy, put the thyrsus in your hand, and do not be surprised when tigers and panthers lie down, fawning, at your feet.
Only dare to be tragic men; for you are to be redeemed. You shall
accompany the Dionysian pageant from India to Greece. Prepare
yourselves for hard strife, but believe in the miracles of your
god.[11]

It was just such a communitarian, Dionysian unit that Tönnies
had in mind with his concept of Gemeinschaft, which is roughly
translated into English as "community." Tönnies' vision of Gemeinschaft was of just such a small, blood-related, and geo-
graphically localized self-sufficient communal lifestyle that was
guided by its essential or organic will toward the common
good. This "organic will" was not necessarily contrary to rational thought, but was not identical with it either. Tönnies' famous book of 1887, *Gemeinschaft und Gesellschaft*, which marks
the beginning of modern German sociology, fatalistically pre-
dicted a decline in bourgeois-Christian civilization or *Gesellschaft* ("society") and a return to communal living.[12] In this immense work of scholarship, there are many references to
Nietzsche and, interestingly, Bachofen. Just such a fantasy was
enacted around 1900 by the various Asconan groups in Switzerland.[13] Among those Germanic Europeans in search of their
long-lost Teutonic spirituality and a return to a Golden Age
of paganism, the "old dreams of a new Reich" were of a very
similar *Volksgemeinschaft* (a mystical blood community of Volk)
through a revolution led by an elite (spiritual and/or political)
or, perhaps, a führer.

We have already seen how Jung was very much attracted to
a philosophy of pagan regeneration based on Bachofen's ideal
image of a prehistorical period of polygamous hetairism (and
its psychoanalytic and Nietzschean interpretation by Gross).
We may add to this Müller's vision of a prehistorical Aryan
"mythopoetic age." By 1916, all of these elements were combined into Jung's own utopian fantasy of a natural analytical
collectivity that too, could transcend even "type and sex."

However, the distinguishing features that make Jung's utopian fantasy a völkisch one are the concentrated references to

261

core völkisch metaphors when proposing the idea of an analytical collectivity, especially its appeal as a secret, elite status. Goethe's poem *"Die Geheimnisse"* ("The Mysteries") not only conjures up images of the hierarchical ancient mystery cults of Greco-Roman antiquity (which were, partially, Goethe's models in this poem) but also the Grail-quest imagery of an elite corp of seekers (like the heretical Templars so beloved of George) who could merge their Christian cross with Wotan's Tree.

"Die Geheimnisse" was published in April 1816 during Goethe's Weimar period. As Jung correctly noted, the poem depicts the idea of a spiritual elite or fraternity (*Bruderschaft*) of men feeling cut off from any sense of meaning in their respective Christian faiths who then find new meaning by coming together to form a new Urreligion that encompasses all religions. The motive for such an all-encompassing religion would be the creation of a revitalized, renewed, spiritualized world. Goethe mixes Christian and pagan imagery in this poem, especially the imagery of Rosicrucianism whose literature Goethe knew well.[14] As early as 1784 Goethe had thoroughly discussed his plan to write a poem with such a utopian theme with Herder, and then later Frau von Stein. Not surprisingly, this poem was a favorite of many in völkisch circles and especially in the German Youth Movement and of course is echoed in the work of George.

In Germanic Europe these were indeed powerful symbols that could (and did) stir the souls of millions. Jung's deliberate use of them created the attractive (if vaguely outlined) fantasy of a true Volksgemeinschaft based on a deep spiritual connection between the analyzed and the primordial images of the god within, and of the ancestors of the inner world (the dead) as well as the forces of the natural world (the sun, astrological influences, the mystical influence of geography). Jung, as it must be emphasized again, wanted a spiritual reawakening in Europe through participation in his own mysteries. Other groups who also employed these potent völkisch symbols for their ability to mobilize the masses sought political ends, resulting in the tragic realization of the völkisch utopia of National Socialist Germany and its occult symbols and secret societies (like the SS) and racially based mystery-cult practices.[15]

Thus, the public Jung was, perhaps, an eccentric psychiatrist and psychoanalyst in the eyes of the academic and scientific community in 1916. The private Jung, however, within the supportive enclave of Küsnacht-Zurich and his circle of disciples, was very much the völkish prophet.

THE MASTER RACE OF INDIVIDUATED SUPERMEN

Jung's Nietzschean religion includes additional aspects that seem to vindicate the approach of his "twin brother," Otto Gross, in his obsession with using Nietzscheanism as the theory and psychoanalysis as the praxis to bring about individual and cultural rebirth. There are similarities between Nietzsche's purely theoretical idea of the übermensch and Jung's concept of an individual or an individuated person who is brought into being through the practice of analysis.

Both the übermensch and the individuated illustrate the epitome of a human being. Neither Jung nor Nietzsche left a fully developed description of just what, in practice, such a being would be like. Because of this lack of any clear-cut description of an individuated human being in the entire corpus of Jung's extensive written works, the idealized cult legend of Jung in *Memories, Dreams, Reflections* is used as the yardstick by Jungians today. Literally volumes of speculation exist on just what Nietzsche meant by an übermensch. Perhaps Nietzsche scholar Kurt Rudolph Fischer's assessment is the best:

> We undercut Nietzsche if we wish to determine what the "Übermensch" is. Because I think it is part of the determination of the "Übermensch" not to be determined—that we shall have to experiment, that we shall have to create. Nietzsche puts emphasis on the creativity of man and therefore we should accentuate that the conception of the "Übermensch" is *necessarily not* determined. We cannot ask whether an author has confused the issue, or has presented us with a dangerous alternative.[16]

According to Jung, one is reborn or renewed through access to the impersonal or collective unconscious that contains the accumulated wisdom and experiences of one's racial ancestors.

Although Jung is paradoxical and vague on this issue, it is arguable that in 1916—and, certainly by the late 1920s when Wilhelm introduced him to Chinese alchemy—contact with the collective unconscious meant one could theoretically access the wisdom and experiences of the whole human species. Becoming a true individual who follows one's own inner law and not that of the herd necessitates an initiation into this transcendent depository of the species. Jung's analysis enables the individual to transcend one's genetic heritage and draw upon the richness of all the races through the Platonic Realm of the Collective Unconscious. Throughout his life, whenever Jung referred to individuation, he resorted to just such Nietzschean metaphors.

Nietzsche may have proposed a very similar idea. As Jung well knew, Nietzsche called such persons *Übermenschen* ("supermen"), humans who have overcome themselves, who have transcended the shackles of heredity, family, society, and deity. As Kaufmann interprets it, "To Nietzsche these *übermenschen* appear as symbols of the repudiation of any conformity to a single norm: antithesis to mediocrity and stagnation."[17] In quite the contrast to the Nazified legend of Nietzsche, as Kaufmann has shown us, Nietzsche the Lamarckian or Darwinian "pangeneticist" believed that the inherited characteristics of all the races, when blended in the future, would predispose an individual to draw upon the advantage of this accumulated biological capital and overcome him- or herself, and to become an übermensch. In the posthumously published *The Will to Power*, according to Kaufmann's interpretation, Nietzsche envisions a master race of supermen, "a future, internationally mixed, race of philosophers and artists who cultivate iron self-control."[18]

Nietzsche's ideal theory of the future is brought into the present through Jung's practice of analysis as initiation. Rather than wait millennia for the races to mix blood and thereby gain access through biology to the riches of the entire species, Jung promises a short-cut method that bypasses the constraints of heredity and gives his few initiates the capacity to become *übermenschen* now. However, it is only those of Aryan heritage that Jung first considered capable of using such capital to achieve rebirth. The growing future analytical collectivity of human beings that follow the new paths offered by Jung would then comprise an elite "master race."

INDIVIDUATION AS REDEMPTION FROM DEGENERACY

"Tell me, my brothers: what do we consider bad and worst of all? Is it not *degeneration*?" Nietzsche could rhetorically ask the world in *Also Sprach Zarathustra*.[19] In addition to the redemption of culture from Judeo-Christianity, and the freeing of the individual from this "alien growth" with his own Nietzschean religion, Jung may have also been offering the average person of his age with an intense concern about heredity a way to transform one's status from "degenerate" to "genius."[20] Indeed, because Jung and Nietzsche shared the same intellectual master—Schopenhauer through his *The World as Will and Representation*—both the Nietzschean übermensch and the Jungian individuated resemble the Schopenhauerian ideal of genius.

Jung's familiarity with Schopenhauer's characteristics of genius from the 1844 second volume of *The World as Will and Representation* is evident as early as January 1899 when, in a Zofingia lecture, Jung describes Jesus of Nazareth as a "god-man" with the exact characteristics of a Schopenhauerian genius.[21] His early fascination with the relationship of genius to madness (the famous "mad genius controversy" of the nineteenth century)[22] is evident in his first publication in 1902. In the third paragraph of this document, his dissertation on his mediumistic cousin, Jung refers to the mad genius controversy, admitting that hysteria and other forms of psychopathology have features in common with "normal psychology, and even the psychology of the supernormal, that of genius."[23]

In his essay "Cryptomnesia" (1905), Jung discusses the relationship between genius and madness, perhaps with no small relevance to his own case. At the age of twenty-nine or thirty, when this essay was written, Jung seemed to have been writing in the nineteenth-century autobiographical mode of a genius, revealing his preoccupation with his own uniqueness, sensitivity, and capacity for innovation, all barely hidden behind the prose of his physician persona:

> One of the commonest and most unusual marks of degeneracy is hysteria, the lack of self-control and self-criticism. Without succumbing to the pseudo-psychiatric witch-hunting of an author like Nordau, who sees fools everywhere, we can assert with confi-

dence that unless the hysterical mentality is present to a greater
or lesser degree genius is not possible. As Schopenhauer rightly
says, the characteristic of the genius is great sensibility, something of a mimosa-like quality of the hysteric. Geniuses also have
other qualities in common with hysterical persons.[24]

A genius, like an hysteric, puts ideas together in unconventional patterns. New combinations of memories of previously
experienced events or previously learned material are the wellsprings of creativity, yet the genius mistakes their novelty as
his own creation and forgets their true source, Jung argues in
his essay. Thus Jung tells us that cryptomnesia is the root of all
genius.

Since the late eighteenth century, the conventional wisdom
was that a genius is an original, born and not made. Generations
of young men in the nineteenth century (including Wagner,
Nietzsche, and Jung) imitated genius using the blueprint provided by Schopenhauer in 1844: "Genius is its own reward; for
the best that one is, one must necessarily be for oneself."[25] Direct
perception of the realm of Platonic ideas operating in life is his
gift, for as Schopenhauer tells those aspiring to greatness, "always to see the universal in the particular is precisely the fundamental character of genius."[26] The creative life of a genius
stands outside convention, often even outside human society,
and like the Nietzschean übermensch he obeys only his own
inner law. He is misunderstood in his own time and therefore
must live "essentially alone." His creations are of eternal value
and created *ex nihilo*, that is, without leaving footprints on the
shoulders of any giants. As Pletsch observes, "The 'genius,' in
other words, emerged to replace God as the guarantor of artistic
and intellectual novelty and cultural innovation generally."[27]

Genius is godlikeness. Or, rather, it is making manifest the
latent god within. A man becomes great, according to Schopenhauer, if his works have a superhuman quality, "and accordingly, what he produces or creates is then ascribed to a *genius*
different from him, which takes possession of him."[28] Following
this ancient Roman view of human nature, genius "indicates
something foreign to the will, i.e., to the I or ego proper, a *genius*
added from outside, so to speak, seems to become active here."
The ancient Roman conception of genius was of a life-spirit liv-

ing in the head, active in procreation, and was the eternal part of the individual that went to the underworld (Hades, or the realm of shades). The *genius* was a separate, impersonal force different from the seat of consciousness and personal identity that the Romans called *animus* and that was located in the chest. The genius was a force of inspiration that moved in and through the individual but that was not experienced as being moved by that individual. The Roman *genius* appears to have been equivalent to another Roman term for this phenomenon, the *anima*, or to the Greek concept of *psyche*.[29]

A Schopenhauerian great man, or a Nietzschean übermensch, therefore, allows him- or herself to be possessed by the divine genius within, and thereby becomes deified. Jung, very much aware of the relationship between the average ancient Greek and his "daimon" or the average ancient Roman and his genius, added this pagan dimension to his view of the human personality.

In Jung's day, especially in the era before the Great War, most medical authorities of the day would probably say that most so-called men of genius were in fact "highly gifted degenerates." Although degeneracy was literally thought to be transmitted in the "protoplasm" of the sperm of the father to his progeny, the physical and mental stigmata were thought to worsen with each new generation, leading to idiocy, further vegetation, and eventually death. "The clearest notion of degeneracy is to regard it as a *morbid deviation from an original type*," the French *alieniste* Benedict Augustin Morel writes in 1857.[30] In German medical texts (following the morphological idealist or essentialist tradition of Goethe's Urform) this original type was known as the Urtyp. A genius would be a fluke, the result of a rare confluence of degenerative hereditary and environmental factors, and would not be preceded or followed in the family by additional genius. Severe mental or physical illness in one generation weakens the family until the line dies out.

Given Jung's "hereditary taint," his idea of individuation has an additional redemptive function for him personally and for society as a whole: individuation is the struggle to free oneself from the shameful burden of degeneracy—and therefore it becomes a liberation. Perhaps this corresponds in part to what Jung meant by the necessity to free oneself from the clutches of the Terrible Mother, the "regressive libido," or doing battle with the dead.

It must be emphasized that Jung's reversal of degeneration theory was a means of liberation for many "nervous" persons who came to Jung for treatment and who were afraid of passing on their hereditary taint to their offspring. The frequent anxiety, fear, and dread over one's hereditary taint was a burden to the average fin-de-siècle person and Jung's ideas—coming as they did from an eminent medical authority and a world-famous psychiatrist—were reassuring. In a compassionate letter to Katz dated 30 July 1918, Jung responds to the recently wedded Katz's fears of passing on her emotional instability to the child she and her husband wish to have. Jung writes: "The factor of inheritance has to be considered as a serious point in the discussion of the problem, *but not as an absolute counter-argument*. The quality and disposition of the whole family and of the ancestors play a much greater role in the creation of the child's disposition than the individual disposition of the father or mother."[31] Here Jung not only disregards degeneracy theory, but also may be disregarding genetics itself with the reference to the role of the ancestors.

Jung found a way to expiate the guilt of his hereditary taint, and with the promise of sharing the secrets of individuation with those who would follow his new path, Jung the Nietzschean "liberator" deliberately reversed the notion of hereditary degeneration and thereby redeemed generations of his followers from the burden of original sin. Society as a whole could thus potentially be reformed, and he could lead us all into the temptations of the promised land of genius from the captivity of degeneration. The collective unconscious then indeed becomes an impersonal one: it was not dependent upon one's own recent heredity and therefore one was not enslaved by one's immediate biological ancestors. When Morel posited in 1857 that this biological *principium degenerationis* was passed on through "the germ" (that is, the sperm) it was soon thereafter taught as scientific dogma to subsequent generations of medical students. With his introduction of the notion of inherited dominants (1917) or archetypes (1919) using biological terms, Jung maintains that the universal potential for individuation then, too, is found in

the Weismannian "embryonic germ-plasm."[32] The potential for
constant renewal and rebirth is what is invariantly inherited,
not degeneracy. This is the degenerating world turned upside
down.

Thus, it may be argued that Jung conceived of the individuated person as one who was reborn as a genius, as one who
could directly perceive the universal in the particulars of life, as
Schopenhauer suggested. But this gift only developed after participation in the initiatory mystery of analysis. When Jung's
early disciple and translator Beatrice M. Hinckle published one
of the very first Jungian "how-to" manuals, aptly titled *The Re-
Creating of the Individual* in 1923, she explicitly compares the
mentality of the genius with that of the re-created or individuated person.[33]

1917–1919: A Return to
Romantic "Naturphilosophie"

Besides Jung's vigorous rejection of the Christian god and his
guerilla war against the organized Judeo-Christian religions of
his day, Jung also rejected the science of the early twentieth century and instead embraced the worldview and methodologies of
early nineteenth-century romantic conceptions of science. With
the creation of his religious cult and its transcendental notions
of a collective unconscious in 1916 Jung had already left the scientific world and academia, never to really return (despite later
pleas for the scientific nature of his analytical psychology). The
adoption of the additional theory of dominants or archetypes
completed this break and formally allied Jung with Goethe,
Carus, and the morphological idealists of the romantic or metaphysical schools of Naturphilosophie that reigned supreme between 1790 and 1830 in German scientific circles.[34]

This rejection of twentieth-century science had its roots in
Jung's medical-school days, where he preferred the vital materialism of nineteenth-century German biology over mechanistic
materialism in his study of evolutionary biology and comparative anatomy. His interest and participation in spiritualism and
psychoanalysis—two marginal fin-de-siècle movements—led

him further from the scientific mainstream. By 1916, in "The Structure of the Unconscious," Jung attacks the scientific world-view and defends the validity of occult movements like Theosophy, Christian Science, the Rosicrucians, and those who practice "folk magic" and astrology by arguing that, "No one who is concerned with psychology should blind himself to the fact that besides the relatively small number of those who pay homage to scientific principles and techniques, humanity fairly swarms with adherents of quite another principle." This other "principle" is in each of us, for Jung says that, "For if such a large percentage of the population has an insatiable need for this counterpole to the scientific spirit, we can be sure that the collective psyche in every individual—be he never so scientific—has this psychological requirement in equally high degree."[35] Jung, in typical fashion, removed these passages attacking the scientific establishment in later editions of this essay. Yet, given what we now know about Jung's religion-building proclivities, with this passage he was equally justifying his own movement's role in providing a therapeutic, occultist "counterpole" to the scientism and the scientific establishment.[36]

In 1917 the English-language version of "The Structure of the Unconscious," which Jung retitled "The Psychology of Unconscious Processes," appeared, in which Jung no longer refers specifically to the central organizing principles of the phylogenetic or collective unconscious as primordial images, but as dominants.[37] The primordial image (Urbild) is no longer just an ancestor or the dead: the primordial images are now gods, although derived from "secular" processes, which is Jung's way of maintaining a minimal scientific persona by not directly offering polytheism to his readers. Furthermore, the clear link with phylogeny is broken, and the dominants now seem very much to resemble the transcendental realm of Platonic ideas. Jung writes:

> The collective unconscious is the sediment of all the experience of the universe of all time, and is also the image of the universe that has been in the process of formation for untold ages. In the course of time certain features have become prominent in this image, the so-called *dominants*. These dominants are the ruling powers,

the gods; that is, the representations resulting from dominating laws and principles, from average regularities in the issue of the images that the brain has received as a consequence of secular processes.[38]

These dominants, such as the "magical demon" that is "always met" according to Jung in this essay, are projected from the transpersonal, collective unconscious out onto other things and persons, making them either demons or gods. In 1919, Jung borrowed a term from the Romantic biological sciences of the Naturphilosophen and called these organizing principles archetypes. Jung first used this term in a talk on "Instinct and the Unconscious" at Bedford College, London University in July 1919, which was published in the same year in the *British Journal of Psychology*.[39]

Several points need to be addressed about Jung's archetypal theory. First, it appears to be merely a transcendental and therefore nonscientific or mystical reinterpretation of the "complex theory," which at least had a basis in the quantitative science of his day through the word-association experiments. Here Jung merely takes a commonly observed clinical phenomenon—the operation of personal complexes based on personal memories (clusters of personal images, feelings, and thoughts organized around a core theme or motif)—and elevates it to a cosmic scale. Behind the personal complexes are now found gods. This is a Schopenhauerian trope of genius: the universal is now to be seen in the particular.

Second, although Jung makes vague analogies to the "universality of brain structure" and even to "Mendelian units" as the biological sources of the transmission of the archetypes, his concept is clearly incompatible with these theories from the materialistic and mechanistic biological sciences. This did not stop Jung from making references to biology throughout the remainder of his career when attempting to explain how mind and body are congruent at the deepest levels of existence. His shift to a theory of the collective unconscious and the archetypes that transcends personal genetic history goes beyond science and is essentially an occult or mystical notion—an article of faith that one either believes in uncritically or not. The evidence for the role of genetics in heredity is compelling, and Jung's theories simply cannot fit in with the wider body of twentieth-century scientific theory concerning this. This more than anything else shut him out of any opportunities for immortalization through the established medical, scientific, and academic institutions of his day. However, if viewed as a prophet of a new religion of rebirth, his continuing popularity outside of these established institutional domains allows us to comprehend the phenomenon of twentieth-century Jungism.

Third, Jung's promotion of völkisch landscape mysticism (i.e., Bodenbeschaffenheit) in his writings until at least the late 1920s presents a problem as well when trying to make any sense of the archetypes from the biological sciences. In many passages (discussed previously) Jung seems to indicate that forces from the soil or landscape can cause major physiological and especially physiognomic changes independent of biological genetic transmission—indeed, even within a single generation. Although this concept is incongruent with twentieth-century biology, it matches the morphological idealism or Romantic Naturphilosophie of Goethe and the Romantics, whose "types" pointed to underlying organizing principles in animate and inanimate nature. If analytical psychology is a science, as Jung would continue to claim throughout the rest of his life, then it was only so in the sense of that word circa 1830. Furthermore, after 1916 Jung's psychological theory is placed squarely within the tradition of speculative or metaphysical Naturphilosophie due to their commonly shared fundamental concepts such as *Einheit* (unity), *Stufenfolge* (succession of stages of gradual development), *Polarität* (polarity, or the interplay of opposing vital forces), *Metamorphose* (metamorphosis), *Urtyp* (archetype), and *Analogie* (analogy). Jung's psychology is a twentieth-century regression or degeneration to nineteenth-century Naturphilosophen.[40]

Fourth, the fact that Jung's psychological theories fit within these traditions of Romantic or metaphysical Naturphilosophie is intellectually consistent with his völkisch agenda. It was precisely these schools of Naturphilosophie that maintained a long tradition of association with the conservative political ideology of the German Idealists and Romantics and had specific social and political ends that they hoped to realize, unlike the Göttingen school of transcendental Naturphilosophie, which was associated with more liberal political philosophies but maintained a narrower focus on empirical scientific goals. As Lenoir observes:

> The principle elements of Volkish Ideology, which underpinned conservative culture throughout the nineteenth century, are present in the biological theories of the Idealists; and the fact that Hegel was one of the major theoreticians of both conservative political theory and the Romantic-Idealist conception of nature cannot fail to alert us to the mutual affinity of these two aspects of German intellectual culture in the early nineteenth century.[41]

Therefore, the theories of the archetypes and the collective unconscious comprise Jung's transcendental or occult religious doctrine of an extramundane reality and its forces (the dead, gods, archetypes). It is his creed, his faith. This is Jung's own version of the secret doctrine, and the metaphysical basis of his Nietzschean religion. Jung found many believers in his völkisch faith—particularly from England and America—and due to their efforts the Jungian movement became the most successful of all of the fin-de-siècle occult traditions.

Why Didn't We Know
These Things about Jung Before?

No one who was in Jung's innermost circle in Küsnacht-Zurich circa 1916 has been alive for almost forty years, so we have no recorded interviews from anyone who could directly tell us what Jung said and how he behaved during this early period. Blinded by the evils of Hitler and Nazism, very few historians, let alone the very few persons of, say, 1950, interested in the historical development of Jung's movement would be able to see the possible völkisch elements in Jung during the first six full decades of his life. There were many successive generations of disciples in the Jungian camp, and the testimony of these early individuals is unfortunately lost to history. No interviews with his wife, Emma, or his colleague and intimate companion, Antonia Wolff, both of whom knew Jung better than anyone, can be found to shed light on these mysterious years or on the behind-the-scenes origins of analytical psychology.

The well-known disciples of Jung's last thirty years (von Franz, Jaffé, Jolande Jacobi, Maier, Lilliane Frey-Rohm, Joseph Henderson, Joseph and Jane Wheelwright, James Hillman) and the editors of his *Collected Works* (Sir Herbert Read, Michael Fordham, Gerhard Adler, and McGuire) all had their closest association with him in a Nazi or post-Nazi period of European history that occluded the earlier Central European world of Jung's thirties and forties (1905–1925) in which völkisch ideas permeated the learned elites and popular culture of German-speaking enclaves.[42] Almost all of the disciples that Jungians today know and read only became associated with Jung in the 1930s when Jung was in his late fifties and early sixties, after he had begun a revision of the basic metaphors of his psychology when his cult began to grow into an international movement. Indeed, since so many of them arrived from the United States and England (especially the generation of disciples that did know Jung in the 1910s and 1920s, such as Hinckle, Long, Esther Harding, Baynes, Eleanor Bertine, and Mann), as foreigners the darker völkisch nuances in Jung's transcendental theories would have bypassed them completely.

Many of these disciples would no doubt have major objections to the "völkisch Jung" image that I argue typifies his work in the first sixty years of his life. Jung's later use of metaphors from alchemy that framed the context of analytical psychology by 1940 were less nakedly völkisch, and it was largely during this period when Jung had already begun the process of revising his theory in terms of alchemical metaphors that these disciples came to know him. With Hitler's shocking assumption of power in January 1933 the world forgot this earlier, multifaceted netherworld of Germanic mysticism and occultism, partially because Hitler himself began to persecute the most apolitical of the völkisch mystics in order to establish the sole spiritual hegemony of National Socialism as the religion of the German peoples.[43]

"The Secret Church"

THE TRANSMISSION

OF CHARISMATIC AUTHORITY

Iₙ ₕᵢₛ ₚₒₛₜₕᵤₘₒᵤₛₗY published masterpiece, *Wirtschaft und Gesellschaft* (*Economy and Society*) of 1922, Max Weber develops his concept of leadership in charismatic groups by dividing it into two separate sociological processes.[1] These processes resoundingly typify the development of Jung's cult into a movement, and thereby also allow us to see how appropriate it is for us to view this phenomenon as a twentieth-century religious movement that has developed in a strikingly similar fashion as the other movements analyzed by Weber in his *Religionssoziologie*.

This final chapter therefore departs somewhat from the exploration of the relationship of Jung's theories to history and instead ventures into a sociological analysis of Jungism as a cultural force. This is intended as a first step to understanding how Jung and his theories are used, to again quote Danzinger, not only "*by* but also *for* and *about* people with particular interests and preferences." Such an analysis is crucial for understanding the persistence of Jung's popularity in our culture in the absence of any concerted institutional process of immortalization by members of established scientific or academic communities. In the history of science and in the history of psychiatry and psychology, Jungism is a unique phenomenon. It would be difficult, for example, to find any comparable parallels in the important comparative historical and structural study of scientific "research schools" that historian Gerald Gieson published in the *History of Science* a decade ago, other than that the most successful of these schools had "charismatic leader(s)" and high levels of "social cohesion" and "discipleship."[2]

According to Weber, the first process is the establishment of charismatic authority, a period is marked by the often arbitrary rule of the charismatic leader and those within his intimate circle upon whom his (or her) halo shines inclusively. This inner circle is perceived by those at lower strata within the movement as possessing, in a sense, "divinity by association." This is also the phase of the initial excitement and high hopes that characterize new movements of this type and that attract outsiders who are seeking similar experiences of revitalization or renewal, whether spiritual, emotional, or intellectual.

The second phase is marked by what Weber refers to as the "routinization of charisma." Weber was fascinated with the ways in which the initial sparks of liberating excitement and hopes of salvation that a charismatic individual could inspire in others in all cases eventually led to a rationalization or routinization of the authority structure and intellectual system of the cult. Charismatic exuberance becomes bureaucratized, and Dionysian spontaneity is replaced by Apollonian regimentation. The process of routinization reduces dependence on the direct authority of the charismatic leader. Although the seeds of this process are almost always present while the charismatic leader is at his strongest, usually the routinization is hastened by the incapacitation of the leader through sickness, age, or death. Association with a divinely inspired charismatic leader then becomes a major vehicle for material and economic gain when the leader's charisma is institutionally, rather than supernaturally, conferred on the elect. As Weber observes:

> In its pure form charismatic authority has a character specifically foreign to everyday routine structures. The social relationships directly involved are strictly personal, based on the validity and practice of charismatic personal qualities. If this is not to remain a purely transitory phenomenon, but to take on the character of a permanent relationship forming a stable community of disciples or band of followers or a party organization or any sort of political or hierarchical organization, it is necessary for the character of charismatic authority to become radically changed. *Indeed, in its pure form charismatic authority may be said to exist only in the process of originating.* It cannot remain stable, but becomes either traditionalized or rationalized, or a combination of both.
>
> The following are the principal motives underlying this transformation: (a) the ideal and also the material interests of the followers in the continuation and the continual reactivation of the

community; (b) the still stronger ideal and also stronger material interests of the members of the administrative staff, the disciples or other followers of the charismatic leader in continuing their relationship.[3]

With regard to bourgeois-Christian European civilization, Jung's neopagan and völkisch charismatic cult marks what Weber calls a "prophetic break" with the religious, social, and economic status quo. In Weberian terms, Jung was indeed a prophet who, through his "personal call," was both a "renewer of religion" and a "founder of religion." Weber writes:

> We shall understand "prophet" to mean a purely individual bearer of charisma, who by virtue of his mission proclaims a religious doctrine or divine commandment. No radical distinction will be made between a "renewer of religion" who preaches an older revelation, actual or supposititious, and a "founder of religion" who claims to bring completely new deliverance. The two types merge into one another. In any case, the formation of a new religious community need not be the result of doctrinal preaching by prophets, since it may be produced by the activities of non-prophetic reformers.[4]

Let us now briefly examine the first stage of the development of charismatic authority in the Jungian movement from the 1920s to the 1950s, a time when the charismatic leader and prophet Jung led a cult or religious renewal from his base of operations—his Küsnacht home where he lived with his wife and family and which was the site of his private practice, and Zurich, the site of the Psychological Club that was presided over by his intimate companion, Toni Wolff.

THE BAYREUTH OF THE JUNGIANS:
KÜSNACHT-ZURICH
FROM THE 1920s TO THE 1950s

A book-length history of the Jungian movement could and should be written. However, this is not that volume, for this is an analysis of the intellectual and historical foundations of Jung's cult or personal religion and not of the resulting movement. Many of the various disciples that came and went in the Jungian camp have interesting stories of their own that should be told one day. The best source of historical information on Jung's disciples and his movement at present is the several short introductions to Jung's published seminars by William Mc-Guire. What follows, therefore, is a preliminary sketch of some aspects of the early days of the Jungian movement when it existed in its most cult-like form.

The first thing that is apparent when the Jungian movement is examined historically and sociologically is that Jung deliberately kept his movement centered on his personality and on direct contact with him and his most intimate associates in Zurich for at least thirty-six years (1912–1948). This was twice the period of sole charismatic authority that Freud allowed for his movement (which formally may be said to have begun in 1902 with his Wednesday circle). By 1920 Freud allowed the formation of associations that could train new analysts in the largely intuitive methods of psychoanalysis through the oral tradition carried on by those who were indeed first analyzed by Freud and then personally approved by him. This therefore removed the necessity for all psychoanalysts to be trained by him personally.[5] Jung did not allow this until the 1940s. Jung himself *was* the method, a living exemplar of individuation, and others were not allowed to practice psychotherapy in his name unless personally approved by him after extensive therapeutic contacts with him or his most intimate circle of disciples.

Michael Fordham, a British disciple and one of the editors of the *Collected Works*, who began his association with Jung in the 1930s, confirms this essential charismatic nature of Jung's cult when he remarks that, "How anyone became an analytic therapist in those days is vague and must be regarded as largely a matter of vocation, though there was an unwritten law that any person who wanted to be called a Jungian analyst was expected to go out to Zurich, make a relation with Jung himself, and undergo analysis with either himself or one or more of his close colleagues."[6] Like Wagner in Bayreuth, Jung presided over Küsnacht-Zurich in the continuation of the same model of a philosopher-genius who offered mysteries that could only be experienced at that one sacred place.

The second striking fact that becomes apparent when analyzing the history of the Jung cult is the prominent role played by women—particularly American women—in its earliest years. In this respect it mirrors the nineteenth-century occult movements of spiritualism and Theosophy, and probably for the same reason: participation in the Jung cult and the conferring of Jungian analyst status allowed for participation in roles of spiritual authority within an organized religious context, whereas women were shut out of such prominent positions of power in Christianity and Judaism. For example, at the famous 1925 seminars on analytical psychology, out of the twenty-seven participants eighteen were women. Only seven analysts from Jung's inner circle participated, and all seven were female. Between November 1928 and June 1930, a total of thirty-one women and twenty-three men attended Jung's dream analysis seminar in Zurich.

Jung's movement gained its first foothold in the United States. This began in the 1920s with female analysts such as Hinkle, Harding, Bertine, Mann, Frances Wickes, Margaret Nordfeld, and Elizabeth Whitney. They would have been joined by another prominent Jungian and translator of Jung's, Constance Long, had she not died in 1923. Joseph Henderson, an analyst who was one of Jung's disciples in the 1930s, remarks that, "It is somewhat awesome to realize what a strong influence American women had on the movement associated with Jung."[7] A later disciple, Mary Mellon, and her husband Paul, provided the necessary financial backing to set up Bollingen Foundation in 1945 (named after the place in Switzerland where Jung had built his tower), which financed the translation and publication of the *Collected Works of C. G. Jung*, thus paving the way for the contemporary explosion of interest in Jung by providing the "sacred texts" for the movement.[8] Indeed, today women make up the vast majority of the "laity" in the various local Jungian groups around the world. Like the Dionysian cults of antiquity, the Jung cult seems to have started (and then prospered) as primarily a cult of women.

In previous chapters the development of the essential ideas and charismatic structure of the Jung cult has been established. Most notably, Jung seems to have deliberately developed his psychological method and organizational plans along an ancient-mysteries model from at least, perhaps, 1912 onwards. Given his specific reference to Goethe's 1816 poem on "The

Mysteries" in his 1916 talk to the newly founded Psychological Club, it is clear that Jung consciously viewed his cult as one that offered *mysteria* in the ancient Hellenistic sense, and we have evidence that Jung deliberately used mystery-cult metaphors when interacting with patients and disciples during this early period.

In an entry for 5 July 1922 in the notes that Harding kept from her analysis, Jung interprets the figure of an "abbot, and arichmandrite" in one of her dreams as a message from the unconscious that, "You are a Priest of the Mysteries," and that therefore Harding was inflated and needed more humility. She also then notes from her discussion with Jung the following Nietzschean ideas of liberation and of belonging to a new nobility. Notice the oracular reference to obeying the law that echoes the remarks of Hesse's analyst in 1917:

> If we are conscious, morality no longer exists. If we are not conscious, we are still slaves, and we are accursed if we obey not the law. [Jung] said that if we belong to the secret church, then we belong, and we need not worry about it, but can go our own way. If we do not belong, no amount of teaching or organization can bring us there.[9]

The "secret church" is a term Jung used frequently during this early period in formal reference to the underground churches that he thought, based on the scholarship of his day, belonged to the Mithraic mysteries of late antiquity. Used in this informal sense here with his patient, the secret church is none other than the Jung cult, whose mysteries offer the initiate consciousness as the key to freedom and individuality—or as the ancients would seek from their mysteries, "hopes for a better life."[10] Given his initiatory deification experience into the Mithraic mysteries (at least as he interpreted the experience), Jung is identifying his cult with Mithraism as a natural religion with ancient Aryan roots.

Jung tells Harding during her sessions with him (in her paraphrase), "We need to reach a higher state of consciousness. . . . Then we discover a new country. And it is our responsibility to cultivate it."[11] Her experience with Jung was so inspiring that the following year (1923) she moved to New York City and started a private practice and a Jungian organization. By doing so, Harding transplanted the Jungian mysteries to a new country and became the *mater magna* of American Jungism.

Starting in the late 1910s and throughout the 1920s, it was clear that to become a member of the secret church one must undergo a subterranean initiation in the mystery grotto of the collective unconscious in Switzerland—and for a fee. Individuation—then as now—was primarily developed through a fee-paying arrangement with Jung or one of his approved analysts. Analyst status within this subculture meant that one was an exemplar of individuation and therefore also a charismatic spark derived from Jung. The fantasy of individuation is based upon the fantasy of being a Jungian analyst and quickly became the driving source of new income for the Jungian analytic elite. It remains so today, and with the manufactured pseudocharisma of Jung widely distributed in the mass media, many in today's society are attracted to the idea of becoming closer to Jung or to becoming like him in a spiritually charismatic way. Within the Jungian subculture the only objective standard by which one can recognize such a vague quality as individuation in another is by the "charisma of office": i.e., the title "Jungian analyst." To be individuated is to be like Jung and add his name as the "cult totem" to one's own identity. Today, one must pay for several years of analysis (usually one hundred hours at a cost of perhaps $10,000 to $15,000) before even applying to an approved Jungian training institute, which then requires six to ten more years of training (analysis, readings in the Jungian literature, and, in some institutes, instruction in the occult sciences such as astrology, palmistry, the *I Ching*, and other "intuitive" methods), which can cost up to another $100,000 or so.

Today, the entire routinized system operates with an economic structure like a multilevel marketing pyramid, with individuation as the vague product sold, and Jungian analyst status essentially equivalent to a distrubutorship that can be bought. Most Jungian analysts see primarily those attracted to Jung and his works, people who, as consumers, want the next best thing to Jung: hence, the usual patient of a Jungian analyst is always a possible trainee whose economic input into the system is potentially significant. Money, perceived power, and perceived spirituality all flow to the few certified Jungian analysts in the elite at the top in this pyramidal economic system.[12]

One of the selling points in the marketing of Jungian analysis today was also one of its attractions to the spiritual elitism of Jung's early contemporaries: the idea of analysis as initiation into mysteries. In Hesse's 1917 analysis, this initiation was depicted by his analyst as an encounter with the dead and with chthonic powers in a mine shaft. A descent into the depths is still today a favorite buzzword of Jungism, a reframing of Bleuler's term "depth psychology" (which he coined around 1911) into the sacred language of mystery-cult initiation. After the appearance of Rudolph Otto's *Das Heilige* (*The Idea of the Holy*) in 1917, Jung referred to the mystery initiations forged by his psychological method as an experience of the *numinosum*. "Everyone who has achieved this breakthrough always describes it as overwhelming," the hierophant Jung says in 1931 about those who sacrifice themselves in the Jungian mysteries of analytical psychology.[13]

Even more revealing is his 1918 statement: "The connection with the suprapersonal of *collective* unconscious means an extension of man beyond himself; it means death for his personal being and a rebirth in a new dimension, as was literally enacted in certain of the ancient mysteries."[14] When Jung says that, "artificial aids have always been needed to bring the healing forces of the unconscious into play. It was chiefly the religions that performed this task,"[15] he is admitting the usurpation of the authority of the world's great religions to heal the spiritually bankrupt and, therefore, the legitimate dispensation of these sacraments by cults like his own.

Jung was openly and avowedly religious in his psychotherapeutic practice. We have evidence that he used paradoxical techniques that seemed to reflect his völkisch beliefs in the transformative effect of experiencing the god within. For example, another female disciple, Käthe Bügler from Germany, says that when she began her training analysis with Jung in 1927 she reports being "shocked" when one of Jung's first questions to her was: "Where is God? Outside or inside?" As he asked her this he held his palm over his heart, then dramatically pointed outward and then placed it over his breast again.[16]

1925 was a significant year in Jung's life and in the development of his cult. Jung turned fifty in July 1925. At the beginning of the year Jung was on an extensive trip throughout the United

States during which he visited the Indians on the Taos Pueblo reservation north of Santa Fe. At the end of the year, he was on an extended safari in Africa. His many remarks about these voyages seem to indicate that they verified the primacy of sun worship among primitive peoples and therefore his notions of the central image of the god within, the collective unconscious as a sun, star, or mandala. Jung, like Haeckel and Keyserling, found authentic sun worship in his travels to "primitive" cultures and thus, in his mind, independently verified his theory of a collective unconscious in which memory was in all matter, not just the neurons of the brain.

By 1925 Jung's fame as a modern prophet or seer had spread, and many wealthy pilgrims were arriving in Zurich from English-speaking lands that had not been destroyed by the war (as Germany and the dismantled Austrian empire had been). He therefore delivered his famous 1925 seminars on analytical psychology in English. The symbolism of this decision cannot be underestimated, for it signals Jung's willingness to spread the gospel of his mysteria around the world. It was no accident, either, that this was the time and place at which he talked of his "confrontation with the unconscious." At this seminar, it can be said that for the first time, with this sort of mythic self-disclosure, a cult of personality was born that continues even today.

The text of this seminar was faithfully transcribed and mimeographed. However, in true mystery-cult or secret-society fashion, access to it was restricted only to those initiates who had one hundred hours of analysis and Jung's personal permission.[17] This forbidden fruit has only been available for general public consumption since 1989, when Princeton University Press was finally allowed to publish it.

Jung's disclosure of his personal myth gave his energetic disciples all the material they needed to make him into a legend. Word spread. By the 1930s, Jung's personality, not his ideas or books (which were, admittedly, difficult for nonacademics to read), became the focus of intense interest and idealization. The legend of Jung as a Keyserling-type sage or holy man was promoted in no small measure in the English-reading world by the biographical pastiche, "Dr. Jung: A Portrait," which was written by an ex-patient of Jung's and appeared in *Harper's Magazine* in

May 1931.[18] For the rest of his life, idealizing biographical sketches about Jung that were slanted toward his persona as a *pater pneumatikos* were all that seemed to appear in the world media, climaxing with Jung's picture on the cover of the 14 February 1955 issue of *Time*.

Jung's 1925 self-disclosure made him an example of what Weber has identified as an "exemplary prophet" who shows the way, as opposed to an "ethical prophet" who demands obedience and has a strict ethical code. "The preaching of this type of prophet says nothing about a divine mission or an ethical duty of obedience, but rather directs itself to the self-interest of those who crave salvation, recommending to them the same path as he himself traversed."[19] Ethical prophets and exemplary prophets tend to produce movements with very different social structures regarding the relationship of the prophet with his religious community. Of the two, Weber notes, the charismatic authority of the exemplary prophet most often leads to the production of elitist cults with strict hierarchical divisions within the laity, rather than leading to the development of "churches" that can encompass many different categories of persons in a more egalitarian manner. The Jung cult and movement, as the result of Jung acting as an exemplary prophet, seem to vindicate Weber's model.

By the early 1930s Jung had begun the process of revising the basic system of völkisch and mystery-cult metaphors, instead becoming more and more intrigued with the rich symbolism of alchemy. In 1925, for example, he framed his confrontation with the unconscious in terms of its parallels with the initiation processes of the Hellenistic mystery cults. Yet, as he is quoted by Jaffé in *Memories, Dreams, Reflections*, Jung says that with the publication of *Psychology and Alchemy* in 1944, "I had at last reached the ground which underlay my own experiences of the years 1913 to 1917; for the process through which I had passed at that time corresponded to the process of alchemical transformation discussed in that book."[20] Jung was very much attracted to alchemy's essential theme of redemption, which it had in common with the ancient mysteries, and one of his first public presentations was a lecture on "The Idea of Redemption in Alchemy" at the 1936 Eranos Conference.[21]

By the testimony of Jung's disciples themselves in the 1930s,

1940s, and 1950s, the atmosphere in Jung's circle had very much taken on the air of a charismatic cult of personality. Küsnacht-Zurich had become the Bayreuth of the Jungians, the only place to experience the master himself in performance. The 1925 seminar on analytical psychology was perhaps the turning point in the veneration of Jung, and it shares more than a few characteristics with the impact of the first Bayreuth festival of 1876 on the subsequent development of institutions of "Wagnerism": the journals, the innumerable Wagner societies, the pilgrimages to Bayreuth, the attempt to imitate the Bayreuth festivals elsewhere in Germany and around the world, etc.[22] *Jungismus* thus began to resemble *Wagnerismus*.

Many of Jung's disciples from this period have remarked on the cult-like nature of the Jungian movement during these years. In the 1983 documentary film, *Matter of Heart*, which contained excerpts from interviews with many of the disciples who knew Jung personally from the 1930s onward, California analyst Jane Wheelwright claims that when she first arrived in Zurich with her husband in 1932 to undergo treatment for marital problems she was put off by the "cultism" that made everyone seem "goofy" to her.[23] There are many additional such references to be found in the nearly two hundred unpublished interviews in the Jung Oral Archives at Harvard Medical School, but two in particular stand out.

In an interview given in December 1969 to Gene Nameche (the interviewer for the Jung Oral Archives project), Jungian analyst Liliane Frey (who had entered analysis with Jung in 1934) says concretely, "It was like a cult."[24] Furthermore, like most charismatic religious movements that promise a direct experience of the transcendent, organized religions with their clerical intercessors were the enemy: "He was very much attracted to the Catholic Church, and at the same time, he was in revolt against the authoritarian system."[25]

A more disturbing picture of the heresiarch Jung and his secret church is given in the astounding interview with Jolande Jacobi, an analyst and, historically, a very influential force in the Jungian movement. Jacobi first met Jung in 1927 and went into analysis with him a few years later. Throughout the 1930s, at Jung's suggestion, she concurrently had analysis with Jung and also with a Freudian and an Adlerian analyst in Vienna where she lived. Jacobi, interestingly, was prominent in certain circles of Viennese society and knew the Freud family well. She attended Freud's eightieth birthday party in 1936. In 1933 Jacobi's lover—a Catholic—was on his deathbed, and so in a symbolic act of love she converted to Catholicism.

After telling Jung of her actions in a letter, Jacobi says Jung wrote back to her "in a furious letter like a fiancé who had been betrayed."[26] In her interview, she then either quotes from Jung's actual letter or paraphrases it: "With me," Jung writes, "nobody has his place who is in the Church. I am for those people who are out of the Church." Jacobi claims that Jaffé refused to publish this particular letter of Jung's in the two volumes of his collected *Letters* because, as Jaffé allegedly told Jacobi, "it doesn't throw a good light on Jung."[27] Perhaps most revealing is Jacobi's final assessment of her experience in Jung's inner circle, which spanned decades: "He himself behaved as if his psychology was another religion."[28]

THE ROUTINIZATION OF THE JUNG CULT

After the initial phase of charismatic authority when shifts in core beliefs or procedures are the prerogative of the charismatic leader, Weber has noted that the process of routinization soon begins through the efforts of disciples who see the need to construct a more permanent authority structure and a static belief system. This process began in the Jungian movement in earnest in the mid-1930s and was fully accomplished by 1948 with the founding of the C. G. Jung Institute in Zurich.

Weber identified several ways in which the "gift of grace" of the original charismatic leader is transmitted to others, but only three are relevant here: first, a charismatic leader may designate a successor whose charisma is therefore conferred but not necessarily an innate characteristic of the candidate; thus, such a hand-picked successor may not maintain the necessary legitimacy for authority within the group. Freud attempted to do this with Jung, but Jung himself never designated a successor in this way. Second, the charismatic leader may have blood relatives, spouses, or other kin who may be able to step in as successors. Weber called this method of routinization "clan charisma," and it appears to have been the method used in Wagner's Bayreuth Circle when his wife, Cosima, and eventually his son, Siegfried, assumed command of the Wagnerian movement after his death in 1883.[29] Similarly, after Freud's death it was his daughter Anna who assumed central charismatic authority in the psycho-analytic movement as an innovator and analyst in her own right. Since both his wife, Emma, and Toni Wolff both died before Jung, there were no analysts in his clan who could step into the role of charismatic leader after his death in 1961. Thus, in the case of the Jungian movement, clan charisma was not the mode of routinization either.

The third method is often known as institutional charisma, or, the charisma of office. According to Weber, it is "the concept that charisma may be transmitted by ritual means from one bearer to another or may be created in a new person. . . . It involves a dissociation of charisma from a particular person, making it an objective, transferable entity."[30] In the case of institutional charisma, legitimacy (that is, the consent of the followers to be led) derives from the perception of qualities acquired through institutionalized rituals, and not the inherent personal characteristics of the individual. Thus, in the case of the Jungian movement, which did indeed have such institutions and rituals in place before Jung's death, the authority of the Jungian analysts who succeeded Jung in diverse international localities becomes the institutionally conferred charisma that derives from their perceived association with the manufactured pseudocharisma of Jung. This pseudocharisma continues to be manufactured by the mass media and by the publications of the Jungian movement, especially after his death. The Jung depicted in his cult legend—*Memories, Dreams, Reflections* and its many imitators—thus becomes the cult totem from which Jungian analysts derive their authority within the movement and not necessarily from any personal charisma of their own.

Jung was not succeeded by a single charismatic authority, but by conferring his name institutionally on others as part of their new identity after training in institutes, he was therefore succeeded, in a sense, by his own manufactured image, kept alive in films, videos, publications, and innumerable local Jungian organizations and in the imitation of his life and the assumption of his name by others as Jungian analysts. These are individuals who willingly imitate Jung and take on his name to secure the social recognition of those who find Jung's legend full of charisma and who therefore transfer such admiration for Jung to the representatives who bear his name.

The Jungian movement grew rapidly because of this, since by the mid-1930s Jung was mostly portrayed in friendly media accounts as a modern prophet, spiritual guru, or wizard-like sage. The unfriendly accounts often hinted at possible connections with Nazism or charges of anti-Semitism. Jungians then and now have generally perceived the *New York Times* in particular as overly sympathetic to Freud and quite dismissive of Jung. A reviewer of a recent biography of Henry A. Murray that contains material on his relationship with Jung stated recently in a notable Jungian journal that, "When the *New York Times* (which consistently takes the view that Jung equals Hitler) deigned to review it (and for them to do even that with a Jungian subject they had to hold their nose), they tapped the same academic vein, and got the same scornfully smug copy."[31]

The charisma of office that extended to those individuals who Jung said could practice in his name included being viewed by believers in the transcendental Jungian "secret doctrine" as not only direct extensions of Jung, but also as interpreters of transcendental occult forces (the archetypes) in their own right. Such Jungian analysts learned quickly how lucrative such institutionalized charisma could be for them. Weber identified this underlying economic motivation for the routinization of charisma that has absolutely nothing to do with the inherent charisma of disciples or their professed "otherworldly" or altruistic motives (also characteristic of charismatic movements identified by Weber):

> Only the members of the small group of enthusiastic disciples and followers are prepared to devote their lives purely idealistically to their call. The great majority of disciples will in the long run "make their living" out of their "calling" in a material sense as well. Indeed, this must be the case if the movement is not to disintegrate.[32]

The first attempts at forming a professional group of Jungian analysts that could train others independent of Jung's direct involvement were made (unsuccessfully) in Great Britain between

1936 and 1939 by Zurich-anointed disciples such as Fordham and E. A. Bennett, followed in 1944 by the formation of the Society of Analytical Psychology. The eight original members of this Society were Gerhard Adler, Culver Barker, Freida and Michael Fordham, Robert Moody, Philip Metman, Lotte Paulsen, and Erna Rosenbaum. The interesting fact that men outnumbered women in this first training society soon became the rule and not the exception as the cult was routinized and became a movement. After the first generations of Jungian analysts were trained in Zurich after 1948 (and then London, New York, San Francisco, and Los Angeles), the power structure shifted from female dominated to male dominated. Today in the Jungian movement men still predominate in the caste of analysts.

Jung's own legendary disdain for imitators and the stagnancy such imitation produced is the official reason for his reluctance to set up his own school or institute until late in life. Given Jung's deliberate efforts to set up an anti-orthodox Christianity cult of redemption or Nietzschean religion, he also no doubt wanted to keep the charismatic quality of his movement as long as possible, which would mean continued focus on his own person, personality, and transcendental ideas, which he reserved the right to change as he saw fit as he grew older. As a Nietzschean, Jung did not need to be a sociologist to understand the potential ossification of the soul or the degeneration from dogma that founding institutions could bring.

However, according to information in the Jung Oral Archives, we now know that in 1939 Jung asked Jacobi to research the possibility of establishing a "Jungian university."[33] After turning in a detailed written analysis of the financial and organizational aspects of such a venture, Jung decided not to go ahead with the project. After the war, there was a push by Jacobi and others to establish such a center, and this time Jung (reluctantly it is said) agreed. Subsequently, on 24 April 1948, due to the efforts of Swiss, English, and American disciples, the C. G. Jung Institute was formally founded in Zurich.

Why did Jung finally begin to rethink his opposition to the routinization of his personal charisma? One can only speculate, but it is interesting to note that Jung's initial interest in a Jungian university in 1939 and his support of an institute after the war followed two reminders of his own mortality, for as Jaffé put it

289

in her reminiscences of Jung: "Jung's health and vitality had been weakened by an attack of amoebic dysentery in India in 1938, and a severe cardiac infarct in 1944 was the next blow life dealt him." Jaffé then quotes Jung as saying, "'It was then that life busted me, as sometimes it busts everyone.'"[34] The realization of his own mortality may have been impetus enough for Jung to consider the symbolic immortality of having the teaching of his ideas formalized and his charisma institutionally conferred through office.

On the occasion of the founding of the Institute, Jung himself gave a brief address. "I am honored that you have come here for the purpose of establishing this institute of research which is designed to carry on the work begun by me."[35] Looking to the future, Jung then listed a multitude of research project ideas concerning the history of religions, mythology, the amplification of symbols in "paranoid patients," and so on. What is remarkable about this brief address is what is missing: nowhere does Jung mention that the role of the Institute was to train and certify "Jungian analysts. This, however, quickly became its primary function and is so today. Indeed, it seems as though Jung viewed the Institute as a research center that would produce a body of scholarly literature that would further validate his transcendental theories of the collective unconscious and its archetypes.

The very first publication of the Institute did just that. In 1949 Jung's longtime disciple, C. A. Maier, published his magisterial account of the ancient healing cult of Asclepius, *Ancient Incubation and Modern Psychotherapy*.[36] Maier's book is a work of classical scholarship, not a book of psychological or psychotherapeutic theory or technique. Interestingly (and indeed, not surprisingly as a member of the inner circle), as he says in an interview given in September 1970, Maier was against "a factory that turned out analysts," and he was not pleased with the state of the Institute twenty-two years after its inception: "Now the emphasis is on quantity, not quality. They take all the dropouts from all over the world. It is pretty bad."[37]

Maier's statement that the emphasis of the Institute was one of quantity and not quality fits Weber's routinization or charisma model exactly, for it is the administrative staff of training analysts (those who have more institutionally conferred charisma than trainees or candidates) that reaps the benefit of a steady and secure flow of economic resources by such an increase in quantity as well as a dissemination of their own personal influence and power within the local community by mentoring their own disciples. Thus, social status–related and especially economic motives are the driving force behind religious institutions that function in this way, and the Jungian movement is no exception.

JUNGISM AS PERSONAL RELIGION

For literally tens of thousands, if not hundreds of thousands, of individuals in our culture, Jung and his ideas are the basis of a personal religion that either supplants their participation in traditional organized Judeo-Christian religion or accompanies it. For this latter group especially, the Jungian experience, as it is promoted by its specialized caste of analysts, holds out the promise of mystery and the direct experience of the transcendent that they do not experience in any church or synagogue.

Describing the contemporary Jungian movement as a form of personal religion implies that individual decision making plays a key role in determining how involved an individual may become with activities in groups that all have, almost without exclusion, spiritual or religious interests at heart. Although all are united by a common belief in individuation and a transcendent, transpersonal collective unconscious that is said to manifest itself through the individual psyche, the emphasis remains on the personal experience of the universal in the particular. This may be sought through contact with established Jungian social organizations or functionaries or through private visionary exercises, the reading of Jungian material, and self-reflection. The entire pantheon of all the world's mythologies, torn out of any semblance of its original cultural contexts, is utilized as an "objective" reference point for the interpretation of personal experience (a difficulty Lukács noted in all forms of Lebensphilosophie).

However, as I noted above, the behavioral norms of the Jungian movement act as strong social forces to encourage the individual to engage in an *economic* relationship to achieve individuation. Analysis with a Jungian analyst is promoted as a modern form of initiation or rite of passage and that, with the aid of an occult specialist (the analyst), contact with a transcendent realm (the collective unconscious) and its powers (the archetypes) leads to an energizing renewal, rebirth, or redemption (individuation). The Jungian movement thus resembles a twentieth-century version of an ancient Hellenistic mystery cult, which was a pagan form of personal religion that also entailed the paying of fees for transformative experiences.[38]

With the development of the training center system in 1948 (they now exist in several countries) the Jungian movement has established numerous cult sites where there exist communities of analysts and laity (nonprofessional Jungian organizations) where initiation into the Jungian mysteries is possible. The number of such mystery-cult sites that produce Jungian analysts and offer initiations proliferated rapidly after Jung's death.

Most of the popular Jungian literature is written by the analysts themselves. The usual pattern is to focus on a particular area of interpersonal concern (e.g., the problems of modern intimate relationships, masculinity, femininity, child abuse, anorexia) by presenting brief unidimensional, clinical vignettes amplified by (1) quotations from Jung and (2) idiosyncratic interpretations of mythological material taken entirely out of its original context. The term "analyst" is used repeatedly in this literature in a special, almost magical, sense to separate such individuals from other psychotherapists. Interestingly, in much of his writings, Jung used these terms interchangeably and actually appears to have preferred the more generic term "psychotherapist." In actual practice, the personal criteria that separate a Jungian analyst from any psychotherapist are probably moot, if they exist at all.

Part of the problem with trying to make an objective analysis of such distinctions in the popular literature of Jungism (which, in most respects, is indistinguishable from its highly idiosyncratic professional literature) is that such literature is written from the point of view of self-promotion, both economic and social-status related. In particular, and without reservation, the specialness and spirituality of the role of the Jungian analyst is often quite openly promoted in the pages of these works. The publication of a book enhances the perceived charisma of an analyst and may lead to paid invitations to speak at some of the local Jungian groups within the vast international network of such organizations. These local psychology clubs actually serve as vehicles through which new patients are funneled to the analysts, and as such act as local "trade organizations" for the enterprise of Jungian analysis as a business. Most of these groups have nonanalysts as nominal leaders, but the local analysts exert a considerable controlling influence over them anyway as such group leaders are often the current or ex-patients of the analysts. Whereas the majority of analysts are men in most localities, women predominate in the leadership roles of these regional groups. Neither the informed discussion of Jung's theories nor his history play a significant role in the social discourse of the Jungian movement.

The popular literature of Jungism also serves as a marketing strategy for the larger capitalist enterprise of Jungian analysis. A notable example is the book by the Jungian analyst James Hall entitled *The Jungian Experience: Analysis and Individuation.*[39] This book is essentially a promotional appeal for those seeking meaning in their lives to find it through the Jungian experience that can be had only by entering into a fee-paying relationship with a Jungian analyst. Not only are the stages of the perpetual, open-ended process outlined for the prospective patient, the sequence of encounters with certain "transpersonal entities"—the archetypes—is presented so as to prime the prospective patient for what they *should* experience once engaged in psychotherapy. Suggestions on how fees are to be paid to the analyst, and why, are also included. The final sections of the book discuss metaphysical issues such as how we may learn how the content of our dreams prepares us for death. Hall clearly suggests that dreams may provide evidence for life after death. Hence, implicit in this is the message of the cosmic importance of learning how to interpret one's dreams through the experience of analysis, for then Jungian analysis becomes an initiatory preparation for the afterlife. A convenient list of regional organizations of Jungian analysts is provided in the section, "How and Where to Find Jungian Analysts."

Belief in the collective unconscious and in its powers is strong among Jungians, for it forms their central "iconography of the transcendent" or their image of the great chain of being that unites them in a metaphysical belief system. Despite the infusion of the Jungian movement with revisionist doctrines (primarily feminism, with a focus on speculation about Jung's personal "problems" with women) and schisms (Fordham's "developmental school" and James Hillman's "archetypal psychology" school),[40] until 1993 the concept of the collective unconscious had never been openly challenged or rejected in an official Jungian publication.[41] Also because of the essential metaphysical concerns of Jungians and the wish to maintain the cult legend of Jung at all costs for fear of losing institutionally conferred charisma (and therefore continued monetary profits), few detailed and critical historical works have ever appeared from members of the Jungian analytic community, and the few that have are marred by gross factual errors.[42] As is the case when confronted with the facts of the historical Jesus, history is not the bread of the faithful.

The Jungian Movement
and Contemporary Neopaganism

Following the wide dissemination of Jung's writings in English translation by the 1960s, Jung's obvious fascination with mythology, parapsychological phenomena, the *I Ching*, astrology, alchemy, and mystical and religious experience of all kinds made him a source of inspiration and affirmation for the neopagan religious movements that began to proliferate in Europe and North America during that period—a true Renaissance of the Asconan ideals. Such innovative spiritual seekers—acutely aware of their status as outsiders—have adopted Jung as a prophet whose achievements as a respected psychiatrist, physician, philosopher, and associate of Freud, have helped to legitimize their movement.

The role of Jungian ideas in modern American paganism (Wicca, "goddess spirituality," etc.) was noted in many places by Margot Adler in her extensive volume on the subject.[43] This considerable Jungian influence on modern witchcraft and neopaganism is seconded in a recent volume by M. D. Faber, a literature scholar, that offers a psychoanalytic interpretation of "the witchcraft cult" and furthermore purports to be an attempt to "retrieve the theory" from twentieth-century occultists who have "hijacked Jungian psychoanalytic theory to mystical ends."[44] In a study of ritual magic groups in contemporary England, anthropologist Tanya Luhrmann notes the early adoption of Jung's concept of the collective unconscious by occultists in the 1920s and 1930s: "In magicians' writings, the collective unconscious practically became a place, to which magical ritual could be a map which magicians used to travel in the collective human soul."[45] Luhrmann demonstrates, additionally, that Jung is still widely read and invoked by practicing occultists today: "Linked to psychology and its authoritative figures, the metaphor of a separate plane is a magician's intellectual resource that dispenses with ordinary canons of truth."[46]

Perhaps the most ironic—and potentially the most disturbing—link between Jungism and neopaganism is the prominent inspirational role Jung's writings play in the revival of "Germanic Religion" or Norse paganism in contemporary continental Europe, England, and North America. This phenomenon, at least as it appeared in the late 1970s, has been documented in a remarkable article by Stephen Flowers.[47] According to Flowers, these groups do not have a direct historical link with the völkisch neopagan groups of Central Europe at the turn of the century, nor do all of them have connections with the neo-Nazi movement (although apparently some individuals and local groups do). The first of these organizations seems to have originated in Iceland in May 1973 and was called the *Ásatruarmenn*. A related group, the Odinic Rite, was founded in the United Kingdom that same year. In the United States, a group called the Viking Brotherhood was founded in Texas in 1972 and evolved into a much larger group, the Asatru Free Assembly in 1978. "Asatru" is allegedly the Icelandic term that means "faith in the Asir" (the old Nordic gods). The Asatru Free Assembly formally dissolved in 1987 but apparently many of its members still practice Germanic neopagan rituals in smaller groups, read the works of Jung, and also read the growing occultist literature on Norse paganism—which includes a 1988 translation by Flowers of List's *Secrets of the Runes* of 1908.[48]

According to Flowers:

> Many of their ideas are drawn from the most recent scholarly work concerning the old Germanic religion, and traditional religions in general, as well as from the psychological theories of C. G. Jung.

295

The concepts of the *archetypes* and the *collective unconscious* have exerted a tremendous influence on the formation of the ideology of the neo-Germanic religion. . . . Divinities in Asatru/ Odinism are not seen as independent, transcendental beings, but rather as exemplary models of consciousness, or archetypes, which serve as patterns for human development. . . . A principle feature of this view is the idea that humanity is almost "biologically" linked to divinity, and that there has never been any real break in this connection (i.e., there is no concept of "original sin"). . . . Jungian psychology and old Germanic written sources remain the most influential ideas in the formation of neo-Germanic concepts concerning the nature of man and his place in the cosmos.[49]

As with the völkisch neopagan groups at the turn of the century, the summer solstice is celebrated as one of the holidays of the new Nordic paganism movement (as it is in the neopagan movement in general). Flowers notes, however, that the members of these neo-Germanic groups "are more attracted by antiquarian interests or racial sentimentalities than by religious zeal or interest in self-transformation."[50] This observation probably could have been equally made about the many participants in the Volkstumbewegung circa 1900. What does unite these modern Germanic neopagans, however, is a belief in an ideology called "metagenetics": the idea "that the 'biological' and the 'spiritual' heritage of a person or people are ontologically identical, and that through a reimmersion into the 'old way' a transforming 'return to the whole' may be effected."[51] Despite the similarities between the philosophies of other neopagan movements, including a deep foundation in Jungian thought, the pagan movement in the United States has generally shunned the neo-Germanic movement for its persistent connection with neo-Nazism.

THE FAITH OF THE FUTURE?

A very prominent American Jungian analyst, Edward Edinger, openly acknowledges Jung's role as a prophet in the twentieth century and the essential religious nature of the Jungian movement. In one publication Edinger even terms Jung's ideas in the

Collected Works a divinely inspired "new dispensation" to succeed the Jewish and Christian dispensations of the Old and New Testaments.[52] Passages from Jung's works are now often read as part of the sermons of some ministers, and Jung is read as part of the services of a New Age "Gnostic Church" in San Francisco, as they are alongside the works of Emerson at some Unitarian services.

Are we witnessing the birth of another religious movement that will one day develop into ritualized services and even cathedrals à la Emanuel Swedenborg?[53] With the Jungian movement and its merger with the New Age spirituality of the late twentieth century, are we witnessing the incipient stages of a faith based on the apotheosis of Jung as a God-man? Only history will tell if Jung's Nietzschean religion will finally win its Kulturkampf and replace Christianity with its own personal religion of the future.

✖ *Notes* ✖

INTRODUCTION

1. Harry Liebersohn, *Fate and Utopia in German Sociology, 1870–1923* (Cambridge, Mass.: MIT Press, 1988), pp. 23–24. Tönnies slowly became prominent in early German sociological thought in the late nineteenth century, starting with the publication of his famous book, *Gemeinschaft und Gesellschaft* (*Community and Society*) in 1887.

2. Tönnies *did* finally find a way to become closer to Nietzsche by befriending Nietzsche's close companions, Lou Andreas-Salomé (1861–1937) and Paul Ree (1849–1901). Ree and Andreas-Salomé were the hosts of a lively Berlin salon in the 1880s in the "Boulevard under the Lindens" (Unter dem Linden Strasse), and frequent visitors included not only Tönnies, but also the historian Hans Delbrück (1848–1919), philologist Paul Deussen (1845–1919), and the experimental psychologist Hermann Ebbinghaus (1850–1909). Helga Sprung observes that such salons "played a major positive role in the emancipation of women" because "they offered women an immediate possibility for direct participation in the intellectual life of their time." See Helga Sprung, "Bourgeois Berlin Salons: Meeting Places for Culture and the Sciences," in W. R. Woodward and R. S. Cohen, ed., *World Views and Scientific Discipline Formation* (Dordrecht: Kluwer, 1991), p. 402.

3. Thomas Carlyle, *On Heroes, Hero-Worship and the Heroic in History* (Chicago: A. C. McClurg & Co., 1891 [1841]), pp. 8–9. A useful work that discusses many of the objects of hero worship mentioned in this volume (although very much colored by the tragedy of Nazism) is Eric Russell Bentley, *A Century of Hero Worship: A Study of the Idea of Heroism in Carlyle and Nietzsche, with Notes on Wagner, Spengler, Stefan George, and D. H. Lawrence*, 2d ed. (Boston: Beacon, 1957). His argument that the common thread of "Heroic Vitalism" in these important figures should *not* be considered as proto-Nazism is an important analogue to the argument by historians (and supported in this volume) that völkisch philosophies and groups were not all *necessarily* proto-Nazi.

4. Nietzsche's *Also Sprach Zarathustra* was published in four separate parts between 1883 and 1885, but only in very small editions. They were published together for the first time in an 1892 edition that was widely read and had a major impact on European culture in the 1890s.

5. These works were: *Der Fall Wagner* (*The Case of Wagner*) in 1888; *Die Götzen Dämmerung* (*The Twilight of the Idols*) in 1889; *Der Antichrist*

(*The Antichrist*) in 1895; *Nietzsche contra Wagner* in 1895; and the auto-biographical *Ecce Homo* in 1908.

6. Ferdinand Tönnies, *Der Nietzsche-Kultus: Eine Kritik* (Leipzig: O. R. Reisland, 1897).

7. Steven Aschheim, *The Nietzsche Legacy in Germany, 1890–1990* (Berkeley and Los Angeles: University of California Press, 1992), p. 201.

8. Although rarely given credit for originating with Jung, the enormously popular series of televised interviews with mythologist Joseph Campbell (1904–1987) in 1988 was an effective promotion of Jung's transcendental ideas of a collective unconscious and its archetypes working through the lives (and especially the dreams) of contemporary individuals. A transcript of these interviews appears in Joseph Campbell and Bill Moyers, *The Power of Myth* (New York: Doubleday, 1988). Following the multiple rebroadcasts of these interviews there followed a surge in Jungism that caught the attention of the media: see the multipage article in the 7 December 1992 issue of *U.S. News and World Report*; also, see the article, "Interest in Carl Jung Experiences Revival as Some Embrace Wider View of Psychodynamics" in the 7 February 1992 issue of *Psychiatric News*, the professional newspaper of the American Psychiatric Association.

9. George Weisz, "The Posthumous Laennec: Creating a Modern Medical Hero, 1826–1870," *Bulletin of the History of Medicine* 61 (1987): 541–62.

10. Richard Shryock, "The Medical Reputation of Benjamin Rush," *Bulletin of the History of Medicine* 45 (1971): 507–52.

11. See the discussion of this bias, and related issues, in the history of psychology by Roy Porter and Mark Micale, "Reflections on Psychiatry and Its Histories," in Mark Micale and Roy Porter, ed., *Discovering the History of Psychiatry* (New York: Oxford University Press, 1994), pp. 3–36. I wish to thank Micale for supplying me with prepublication proofs of this important essay. On the shift of the center of scientific research to the United States see Roger Geiger, *To Advance Knowledge: The Growth of American Research Universities, 1900–1940* (New York: Oxford University Press, 1990).

12. This issue is the theme of the selections in the annual edited by Hans Rappard, P. J. Van Strien, L. P. Mos, and William Baker, *Annals of Theoretical Psychology* 8 (1993).

13. Kurt Danzinger, "Psychological Objects, Practice, and History," *Annals of Theoretical Psychology* 8 (1993): 43. Also relevant is Kurt Danzinger, "Social Context and Investigative Practice in Early Twentieth-Century Psychology," in Mitchell Ash and W. R. Woodward, ed., *Psychology in Twentieth-Century Thought and Society* (Cambridge: Cambridge University Press, 1987), pp. 13–34.

Chapter One

1. C. G. Jung, *Memories, Dreams, Reflections by C. G. Jung*, ed. Aniela Jaffé (New York: Pantheon, 1962). In the first—and still the best, despite its age—detailed critical examination of Jung's work, *MDR* is termed an "automythology" that is in "a special genre of its own." Peter Homans, *Jung in Context: Modernity and the Making of a Psychology* (Chicago: University of Chicago Press, 1979), p. 29.

2. C. G. Jung, "Answer to Job," *Psychology and Religion: West and East*, CW 11 (Princeton: Princeton University Press, 1969), para. 645.

3. Of the many biographies of Jung, the one most similar to *MDR* in its odd mystical presentation of Jung is Marie-Louise von Franz, *C. G. Jung: His Myth in Our Time* (Boston: Little, Brown, 1975; original German ed., 1972). Von Franz (1915–) met Jung as an eighteen-year-old in 1933 and became one of his closest disciples. She never married, and after Jung built his tower in Bollingen, Switzerland, von Franz bought property nearby and also built her own tower near the house of her companion, Barbara Hannah, who was another close disciple of Jung's and the author of the best (in terms of new historical details) of these works of discipleship, *C. G. Jung: His Life and Work, A Biographical Memoir* (New York: G. P. Putnam's Sons, 1976). A picture of Jung as an intellectual hero by a friend and disciple of Jung's is Laurens van der Post, *Jung and the Story of Our Time* (New York: Random House, 1977). A new generation of Jung biographers for whom Jung was a *spiritus rector* have continued the tradition of idealization. See, e.g., Gerhard Wehr, *Jung: A Biography* (Boston: Shambhala, 1987).

4. I am indebted to Jung scholar Sonu Shamdasani for alerting me to the construction of *MDR* by Jaffé, the Jung family, and editors at Random House, which published the English-language edition. An edited typescript with editorial markings and material missing from the published versions can be found in the rare books collection of the Countway Library of Medicine, Harvard Medical School, Boston. An early chapter on Toni Wolff—one of the few Jung apparently did by hand—was removed by the Jung family very early in the editorial process, directly following Jung's death, and is not at the Countway. It is said to follow the format of *MDR* and contain reports of mutually significant dreams, synchronicities, etc., between Jung and Wolff, who maintained an intimate personal relationship for approximately forty years.

5. On the *theos aner* see David Tiede, *The Charismatic Figure as Miracle Worker* (Missoula: SBLDS, 1972); and Carl Halladay, *Theos Aner in Hellenistic Judaism* (Missoula: SBLDS, 1977). See also the more accessible discussions in Howard Clark Kee, *Medicine, Miracle and Magic in New Testament Times* (Cambridge: Cambridge University Press, 1986),

pp. 84–86; and in Peter Brown, *The Making of Late Antiquity* (Cambridge, Mass.: Harvard University Press, 1978), pp. 59–72. On the "holy man," see Peter Brown, "The Rise and Function of the Holy Man in Late Antiquity," in his *Society and the Holy in Late Antiquity* (Berkeley and Los Angeles: University of California Press, 1982).

6. On an analogous phenomenon, the fifteenth-century revival of "historical ideals of life," see Gabor Klaniczay, "Legends as Life-Strategies for Aspirant Saints in the Later Middle Ages," in his collection of essays, *The Uses of Supernatural Power* (Princeton: Princeton University Press, 1990).

7. Charles Talbert, "Biographies of Philosophers and Rulers as Instruments of Religious Propaganda in Mediterranean Antiquity," *Aufsteig und Niedergang der römischen Welt* II.16.2. (1978): 1619–51. According to Talbert, in the pagan biographical tradition "the life of the philosopher functions as a legitimation of his teaching" (p. 1643). The image of this hero personifies the value system of the community that he founded. "Such a life produced directly by a religious community would correctly be called a 'cult legend'" (p. 1626). Similarly, I argue that the idealized and sacralized image of Jung in *MDR* has become the cult legend of the Jungian movement.

8. Kee, *Medicine, Miracle, and Magic*, p. 84.

9. Ibid., p. 85.

10. Brown, "The Rise and Function of the Holy Man," p. 142, 121.

11. Ibid., p. 132.

12. Jung's frequent retreats to the stone tower that he built at Bollingen to escape civilization are idealized in the chapter entitled "The Tower" in *MDR*. The book presents Jung waxing poetic on his self-imposed solitude in nature: "In Bollingen, silence surrounds me almost audibly, and I live 'in modest harmony with nature.' Thoughts rise to the surface and reach back into the centuries, and accordingly anticipate a remote future. Here the torment of creation is lessened; creativity and play are close together" (p. 226). The images of Jung retreating to nature to receive the wisdom of the ages and to see into the future are of Jung as the pagan ascetic holy man. Jung also seems to have been living out a German Romantic fantasy. See Ilza Veith, "Loneliness and Solitude: Historical and Philosophical Reflections on Voluntary Withdrawal from Society," in Hertha Riese, ed., *Historical Explorations in Medicine and Psychiatry* (New York: Springer, 1978), pp. 87–98.

13. Brown, "The Rise and Function of the Holy Man," p. 101.

14. Ibid., p. 134.

15. See Ronald Glassman, "Manufactured Charisma and Legitimacy," *Social Research* 42 (1975): 615–36.

16. That is, pre-Aniela Jaffé, the editor of *MDR*.

17. Nowhere has this been more problematic than in the literature of New Testament scholarship. Although it is now acceptable to speak of an original pre-Pauline "Christ cult" that formed around Jesus of Nazareth and that later developed into the "Jesus movement" and then, even later, organized Christianity, this was not always so. This controversy is briefly summarized in Talbert, "Biographies of Philosophers and Rulers," pp. 1625–26. A similar sequence of development is posited here for the Jung cult although I use the term "cult" broadly to reinforce the idea that the Jungian movement is in fact made up of many decentralized cults.

18. Wilhelm Bousset, *Kyrios Christos: A History of the Belief in Christ from the Beginnings of Christianity to Irenaeus* (Nashville, 1970), p. 11. For background on the development of the History of Religions School in classical scholarship, see C. Colpe, *Die religionsgeschichtliche Schule: Darstellung und Kritik ihres Bildes vom gnostischen Erlösungsmythos* (Göttingen, 1961).

19. Marc Galanter, *Cults: Faith, Healing and Coercion* (New York: Oxford University Press, 1989), p. 5.

20. Max Weber, *The Sociology of Religion*, trans. Ephraim Fischoff (Boston: Beacon, 1991), p. 3. The original "Religionssoziologie" was published as part of his posthumous *Wirtschaft und Gesellschaft* (Berlin: J.C.B. Mohr, 1922).

21. Weber, *The Sociology of Religion*, p. 2.

22. This is in the extensive revision of a seminal 1916 paper, published in its third and even more expanded form as "The Relations Between the Ego and the Unconscious" (1928), *Two Essays on Analytical Psychology* CW 7 (Princeton: Princeton University Press, 1966). However, as early as 1917 Jung introduced the prototype of this concept with the idea that the image of a "magical demon" is sometimes projected onto the doctor by the patient. "The picture of this demon is the lowest and the most elementary concept of God. It is the dominant of the primitive tribal magic-man, or a singularly gifted personality endowed with magical power" (Jung, "The Psychology of Unconscious Processes," in *Collected Papers on Analytical Psychology*, 2d ed., Constance Long, ed. and trans. (London: Baillière, Tindall and Cox, 1920).

23. Other speakers to this religious youth movement group included Martin Buber and Gertrud Bäumler. See Martin Green, *The Von Richthofen Sisters: The Triumphant and Tragic Modes of Love* (New York: Basic Books, 1974), p. 224.

24. C. G. Jung Institute of Los Angeles, *Matter of Heart* (film script), p. 4. *Matter of Heart* was a documentary produced by the Institute and released in 1983. It was derived from the forty-hour film archive produced by the Jung Film Project between 1975 and 1981.

25. See Guy Oakes, "Weber and the Southwest German School: The Genesis of the Concept of the Historical Individual," in Wolfgang Mommsen and Jürgen Osterhammel, ed., *Max Weber and His Contemporaries* (London: Unwin Hyman, 1987), pp. 434–46.

26. See the chapter on Jung in Henri Ellenberger, *The Discovery of the Unconscious* (New York: Basic Books, 1970), pp. 657–748; and Henri Ellenberger, "Carl Gustav Jung: His Historical Setting," in Riese, *Historical Explorations* pp. 142–50. Also: "C. G. Jung and the Story of Helene Preiswerk: A Critical Study with New Documents [1991]," in Mark Micale, ed., *Beyond the Unconscious: Essays of Henri F. Ellenberger in the History of Psychiatry* (Princeton: Princeton University Press, 1993), pp. 291–305.

27. This controversy over Jung's behavior and beliefs in the 1930s has not disappeared. See, e.g., Aryeh Maidenbaum and Stephen Martin, ed., *Lingering Shadows: Jungians, Freudians, and Anti-Semitism* (Boston: Shambhala, 1991).

28. Goethe has been described as Nietzsche's model of an übermensch by Walter Kaufmann. In *Nietzsche: Philosopher, Psychologist, Antichrist* (Princeton: Princeton University Press, 1950), Kaufmann makes this distinction in his chapter on "Overman and Recurrence," and cites the following remarks by Nietzsche on Goethe that are congruent with the former's written descriptions of an übermensch: " 'he disciplined himself into wholeness, he *created* himself' and became 'the man of tolerance, not from weakness but from strength,' 'a spirit who has *become free*' " (p. 278).

29. Ellenberger, "Carl Gustav Jung: His Historical Setting," p. 149.

30. C. G. Jung, "The Swiss Line in the European Spectrum" (1928), *Civilization in Transition*, CW 10 (Princeton: Princeton University Press, 1970), para. 905.

31. Oswald Spengler, *Untergang des Abendlandes, Gestalt und Wirklichkeit* (Munich: C. H. Beck'sche Verlagsbuchhandlungen, 1918) and its companion volume, *Untergang des Abendlandes, Welthistorische Perspectiven* (Munich: C. H. Beck'sche Verlagsbuchhandlungen, 1922). This massive Nietzschean work of historical and metaphysical speculation takes up some of Jung's concerns at this time. For example, Spengler says, "For every man, whatever the Culture to which he belongs, the elements of the soul are the deities of an *inner mythology*." Oswald Spengler, *The Decline of the West*, 2 vols., trans. Charles Francis Atkinson (New York: Alfred Knopf, 1980), 1:312.

32. "The Psychology of the Transference" (1946), *The Practice of Psychotherapy*, CW 16 (Princeton: Princeton University Press, 1966).

33. George Mosse, *The Crisis of German Ideology: Intellectual Origins of the Third Reich* (New York: Grosset and Dunlap, 1964), 15.

34. According to Mosse, "Not all of nature, therefore, but only its regional manifestations gave the folk its character, potential, and unity. Nature was defined as a landscape: those features of the environment peculiar and familiar to the members of one Volk and alien to all others" (*The Crisis of German Ideology*, p. 15). The soul of the land shapes the soul of the person. Interestingly, this völkisch assumption is the basis of Daniel Noel's biographical investigation of how Jung's ideas were influenced by the terrain of places that he visited in the 1920s. In his article Noel asserts that in the 1920s Jung "had started to formulate what I call an ecological notion of the collective unconscious psyche" (p. 72). See Daniel Noel, "Soul and Earth: Traveling with Jung Toward an Archetypal Ecology," in *Quadrant: The Journal of Contemporary Jungian Thought* 23 (1990): 57–73.

The importance of geography in determining national character was transmitted to the German bourgeoisie in abundance in the 1850s and 1860s through the works of authors such as Bernhard von Cotta, whose book, "Germany's Earth: Its Construction and Influence on the Life of People" (*Deutschland's Boden: Sein Bau und dessen Einwirkung auf das Leben der Menschen* [Leipzig: F. A. Brockhaus, 1853]) was highly influential in the social and political circles of Pan-Germanism. Geographical determinism was also promoted through the many popular science magazines that appeared with the rise of scientific materialism. German culture took on the added dimension of a firm grounding in scientific ideas for the average educated person during this period, and popular periodicals such as *Westermann's Monatsheft* (which began publication in 1857) vigorously promoted a Weltanschauung based on scientific materialism. The central importance of geography as such an all-encompassing science as presented in *Westermann's Monatsheft* is discussed in Robert Brain, "The Geographical Vision and the Popular Order of the Disciplines, 1848–1870," in Woodward and Cohen, *World Views and Scientific Discipline Formation* pp. 367–76.

35. Peter Gay, *Weimar Culture: The Outsider as Insider* (New York: Harper & Row, 1968), pp. 11–12.

36. Basel (or Bâle), which lies on both banks of the Rhine, was the capital of the half-canton Basel-Stadt or Bâle-ville and by 1899, according to a prominent nineteenth-century travel guidebook, had a population of 99,365: Karl Baedeker, *Switzerland, and the Adjacent Portions of Italy, Savoy, and Tyrol: Handbook for Travellers*, 18th ed. (Leipzig: Karl Baedeker, 1899), p. 4. Baedeker also reports data from a census conducted by the government of Switzerland on 1 December 1888 that provides total population figures for each of the twenty-two official cantons. These total figures are further subdivided according to religion. For Bâle-ville in 1888, the total population was listed as 74,247,

out of which 50,326 were Protestant, 22,402 were Roman Catholic, 1,078 were Jews, and 441 belonged to "Sects" (p. xxxiii). These figures give a rough picture of how dominantly Protestant Jung's world was when growing up, and especially how few non-Christians (such as Jews) he would likely meet on any given day.

37. Ellenberger, *The Discovery of the Unconscious*, p. 662.

38. "Not until I was in my thirties was I able to confront Mater Ecclesia without this sense of oppression. The first time was in St. Stephen's Cathedral in Vienna." Jung, *MDR*, p. 17.

39. Fritz Ringer, *The Decline of the German Mandarins: The German Academic Community, 1890–1933* (Cambridge, Mass.: Harvard University Press, 1969).

40. The Swiss elements of Jung's Zofingia fraternity are conspicuously stressed by Marie-Louise von Franz in her introduction to Jung's published Zofingia lectures. See *The Zofingia Lectures*, CW A (Princeton: Princeton University Press, 1983). Jung does indeed refer to the "official displays of public enthusiasm in the pan-German Empire" as "inane" (p. 55) in his 1897 inaugural address. However, in an earlier talk the same year, anti-Semitism (often associated with Pan-Germanism by this time) is evident when he praises his hero, the "noble [Johann] Zöllner" (a psychical researcher), for being "mortally wounded in his struggle against the Judaization of science" (p. 35). This latter phrase is absent from the index of the *Zofingia Lectures*.

41. C. G. Jung, *Analytical Psychology: Notes of the Seminar Given in 1925* (Princeton: Princeton University Press, 1989), p. 37. Mendel's work and its suggestion of genes was rediscovered only in 1900. Jung's description here resembles its conceptual precursor in biology, August Weismann's "germ-plasm" theory. As I have found in many other volumes of Jung's *Collected Works* and seminars, odd, eccentric, unflattering ideas—such as this one—are often conspicuously absent from the index at the back of these books, although such concepts or terms are mentioned repeatedly in the text.

42. Ibid., p. 82.

43. Eliza Marian Butler, *The Tyranny of Greece Over Germany: A Study of the Influence Exercised by Greek Art and Poetry over the Great German Writers of the Eighteenth, Nineteenth, and Twentieth Centuries* (Cambridge: Cambridge University Press, 1935).

44. Ibid., p. 46. See also Johann Joachim Winckelmann, *Reflections on the Imitation of Greek Works in Painting and Sculpture* (1755), trans. E. A. Hyer and Roger Norton (La Salle, Ill.: Open Court, 1987).

45. In his 1867 essay on Winckelmann, Walter Pater points out Winckelmann's avoidance of the irrational elements of Greek culture, so familiar to fin-de-siècle modernity: "Into this stage of achievement

Winckelmann did not enter. . . . His conception of art excludes that bolder type of it which deals confidently with life, conflict, evil. Living in a world of exquisite but abstract and colorless form, he could hardly have conceived of the subtle and penetrative, but somewhat grotesque art of the modern world." Walter Pater, *The Renaissance: Studies in Art and Poetry* (New York: Macmillan, 1909), pp. 235–36.

46. In a 28 February 1932 letter to Swiss author and editor Max Rychner, who wrote to Jung and other celebrities asking them for opinions about Goethe and his work, Jung says, "My mother drew my attention to *Faust* when I was about 15 years old." Jung considered it a Germanic contribution to the world as a sacred text: "*Faust* is the most recent pillar in that bridge of the spirit which spans the morass of world history, beginning with the Gilgamesh epic, the *I Ching*, the Upanishads, the *Tao-te-Ching*, the fragments of Heraclitus, and continuing in the Gospel of St. John, the letters of St. Paul, in Meister Eckhart and in Dante." C. G. Jung, *Letters: I. 1906–1950* (Princeton: Princeton University Press, 1973), p. 89.

47. Largely because of the cultural repercussions of Winckelmann's rediscovery of ancient Greece, the teaching of German Wissenschaft in the nineteenth century originally was not based on the methods of the natural sciences, but instead on those of philosophy and classical philology. Between 1850 and 1880 this emphasis had reversed somewhat. The claims of both Freud and Jung that their psychological theories and methods were indeed science comes from this older view of Wissenschaft that was eventually supplanted by the equation of the scientific with the experimental study of materialist hypotheses. On German education and science during the nineteenth century, see the following: Fritz Ringer, "Higher Education in Germany in the Nineteenth Century," *Journal of Contemporary History* 2 (1967): 125–46; R. Steven Turner, "The Growth of Professional Research in Prussia, 1818 to 1848—Causes and Context," *Historical Studies in the Physical Sciences* 3 (1971): 137–82; and an older but still useful work, Friedrich Paulsen, *German Universities and University Study* (New York: Macmillan, 1906).

48. Ernest Jones, *Free Associations: Memoirs of a Psycho-Analyst* (New York: Basic Books, 1959), p. 35.

49. Jung, *Analytical Psychology*, p. 6.

CHAPTER TWO

1. George Mosse, *The Culture of Western Europe: The Nineteenth and Twentieth Centuries*, 3d ed. (Boulder: Westview Press, 1988). Specifically, according to Mosse, "This change of public spirit after 1870 tended toward a recapturing of the irrational—a revolt against positiv-

ism which was later to form part of the totalitarian movement of this century" (p. 220). The literature on the fin de siècle is quite large, but a useful collection of essays on the technological, economic, social, and scientific innovations of that era can be found in Mikulás Teich and Roy Porter, eds., *Fin de Siècle and Its Legacy* (Cambridge: Cambridge University Press, 1990).

2. An introduction to the nineteenth-century bourgeois European mentality, useful here because of its focus on German Europe, is the section on "Studies in the History of the Bourgeois-Christian World," in Karl Löwith, *From Hegel to Nietzsche: The Revolution in Nineteenth-Century Thought* (New York: Holt, Rinehart and Winston, 1964). A useful perspective can also be found in the general introduction to Peter Gay, *The Bourgeois Experience, Victoria to Freud: Volume 1. Education of the Senses* (New York: Oxford University Press, 1984), pp. 3–70; and the second volume, *The Tender Passion* (New York: Oxford University Press, 1986).

3. In the Jung Oral Archives at the Countway Library of Medicine the lengthy interview with Jolande Jacobi repeatedly brings out her personal observations of Jung's bourgeois conventionality in social situations.

4. Ellenberger, *The Discovery of the Unconscious*; "Carl Gustav Jung: His Historical Setting."

5. Max Nordau, *Degeneration* (New York: D. Appleton, 1895), p. 1. The appearance of the English translation of *Degeneration* in February 1895 was a major cultural event, as the book ignited outrage among modern artists and fear among many everyday individuals when Nordau argued that they were hereditary degenerates. George Bernard Shaw, among many others, counterattacked Nordau with his own publications. The original German edition was *Entartung* (Berlin: C. Dunker, 1892).

6. See J. Edward Chamberlin and Sander Gilman, eds., *Degeneration: The Dark Side of Progress* (New York: Columbia University Press, 1985); Daniel Pick, *Faces of Degeneration: A European Disorder, c. 1848–1918* (Cambridge: Cambridge University Press, 1989); and Ian Dowbiggin, *Inheriting Madness: Professionalization and Psychiatric Knowledge in Nineteenth-Century France* (Berkeley and Los Angeles: University of California Press, 1991).

7. Friedrich Nietzsche, "Thus Spoke Zarathustra, Part I (1883)," in *The Portable Nietzsche*, ed. and trans. Walter Kaufmann (New York: Viking Penguin Books, 1982), p. 187.

8. Jost Hermand, *Old Dreams of a New Reich: Volkish Utopias and National Socialism* (Bloomington: Indiana University·Press, 1992), pp. 31, 35.

9. The term "decadent" meant many things to the fin-de-siècle generation, but it generally referred to something that was luxurious, sensual, and corrupting. For an engaging meditation on the term, see Richard Gilman, *Decadence: The Strange Life of an Epithet* (New York: Farrar, Straus, Giroux, 1979). On the literary movement, see A. E. Carter, *The Idea of Decadence in French Literature* (Toronto: University of Toronto Press, 1958); Arthur Symons's signal "The Decadent Movement in Literature," which first appeared in the November 1893 issue of *Harper's New Monthly Magazine*, is reprinted in Karl Beckson, ed., *Aesthetes and Decadents of the 1890s* (Chicago: University of Chicago Press, 1981), pp. 134–51.

10. On the individual as "Nietzschean hero," see Leslie Paul Thiele, *Friedrich Nietzsche and the Politics of the Soul: A Study of Heroic Individualism* (Princeton: Princeton University Press, 1990).

11. "I was twenty-four when I read *Zarathustra.* I could not understand it, but it made a profound impression upon me." Jung, *Analytical Psychology* p. 7. We know, however, from the dates of the Zofingia lectures that Jung was quite familiar with Nietzsche at age twenty-three.

12. Jung, *MDR*, p. 102.

13. The seminar notes have been edited by James Jarrett and are now available in C. G. Jung, *Nietzsche's Zarathustra*, 2 vols. (Princeton: Princeton University Press, 1988).

14. Steven Aschheim, *The Nietzsche Legacy in Germany* p. 14.

15. This equation of modernity with the dark forces of irrationalism (which has no redeeming value) is a bias argued most recently in Georg Lukács, *The Destruction of Reason*, trans. Peter Palmer (Atlantic Highlands, N.J.: Humanities Press, 1981).

16. The philosophical work of Arthur Schopenhauer (1788–1860) achieved its strongest reception in European culture between 1880 and 1900 and had a great impact on Richard Wagner (1813–1883), Friedrich Nietzsche, and many others who matured during the fin de siècle such as Jung. See David Luft, "Schopenhauer, Austria, and the Generation of 1905," *Central European History* 26 (1983): 53–75. Jung, while a medical student, was led to his ideas of the unconscious mind through studying Schopenhauer and von Hartmann (1842–1906). He was largely ignorant of the growing psychiatric literature (primarily in French) on dissociation and hypnotism at this time and instead turned to these German philosophers to help him formulate his ideas about the human psyche. "My ideas of the unconscious, then, first became enlightened through Schopenhauer and Hartmann. Hartmann, having the advantage of living in a later period than Schopenhauer, formulates the latter's ideas in a modern way," Jung reported in 1925. See Jung, *Analytical Psychology*, p. 5.

17. On the history of French psychiatry in the nineteenth century and the leading role of the Esquirol circle, see Jan Goldstein, *Console and Classify: The French Psychiatric Profession in the Nineteenth Century* (Cambridge: Cambridge University Press, 1987). On the leading role of French *alienistes* such as Benedict Augustin Morel (1809–1873) in establishing hereditary degeneration as the most influential theory of mental illness and therefore the most pressing social concern of the age, see Dowbiggin, *Inheriting Madness*; and Pick, *Faces of Degeneration*.

18. The theoretical differences between Freud and Janet were significant, and each maintained a very different view of the unconscious. Personally, the two men despised one another. See Campbell Perry and J. R. Laurence, "Mental Processing Outside of Awareness: The Contributions of Freud and Janet," in Kenneth Bowers and Donald Meichenbaum, ed., *The Unconscious Reconsidered* (New York: John Wiley, 1984). The best history of this French dissociationist tradition is Ellenberger's *The Discovery of the Unconscious*. Also useful is Onno van der Hart and B. Friedman, "A Reader's Guide to Pierre Janet on Dissociation: A Neglected Intellectual Heritage," *Dissociation* 2 (1989): 3–16.

19. See C. G. Jung, "On the Doctrine of the Complexes" (1911), *Experimental Researches* CW 2 (Princeton: Princeton University Press, 1972); and especially his, "A Review of the Complex Theory" (1934), *The Structure and Dynamics of the Psyche*, CW 8 (Princeton: Princeton University Press, 1969). The dissociationist basis of this theory is explicitly discussed in Richard Noll, "Multiple Personality, Dissociation, and C. G. Jung's 'Complex Theory,'" *Journal of Analytical Psychology* 34 (1989): 353–70; and "Multiple Personality and the Complex Theory: A Correction and a Rejection of C. G. Jung's 'Collective Unconscious,'" *Journal of Analytical Psychology* 38 (1993): 321–23.

20. See, e.g., Wilma Koutstaal, "Skirting the Abyss: A History of Experimental Explorations of Automatic Writing in Psychology," *Journal of the History of the Behavioral Sciences* 28 (1992): 5–27. One such pioneer of the use of experimental automatic writing was Gertrude Stein, who published papers on her work as a student at Radcliffe in the 1890s. See also Sonu Shamdasani, "Automatic Writing and the Discovery of the Unconscious," *Spring* 54 (1993): 100–131.

21. F.W.H. Myers's theory of the subliminal self can be found in his numerous publications in the 1880s and 1890s in the *Proceedings of the Society for Psychical Research* and in his posthumous magnum opus, *Human Personality and Its Survival of Bodily Death*, 2 vols. (London: Longman, Greens, 1903). The crowning achievement of psychical research is the analysis of the "Census of Hallucinations" of apparitions of the living and the dead conducted by Myers and his colleagues, Edmund Gurney and Frank Podmore: *Phantasms of the Living*, 2 vols.

(London: Kegan Paul, Trench, Trubner & Co, 1886). Myers was a close friend of William James (as was Flournoy), who held Myers in such great esteem that he suggested, *"What is the precise constitution of the Subliminal*—such is the problem which deserves to figure in our Science hereafter as the *problem of Myers."* William James, "Frederic Myers' Service to Psychology" (1901), in *The Works of William James: Essays in Psychical Research*, ed. Frederick Burkhardt and Fredson Bowers (Cambridge, Mass.: Harvard University Press, 1986), p. 196.

22. Burckhardt's complaint is in a letter to Johanna Kinke dated 23 August 1843 and is cited in Peter Gay, *Education of the Senses*, p. 52n.

23. On Jewish identity and typical patterns of assimilation and nationalism among Jews in late nineteenth-century Austria-Hungary, see the excellent volume by Marsha Rosenblatt, *The Jews of Vienna, 1867–1914: Assimilation and Identity* (Albany: State University of New York Press, 1983). By the end of the First World War there were 200,000 Jews in Vienna, according to Rosenblatt (p. 196).

24. Löwith, *From Hegel to Nietzsche*, p. 334.

25. Ibid., p. 22.

26. Roy Pascal, *From Naturalism to Expressionism: German Literature and Society, 1880–1918* (New York: Basic Books, 1973), p. 167. See especially Pascal's discussion of theological modernists on pp. 167–71.

27. Ibid., p. 167.

28. Wilhelm Hauer, Karl Heim, Karl Adam, *Germany's New Religion: The German Faith Movement*, ed. and trans. by T.S.K. Scott-Craig and R. E. Davies (New York: Abingdon Press, 1937).

29. George Bernard Shaw, *The Perfect Wagnerite*, 4th ed. (London: Constable & Co., 1923). Shaw's first edition of this work appeared in 1898.

30. Albert Schweitzer, *The Quest of the Historical Jesus: A Critical Study of Its Progress from Reimarus to Wrede*, trans. by W. Montgomery (New York: Macmillan, 1968), p. 1. This translation is based on the first German edition: *Von Reimarus zu Wrede: Eine Geschichte der Leben-Jesu-Forschung* (1906); an enlarged and retitled edition appeared in 1913 as *Geschichte der Leben-Jesu-Forschung*. Schweitzer believed he was improving on the advances made by Strauss and by the Tübingen school in this work. Jung was familiar with Schweitzer's works and refers to the 1913 volume in some of his writings. Both men were born in Germanic Europe in the same year—1875—which makes them contemporaries in many ways.

31. David Friedrich Strauss, *The Life of Jesus Critically Examined*, trans. George Eliot, ed. Peter Hodgson (Philadelphia: Fortress Press, 1972). See also Horton Harris, *David Friedrich Strauss and His Theology* (Cambridge: Cambridge University Press, 1973).

32. This tradition continues today, but with much less controversy. See, e.g., John Dominic Crossan, *The Historical Jesus: The Life of a Mediterranean Jewish Peasant* (New York: Harper & Row, 1991). For the earliest speculations on the historical Jesus, and the eighteenth-century theologian who provided Schweitzer's starting point, see Charles Talbert, ed., *Reimarus: Fragments* (Philadelphia: Fortress Press, 1970).

33. Due to Renan's talents, it was thought that he would become a doctor of theology and teach Oriental languages (Hebrew, Arabic, Aramaic) in a Catholic seminary. Instead, as a disciple and early biographer puts it, "Every month of study led him further and further away from the Church." Madame James Darmesteter, *The Life of Ernest Renan* (Boston: Houghton, Mifflin, & Co., 1897), p. 48.

34. Strauss's most famous work in this vein was *Der alte und der neue Glaube* [*The Old Faith and the New*] (Leipzig, 1872). On Strauss's mixture of biological evolutionary ideas with political views, see Richard Weikart, "The Origins of Social Darwinism in Germany, 1859–1895," *Journal of the History of Ideas* 54 (1993): 469–88. For the most detailed assessment of the later work of Strauss, which was much informed by Darwin, see Frederick Gregory, *Nature Lost? Natural Science and the German Theological Traditions of the Nineteenth Centuries* (Cambridge, Mass.: Harvard University Press, 1992), pp. 67–111.

35. Friedrich Nietzsche, "David Strauss, the Confessor and the Author," *Untimely Meditations*, trans. R. J. Hollingdale (Cambridge: Cambridge University Press, 1983), pp. 1–55. For discussions of Nietzsche's evaluation of Strauss, see Kauffman, *Nietzsche: Philosopher, Psychologist, Antichrist* pp. 114–16, 120, 130, 148, 367n; and Carl Pletsch, *Young Nietzsche: Becoming a Genius* (New York: The Free Press, 1991), pp. 165–67.

36. Jung's personal library contains a German translation of Renan's famous work. Interestingly, Strauss and Jung shared a similar fascination with the famous early spiritualist medium, "the Seeress of Prevorst." Schweitzer notes in *The Quest of the Historical Jesus*: "Two journeys which Strauss made along with his fellow-student Binder to Weinsberg to see Justinius Kerner made a deep impression upon him. He had to make a deliberate effort to escape from the dream-world of the 'Prophetess of Prevorst.' Some years later, in a Latin note to Binder, he speaks of Weinsberg as 'Mecca nostra'" (pp. 68–69). In a May 1897 lecture to his Zofingia fraternity, Jung quotes from the writings of Strauss on the "Seeress." C. G. Jung, "Some Thoughts on Psychology," in *The Zofingia Lectures*, paras. 73–75.

37. C. G. Jung, "Thoughts on the Interpretation of Christianity, with Reference to the Theory of Albrecht Ritschl" (1899), in *The Zofingia Lec-*

tures, para. 251. His reference to seeking the opinions of theologians "for more than two years now" probably is in reference to the freedom he felt in doing so after the death of his father, with whom he had many theological disagreements, in 1896.

38. Ibid., p. 107.

39. This more critical approach of Protestantism fostered a distinctly American form of psychotherapy in the Boston area starting around 1880 that seems to have been based on (1) the spiritual and moral principles of the New England Transcendentalism of Ralph Waldo Emerson (and others) and (2) on strengthening the volition ("will training"). See George E. Gifford, Jr. ed., *Psychoanalysis, Psychotherapy, and the New England Medical Scene, 1894–1944* (New York: Science/History Publications, 1978); the "Emmanuel Movement" led by Rev. Elwood Worcester of Boston's famous Emmanuel Church spawned a psychotherapeutic movement and even a journal (in 1909) entitled *Psychotherapy* that was a forum for discussion on the common bond between psychology, medicine, and religion. The works of William James, Henri Bergson, and Emerson were the foundation of most of the discussions. Besides clergymen, eminent physicians and psychiatrists contributed to its early issues. See Robert Fuller, *Americans and the Unconscious* (New York: Oxford University Press, 1986), pp. 100–108.

40. A. D. Nock, "Hellenistic Mysteries and Christian Sacraments," in *Essays on Religion and the Ancient World*, ed. Zeph Stewart, 2 vols. (Cambridge, Mass.: Harvard Univerisity Press, 1972), 2:791. Similarly, historians of science who research astrology, magic, and divination within their ancient cultural contexts are also viewed with suspicion. For an argument against such taint, see David Pingree, "Hellenophilia versus the History of Science," *Isis* 83 (1992): 554–63.

41. James Gilman, "R. G. Collingwood and the Religious Sources of Nazism," *Journal of the American Academy of Religion* 54 (1986): 111–28. This thesis is also argued in a broader context in George Mosse, *The Nationalization of the Masses: Political Symbolism and Mass Movements in Germany from the Napoleonic Wars through the Third Reich* (Ithaca: Cornell University Press, 1975).

42. Georg Lukács, "Vitalism (*Lebensphilosophie*) in Imperialist Germany," in *The Destruction of Reason*, p. 415.

43. Ibid., p. 414. On themes related to mythology and Lebensphilosophie, see Ivan Strenski, "Ernst Cassirer's Mythical Thought in Weimar Culture," *History of European Ideas* 5 (1984): 363–84; and Jonathan Wagner, "Nazism and Sentimentalism: The Propaganda Career of Karl Goetz," *Canadian Journal of History* 24 (1989), pp. 63–81.

44. Beatrice Hinkle, "Jung's Libido Theory and the Bergsonian Phi-

losophy," *New York Medical Journal* 99 (1914): 1080–86. See also Pete Gunter, "Bergson and Jung," *Journal of the History of Ideas* 44 (1982): 632–52.

45. See Walter Struve, *Elites Against Democracy: Leadership Ideas in Bourgeois Political Thought in Germany, 1890–1933* (Princeton: Princeton University Press, 1973).

CHAPTER THREE

1. Ernst Mayr makes the argument that "Darwinism" is not one coherent theory, as Darwin presented it in his 1859 book, but instead five separate theories that other evolutionists rejected in one or more of its components. This confusion has led to ambiguous interpretations of the terms "Darwinian" or the "Darwinian revolution" by others during Darwin's lifetime and it continues today, Mayr asserts. These five theories were:

1. The acceptance of evolution as such, as opposed to a constant, unchanging world
2. Evolution of all life through common descent from a single ancestor
3. The gradualness of evolution, as opposed to its suddenness (saltationism)
4. Populational speciation
5. Natural selection.

See Ernst Mayr, *The Growth of Biological Thought: Diversity, Evolution and Inheritance* (Cambridge, Mass.: Harvard University Press, 1982), pp. 505–10.

2. On this issue of variation and descent in Naturphilosophie, see Timothy Lenoir, "Generational Factors in the Origin of *Romantische Naturphilosophie*," *Journal of the History of Biology* 2 (1978): 57–100. See also the paper by William Coleman, "Morphology Between Type Concept and Descent Theory," *Journal of the History of Medicine* 31 (1976): 149–75.

3. On the three basic types of Naturphilosophie (transcendental, romantic, and metaphysical Naturphilosophie) see Timothy Lenoir, "The Göttingen School and the Development of Transcendental Naturphilosophie in the Romantic Era," in William Coleman and Camille Limoges, eds., *Studies in the History of Biology, Volume 5* (Baltimore: Johns Hopkins University Press, 1981), pp. 111–205. See also the following: D. M. Knight, "The Physical Sciences and the Romantic Movement," *History of Science* 9 (1970): 54–75; H.A.M. Snelders, "Romanticism and Naturphilosophie and the Inorganic Natural Sciences, 1798–1840. An

Introductory Survey," *Studies in Romanticism* 9 (1970): 193–215; Charles Culotta, "German Biophysics, Objective Knowledge and Romanticism," *Historical Studies in the Physical Sciences* 4 (1975): 3–38; Elke Hahn, "The Philosophy of Living Things: Schelling's Naturphilosophie as a Transition to the Philosophy of Identity," in Woodward and Cohen, *World Views and Scientific Discipline Formation* pp. 339–50; L. H. LeRoy, "Johann Christian Reil and Naturphilosophie in Physiologie" (Ph.D. diss., University of California, Los Angeles, 1985); Helmut Müller-Sievers, "Epigenesis: Wilhelm von Humbolt und die Naturphilosophie" (Ph.D. diss., Stanford University, 1990); and Gunther B. Risse, "Kant, Schelling and the Early Search for a Philosophical Science of Medicine in Germany," *Journal for the History of Medicine and Allied Sciences* 27 (1972): 145–58. Two useful essays on Naturphilosophie appear in the volume edited by G. S. Rousseau and Roy Porter, *The Ferment of Knowledge: Studies in the Historiography of Eighteenth-Century Science* (Cambridge: Cambridge University Press, 1980): Simon Schaffer, "Natural Philosophy" (pp. 55–91), and J. L. Heilbron, "Experimental Natural Philosophy" (pp. 357–87). The best collection of essays on Naturphilosophie, however, can be found in Herbert Hörz, Rolf Löther, and Siegfried Wollgast, ed., *Naturphilosophie von der Spekulation zur Wissenschaft* (Berlin: Akademie Verlag, 1969).

4. Richard Owen, *On the Archetype and Homologies of the Vertebrate Skeleton* (London: Voorst, 1848). Jung of course later uses it for his own morphology of transcendental Platonic ideas in the human psyche, his own historical taxonomy of human experience, in his theory of dominants (1917) or archetypes (1919).

5. Dieter Oldenburg, *Romantische Naturphilosophie und Arzneimittellehre* (Brunswick, West Germany: Technische Universität Braunschweig, 1979); Frederick Gregory, "Regulative Therapeutics in the German Romantic Era: The Contribution of Jakob Friedrich Fries (1773–1843)," *Clio Medica* 18 (1983): 184–201. Also useful is W. F. Bynum, "Health, Disease and Medical Care," in Rousseau and Porter, *The Ferment of Knowledge*, pp. 211–53.

6. See Paul Lawrence Farber, "The Type-Concept in Zoology during the First Half of the Nineteenth Century," *Journal of the History of Biology* 9 (1976): 110; also Lenoir, "The Göttingen School," pp. 111–205.

7. Timothy Lenoir, *The Strategy of Life: Teleology and Mechanics in Nineteenth-Century German Biology* (Chicago: University of Chicago Press, 1982), p. 69.

8. See Ellenberger, *The Discovery of the Unconscious* pp. 204–7.

9. According to a 1954 statement by W. Leibbrand, " Jung's teachings in the field of psychology are not intelligible if they are not connected with Schelling" (cited in ibid., p. 204). Jung's posthumous *Bi-*

bliothek lists editions of the collected works of Schelling and Goethe among its holdings, as well as the works of Görres and Carus. Whereas the Naturphilosophen are amply represented, the works of the major scientific materialists are almost entirely absent from the shelves of Jung's personal library.

10. *MDR*, pp. 89, 101.

11. C. G. Jung, *Mysterium Coniunctionis*, CW 14 (Princeton: Princeton University Press, 1970), para. 791.

12. See Frank Sulloway, *Freud: Biologist of the Mind: Beyond the Psychoanalytic Method* (New York: Basic Books, 1979), pp. 146–47; Iago Galdston, "Freud and Romantic Medicine," *Bulletin of the History of Medicine* 30 (1956): 489–507; Paul Cranefield, "Some Problems in Writing the History of Psychoanalysis," in George Mora and Jeanne Brand, ed., *Psychiatry and Its History: Methodological Problems in Research* (Springfield, Ill.: Charles Thomas, 1970), pp. 41–55.

13. See Sulloway, *Freud: Biologist of the Mind* pp. 14–28, 65–66; Paul Cranefield, "The Philosophical and Cultural Interests of the Biophysics Movement of 1847," *Journal of the History of Medicine and Allied Sciences* 21 (1966): 1–7; Paul Cranefield, "Freud and the 'School of Helmholtz,'" *Gesnerus* (1966) 23: 35–39.

14. The research program of the "teleomechanists" is identified and described in Lenoir, *The Strategy of Life*. However, it must be noted that not all scholars agree with Lenoir's thesis that a separate school of "teleomechanists" existed along with vitalistic Naturphilosophie and reductionistic materialism. See the criticisms in a review of Lenoir's book by K. Caneva, "Teleology with Regrets," *Annals of Science* 47 (1990): 291–300.

15. See Frederick Gregory, *Scientific Materialism in Nineteenth-Century Germany* (Dordrecht: D. Reidel, 1977). In line with Jung's lifelong allegiance with the vitalists and the Naturphilosophen, in a 9 June 1934 letter to his disciple Gerhard Adler Jung says that Freud's "materialistic, rationalistic view of the world" is due to the fact "he is simply a typical exponent of the expiring 19th century, just like Haeckel, Dubois-Reymond, or that Kraft und Stoff ass Büchner." See Jung, *Letters: 1. 1906–1950*, p. 164.

16. Useful historical reviews of evolutionary biology are Mayr, *The Growth of Biological Thought*; Ernst Mayr, *Charles Darwin and the Genesis of Modern Evolutionary Thought* (Cambridge, Mass.: Harvard University Press, 1991); Robert Richards, *Darwin and the Emergence of Evolutionary Theories of Mind and Behavior* (Chicago: University of Chicago Press, 1987; Robert Richards, *The Meaning of Evolution: Morphological Construction and Ideological Reconstruction of Darwin's Theory* (Chicago: University of Chicago Press, 1992); and Peter Bowler, *Evolution: The His-*

tory of an Idea (Berkeley and Los Angeles: University of California Press, 1984). Also of value are the contributions to Evelyn Fox Keller and Elisabeth Lloyd, ed., *Keywords in Evolutionary Biology* (Cambridge, Mass.: Harvard University Press, 1992).

17. John Kerr, *A Most Dangerous Method: The Story of Jung, Freud and Sabina Spielrein* (New York: Alfred Knopf, 1993).

18. On the influence of nineteenth-century concepts of genius on the Nietzsche-Wagner relationship, and on Nietzsche's development as an intellectual, see Pletsch, *Young Nietzsche*.

19. Josef Breuer and Sigmund Freud, *Studien über Hysterie* (Leipzig and Vienna: Deuticke, 1895); English edition: *Studies On Hysteria*, trans. James Strachey (New York: Basic Books, 1975).

20. Stanley Rothman and Philip Isenberg, "Sigmund Freud and the Politics of Marginality," *Central European History* 7 (1974): 58–78. This same Viennese milieu, with its additional völkisch elements of Teutonic occultism and Pan-Germanism, also forged the psyche of a young and destitute Adolf Hitler, who lived there from 1906 to 1911, the years of first significant fame for Freud and psychoanalysis. "Vienna, the city so widely considered the very essence of innocent gaiety, the festive home of happy crowds, is to me, unfortunately, but a living reminder of the saddest period in my life. . . . But more than this, I formed at this time an image and a concept of the world which have become the rock-ribbed foundation of my present activity. I have had but to learn a little beyond what I then created; there was nothing I had to change." Adolf Hitler, *Mein Kampf* (New York: Stackpole Sons, 1939), 1: 35. The original German edition appeared separately in two volumes, in 1925 and in 1927.

21. See Kerr, *A Most Dangerous Method*.

22. On the nineteenth-century controversy over Jewish ethnicity as degeneracy, see S. Almog, "Judaism as Illness," *History of European Ideas* 13 (1991): 793–804.

23. Sander Gilman, "Sexology, Psychoanalysis and Degeneration: From a Theory of Race to a Race to Theory," in Chamberlin and Gilman, *Degeneration: The Dark Side of Progress*, p. 89. Gilman's article is the single best exploration of Freud's transformation of nineteenth-century medical theories of hereditary degeneration. Freud's rejection of hereditary degeneration theory was noted, but not fully explored, in Sulloway's exemplary work, *Freud, Biologist of the Mind* pp. 289–97, 423.

24. Kerr, *A Most Dangerous Method*.

25. Frank Sulloway, "Reassessing Freud's Case Histories: The Social Construction of Psychoanalysis," in Toby Gelfand and John Kerr, ed., *Freud and the History of Psychoanalysis* (Hillsdale, N.J.: The Analytic

Press, 1992), pp. 154, 180. See also G. Weisz, "Scientists and Sectarians: The Case of Psychoanalysis," *Journal of the History of the Behavioral Sciences* 11 (1975): 350–64. The work of Sulloway, Jeffrey Masson, and Peter Swales in the 1970s and 1980s may be credited for sparking the diminution of charisma from Freud as evidenced by the following: Frederick Crews, "The Unknown Freud," *The New York Review of Books* 40 (19), 18 November 1993; and especially the cover story of the 29 November 1993 issue of *Time* ("Is Freud Dead?") by Paul Gray, "The Assault on Freud," pp. 47–51. For a sociological discussion of "Freudian psychotherapy" as a "client cult," see Rodney Stark and William Bainbridge, "Who Joins Cult Movements?" in R. Stark and W. Bainbridge, eds., *The Future of Religion: Secularization, Revival, and Cult Formation* (Berkeley and Los Angeles: University of California Press, 1985), pp. 394–424.

26. See Georg Lukács, "Vitalism (*Lebensphilosophie*) in Imperialist Germany," which comprises chapter 4 of his *Destruction of Reason*, pp.403–546.

27. The charismatic nature of Freudism is observed by Weber in a 13 September 1907 letter to Else Jaffe. Excerpts can be found in Marianne Weber, *Max Weber: A Biography*, trans. Harry Zorn (New Brunswick: Transaction Books, 1988), p. 379. The sociological phenomenon of groups like Freud's and similar "aesthetic sects"—such as that centered on poet Stefan George—were Weber's living models of charismatic cults or sects that had the potential to "routinize" and form quasi-religious institutions. In a talk given at the very first meeting of the Society of German Sociologists in 1910 he cited George and his fanatic circle in this connection. For the text of Weber's brief remarks on the charismatic group of the *George-Kreis*, see Max Weber, "Geschäftsbericht und Diskussionsreden auf den deutschen soziologischen Tagungen," (1910, 1912) in *Gesammelte Aufsätze zur Soziologie und Sozialpolitik* (Tübingen: Verlag von J.C.B. Mohr [Paul Siebeck], 1924), pp. 446, 453. Weber had his initial personal encounter with George in August 1910 and, impressed with the eccentric poet, maintained a fruitful personal relationship with him until June 1912. On the Weber-George relationship, and Weber's public defense of the *George-Kreis*, see Arthur Mitzman, *The Iron Cage: An Historical Interpretation of Max Weber* (New York: Alfred Knopf, 1970), pp. 262–71.

28. The Clark Conference is exhaustively covered in the useful, but somewhat eccentric, volume by Saul Rosenzweig, *Freud, Jung and Hall the King-Maker: The Expedition to America (1909)* (Seattle: Hogrefe & Huber, 1992).

29. Robert S. Woodworth, letter to the editor, *The Nation* 103 (1916): 396.

30. Knight Dunlap, *Mysticism, Freudianism, and Scientific Psychology* (St Louis, Mo.: Mosby, 1920), p. 8.

31. An excellent review of the rejection of psychoanalysis on these grounds in the United States is found in Gail Hornstein, "The Return of the Repressed: Psychology's Problematic Relations with Psychoanalysis, 1909–1960," *American Psychologist* 47 (1992): 254–63.

32. William Montgomery, "Germany," in Thomas Glick, ed., *The Comparative Reception of Darwinism* (Austin: University of Texas Press, 1974), p. 107.

33. Ernst Haeckel, *Natürliche Schöpfungsgeschichte* (Berlin: G. Reimer, 1868), pp. 5, 93. His view on the struggle for the "survival of the fittest" in human society also appear in this book. See Weikart, "The Origins of Social Darwinism in Germany," pp. 469–88.

34. Mayr, *The Growth of Biological Thought* p. 70.

35. Cited in the exemplary paper by Niles Holt, "Ernst Haeckel's Monistic Religion," *Journal of the History of Ideas* 32 (1971): 270.

36. Haeckel's explicit call for a revolutionary *Kulturkampf* through a monistic religion comes in his chapter, "Our Monistic Religion," in this famous book, which sold more than 300,000 copies in Germany alone by Haeckel's death in 1919. For a review of the many twists and turns in the development of monistic religion, see ibid.

37. See especially Ernst Haeckel, *Kunstformen der Natur: 100 Illustrationstafeln mit beschreibendem Text* (Leipzig: Verlag der Bibliographischen Instituts, 1899–1904). On the "evolutionary aesthetics" movement inspired by Haeckel, see C. Kockerbeck, *Ernst Haeckel's 'Kunstformen der Natur' und ihr Einfluss auf die deutsche bildene Kunst der Jahrhundertwende* (Frankfurt, 1986), and Kurt Bayertz, "Biology and Beauty: Science and Aesthetics in *Fin-de-Siècle* Germany," in Teich and Porter, *Fin de Siècle and Its Legacy*, pp. 278–95.

38. A poster announcing performances by Haeckel in Berlin in April 1905 is reproduced between pp. 8 and 9 in the exemplary volume by Daniel Gasman, *The Scientific Origins of National Socialism: Social Darwinism in Ernst Haeckel and the German Monistic League* (London: Macdonald, 1971), which is the best book on Haeckel in English. An image on the poster shows a lecture hall with skeletons and all of Haeckel's nature drawings prominently displayed in what Gasman refers to as "a sinister environment for a Darwinian Passion Play." Compare Jung's dream with the images in Ernst Haeckel, *Die Radiolarien (Rhizopoda radiaria): Eine Monograph*, 2 vols. (Berlin: G. Reimer, 1862). The illustrations from these technical works of Haeckel found their way into innumerable popular magazines and other readily accessible publications. They may have appeared in the books or the "scientific periodical" Jung "read with a passionate interest" when an ado-

lescent and which his parents paid for him to receive (see *MDR*, pp. 83–85).

39. Ernst Haeckel, *The Riddle of the Universe at the Close of the Nineteenth Century*, trans. Joseph McCabe (New York and London: Harper & Brothers, 1900), p. 382.

40. Montgomery, "Germany," p. 85.

41. Duncan read the English translation of *The Riddle of the Universe* and other works by Haeckel, and after reading the press reports of Haeckel's seventieth birthday in February 1904 sent him a letter of congratulations in which she told him, "Your works had brought me also religion and understanding, which count for more than life." A correspondence between Duncan and Haeckel ensued, and while performing at Bayreuth she held a dinner party in his honor and sat with him in the Wagner family box at the Festspielhaus through a performance of *Parsifal*, which Duncan said did not appeal to Haeckel because "his mind was too purely scientific to admit the fascination of a legend." This story is cited in Victor Seroff, *The Real Isadora* (New York: Dial Press, 1971), pp. 66–67. See also the earlier biography by Allan Ross Macdougall, *Isadora, a Revolutionary in Art and Love* (New York: Thomas, 1960), pp. 90, 92, 132, 258.

42. Steiner and Haeckel corresponded in the 1890s and recognized a common bond in their philosophical work. This was prior to Steiner's break with the Theosophical movement. Gasman says, "Haeckel, however, eventually dissociated himself from Steiner, fearing the idealistic implications of the word, theosophy" (*The Scientific Origins of National Socialism*, p. 79). See Johannes Hemleben, *Rudolph Steiner und Ernst Haeckel* (Stuttgart: Verlag Freies Geistesleben, 1965); also, Rudolph Steiner, *Haeckel, die Welträtsel, und die Theosophie* (Dornach, Switzerland: Philosophisch-Anthropologischer Verlag, 1926).

43. Forel is open about his participation in the Monistic movement, and his rejection of its support of German imperialism during the First World War in his autobiography *Out of My Life and Work* (New York: Norton, 1937).

44. In *The Discovery of the Unconscious*, Ellenberger does not mention Forel's advocacy of eugenics, Social Darwinism, or the monistic religion, although his great achievements as director of the Burghölzli and in psychiatric treatment are deservedly lauded (see, e.g., pp. 285–86). Forel's lifelong passion was not psychiatry, but ants; he was an internationally recognized expert on their biology and behavior. His observations of ants and the results of his eugenics experiments with them led to analogies with human society and suggestions for its improvement. In his epilogue to his two-volume magnum opus, *The Social World of Ants*, trans. C. K. Ogden (New York: Albert & Charles Boni,

1930; original English edition, 1928), Forel outlines his utopian vision. "We may hope that the eugenics of the future, if well applied, will even be able to improve by small degrees the quality of our higher races" (2:350), he writes, and, to accomplish this, advocates the establishment of a "scientific religion of man's well-being" that "must be the religion of the future" and "must be free from doctrine and metaphysics, uniting all that is truly good and purely human in the ancient religions" (2:351). Neither Haeckel nor the monistic religion are mentioned by name here, but Forel's ideas clearly reflect these influences. Forel's remarks demonstrate how tempting it was for psychiatric authorities at the turn of the century to use their influence to advocate avenues of Lebensreform for society as a whole, including proposals for new religions.

45. For more on Ostwald, and his prominent role in promoting eugenics and Social Darwinism in Germany, both later incorporated into Nazi culture, see Gasman, *The Scientific Origins of National Socialism*. Jung's personal library contains several volumes by Ostwald from this Monistenbund period: *Grosse Männer* (1910), *Modernenaturphilosophie. 1. Die Ordnungswissenschaften* (1914), and *Die Philosophie der Werte* (1913). See *C. G. Jung Bibliothek: Katalog* (Küsnacht-Zurich, 1967), pp. 55–56.

46. See the interesting interview with Ostwald and the background details of his life in Edwin E. Slosson, *Major Prophets of To-Day* (Boston: Little, Brown, 1914), pp. 190–241. Slosson even includes a very useful bibliographic section on "How to Read Ostwald" (pp. 238–41). Other modern "prophets" of the prewar era interviewed and profiled by Slosson, the literary editor of *The Independent*, include Maurice Maeterlinck, Bergson, Henri Poincaré, Élie Metchnikoff, and Haeckel.

47. C. G. Jung, "A Contribution to the Study of Psychological Types" (1913), *Psychological Types*, CW 6 (Princeton: Princeton University Press, 1971), para. 870.

48. Ibid., chapter 9.

49. Ibid., para. 699. This appears in the "Definitions" section at the end of *Psychological Types* under the entry for "concretism."

50. Jung mentions the *Annalen der Naturphilosophie*, which was a place for prominent members of the scientific community to publish their own speculative philosophies, in a lecture given in December 1922 to the students of Zurich University but published years later: "The Love Problem of a Student" (1928), *Civilization in Transition*, para. 214. Ostwald's theory of energetics is clearly a reference point in his "On Psychic Energy" (1928), *Structure of Dynamics of the Psyche* where Ostwald and his theory are briefly dismissed in two early footnotes.

51. See the chapter on "Monism and Marxism" in Gasman, *The Sci-*

entific Origins of National Socialism, pp. 106–25. For a sampling of the East German literature on the cross-correspondences between monism and Marxism, and a brief discussion of early German communists who were also monists, see the following: Hermann Ley, "Der Deutsche Monistenbund—zur Aktualität seiner Aufgaben und Ziele," in Uwe Niedersen, ed., *Komplexität-Zeit-Methode (I): Komplexitätsbewältigung— eine Einführung* (Halle-Wittenberg, DDR: Martin-Luther-Universität, 1986), pp. 179–94; E. Teumer, "Aus dem Kampf des 'Deutschen Monistenbundes' um eine wissenschaftliche Weltanschauung," in H. Hörz, R. Löther and S. Wollgast, ed., *Naturphilosophie—von der Spekulation zur Wissenschaft* (Berlin, DDR: 1969); Reinhard Mocek, "Two Faces of Biologism: Some Reflections on a Difficult Period in the History of Biology in Germany," in Woodward and Cohen, *World Views and Scientific Discipline Formation*, pp. 279–91.

52. I am indebted to Peter Swales for this information about the Haeckel Museum in Jena and for directing my attention to the importance of Haeckel for understanding Fliess and Freud.

53. *MDR*, pp. 100–101.

54. Haeckel, *The Riddle of the Universe* pp. 148–49.

55. See C. G. Jung, *The Psychology of the Unconscious: A Study of the Transformation and Symbolisms of the Libido*, CW B, (Princeton: Princeton University Press, 1991), paras. 36, 43.

56. Ibid., para. 36.

57. Ibid., para. 43.

58. Ibid., para. 51.

59. See Bernice Glatzer Rosenthal, "Wagner and Wagnerian Ideas in Russia," in David Large and William Weber, ed., *Wagnerism in European Culture and Politics* (Ithaca: Cornell University Press, 1984), pp. 198–245.

60. On the Marxist god-building movement," see George Kline, "The God-Builders: Gorky and Lunacharsky," chap. 4 in his *Religious and Anti-Religious Thought in Russia* (Chicago: University of Chicago Press, 1975); and Leszek Kolakowski, *Main Currents of Marxism. Volume 2: The Golden Age*, trans. P. S. Falla (Oxford: Oxford University Press, 1985), pp. 446–47.

61. Nina Tumarkin, *Lenin Lives! The Lenin Cult in Soviet Russia* (Cambridge, Mass.: Harvard University Press, 1983). The quote from the 1913 letter of Lenin is reproduced on p. 22 of Tumarkin's book. For an account of the gradual demise of the Lenin cult in Russia, and a return to the reverence of ancestors, see Nina Tumarkin, "Myth and Memory in Soviet Society," *Society* 24 (1987): 69–72. Nietzschean god-building and Carlylian hero worship were very much a part of communism and fascism: Jeremy Paltiel, "The Cult of Personality: Some

NOTES TO CHAPTER FOUR

Comparative Reflections on Political Culture in Leninist Regimes," *Studies in Comparative Communism* 16 (1983): 49–64; Graham Gill, "Personality Cult, Political Culture and Party Structure," *Studies in Comparative Communism* 17 (1984): 111–21; and Romke Visser, "Fascist Doctrine and the Cult of the Romanita," *Journal of Contemporary History* 27 (1992): 5–22.

62. Nietzsche, "Also Sprach Zarathustra: Third Part," in *The Portable Nietzsche*, p. 315.

63. Struve, *Elites Against Democracy*. Rather than review the vast literature on elites theory (such as Pareto's, etc.), I refer the reader to the first chapter of Struve's book and to its bibliographical essay, which contain extensive references to both the English and German literatures.

64. Ibid. pp. 41–45.

65. Jung, "Introduction to Toni Wolff's 'Studies in Jungian Psychology,'" *Civilization in Transition*, para 887. This "silent experiment" was the Psychological Club—the germ-cell of Jung's movement.

CHAPTER FOUR

1. For a colorful description of these völkisch examples of politics conducted in "a sharper key," see Carl Schorske, *Fin-de-Siècle Vienna: Politics and Culture* (New York: Alfred Knopf, 1980), pp. 116–80. For a brief critique of the historical work of Schorske and others on fin-de-siècle Vienna and Austria-Hungary, see M. P. Steinberg, "'Fin de Siècle Vienna Ten Years Later: Viel Traum, Wenig Wirklichkeit," *Austrian History Yearbook* 22 (1991): 151–62. On the intellectual sources of German Jews in the nineteenth-century see George Mosse, *German Jews Beyond Judaism* (Bloomington: Indiana University Press, 1985).

2. See George Drinka, *The Birth of Neurosis: Myth, Malady and the Victorians* (New York: Simon and Schuster, 1984).

3. This sociological hypothesis has also been put forth to explain the preponderance of female mediums or "wise women" in possession and trance-type religious practices in traditional societies that are otherwise male-dominated. See I. M. Lewis, *Ecstatic Religions: An Anthropological Study of Spirit Possession and Shamanism* (Middlesex: Penguin, 1971).

4. Pierre Chuvin, *A Chronicle of the Last Pagans*, p. 16.

5. Roman pagans burned their corpses, which were considered unclean, and were horrified at the Christian practice of saving body parts and (through pagan eyes) defiling sacred sites by keeping such relics on or near altars. See Peter Brown, *The Cult of the Saints: Its Rise and Function in Latin Christianity* (Chicago: University of Chicago Press,

1981). During the European Middle Ages, monasteries and other Christian orders would have an envied or ridiculed social status depending on the nature and source of their relics (i.e., the more noted or powerful a saint, the more supernatural power accrued in that Christian community). Thus, it has been documented that Indiana Jones–like raids by monks from one monastery to steal the relics of another took place and resulted in the passage of ecclesiastical codes to ban such theft. See Patric Geary, *Furta Sacra: Thefts of Relics in the Central Middle Ages* (Princeton: Princeton University Press, 1990).

6. Ross Shepard Kraemer, *Her Share of the Blessings: Women's Religions Among Pagans, Jews, and Christians in the Greco-Roman World* (New York: Oxford University Press, 1992), p. 174.

7. Emile Durkheim, *The Elementary Forms of the Religious Life*, trans. Joseph Ward Swain (London: George Allen and Unwin, 1915), p. 61.

8. Mircea Eliade, "The Occult and the Modern World," (1974) in *Occultism, Witchcraft and Cultural Fashions* (Chicago: University of Chicago Press, 1976), pp. 64–65. The scholarly opinion on Christianity's rejection of pagan mysteries–type "secret initiations" is reviewed in Mircea Eliade, *Rites and Symbols of Initiation: The Mysteries of Birth and Rebirth* (New York: Harper Colophon, 1958), pp. 115–38. See also Nock, "Hellenistic Mysteries and Christian Sacraments," 2:791–820.

9. Erika Bourguignon, *Possession* (San Francisco: Chandler and Sharp, 1976).

10. For spiritualistic traditions in pagan antiquity, see the following: E. R. Dodds, "Supernormal Phenomena in Classical Antiquity," *Proceedings of the Society for Psychical Research* 55 (1971): 189–237; E. R. Dodds, *The Greeks and the Irrational* (Berkeley and Los Angeles: University of California Press, 1951); John Pollard, *Seers, Shrines, and Sirens: The Greek Religious Revolution in the Sixth Century B.C.* (New York: A. S. Barnes, 1965); Joseph Fontenrose, *Python: A Study of Delphic Myth and its Origins* (Berkeley and Los Angeles: University of California Press, 1959); H. W. Parke, *Sybils and Sibylline Prophecy in Classical Antiquity*, edited by B. C. McGing (London: Routledge, 1988); and H. W. Parke and D.E.W. Wormell, *The Delphic Oracle*, 2 vols. (Oxford: Basil Blackwell, 1956).

11. Morton Smith, *Jesus the Magician* (San Francisco: Harper & Row, 1978). A brief (and unconvincing) critique of Smith's hypothesis can be found in Kee, *Medicine, Miracle and Magic* pp. 112–14.

12. See David Aune, *Prophecy in Early Christianity and the Ancient Mediterranean World* (Grand Rapids, Mich.: William B. Eerdmanns, 1983).

13. See James Webb, *The Occult Underground* (La Salle, Ill.: Open

Court, 1974), and his scholarly companion volume, *The Occult Establishment* (La Salle, Ill.: Open Court, 1976).

14. This was not as true in many Roman Catholic countries, especially Spain, where inquisitions in 1808 and 1815 forced many to flee to more tolerant Catholic countries, such as France.

15. Sydney Ahlstrom, *A Religious History of the American People* (New Haven: Yale University Press, 1972).

16. Emma Hardinge, *Modern American Spiritualism; or, A Twenty Years Record of the Communion Between Earth and the World of Spirits, From 1848 to 1868* (New Hyde Park, N.Y.: University Books, 1970). This is a modern reprint of the first edition of 1869. An excellent contemporary historical narrative can be found in Ruth Brandon, *The Spiritualists: The Passion for the Occult in the Nineteenth and Twentieth Centuries* (New York: Alfred Knopf, 1983).

17. See James, *The Works of William James*. His final assessment of spiritualism and psychical research, published in the year before his death and included in this volume, especially rewards consulting: "The Confidences of a 'Psychical Researcher'" (1909). See especially Eugene Taylor, *William James on Exceptional Mental States: The 1896 Lowell Lectures* (New York: Scribner's, 1982).

18. Mesmeric circles waxed and waned in European and American cultures in the nineteenth century. Ultimately, the greatest cultural influence of Mesmerism came in the legitimization of hypnosis in late nineteenth century French psychiatry, which formed the basis of Jung's clinical training. Useful cultural histories of Mesmerism are: Robert Darnton, *Mesmerism and the End of the Enlightenment in France* (Cambridge, Mass.: Harvard University Press, 1968); Jean-Roch Laurence and Campbell Perry, *Hypnosis, Will & Memory: A Psycho-Legal History* (New York: Guilford, 1988); Robert Fuller, *Mesmerism and the American Cure of Souls* (Philadelphia: University of Pennsylvania Press, 1982): and Fuller's *Americans and the Unconscious* (New York: Oxford University Press, 1986).

19. John Symonds, *Madame Blavatsky, Medium and Magician* (London: Yoseloff, 1960); Geoffrey Barborka, *H. P. Blavatsky: Tibet and Tulku* (Adyar, India: Theosophical Society, 1966).

20. Annie Besant (1847–1933) was a remarkable woman in her own right. She played an early key role in the Indian nationalist movement against British rule and was jailed for a short while following her founding of the Home Rule for India League in 1916. See A. H. Nethercot, *The First Five Lives of Annie Besant* (Chicago: University of Chicago Press, 1960); and also A. H. Nethercot, *The Last Four Lives of Annie Besant* (Chicago: University of Chicago Press, 1963).

21. John Symonds, "Mme. Blavatsky," in Richard Cavendish, ed., *Man, Myth and Magic, Volume 2*. (New York: Marshall Cavendish Corporation, 1970), pp. 286–89.

22. Such was the case for the Paris daily, *Le Petit Journal*. Similar gigantic increases in circulation due to innovative technologies and a greater literacy among European and American populations could be found in London, Berlin, and New York newspapers. See Patrick Bratlinger, "Mass Media and Culture in *Fin-de-Siècle* Europe," in Teich and Porter, *Fin de Siècle and Its Legacy*, pp. 98–114.

23. The only historical work on the Theosophical movement at the turn of the century that is not written by a believer traces its influence among the occultist intelligentsia of Russia. See Maria Carlson, *"No Religion Higher than Truth": A History of the Theosophical Movement in Russia, 1875–1922* (Princeton: Princeton University Press, 1993).

24. See Martin Green, *Mountain of Truth: The Counterculture Begins: Ascona, 1900–1920* (Hanover: University Press of New England, 1986).

25. Jung, *Letters, Volume I*, p. 24.

26. Jung, "The Structure of the Unconscious" (1916), *Two Essays*, para. 494.

27. Nicholas Goodrick-Clarke, *The Occult Roots of Nazism: Secret Aryan Cults and Their Influence on Nazi Ideology* (New York: New York University Press, 1992), pp. 265–87.

28. According to the *C. G. Jung Bibliothek: Katalog*, pp. 49–50, these are as follows: *Apollonius of Tyana, the Philosopher-Reformer of the First Century A.D.* (1901); *The Chaldean Oracles*, 2 vols. (1908); *Did Jesus Live in 100 B.C.?* (1903); *The Doctrine of the Subtle Body in Western Tradition* (1919); *Fragments of a Faith Forgotten: Some Short Sketches Among the Gnostics Mainly of the First Two Centuries* (1906); *The Gnostic Crucifixion* (1907); *The Gnostic John the Baptizer* (1924); *The Hymn of Jesus* (1907); *The Hymn of the Robe of Glory* (1908); *A Mithraic Ritual* (1907); *Simon Magus, an Essay* (1892); *Some Mystical Adventures* (1910); *Pistis Sophia, a Gnostic Miscellany* (1921); *Thrice-Greatest Hermes*, 3 vols. (1906); *The Vision of Aridaeus* (1907); *The Wedding-Song of Wisdom* (1908); and *The World-Mystery* (1907). Most scholars who analyze the Gnostic elements in Jung's work ignore the materials that initially attracted Jung to Gnosticism—Mead's "occult" writings—and instead focus on mainstream academic scholars of Gnosticism (such as Gilles Quispel) who entered Jung's life much later. Despite his importance, Mead is not even mentioned, for example, in Robert Segal, *The Gnostic Jung* (Princeton: Princeton University Press, 1992). Also on Jung's shelves were the following works of major Theosophists, some perhaps purchased during Jung's student years: by H. P. Blavatsky: *The Secret Doctrine*, 2 vols. (1893, 1897); *Höllen Träume* (1908); and *The Theosophical Glossary* (1930);

by C. W. Leadbeater: *Die Astral-Ebene* (1903); and *Die Devachan-Ebene: Ihre Charakteristik und ihre Bewohner* (n.d.).

29. This is how Mead describes this series, which he edited:

ECHOES FROM THE GNOSIS

Under this general title is now being published a series of small volumes, drawn from, or based upon, the mystic, theosophic and gnostic writings of the ancients, so as to make more easily audible for the ever-widening circle of those who love such things, some echoes of the mystic experiences and initiatory lore of their spiritual ancestry. There are many who love the life of the spirit, and who long for the light of gnostic illumination, but who are not sufficiently equipped to study the writings of the ancients first hand, or to follow unaided the labours of scholars. These little volumes are therefore intended to serve as introduction to the study of the more difficult literature of the subject; and it is hoped that at the same time they may become for some, who have, as yet, not even heard of the Gnosis, stepping-stones to higher things.

Mead, *A Mithraic Ritual*, 1907), p. 6.

30. Ulrich Müller, "Wagner and Antiquity," in U. Müller and Peter Wapnewski, ed., *Wagner Handbook*, trans. John Deathridge (Cambridge, Mass.: Harvard University Press, 1992), pp. 227–35.

31. Richard Wagner, *Sämtliche Schriften und Dichtungen*, 16 vols. (Leipzig: 1911–1913). The first ten volumes were originally published under Wagner's supervision in Leipzig between 1871 and 1883. An incomplete English translation by William Ashton Ellis is the eight-volume *Richard Wagner's Prose Works* (London: 1892–1899; reissued 1972). An unparalled summary is Jürgen Kühnel, "The Prose Writings," in Müller and Wapnewski, *Wagner Handbook*.

32. The best source are the superb literature reviews in Müller and Wapnewski, *Wagner Handbook*.

33. See. e.g., Jacques Barzun, *Darwin, Marx, Wagner: Critique of a Heritage*, 2d ed. (New York: Vantage, 1958).

34. Cited in Léon Poliakov, *The Aryan Myth: A History of Racist and Nationalist Ideas in Europe*, trans. Edmund Howard (New York: Basic Books, 1974), p. 313.

35. Mark Twain, *What Is Man? And Other Essays* (Ann Arbor, Mich.: University of Michigan Press, 1972), pp. 226–27.

36. George Bernard Shaw, *The Perfect Wagnerite*, 4th ed. (London: Constable, 1923), p. 3.

37. On Wagnerism, see especially the following: Erwin Koppen, "Wagnerism as Concept and Phenomenon," in Müller and Wapnewski, *Wagner Handbook*, pp. 343–53; Large and Weber, *Wagnerism in Eu-*

ropean Culture and Politics; and Anne Dzamba Sessa, *Richard Wagner and the English* (Rutherford, N.J.: Farleigh Dickinson University Press, 1979).

38. This is from an entry on 19 April 1878. Cosima Wagner, *Cosima Wagner's Diaries*, 2 vols. (New York: Harcourt Brace Jovanovich, 1977), 2:63.

39. His first visit to Bayreuth as führer is described in vivid detail in the memoirs of Siegfried Wagner's daughter. See Friedelind Wagner and Page Cooper, *Heritage of Fire: The Story of Richard Wagner's Granddaughter* (New York: Harper and Brothers, 1945), pp. 97–124.

40. Geoffrey Field, *Evangelist of Race: The Germanic Vision of Houston Stewart Chamberlain* (New York: Columbia University Press, 1981), p. 444.

41. Aldo Carotenuto, *A Secret Symmetry: Sabina Spielrein Between Jung and Freud* (New York: Pantheon, 1982).

42. Trigant Burrow, *A Search for Man's Sanity: The Selected Letters of Trigant Burrow* (New York: Oxford University Press, 1958), pp. 25, 27.

43. Laurens van der Post, *Jung and the Story of Our Time* (New York: Random House, 1976), p. 67. Despite this testimony by van der Post—and the evidence from others who knew Jung earlier in life—Wagner is conspicuously absent from the list of Jung's musical "favorites" given by Jaffé in an essay of fond reminiscences concerning her experiences with Jung. Bach, Handel, Mozart, "pre-Mozartians," and "Negro spirituals" were all mentioned by Jaffé as Jung's preferred tastes in music. This is oddly conflictual with van der Post's statement since they both knew Jung during the same period, and as such this may be yet another indication of how Jung's disciples have taken it upon themselves to wash away any potential taint of Nazism from Jung's image. See Aniela Jaffé, "From Jung's Last Years," in *From the Life and Work of C. G. Jung*, trans. R.F.C. Hull (New York: Harper Colophon, 1971), p. 116. Original German edition: *Aus Leben und Werkstatt von C. G. Jung: Parapsychologie, Alchemie, Nationalsozialismus, Erinnerungen aus den Letzten Jahren* (Zurich: Rascher & Cie, 1968).

44. This is an often-analyzed dream that appears time and again in the secondary Jungian literature. Jung's first public report of this dream was during his 1925 seminar on analytical psychology. See Jung, *Analytical Psychology*, pp. 48, 56–57, 61–62. Jaffé used the transcript of this 1925 seminar to construct the chapter "Confrontation with the Unconscious" in *MDR*, which also mentions this dream, but with many details left out.

45. Jung, *The Psychology of the Unconscious*, pp. 335–36. In his 1952 rewrite of this book, Jung expands this discussion and attempts to ground Wagnerian mythology into his archetypal theory (see C. G.

Jung, *Symbols of Transformation*, CW 5 (Princeton: Princeton University Press, 1967), paras. 357–569.

46. Cartotenuto, *A Secret Symmetry*, p. 86.

CHAPTER FIVE

1. "Zu stark is die Fixierung der Historiker auf den griechisch-römischen Raum als die eigentliche Kulturwelt." Ekkehard Hieronimus, "Von der Germanen-Forschung zum Germanen-Glauben. Zur Religionsgeschichte des Präfaschismus," in Richard Farber and Renate Schlesier, ed., *Die Restauration der Götter: Antike Religion und neo-Paganismus* (Würzburg, Germany: Königshausen and Neumann, 1986), p. 242.

2. Hermand, *Old Dreams of a New Reich*, p. 7. On völkisch pietism, see Koppel Pinson, *Pietism as a Factor in the Rise of German Nationalism* (New York: Columbia University Press, 1934).

3. Ibid.

4. Translated into English by Beatrice M. Hinkle, and published under the title *The Psychology of the Unconscious: A Study of the Transformations and Symbolisms of the Libido*. In 1991 this translation was republished as CW B.

5. Ernest Jones, *The Life and Work of Sigmund Freud. Volume 1: The Formative Years and the Great Discoveries, 1856–1900* (New York: Basic Books, 1953), p. 22.

6. Nicholas Goodrick-Clarke, "The Modern Occult Revival in Vienna 1880–1910," *Durham Univerisity Journal* 49 (1987): 63–68.

7. Ibid., p. 67.

8. Jost Hermand, "The Distorted Vision: Pre-Fascist Mythology at the Turn of the Century," in Walter Wetzels, ed., *Myth and Reason: A Symposium* (Austin: University of Texas Press, 1973), p. 111.

9. See, for example, the extensive bibliography of such material in Goodrick-Clarke, *The Occult Roots of Nazism*, pp. 265–87.

10. On these aspects see, especially, George Mosse, *Nationalism and Sexuality: Middle-Class Morality and Sexual Norms in Modern Europe* (Madison, Wisc.: University of Wisconsin Press, 1985).

11. A völkisch publication from 1913 contains a statement by Heinrich Driesmans that unites a racially sanitized "eugenetic" Christ with "Siegfried the sun-hero" and "Parsifal the grail-seeker." See Hermand, "The Distorted Vision," p. 123. Völkisch proponents uncomfortable with abandoning Christianity often sought syncretism through Parsifal-like grail symbolism.

12. George Mosse, "The Mystical Origins of National Socialism," *Journal of the History of Ideas* 21 (1961): 84. The most comprehensive

information in English on List can be found in Goodrick-Clarke, *The Occult Roots of Nazism*. For more on List see: Mosse, *The Crisis of German Ideology*; Goodrick-Clarke, "The Modern Occult Revival in Vienna," and Hieronimus, "Von der Germanen-Forschung zum Germanen-Glauben," pp. 254–56. The only biography of List is Joseph Baltzli, *Guido von List: Der Wiederentdecker Uralter Arischer Weisheit. Sein Leben und sein Schaffen* (Vienna: Guido von List Bücherei, 1917).

13. Fritz Stern, *The Politics of Cultural Despair: A Study in the Rise of the Germanic Ideology* (Berkeley and Los Angeles: University of California Press, 1961), p. 50. Stern summarizes Lagarde's plan for a new "Germanic Religion" on pp. 35–52.

14. Paul Branwell Means, *Things That Are Caesar's: The Genesis of the German Church Conflict* (New York: Round Table Press, 1935), p. 166.

15. On Indo-European horse sacrifices, see Jaan Puhvel, "Aspects of Equine Functionality," in Jaan Puhvel, ed., *Myth and Law Among the Indo-Europeans* (Berkeley and Los Angeles: University of California Press, 1970), pp. 159–72; also, Jaan Puhvel, "Victimal Hierarchies in Indo-European Animal Sacrifice," *American Journal of Philology* 99 (1978): 354–62.

16. For background on the neopagan movement at the turn of the century, an excellent source is Faber and Schlesier, *Restauration der Götter*. For a recent documentation of European solar worship, see the well-illustrated volume by Miranda Green, *The Sun-Gods of Ancient Europe* (London: Hippocrene Books, 1991).

17. Members of the neo-Nazi movement in the Germany of the 1990s continue to celebrate the summer solstice as well as the birthday of Hitler. See Craig Whitney, "Germans Begin to Recognize Danger in Neo-Nazi Upsurge," *The New York Times*, 21 October 1993, p. A10. Also, J. F. Pilat, "Euroright Extremism," *The Wiener Library Bulletin* 34 (1981): 48–64. See also the section on Norse paganism in J. Gordon Melton and Isotta Poggi, *Magic, Witchcraft and Paganism in America: A Bibliography*, 2d ed. (New York: Garland, 1992), pp. 233–36. Also, the article by one of the leading proponents of Norse neopaganism (who published an English translation of List's book, *The Secret of the Runes* in 1988): Stephen Flowers, "Revival of Germanic Religion in Contemporary Anglo-American Culture," *Mankind Quarterly* 21 (1981): 279–94.

18. Johann Wolfgang von Goethe, *Gespräche*, 5 vols. (Leipzig: 1909), 4:441–42. The translation appears in Karl Löwitz, *From Hegel to Nietzsche*, pp. 24–25.

19. On Müller's life, see the biographies by Nirad Chaudhuri, *Scholar Extraordinary: The Life of Professor the Rt. Hon. Freidrich Max*

Müller (New York: Oxford University Press, 1974), and by Johannes Voigt, *Max Müller: The Man and His Ideas* (Calcutta: K. L. Mukhopadhyay, 1967). Also useful is the posthumous collection by his wife, Georgina Müller, *The Life and Letters of the Rt. Honorable Friedrich Max Müller* (London: Longmans, Green & Co., 1902).

20. See the historical review by Mircea Eliade, "The 'History of Religion' as a Branch of Knowledge," which is the last chapter in his *The Sacred and the Profane: The Nature of Religion* (New York: Harcourt, Brace & World, 1959).

21. This accolade came from no less a figure than Sir Edward Evans-Pritchard. His fascination with pagan solar myths caused anxiety in some of his staid Oxfordian colleagues who were bourgeois Christians. As Evans-Pritchard tells it, "He was a staunch Protestant ('the Protestants are better Christians than the Romans') and a devout one, but one of the reasons he was not elected to the Chair of Sanskrit at Oxford in 1860 was that it was said his teaching was subversive of the Christian faith—'unsettling.' Furthermore, he was a German." Sir Edward Evans-Pritchard, *A History of Anthropological Thought* (New York: Basic Books, 1981), p. 185.

22. The best single introduction to the debate over the solar mythologists is Richard Dorson, "The Eclipse of Solar Mythology," in Thomas Sebeok, ed., *Myth: A Symposium* (Bloomington: Indiana University Press, 1958), pp. 25–63.

23. Max Müller, *Lectures on the Science of Language, delivered at the Royal Institution of Great Britain in February, March, April, and May, 1863*, 2d series (New York: Scribner's, 1869), p. 520.

24. Max Müller, *India: What Can It Teach Us? A Course of Lectures Delivered before the University of Cambridge* (New York: 1883), p. 216.

25. For an excellent discussion of nineteenth-century philology, see Maurice Olender, *The Languages of Paradise: Race, Religion and Philology in the Nineteenth Century* (Cambridge, Mass.: Harvard University Press, 1992). Also, Edward Said, *Orientalism* (New York: Vintage, 1978).

26. Léon Poliakov, *The Aryan Myth: A History of Racist and Nationalist Ideas in Europe*, trans. E. Howard (New York: Basic Books, 1974; original French edition, 1971), p. 255.

27. Both Renan and Müller were major influences on Jung and are cited in *Wandlungen und Symbole der Libido*. According to Poliakov in *The Aryan Myth*, Renan, influenced greatly by his friend Müller and the German Aryanists actually referred to the Aryan race as "masters of the planet" (p. 208) and Müller once wrote as late as 1883 that "the Aryan nations have become the rulers of history" (p. 213). As Poliakov comments:

As propagandist for the Aryan Myth Renan deserves to be placed side by side with his friend Max Müller. If the influence of one was exercised in Latin countries and that of the other in the Anglo-Saxon and Germanic world, Renan was nevertheless regarded as an authority by the whole of international learned society. The warnings which both of them issued after 1870–71 against seeking political advantage from the confusion between languages and races must be placed to their credit. This implied self-criticism had little effect, however, while their writings before the Franco-Prussian war continued to make headway in one encyclopedia after another and to spread their influence through a series of textbooks. (p. 206)

28. On Schleicher and the history of scholarship on the Indo-Europeans, see J. P. Mallory, *In Search of the Indo-Europeans: Language, Archeology and Myth* (London: Thames and Hudson, 1989), pp. 9–23. Mallory's book is perhaps the single best volume to consult on the Indo-Europeans. Also useful as an introduction to the scholarship on historical linguistics and comparative mythology is C. S. Littleton, *The New Comparative Mythology* (Berkeley and Los Angeles: University of California Press, 1982).

29. Mallory, *In Search of the Indo-Europeans*, pp. 16, 18.

30. Blavatsky, *The Secret Doctrine* 1:688. This tree diagram begins with the "Primeval Astral Man" and traces our esoteric descent through the "Second Astral Race," and the third, which separates a separate line of "astrals" from the "Semi-Astral Third Race of Men." Men and primates enter the physical world at this point and sexual differentiation occurs as they follow separate lines of development. A fourth physical race of mankind (the Atlanteans, who died in the deluge) is followed by our present fifth race. "Aryan" is used in a generic way to refer to all of the present races of mankind, which Blavatsky claimed were new and originated in Central Asia, although they later separated and migrated. "But this separation did not take place either in the localities assigned for it by modern science, nor in the way the Aryans are shown to have divided and separated by Mr. Max Müller and other *Aryanists*," Mme. Blavatsky asserted in her esoteric tract, thus superceding the authority of academic scholars concerning the legitimacy of her ideas. On the spiritual primacy of the Aryan race as communicated from the great beyond by the mahatmas, see A. P. Sinnett, *The Mahatma Letters to A. P. Sinnett*, ed. Trevor Barker (New York: Frederick Stokes, 1924), p. 154. For an interesting and scholarly discussion of these issues from an occultist perspective, see Joscelyn Godwin,

Arktos: The Polar Myth in Science, Symbolism, and Nazi Survival (Grand Rapids, Mich.: Phanes Press, 1993), pp. 37–45.

31. Jakob Grimm, *Deutsche Mythologie*, 4 vols. (Berlin: F. Dümmler, 1875–1878; original edition, 1835).

32. Max Müller, *Introduction to the Science of Religion* (London: Longmans, 1873), p. 44.

33. It should be noted that Müller had fundamental reservations about Darwin's materialistic and mechanistic theories of natural selection and common descent as, in his view, they did not account for the uniquely human adaptation of language in any meaningful way. Müller, relying somewhat on Kantian idealism and some related ideas of the Naturphilosophen, argued that any new science devoted to the study of the human mind should be founded on the *Geisteswissenschaft* of the "science of language" and not on the *Naturwissenschaft* of Darwinian evolutionary biology. For a summary of Müller's views on this issue, see Elizabeth Knoll, "The Science of Language and the Evolution of Mind: Max Müller's Quarrel with Darwinism," *Journal of the History of the Behavioral Sciences* 22 (1986): 3–22.

34. On Charles Darwin's pangenesis as a form of quasi-Lamarckian "soft inheritance," see the discussion by Mayr, *The Growth of Biological Thought* pp. 693–94.

35. Haeckel, *The Riddle of the Universe*, p. 328.

36. On Diederichs's life and his ambivalent relationship with other, more actively anti-Semitic and politically extreme publishers, see the volume by Gary Stark, *Entrepreneurs of Ideology: Neoconservative Publishers in Germany 1890–1933* (Chapel Hill: University of North Carolina Press, 1981). Also useful is William Mahoney, "The Publisher as *Zeitkritiker*: Eugen Diederichs and the Frustrated Response to German Culture, 1896–1930" (Ph.D. diss., University of Connecticut, 1989). Mahoney's dissertation provides a complete list of Diederichs's own published works as well as a useful but incomplete list of the works published in *Die Tat* by others between 1913 and 1930. Useful primary materials by Diederichs can be found in Lulu von Strauss and Torney Diederichs, *Eugen Diederichs: Leben und Werk* (Jena: Eugen Diederichs Verlag, 1936).

Besides republishing the works of Paul de Lagarde, whom he very much admired, and ancient German texts such as the Elder Edda, Diederichs also was the publisher of many of Richard Wilhelm's works, notably his translation of the I Ching. The divinatory methods of the I Ching, used often by Jung in the 1920s and 1930s, were a part of the initial training program of the C. G. Jung Institute of Zurich in 1948 and its use is widely advocated today in Jungian analytic-training

institutes throughout the world. Diederichs also influenced generations of Jung's disciples through the folk tales, German mysticism, and
mythological material in some of his publications. In the late 1970s a
Jungian closely associated with the educational methods of the Jung
Institute claimed that "it seems that what many Jungians have learned
and know about the Germanic Gods is based on one single book,
M. Ninck's *Wodan und germanischer Schicksalsglaube*," which was a
völkisch-oriented book published by Eugen Diederichs Verlag in 1935.
See Margrit Burri, "Repression, Falsification, and Bedeviling of Germanic Mythology," *Spring* (1978): 88.

37. In addition to the Eugen Diederichs Verlag, Stark examines four
other German publishing houses that legitimized the mystical, anti-
Semitic and elitist philosophies of the völkisch movement by publishing their works along with volumes of Germanic high culture.
These four other companies—J. F. Lehmanns Verlag (Munich), the
Hanseatische Verlagsanstalt (Hamburg), the Gerhard Stalling Verlag
(Oldenburg), and the Heinrich Beenken Verlag (Berlin)—were also
not merely propaganda machines for specialized neoconservative
groups as some other publishers were, and therefore they brought
the völkisch fusion of occultism, political reform, and anti-Semitism
into the cultural mainstream. See Stark, *Entrepreneurs of Ideology*, pp.
9–14.

38. The earliest of Keller's works, *Eine Philosophie des Lebens* (Jena:
Eugen Diederichs Verlag, 1919), does not appear in Jung's *Bibliothek*
listings, but two others do.

39. This is from a 1927 Eugen Diederichs Verlag advertisement and
is cited in Stark, *Entrepreneurs of Ideology*, p. 68.

40. Ibid., p. 70.

41. Ibid.

42. Cited in Mosse, *The Crisis of German Ideology*, p. 60. The use of the
Rosicrucians as a symbol of the new spiritual elite that would lead the
world to a spiritual reawakening was also used by Goethe in a poem
that was highly regarded by those in the völkisch movement, *Die Geheimnisse* ("The Mysteries"), written in 1816.

43. Jung's personal library at Küsnacht contains no fewer than
seven volumes by Arthur Drews, all published by Diederichs: *Die
Christusmythe* (1910 and 1911 editions); *Die Entstehung des Christentums aus dem Gnostizismus* (1924); *Lehrbuch der Logik* (1928); *Die Mari-
enmythe* (1928); *Plotin und der Untergang der antiken Weltanschauung*
(1907); and *Der Sternhimmel in der Dichtung und Religion der alten Völker
und des Christentums* (1923), which contains typically völkisch expositions on the star or sun as representations of god in the natural religion
of the ancients.

44. Stark, *Entrepreneurs of Ideology*, p. 73.

45. Mosse, *The Crisis of German Ideology* p. 59.

46. Hermand, "The Distorted Vision," p. 123. The swastika is an ancient Indian symbol of auspiciousness or of good luck. Blavatsky adopted it as part of the official insignia of the Theosophical Society and also as part of her own personal crest. On the solar basis of swastika symbolism and its prevalence in archaic Celtic and Germanic symbolism, see Green, *The Sun-Gods of Ancient Europe* pp. 46–49.

47. Mosse, *The Crisis of German Ideology*, p. 59.

48. These dates are Stark's and conflict with the later dates of other scholars. For example, Mahoney claims the *Serakreis* was "founded during the summer of 1910 and named after a *Tanzlied* ("Sera, Sera, Sancti nostri Domine")," ("The Publisher as *Zeitkritiker*, p. 132). For background on the Youth Movement, see Walter Laquer, *Young Germany: A History of the Youth Movement* (New York: Basic Books, 1962); and Peter Stachura, *The German Youth Movement, 1900–1945: An Interpretation and Documentary History* (London: Macmillan, 1981). On the Sera Circle, see Stark, *Entrepreneurs of Ideology*, pp. 74–75, 104–5; and Mahoney, "The Publisher as *Zeitkritiker*," pp. 69, 132–34. Diederichs has been given credit by many as perhaps *the* leading force that made the pre–WW I German Youth Movement possible as its financial backer, public relations director, and publisher of its manifestos and philosophical works. See Stark, *Entrepeneurs of Ideology*, pp. 105–6.

49. Stark, *Entrepreneurs of Ideology*, p. 75.

50. Max Weber, "Science as Vocation," (1919) in H. H. Gerth and C. Wright Mills, ed., *From Max Weber: Essays in Sociology* (New York: Oxford University Press, 1946), p. 155.

51. See his final comprehensive statements on the circular mandala as an image of the "god within" in the following: C. G. Jung, "Concerning Mandala Symbolism," (1950) and "Appendix: Mandalas" (1955) in *Archetypes and The Collective Unconscious*, CW 9,i (Princeton: Princeton University Press, 1968).

52. Holt, "Ernst Haeckel's Monistic Religion," p. 273.

53. Haeckel, *The Riddle of the Universe*, p. 10. It should be noted, however, that despite his criticisms of Haeckel, Ludwig Büchner softened his rhetoric as he grew older, and in the 1875 second edition of his *Physiologische Bilder* he stated that he preferred the label "monist" to "materialist" as a description of his philosophical stance, thus very much resembling Haeckel. See Gregory, *Scientific Materialism in Nineteenth-Century Germany*, p. 118.

54. On the multiple meaning of "natural religion" and "nature religion" in German culture from Schleiermacher to Müller and then the *Naturmenschen*, see Karl-Heintz Kohl, "Naturreligion: Zur Transforma-

tionsgeschichte eines Begriffs," in Faber and Schledier, *Die Restauration der Götter*, pp. 198–214.

55. Gasman, *The Scientific Origins of National Socialism*, p. xiv–xv. Gasman's book should be read in concert with those of Mosse (*The Crisis of German Ideology*) and Goodrick-Clarke (*The Occult Roots of Nazism*) to get a complete picture of the important role of occult ideas at the highest levels of the völkisch movement (the learned elites) and at the lowest levels (the fluid occult underground of neopaganism) to understand the full impact of these ideas in the development of both National Socialism and Jung's analytical psychology. Gasman is not without his critics. See, e.g., the unconvincing critique of Gasman's thesis by East German scholar Reinhard Mocek, "Two Faces of Biologism: Some Reflections on a Difficult Period in the History of Biology in Germany," in Woodward and Cohen, *World Views and Scientific Discipline Formation*, pp. 279–91.

56. Haeckel, *The Riddle of the Universe*, pp. 280–81.

57. In Gasman, *The Scientific Origins of National Socialism*, p. 69, trans. from Wilhelm Ostwald, "Die Sonne," *Sonne* 1 (1914): 2. *Die Sonne* was a typical völkisch/monist periodical of this time.

58. Anonymous, "Sonnwendfest," *Der Monismus: Zeitschrift für einheitlische Weltanschauung und Kulturpolitik* 5 (1910): 126. This translation and citation are by Gasman, *The Scientific Origins of National Socialism*, p. 70.

59. James Webb, *The Occult Establishment* (La Salle, Ill.: Open Court, 1976), p. 182. The best source in English on Keyserling's life and ideas is Struve, "Count Hermann Keyserling and the School of Wisdom: Grand Seigneurs, Sages and Rulers," a chapter in his *Elites Against Democracy*, pp. 274–316.

60. Houston Stewart Chamberlain, *Immanuel Kant: Die Persönlichkeit als Einführung in das Werk* (Munich: Bruckmann, 1905).

61. An interesting short summary of these works can be found in the section entitled "H. S. Chamberlain as the Founder of Modern Racialism" in Lukács, *The Destruction of Reason*, pp. 697–714.

62. Graf Hermann Keyserling, *Das Gefüge der Welt: Versuch einer kritischen Philosophie* (Munich, 1906).

63. Field, *Evangelist of Race*, p. 323. The details of the personal relationship between Chamberlain and Keyserling are adeptly covered by Field (pp. 321–24).

64. Count Hermann Keyserling, *The Travel Diary of a Philosopher*, 2 vols., trans. J. Holroyd Reece (New York: Harcourt, Brace & Co., 1925), pp. 223–25. From April to August 1925 this work went through three printings. The third printing appeared as an attractive boxed set. Key-

serling's picture appears on the box with such accolades from reviewers as, "The publication of this diary is a spiritual event of national importance" (*Century Magazine*), and "The writer may yet emerge as among the great ones of the earth" (*New York Times*).

65. On the founding and operation of the School of Wisdom, and for an autobiographical summary of the life and work of Keyserling, see Count Hermann Keyserling, "My Life and Work as I See Them," in his *The World in the Making* (New York: Harcourt, Brace & Co., 1927), pp. 3–104. Keyserling's motives were based on ideas of cultural *renovatio* through occult practices such as yoga, Eastern meditation, and Jungian psychology: "The School of Wisdom should much rather be called a strategic headquarters than a center of study; it is precisely for this reason that it evokes so much enmity. It undertakes, by means of the proper psychological methods, to assimilate the impulse of life-renewal on the basis of the spirit, which I stand for, into the broad body of spiritual reality" (p. 67). Keyserling's own psychoanalysis was a Jungian one and included sessions with Jung, who continued to analyze Keyserling's dreams through the mail. Keyserling says: "Thanks to psychoanalysis, with the practice of which I first became acquainted in December 1922, through Oskar A. H. Schmitz, and the theory and practice of which occupied me for two years afterward, the hypertensions of my nature, as they had been until then, were converted into normal tensions. I became more calm, saw myself more clearly" (p. 69).

66. Cited in Struve, *Elites Against Democracy*, p. 300.

67. Ibid., p. 301.

68. Count Hermann Keyserling, *America Set Free* (New York: Macmillan, 1929), p. 582.

69. Other prominent lecturers included Ernst Troeltsch, Rabbi Leo Baeck, Friedrich Gogarted, Leopold Ziegler, and Leo Frobenius.

70. Jung, *MDR*, p. 373.

71. See Jung, *Letters: I. 1906–1950*, pp. 46–76. Wilhelm died in 1930, but other letters to Keyserling also appear from 1931 (pp. 82–86), 1932 (pp. 92–93), and 1945 (p. 401).

72. In a letter to Wilhelm dated 26 April 1929, Jung tells Wilhelm: "You are *too important* for our Western world. I must keep on telling you this." Ibid., p. 63.

73. See the following in *Civilization in Transition*: "The Swiss Line in the European Spectrum" (1928); "The Rise of a New World" (1930); and "La Révolution Mondiale" (1934).

74. Jung, "La Révolution Mondiale," para. 945.

75. Bernhard von Cotta, *Deutschlands Boden. Sein Bau und dessen Einwirkung auf das Leben der Menschen* (Leipzig: F.A. Brockhaus, 1853).

76. Cited by Robert Brain in "The Geographical Vision and the Popular Order of Disciplines, 1848–1870," in Woodward and Cohen, *World Views and Scientific Discipline Formation*, p. 374.

77. Jung, "Mind and Earth" (1927), ibid., para. 93.

78. Ibid., para. 94.

79. William McGuire, *The Freud/Jung Letters* (Princeton: Princeton University Press, 1974) p. 305 (letter 184 J). See also Maurice Low, *The American People: A Study in National Psychology*, vol. 1 (Boston: Macmillan 1909).

80. C. G. Jung, "Über des Unbewusste," *Schweitzerland: Monatshefte für Schweitzer Art und Arbeit* 4 (1918): 464–72, 548–58. See C. G. Jung, "The Role of the Unconscious" (1918), *Civilization in Transition*.

81. Ibid., para. 17.

82. Ibid., para. 18.

83. Ibid.

84. Mosse, *The Crisis of German Ideology*, p. 16.

85. Jung, "The Role of the Unconscious," para. 19.

86. Ibid.

87. Ibid., para. 20.

88. Ibid., para. 45.

89. See "From Esther Harding's Notebooks: 1922, 1925," in William McGuire and R.F.C. Hull, *C. G. Jung Speaking: Interviews and Encounters* (Princeton: Princeton University Press, 1977), p. 30.

90. Jung, *Analytical Psychology* p. 133.

91. Ibid., pp. 133–34.

92. A photograph of it appears in Aniela Jaffé, *C. G. Jung: Word and Image* (Princeton: Princeton University Press, 1979), p. 76.

93. An example is William Hobbs, *The Earth Generated and Anatomized: An Early Eighteenth-Century Theory of the Earth* (Ithaca: Cornell University Press, 1981). Hobbs's theory proposed that the earth had a "heart" that pulsated and guided the ebb and flow of the tides.

94. For the history of this geophysical debate, see Stephen Brush, "Nineteenth-Century Debates about the Inside of the Earth: Solid, Liquid or Gas?" *Annals of Science* 36 (1979): 225–54; Philip Lawrence, "Heaven and Earth—The Relation of the Nebular Hypothesis to Geology," in W. Yourgrau and A. D. Breck, ed., *Cosmology, History and Theology* (New York: Plenum, 1977), pp. 253–81; C. S. Gillmor, "The Place of the Geophysical Sciences in 19th Century Natural Philosophy," *Eos* 56 (1975): 4–7; and John Burke, "The Earth's Central Heat: From Fourier to Kelvin," in *Actes du VIIIᵉ Congrès International d'Histoire des Sciences, 1971* (1974), pp. 91–96. Buffon's comet theory of the origin of planets is illustrated and discussed in Bowler, *Evolution: The History of an Idea*, pp. 33–36, including an assessment of Buffon's abandonment

NOTES TO CHAPTER FIVE

of Vulcanism for Neptunism (the retreating-ocean theory of the origin of rocks).

95. Ibid., p. 131.

96. Eugen Bleuler, *Naturgeschichte der Seele und ihres Bewusstwerdens* (Berlin: Springer, 1921). See the discussion in Ellenberger, *The Discovery of the Unconscious*, pp. 839–40.

97. Jung attempts this in his introduction of the term in print in 1947 after presenting it at an Eranos Conference in Ascona in 1946. See Jung, "On the Nature of the Psyche," (1947) *Structure and Dynamics of the Psyche*, para 368.

98. Ibid., p. 131.

99. See especially the section on "Psyche and Swastika" in Geoffrey Cocks, *Psychotherapy in the Third Reich* (New York: Oxford University Press, 1985), pp. 50–86. An acknowledgment of Jung's völkisch influences is specifically noted in Geoffrey Cocks, "The Nazis and C. G. Jung," in Maidenbaum and Martin, *Lingering Shadows*, pp. 157–66. See also the following: Andrew Samuels, "National Psychology, National Socialism, and Analytical Psychology: Reflections on Jung and Anti-Semitism," *Journal of Analytical Psychology* 37 (1992): 3–28, 127–48; and Arvid Erlenmeyer, "Jung und die Deutschen," *Analytische Psychologie* 23 (1992): 132–61.

100. On Swiss heretical movements during the Middle Ages, see Norman Cohn, *In Pursuit of the Millennium: Revolutionary Millenarians and Mystical Anarchists of the Middle Ages*, 2d ed. (New York: Oxford University Press, 1970). See also the consecutive chapters, "The Swiss Reformation" and "The Sectarian Spectrum: Radical Movements within Protestantism" in Steven Ozment, *The Age of Reform, 1250–1550: An Intellectual and Religious History of Late Medieval and Reformation Europe* (New Haven: Yale University Press, 1980), pp. 318–51. Useful background on Swiss culture is provided in Nicholas Bouvier, Gordon Craig, and Lionel Gossman, *Geneva, Zurich, Basel: History, Culture and National Identity* (Princeton: Princeton University Press, 1994).

101. These statistics are reported in Baedeker, *Switzerland, and the Adjacent Portions of Italy, Savoy and Tyrol*, p. xxxiii.

102. On Rorschach's analysis of the cult of the Schwartzenburg *Waldbruderschaft* (Forest-brotherhood) of Johannes Binggeli and his precursor, Anton Unternährer, which Rorschach based on his own original fieldwork and historical investigation, see the following: "Einiges über schweizerische Sekten und Sektgründer" ["On Swiss Sects and Founders of Sects"], *Schweitzer Archiv für Neurologie und Psychiatrie* 1 (1917): 254–58; "Weiteres über Schweitzerische Sektenbildungen" ["Further Studies on the Formation of Swiss Sects"], *Schweitzer Archiv für Neurologie und Psychiatrie* 2 (1919): 385–88; "Sek-

tiererstudien" ["Studies on the Founders of Swiss Sects"], *Internationale Zeitschrift für ärztliche Psychoanalyse* 6 (1920): 106–7; and "Zwei Schweitzerische Sektensifter (Binggeli und Unternährer)" ["Two Swiss Founders of Sects"], *Imago* 13 (1927): 395–441. All of these have been reproduced in Hermann Rorschach, *Gesammelte Aufsätze* (Bern and Stuttgart: Verlag Hans Huber, 1965).

According to Ellenberger, Rorschach became so fascinated with his ethnographic fieldwork that "at one point, Rorschach firmly believed that this study of Swiss sects would be his life's work." See Henri Ellenberger, "The Life and Work of Hermann Rorschach (1884–1922)," in Micale, *Beyond the Unconscious*, p. 204.

103. See Pascal, *From Naturalism to Expressionism*.

104. Aschheim, *The Nietzsche Legacy in Germany*, pp. 201–31.

105. Mitzman, *The Iron Cage*, p. 288.

106. Green, *The von Richthofen Sisters*; and especially his *Mountain of Truth*.

107. For a general overview, see Walter Burkert, *Ancient Mystery Cults* (Cambridge: Cambridge University Press, 1987); the most persuasive rejection of the Persian origins of Mithraism can be found in David Ulansey, *The Origins of the Mithraic Mysteries: Cosmology and Salvation in the Ancient World* (New York: Oxford University Press, 1989).

108. On Fechner's significance in the history of psychology, see L. Sprung & H. Sprung, "Gustav Theodor Fechner in der Geschichte der Psychologie—Leben, Werk und Wirken in der Wissenschaftsentwicklung des 19. Jahrhunderts," in *Psychologiehistorische Manuskript* 9 (1987): 1–54.

109. G. T. Fechner, *Zend-Avesta, oder über die Dinge des Himmels und des Jenseits*, 2 vols. (Leipzig: Voss, 1851). Fechner was extremely well known in the nineteenth century and some aspects of his experimental work on psychophysics are still regarded highly. Fechner's scientific works were read and admired by Freud and Jung, and he was Wilhelm Wundt's mentor. See Ellenberger, *The Discovery of the Unconscious*, pp. 215–18.

110. Webb, *The Occult Establishment*, p. 32. Ha'nish published several books: *Mazdaznan Health and Breath* (London, 1913; originally in the U.S.A., 1902); *Inner Studies* (Chicago, 1902); and a book that won a "Medal of Progress" award at the International Cookery Exhibition held in Luxembourg in 1911, his *Mazdaznan Dietetics and Cookery Book* (London, 1911). The cult also put out a short-lived journal, *The British Mazdaznan Magazine* in 1914. On these references, see Webb, p. 74. Webb's book is an indispensable scholarly source for tracing the influence of the occult popular culture on learned European elites, especially at the turn of the century.

NOTES TO CHAPTER SIX

111. A bibliography of Heise's works, and the occult context in which he lived, can be found in Goodrick-Clarke, *The Occult Roots of Nazism*, pp. 27, 44, 45, 55, 234, 270.

112. Green, *The Mountain of Truth*, p. 235. For a brief description of the Mazdaznans that still remained in Switzerland, see the report in a Theosophical Society journal by H. R. Ecroyd, "A Strange Adventure in Switzerland," *The Quest* 21 (October 1939).

113. See McGuire, "Introduction," *The Psychology of the Unconscious*, p. xviii; also, Noll, "Jung the *Leontocephalus*," pp. 12–60. The *Deus Leontocephalus*, the "lion-headed god" was a ubiquitous image found in ancient Mithraic cult sites and—as this article argues—was particularly fascinating to Jung for a variety of reasons.

114. Jung, "On Psychic Energy," para. 92.

115. C. G. Jung, *Nietzsche's "Zarathustra": Notes of the Seminar Given in 1934–1939*, 2 vols. (Princeton: Princeton University Press, 1988), 1:4.

116. See William McGuire, *Bollingen: An Adventure in Collecting the Past* (Princeton: Princeton University Press, 1982), pp. 31ff. The neo-pagan, vegetarian counterculture at Ascona circa 1900 caught the attention of some journalists and social commentators. An early study of a colony of forty vegetarians is Adolph Grohmann, *Die Vegetarier-Ansiedlung in Ascona und die sogenannten Naturmenschen im Tessin* (Halle, 1904).

117. Jung delivered fourteen lectures in all at the annual Eranos Conferences, which were organized by Olga Fröbe, whom Jung met at Keyserling's School of Wisdom in 1930. According to Fröbe, the name "Eranos" was proposed to her by the theologian Rudolph Otto in Marburg in November 1932. See Aniela Jaffé, "C. G. Jung and the Eranos Conferences," *Spring* (1977): 201–12.

Chapter Six

1. It is Letter 199a F in McGuire, *Freud/Jung Letters*, pp. 332–35.

2. On the talented actress and lecturer, whose birth name was indeed Frank Miller, see the stunning photographs of her in costume and the discussion of her case and its relevance to Jung in the exemplary paper by Sonu Shamdasani, "A Woman Called Frank," *Spring* 50 (1990): 26–56. For a brief period (1899–1900) Miller was a student of Flournoy's in Geneva, and her brief report of her fantasies (which includes an introduction by Flournoy) attempts to trace the source of her visions and reveries to cryptomnesia, not to otherworldly or transcendent sources such as the spiritualist mediums were claiming. See Frank Miller, "Some Instances of Unconscious Creative Imagination," *Journal of the American Society for Psychical Research* 1 (1907): 287–308.

3. This is argued throughout by Peter Homans in his *Jung in Context: Modernity and the Making of a Psychology* (Chicago: University of Chicago Press, 1979). See especially pp. 64–73.

4. Ibid., p. 66.

5. John Kerr, "Beyond the Pleasure Principle and Back Again: Freud, Jung and Sabina Spielrein," in Paul Stepansky, ed., *Freud: Appraisals and Re-Appraisals*, Contributions to Freud Studies, vol. 3 (Hillsdale, N.J.: The Analytic Press, 1988), p. 40. I highly recommend this work to anyone wishing to understand *Wandlungen* from a psychoanalytic perspective, and from the perspective of psychoanalytic history. Pages 40–50, in my opinion, contain the clearest and most critical summary of *Wandlungen* to be found in the English language.

6. Ibid., p. 40.

7. This is argued at length in Noll, "Jung the *Leontocephalus*," pp. 12–60.

8. Jung, "New Paths in Psychology" (1912), *Two Essays*.

9. Jung, *Analytical Psychology*, p. 25.

10. Jung, *The Psychology of the Unconscious*, p. 5.

11. Ibid., p. 6.

12. After determining to his satisfaction what the vocabulary of this reconstructed proto–Indo-European language was, Schleicher wrote a folk tale in it entitled *Avis akvasas ka*, or "The Sheep and the Horses."

13. Just one of several examples: After analyzing one of Miller's creations as a "religious hymn" down to its "erotic root," Jung says that,

> It is not too much to say that we have herewith dug up the erotic root, and yet the problem remains unsolved. Were there not bound up with that a mysterious purpose, probably of the greatest biological meaning, then certainly twenty centuries would not have yearned for it with such intense longing. Doubtless this sort of libidian current moves in the same direction as, taken in the widest sense, did that ecstatic ideal of the Middle Ages and of the ancient mystery cults, one of which became later Christianity. There is to be seen biologically in this ideal an exercise of psychologic projection (of the paranoian mechanism, as Freud would express it. (Jung, *The Psychology of the Unconscious*, pp. 62–63)

14. Ibid., para. 56.

15. Interestingly, Müller's ideas did not enter into Freud's thinking—perhaps yet another of the fundamental distinctions between the two men. Freud admits that Jung's researches into ethnology and comparative mythology that later formed *Wandlungen* were the initial stimulus for researching and writing *Totem and Taboo*, published in toto in 1913 after appearing in multiple parts in the psychoanalytic

journal *Imago*, starting with its first issue in 1912. On Freud's sources, which include Wundt, James Frazer, and Müller's arch-nemesis Andrew Lang, see the exemplary volume by Edwin Wallace, *Freud and Anthropology: A History and Reappraisal* (New York: International University Press, 1983).

16. The distillation of Müller's basic ideas is drawn from several of his many works, but primarily from his *Lectures on the Science of Religion* (London: Houghton, 1870).

17. Later F.W.H. Myers, the psychical researcher from Cambridge, borrowed this term from Müller to describe the apparent myth-making functions of the subliminal self.

18. Müller, *Lectures on the Science of Religion*, p. 71.

19. Jung, *The Psychology of the Unconscious*, para. 45.

20. To be fair and accurate, however, this would fit in with Jung's greater methodological assumptions, as Miller was of Aryan (Indo-European) ancestry.

21. For a typical example of Jung's lengthy etymological excursions, see the two full pages of etymological connection between "nightmare" and "mare" in Jung, *The Psychology of the Unconscious*, paras. 378–81.

22. See McGuire, *Freud/Jung Letters*, letter 2977. See also McGuire's introduction in Jung, *Psychology of the Unconscious*, p. xxiii.

23. See ibid., pp. 76–77.

24. Ibid., para. 145.

25. Ibid., para. 149.

26. Ibid., para. 150.

27. See the discussion in Homans, *Jung in Context*, pp. 130–32.

28. Jung, *The Psychology of the Unconscious*, paras. 150–51.

29. Ibid., para. 152.

30. Ibid., paras. 173–75.

31. Ibid., para. 155.

32. Ibid., para. 158.

33. Ibid., para. 163.

34. Ibid., para. 180.

35. Ibid., para. 155n.

36. Ibid., para. 201.

37. Ibid., para. 203.

38. Ibid., para. 204n.

39. Jung, *Analytical Psychology*, p. 26.

40. Jung, *The Psychology of the Unconscious*, pp. 335–41.

41. Homans, *Jung in Context*, p. 67. Homans's language is stronger elsewhere: "Still, *Symbols of Transformation* was an attempt to come to terms with the two modes of experience of religion, assimilating to a

limited degree the personal mode and strongly repudiating the traditional mode" (p. 130).

42. I discuss the historical context of this fin-de-siècle classical scholarship concerning the mystery cults at length in my introduction to *Mysteria: Jung and the Ancient Mysteries* (Princeton: Princeton University Press, 1994). See also the very useful paper by Bruce Metzger, "Considerations of Methodology in the Study of the Mystery Religions and Early Christianity," *Harvard Theological Review* 48 (1955): 1–20.

43. Franz Cumont, *Textes et monuments figurés relatifs aux mystères de Mitra*, 2 vols. (Brussels: H. Lamertin, 1896 [1], 1899 [2]).

44. The work appeared rather quickly in an English translation as well. See Franz Cumont, *The Mysteries of Mithra* (New York: Open Court, 1903).

45. Luther Martin explains the problem in his extremely useful book, *Hellenistic Religions: An Introduction* (New York: Oxford University Press, 1987), pp. 114–15:

> Unlike the myths of the other mystery deities, no received myth of Mithras survives, nor does the iconographic evidence seem to reflect any such official narrative of the deity's life. Mithraic iconography seems rather to depict isolated scenes of Mithraic activity from which modern attempts to reconstruct a mythic narrative have been made. Even the scenes, with several exceptions, seem to express regional variations of the cult expression.

46. For Weber's participation in this early Eranos group, see Weber, *Max Weber: A Biography*, p. 356. It is not known whether this prominent Heidelberg circle of scholars was Rudolph Otto's inspiration for the name of the later (1933) Eranos Conferences at Ascona. What is certain is that Dieterich was disseminating his knowledge of Mithraism and the Mithraic Liturgy to Weber and other scholars, and Weber mentions Mithraism in his works on the sociology of religion.

47. Albrecht Dieterich, *Eine Mithrasliturgie* (Leipzig: Verlag B. G. Teubner, 1903; 2d ed., 1910). Dieterich dedicated this work to Cumont.

48. The English translation of the Mithraic Liturgy can be found in H. D. Beck, *The Greek Magical Papyri in Translation* (Chicago: Chicago University Press, 1986), pp. 48–54.

49. McGuire, *Freud/Jung Letters*, letter 210 J.

50. Jung, *The Psychology of the Unconscious*, p. 66

51. Burkert translates Renan's famous line as follows: "If the growth of Christianity had been halted by some mortal illness, the world would have become Mithraic" (Ernest Renan, *Marc Aurèle et la fin du monde antique* [Paris, 1882]). Burkert, *Ancient Mystery Cults*, p. 3.

52. Jung, *Analytical Psychology*, p. 99.

53. Cumont, *The Mysteries of Mithras*, p. 4.

54. Ibid., p. 1.

55. Jung, *The Psychology of the Unconscious*, para. 127.

56. Ibid., para. 124.

57. See Gunter, "Bergson and Jung," 635–52.

58. A similar idea concerning the continuity of animate and inanimate matter through their status as constraints for "invariant free dynamics" (laws and forces of nature) is discussed by Wolfgang Köhler. Köhler, however, was avowedly nonvitalistic as well as nonmechanistic in this theoretical contribution to gestalt psychology. The result was a very monistic position that resembles Haeckel's in many respects (including a lingering reputation for its philosophical vagueness). See the various discussions of this "postulate of invariance in evolution" in Mary Henle, ed., *The Selected Papers of Wolfgang Köhler* (New York: Liveright, 1971), pp. 72–77, 330, 349–50, 371. For an intriguing discussion of holism as a German cultural style of psychobiological theory and research in the 1920s and 1930s as, in part, an answer to the spiritual crisis of modernity, see Anne Harrington, "Interwar 'German' Psychobiology: Between Nationalism and the Irrational," *Science in Context* 4 (1991): 429–47.

59. Dieterich, *Eine Mithrasliturgie*, p. 161.

60. On the separate and distinct differences between pagan *mysteria* and the mysteries mentioned in the texts of Hellenistic Judaism and early Christianity, see Nock, "Hellenistic Mysteries and Christian Sacraments," 2:791–820; and Hugo Rahner, "The Christian Mystery and the Pagan Mystery (1944)," in Joseph Campbell, ed., *The Mysteries: Papers From the Eranos Yearbooks* (Princeton: Princeton University Press, 1955), pp. 337–404.

61. See Poliakov, *The Aryan Myth*.

62. Peter Gay, *Freud: A Life for Our Time* (New York: W. W. Norton, 1988), p. 239. On Freud's own implicit cognitive categories of racial differences, see Sander Gilman, *Freud, Race, and Gender* (Princeton: Princeton University Press, 1993).

63. Houston Stewart Chamberlain, *Die Grundlagen des Neunzehnten Jahrhunderts*, 2 vols. (Munich: Bruckmann, 1899). This work was a bestseller and went through multiple editions. It first appeared in English as *The Foundations of the Nineteenth Century*, 2 vols. (London: John Lane, 1911). According to Field, "Cosima [Wagner] strongly encouraged him, for she believed the book would be a Wagnerian *Kulturgeschichte*" (p. 171). On the writing and reception of *Grundlagen*, see Field, *Evangelist of Race* pp. 169–224.

64. Jung, *The Psychology of the Unconscious*, para. 136n.

65. Mosse, *The Crisis of German Ideology*, pp. 93, 97.

66. Field, *Evangelist of Race*, p. 223.

67. Gasman, *The Scientific Origins of National Socialism*, p. 177.

68. Mosse, "The Mystical Origins of National Socialism," p. 93.

69. R. Andrew Paskauskas, ed., *The Complete Correspondence of Sigmund Freud and Ernest Jones, 1908–1939* (Cambridge, Mass.: Harvard University Press, 1993), pp. 180, 182 (letters 107 and 108).

70. James Jackson Putnam, *Letters* (Cambridge, Mass.: Harvard University Press, 1971), p. 376.

71. Historians of this period have mentioned Jung's book in this regard, usually in one-sentence statements without elaboration. Mosse (*The Culture of Western Europe*, p. 275) charges Jung with fostering a "racial mysticism, which, in turn, derived some scientific respectability through its incorporation in his psychoanalytical theories." According to Green (*Mountain of Truth*, p. 137), "[1912] was the year of Jung's *Wandlungen und Symbole der Libido*, a book that gave scholarly respectability to one of Ascona's most prized truths, the value of sun worship."

72. Although there were scattered Germanic cults actually attempting to revive a votive religion with mystery-cult elements based on the worship of the Germanic Gods (such as Wotan), nothing much came of this. However, Hauer's German Faith Movement was a revival of völkisch religion in other respects during the Nazi era. See Hauer, Heim, and Adam, *Germany's New Religion*. Formally founded in July 1933, it incorporated many traditional völkisch elements. Hauer argued that there is "an antithesis between an alien faith and the German genius" (p. 42)—the "alien faith," of course, being Christianity. The use of the word "genius" is significant here, as it directly refers to the ancient Roman pagan belief that a genius (or anima) resided in the head and was the source of inspiration when it possessed a like and alien spirit. The "German genius" is another way of saying the "German god within." Mediation through "a sacred person, a sacred book, or a sacred rite" is rejected by Hauer "not indeed because we deny the existence of God or of the eternal powers which govern life, but because we have found from experience that it is possible to have immediate contact with those powers" (p. 48). This was also the appeal of the ancient Hellenistic mysteries of pagan antiquity and modern groups based on this model. Hauer was an associate of Jung's and participated in the Eranos Conference in 1934, during which he spoke on "Symbols and Experience of the Self in Indo-Aryan Mysticism."

73. Self-deification, or becoming one with the god within, was a pagan appeal to reject Christianity, its symbols, and its Semitic god. The dynamic swastika was hailed as the alternative to the cross. An article on the swastika in a 1918 issue of *Die Tat* by Illse Alma Drews

exemplifies the use of metaphors in a neopagan (but not political) sense, much as Jung sometimes uses them through *Wandlungen* and elsewhere: "As the Christians joyfully gather round their cross symbol, so should all of us, too, who confess the new religion, meet each other under the common sign of the swastika. . . . The swastika can, like no other sign, warn and arouse us, light the holy flame in us, so that we become joyful sacrifices to the highest . . . a victory sign of the new, inner-world God." Green, *Mountain of Truth*, p. 241.

74. Jung, *Civilization in Transition*.

75. Jung, *Letters: 1. 1906–1950*, pp. 39–40.

76. Jung, *Psychological Types*, para. 324.

77. Means, *Things That Are Caesar's*, p. 163. Means's book provides an introductory summary of the various neopagan völkisch movements in German Europe from the fin de siècle to Nazi Germany in his chapter on "Nationalist Religion, the New Paganism of the Young Germanic Folk Movement" (pp. 163–84).

78. Mosse, *The Crisis of German Ideology*, pp. 15–151. Mosse's chapter, "Education Comes to the Aid," traces the widespread infiltration of völkisch thought into the educational system in Germanic lands between 1873 and 1918 (pp. 152–70).

79. Fritz Stern, *Dreams and Delusions: National Socialism in the Drama of the German Past* (New York: Vintage, 1989), p. 122.

80. Although other examples will be provided in this book, the language of a contemporary Jungian analyst is typical for Jungian publications and contains Nietzschean metaphors of liberation and individuation (a term Jung borrowed from Schopenhauer, von Hartmann, and Nietzsche): "Analysis is a formal process of self-reflection and understanding, meant to free one from unnecessary bondage to complexes that are dominant in one's personal psychology. Jungian analysis is also intended to help one find the path of one's own individuation, which can never be defined in general or cultural terms." James Hall, *The Jungian Experience: Analysis and Individuation*, p. 121.

CHAPTER SEVEN

1. Jung, "Some Thoughts on Psychology," p. 31.

2. Ibid., pp. 31–32.

3. Jung rhetorically asks: "Why do the sermons about the historical Jesus make no sense? Why are people more interested in attending scientific lectures than in going to church? Why is their interest focused on Darwin, Haeckel, and Büchner?" *The Zofingia Lectures*, p. 107.

4. The similarity between the later monism of Haeckel and the "philosophy of the unconscious" of von Hartmann has been noted by

David DeGroot, *Haeckel's Theory of the Unity of Nature: A Monograph in the History of Philosophy* (Boston: The Christopher Publishing House, 1965), p. 38. Jung's personal library contains the fifth edition of von Hartmann's work: Eduard von Hartmann, *Philosophie des Unbewussten* (Berlin: Carl Dunkers Verlag, 1873). Von Hartmann's work is Schopenhauerian philosophy combined with evolutionary Wissenschaft circa 1870. This work therefore made sense to many at the end of the nineteenth-century who were trying to reconcile personal iconographies of the transcendent with the compelling contradictions provided by evolutionary biology. *Philosophie des Unbewussten* went through many editions and was one of the most popular books in fin-de-siècle Central Europe. The evolutionary works of Haeckel (as well as Darwin, Wallace, Büchner, etc.) are cited by von Hartmann, but Haeckel's Monism is not, as Haeckel was at the time only just mentioning such an idea without elaboration. Von Hartmann seizes upon this lack of a vitalistic element in the evolutionary work of Haeckel of this period and points out the inconsistencies in his biological statements on the *"Begriff der Individualität"* (the concept of the individual). Von Hartmann instead argues for a "unitary concept of organic individuals [*einheitlichen Begriff des organischen Individuums*]" (p. 491) that can include vitalism. Haeckel, as has been noted, adopted a similar view in later years.

5. Jung, "Some Thoughts on Psychology," para. 136. For an exemplary examination of the ideas of these materialists (and a critique of von Hartmann), see the translation of the second edition (1873) of Friedrich Albert Lange, *The History of Materialism: And Criticism of Its Present Importance* (New York: Humanities Press, 1950). Lange's critique of von Hartmann is in the chapter on "Darwinism and Teleology," and his opinion is clear: "It will hardly be necessary for our readers once more to disturb the illusion that the 'Philosophie des Unbewussten' contains 'speculative results on the inductive scientific method.' There can hardly be another modern book in which the scientific material swept together stands in such flagrant contrast to all the essential principles of scientific method" (p. 80).

The scientific materialism that arose in Germany in the 1850s in response to the Idealist and Naturphilosophie establishment was led by Karl Vogt, Jacob Moleschott, Ludwig Büchner, and Heinrich Czolbe in academic circles and supported in popular science journals such as *Die Natur* (which first appeared in 1852) that also appeared during this decade. Jung read such journals as a youth. See Gregory, *Scientific Materialism in Nineteenth-Century Germany*.

6. Jung, *The Zofingia Lectures*, p. 105.

7. Ibid., p. 93. On Schopenhauerian genius, see below.

8. Ellenberger discusses this controversy in detail in his "Carl Gus-

tav Jung," pp. 147–48. See also James Hillman, "Some Early Background to Jung's Ideas: Notes on *C. G. Jung's Medium* by Stefanie Zumstein-Preiswerk," *Spring* (1976): 123–36.

9. C. G. Jung, *Psychiatric Studies*, CW 1 (Princeton: Princeton University Press, 1970).

10. James Witzig, "Théodore Flournoy—A Friend Indeed," *Journal of Analytical Psychology* 27 (1982): 138–41. Jung actually states that Flournoy was perhaps more of a long-lasting influence on him than Freud, and also acknowledges the importance of William James on his work, in sections of *MDR* not included in the published edition but which can be found in the editorial prepublication manuscript of *MDR* at the Countway Library of Medicine. Further information on Jung's relationships with Flournoy, James, and others can be found in the works of Eugene Taylor: "William James and Jung," *Spring* (1980): 157–68; "C. G. Jung and the Boston Psychopathologists, 1902–1912," *Voices: The Art and Science of Psychotherapy* 21 (1985): 132–45; and in "Jung and His Intellectual Context: The Swedenborgian Connection," *Studia Swedenborgiana* 7 (1991): 47–69.

11. Ellenberger, "Carl Gustav Jung," p. 149.

12. *MDR*, pp. 30–32.

13. Drinka, *The Birth of Neurosis*, p. 53.

14. For further exploration of this theme, see Richard Noll, "Max Nordau's *Degeneration*, C. G. Jung's Taint," *Spring* 55 (1994).

15. Mitchell Ash, "Academic Politics in the History of Science: Experimental Psychology in Germany, 1879–1941," *Central European History* 13 (1980): 263. See also Marilyn Marshall and Russel Wendt, "William Wundt, Spiritism, and the Assumptions of Science," in Wolfgang Bringmann and R. D. Tweny, ed., *Wundt Studies* (Toronto: Hogrefe, 1980), pp. 158–75.

16. Ellenberger, *The Discovery of the Unconscious*, p. 674. See also Aniela Jaffé, "Parapsychology: Experience and Theory, Occultism and Spiritualism, Synchronistic Phenomena," in her *From the Life and Work of C. G. Jung*.

17. On the importance to nineteenth-century German Europe of the Seeress of Prevorst (Friedericke Hauffe), whose trances between 1827 and 1829 included visionary travels to other worlds, communications with the dead, the articulation of neo-Platonic philosophy, and the prescription of medicinal and herbal cures, and were recorded by the Kerner (1786–1862), see Ellenberger, *The Discovery of the Unconscious*, pp. 79–81. The book that fascinated Goethe, Jung, Nietzsche, and many others was Justinius Kerner, *Die Seherin von Prevorst, Eröffnen über das innere Leben und über das Hineinragen einer Geistwelt in die unsere*, 2 vols. (Stuttgart-Tübingen: Cotta, 1829).

18. In future publications, Shamdasani will argue that Jung's work was in actuality a "project for a mediumistic psychology."

19. Jung's publications in this area appear in *Experimental Researches*.

20. See Daniel Schacter, "Implicit Memory: History and Current Status," *Journal of Experimental Psychology: Learning, Memory, and Cognition* 13 (1987): 501–8. Implicit memory is in evidence when "information that was encoded during a particular episode is subsequently expressed without conscious or deliberate recollection" (p. 501). This is precisely what Jung and his coworkers were trying to experimentally demonstrate through the word-association protocol and reaction-time differentials that hinted at affectively toned memories that influenced the present behavior of the subjects, but without their awareness. Schacter credits the nineteenth-century literature of psychical researchers as "the first to document implicit memory phenomena on the basis of controlled empirical observation" (p. 503). Although Schacter does not mention Flournoy in his review, another expression for a form of implicit memory is, of course, cryptomnesia. This, too, has undergone recent experimental study by cognitive psychologists: Alan Brown and Dana Murphy, "Cryptomnesia: Delineating Inadvertent Plagiarism," *Journal of Experimental Psychology: Learning, Memory, and Cognition* 15 (1989): 432–42.

21. For example, *Psychiatric Studies* contains such scientific papers as "On Hysterical Misreading" (1904) and "Cryptomnesia" (1905), and his doctoral dissertation on the case of the medium "S. W.," which also analyzes the content of her trance utterances in terms of cryptomnesia. *Experimental Researches* contains his "Experimental Observations on the Faculty of Memory" (1905) and his word-association studies.

22. Jung, *The Zofingia Lectures*, p. 102.

23. Ibid., pp. 103–4.

24. See, e.g., Douglas Hermann, ed., *Memory in Historical Perspective: The Literature Before Ebbinghaus* (New York: Springer, 1988).

25. The original German publication of Jung and Riklin appears in English translation as "The Associations of Normal Subjects" (1904), in *Experimental Researches*. *CW* 2. See also William McGuire, "Jung's Complex Reactions (1907): Word Association Experiments Performed by Binswanger," *Spring* (1984): 1–34.

26. Jung and Riklin, "The Associations of Normal Subjects," para. 210.

27. Peter Swales, "What Jung Didn't Say," *Harvest: Journal of Jungian Studies* 38 (1992): 30.

28. The best source is, of course, Kerr, *A Most Dangerous Method*

What sparked interest in the Spielrein/Jung relationship—which was apparently unknown to his later generations of disciples although quite well known before World War I—is the collection of Spielrein's letters and diary entries in Carotenuto, *A Secret Symmetry*. See also: Aldo Carotenuto, "Sabina Spielrein and C. G. Jung: Some Newly Discovered Documents Bearing on Psychotic Transference, Counter Transference, and the Anima," *Spring* (1980): 128–44; Aldo Carotenuto, "More About Sabina Spielrein: A Response to Bettelheim," *Spring* (1985): 129–36; Aldo Carotenuto, "Jung's Shadow Problem with Sabina Spielrein," in Mary Ann Mattoon, ed., *The Archetype of Shadow in a Split World: Proceedings of the Tenth International Conference on Analytical Psychology, Berlin 1986* (Zurich: Daimon Verlag, 1987), pp. 240–53, and see also the discussion by Peter Mudd that follows (pp. 254–60); and Swales, "What Jung Didn't Say," pp. 30–37.

29. Carotenuto, *A Secret Symmetry*, p. 100.

30. The choice of this pseudonym for the "Jewish girl" in the earlier protocol was "Alice Stern," and *Stern* is the German word for star.

Chapter Eight

1. Eugen Bleuler, "Die Prognose der Dementia Praecox—Schizophreniengruppe," *Allgemeine Zeitschrift für Psychiatrie* 65 (1908): pp. 436–64.

2. C. G. Jung, "The Content of the Psychoses" (1908), *Psychogenesis of Mental Disease*, CW 3 (New York: Pantheon, 1960).

3. It is often incorrectly understood (and often incorrectly reported in Jungian publications) that Jung came up with the first biochemical theory of schizophrenia. His only innovation was that this "toxin" could be produced environmentally, through trauma, rather than through strict heredity. In fact, Jung's talk of a toxin in the etiology of schizophrenia echoes one of the first published descriptions of dementia praecox, as a metabolic disorder. He thought that it was caused by auto-intoxication through a "tangible morbid process occurring in the brain." Emil Kraepelin, "Dementia Praecox," in John Cutting and Michael Shepherd, ed., *The Clinical Roots of the Schizophrenia Concept: Translations of Seminal European Contributions on Schizophrenia* (Cambridge: Cambridge University Press, 1987), p. 23.

4. This was published in an English translation by William Alanson White as *Wishfulfillment and Symbolism in Fairy Tales*, Nervous and Mental Disease Monograph Series, No. 21 (New York: Journal of Nervous and Mental Disease, 1915). On Riklin, see Dieter Baumann, "In Memory of Franz Riklin," *Spring* (1970): 1–6.

5. Wolfgang Schwentker, "Passion as a Mode of Life: Max Weber, the Otto Gross Circle and Eroticism," in Mommsen and Osterhammel, *Max Weber and His Contemporaries*, p. 488.

6. The literature on Gross is small but growing. The best single work is Emanuel Hurwitz, *Otto Gross: 'Paradies'—Sucher zwischen Freud und Jung* (Zurich and Frankfurt: Suhrkamp Verlag, 1979); in English, see the volumes by Green, *The von Richthofen Sisters*, and *Mountain of Truth*; in French, see J. Le Rider, *Otto Gross: révolution sur le divan* (Paris: Solin, 1988). Most of the scant nonpsychoanalytic literature on Gross concerns his connections with the circle of Max Weber. See Nicolaus Sombert, "Max Weber and Otto Gross: On the Relationship Between Science, Politics and Eros in Wilhelmine Germany," *History of Political Thought* 8 (1987): 131–52; Schwentker, "Passion as a Mode of Life"; and Guenther Roth, "Marianne Weber and Her Circle," in Weber, *Max Weber*. The only significant paper that attempts to illuminate the connection between Jung and Gross is Martin Stanton, "Otto Gross's Case Histories: Jung, Stekel, and the Pathologization of Protest," in Renos Papadopoulos, ed., *Carl Gustav Jung: Critical Assessments*, 4 vols. (London: Routledge, 1992), 1:200–208.

7. Ernest Jones, *The Life and Work of Sigmund Freud. Volume 2: Years of Maturity, 1901–1919* (New York: Basic Books, 1955). Jones took this from Freud's letter to Jung dated 27 February 1908 (see McGuire, *Freud/Jung Letters*, p. 126, letter 74 F). Jones gives Gross credit for helping to put psychoanalysis on the map with a 1904 article and 1907 book that compared Freudian theory with the current psychiatric knowledge on dementia praecox and manic depression. Jones describes Gross as "a genius who later unfortunately developed schizophrenia" (p. 29). Jones also reveals that "he was my first instructor in the practice of psychoanalysis and I used to be present during his treatment of a case."

8. J. E. Michaels, *Anarchy and Eros: Otto Gross's Impact on German Expressionist Writers* (New York: Peter Lang [Utah Studies in Literature and Linguistics, no. 24], 1983).

9. On the historical significance of Hanns Gross, and an explanation of why he seems to have been passed over in so many history books, see William Johnston, *The Austrian Mind* (Berkeley and Los Angeles: University of California Press, 1972), pp. 94–95.

10. Henry Murger, *La vie de Bohème* (Paris: 1849), p. 14. This translation is from Jerrold Seigel, *Bohemian Paris: Culture Politics, and the Boundaries of Bourgeois Life, 1830–1930* (New York: Viking, 1986), p. 3. Seigel (pp. 401–4) provides a very useful—if brief—bibliographic essay, "A Note on Histories of Bohemia." A more comprehensive account of antibourgeois or nonbourgeois subcultures throughout Euro-

pean history can be found in the work of the German sociologist Helmut Kreuzer, *Die Bohème. Beiträge zu ihrer Beschreibung* (Stuttgart: 1968). To these volumes must, of course, be added the documentation of Bohemia provided by the works of Green.

11. These can be found in the collection edited by Kurt Krieler: Otto Gross, *Von geschlechtlicher Not zur sozialen Katastrophe* [From Sexual Privation to Social Catastrophe] (Frankfurt: Robinson Verlag, 1980). There is no English language edition of the works of Otto Gross.

12. Green, *The von Richthofen Sisters.*

13. This is according to Eduard Baumgarten, whose comments are reported in summary by Ellen Kennedy following the translation of the paper by Sombart, "Max Weber and Otto Gross," p. 150. For the original German commentary by Sombart and Baumgarten, see the following: Nicolaus Sombart, "Gruppenbild mit zwei Damen: Zum Verhältnis von Wissenschaft, Politik und Eros im wilhelminischen Zeitalter," *Merkur* 30 (1976): 972–90; and Eduard Baumgarten, "Über Max Weber: Ein Brief an Nicholas Sombart," *Merkur* 31 (1977): 296–300.

14. This is cited in Schwentker, "Passion as a Mode of Life," pp. 483, 495. An abbreviated form of the original letter appears in Eduard Baumgarten, ed., *Max Weber: Werk und Person* (Tübingen: Mohr 1964), pp. 644–48.

15. Weber, *Max Weber,* p. 377. Weber's critique of Gross in this letter is reproduced at length on pp. 375–80.

16. Cited in ibid., p. 376.

17. Ibid., p. 379.

18. Weber, *Max Weber,* p. 375. This is a remarkable book that documents in vivid detail the Heidelberg circle of the Webers, which included Georg Simmel, Lukács, Karl Jaspers, and many other noted scholars and political and literary figures.

19. Ibid.

20. Ibid., p. 374.

21. Ibid., p. 380.

22. Ibid., pp. 378–79.

23. McGuire, *Freud/Jung Letters,* p. 90 (letter 46 J).

24. Paskauskas, *The Complete Correspondence of Sigmund Freud and Ernest Jones* p. 1 (letter 1).

25. McGuire, *Freud/Jung Letters,* p. 153 (Letter 95 J).

26. Ibid., p. 156 (letter 98 J). See also Jung's letter to Freud of 9 September 1908 (letter 108 J) in which he looks forward to talking with Freud in person again because his last intelligent conversations were with Gross during their mutual analysis: "In this respect Gross as a contrast, no matter how hard to digest, did me a world of good. In

spite of his prickliness, talk with him is wonderfully stimulating. I have missed that to no end" (p. 171).

27. David Buss, "Toward a Biologically Informed Psychology of Personality," *Journal of Personality* 58 (1990): 1–16; David Buss, "Evolutionary Personality Psychology," *Annual Review of Psychology* 42 (1991): 459–92; David Buss, "Sex Differences in Human Mate Preferences: Evolutionary Hypotheses Tested in 37 Cultures," *Behavioral and Brain Sciences* 12 (1989): 1–49. This essential view of the natural polygamous nature of the human species as a consequence of evolution is argued extensively from a sociobiological perspective in Helen Fisher, *Anatomy of Love: The Natural History of Monogamy, Adultery, and Divorce* (New York: W. W. Norton, 1992). A related and controversial sociobiological theory by University of Western Ontario professor J. Philippe Rushton, the "Differential K Theory," also argues that individual difference in human personality and behavior are determined by one's biologically based inherited "reproductive strategy" along a continuum from "r" to "K": that is, from maximun egg output and no parental care (the extreme r-strategist) to a few offspring intensively nurtured (an extreme K-strategist). Current species such as oysters, who produce five hundred million eggs per year with no parental care, would be among the many r-strategists in evidence today. Although humans are the most K-oriented of all species, Rushton argues that many humans are far more "r-strategists" (i.e., polygamous) than others and that this evolutionary heritage of common descent from our nonhuman ancestors still determines much of human behavior. It must be remembered that according to Darwinian theory, all forms of life evolved from a single ancestor, and so the common ancestors of humans, oysters, and even fungi spent many millions of years as r-strategists. Thus, from the point of view of evolutionary epistemology, the miniscule period of human life and especially civilization could not be a sufficiently long enough period to eliminate such deeply embedded adaptations as the r-reproductive strategies of our ancestors. See J. P. Rushton, "Differential K Theory: The Sociobiology of Individual and Group Differences," *Personality and Individual Differences* 6 (1985): 441–52; also, "Sir Francis Galton, Epigenetic Rules, Genetic Similarity Theory, and Human Life-History Analysis," *Journal of Personality* 58 (1990): 117–40.

28. Carotenuto, *A Secret Symmetry*, p. 107.

29. McGuire, *Freud/Jung Letters*, p. 207 (letter 133 J).

30. Ibid., p. 289 (letter 175 J).

31. See Philipp Wolff-Windegg, "C. G. Jung—Bachofen, Burckhardt and Basel," *Spring* (1976): pp. 137–47.

CHAPTER NINE

1. Green, *Mountain of Truth*, p. 17.
2. Green, *The von Richthofen Sisters*, p. 44.
3. Jung, *The Psychology of the Unconscious*, para. 249.
4. See Ellenberger, *The Discovery of the Unconscious*, pp. 218–23.
5. Ibid., p. 222.
6. In his autobiographical notes to his *Artistic Form and Yoga in the Sacred Images of India*, trans. Gerald Chapple and James Lawson (Princeton: Princeton University Press, 1984), Zimmer reveals the hereditarian concerns, belief in Bachofenian matriarchy, and nineteenth-century cognitive categories of race that also characterized Jung. Zimmer states that:

> [His mother's] father's side was of German-Saxon extraction. . . . Her mother . . . was of Wendish stock. . . . This Saxon-Wendish stock is inclined to mysticism, as are kindred folk in Silesia. . . . This may account for my predilection for mysticism, myths, and symbols, while the Pre-German, Pre-Celtic, Pre-Aryan descent of my father from the ancient European matriarchical civilization explains my penchant for the corresponding stratifications in ancient Pre-Aryan Hindu civilization (the Great Mother, the feminine principle in Tantrism). (p. 253)

7. Johann Jakob Bachofen, *Das Mutterrecht: Eine Untersuchung über die Gynaekokratie der alten Welt nach ihrer religiösen und rechtlichen Natur* (Stuttgart: Kreis & Hoffman, 1861). Selections from this volume and other works by Bachofen can be found in J. J. Bachofen, *Myth, Religion, and Mother Right: Selected Writings of J. J. Bachofen*, trans. Ralph Manheim (Princeton: Princeton University Press, 1967).
8. See Hermann Glaser, ed., *The German Mind of the Nineteenth Century: A Literary and Historical Anthology* (New York: Continuum, 1981).
9. *C. G. Jung Bibliothek: Katalog*, p. 8.
10. The evidence supporting this argument, and a modern reassessment of Bachofen's ideas, are cogently presented by Fisher in *Anatomy of Love*, pp. 281–84.
11. Marianne Weber, *Ehefrau und Mutter in der Rechtsentwicklung* (Tübingen: Mohr, 1907).
12. Roth, "Marianne Weber and Her Circle," p. xxii.
13. Otto Gross, "Zur Überwindung der kulturellen Krise," *Die Aktion* 3 (1913): 384–87. This essay appears in Gross, *Von geschlechtlichter Not zur sozialen Katastrophe*, pp. 13–15.
14. Sombart, "Max Weber and Otto Gross," p. 138.

15. Ibid.

16. The small but influential Cosmic Circle is frequently mentioned in many publications, but the best treatment is in Green, *The von Richthofen Sisters*, pp. 73–85.

17. A useful treatment of George's cultic practices and metaphors in his work is the two-volume work by Hansjürgen Linke, *Das Kultische in der Dichtung Stefan Georges und seiner Schule* (Munich and Dusseldorf: Helmut Küpper vormals George Bondi, 1960). Linke extensively documents just how far George and his circle would go in the practice of their religious cultism in a fascinating, almost ethnographic, style. A lucid account of George's life and cultic activities can also be found in Wayne Andrews, "The Gospel According to Stefan George," a chapter in his book *Siegfried's Curse: The German Journey From Nietzsche to Hesse* (New York: Atheneum, 1972), pp. 171–97.

18. On French decadent "satanism," see James Laver, *The First Decadent: The Strange Life of J. K. Huysmans* (New York: Citadel Press, 1955), pp. 110–55. Huysmans's famous novel, *Là-Bas* (1891), with its graphic descriptions of the satanic black mass, reflected the practices among some of the decadents in the French occult underground. On the Golden Dawn and its practices, see Ellic Howe, *The Magicians of the Golden Dawn: A Documentary History of a Magical Order, 1887–1923* (London: Routledge and Kegan Paul, 1972).

19. Michael Metzger and Erika Metzger, *Stefan George* (New York: Twayne, 1972), p. 35.

20. This is incorrectly reported by Joseph Campbell as happening in the 1920s. See Joseph Campbell, "Introduction," in Bachofen, *Myth, Religion, and Mother Right*, p. xxv.

21. Linke, *Das Kultische in der Dichtung Stefan Georges und seiner Schule*, pp. 60–61.

22. At a ritual gathering of the members of the Sera Circle and Free German Youth on the Hohen Meissner mountain in 1913 that was organized by Diederichs, Klages gave a talk in which he argued that modern civilization was drowning the soul of humanity and that what was needed was a return to nature and to Mother Earth. See Mosse, "The Mystical Origins of National Socialism," p. 83. For a description of this event and the texts of talks by Klages, Julius Langbehn, and others, see Eugen Diederichs, ed., *Freideutsche Jungend: Zur Jahrhundertfeier auf dem Hohen Meissner* (Jena: Diederichs, 1913).

23. Green, *The von Richthofen Sisters*, p. 80.

24. See Webb, *The Occult Establishment*, pp. 395, 397–98.

25. Ludwig Klages, *Ausdrucksbewegung und Gestaltungskraft. Grundlagung der Wissenschaft vom Ausdruck*, 3d ed. (Leipzig: Barth, 1923).

26. The rising influence of characterology and expression analysis

are discussed at length by Ulfried Geuter in *The Professionalization of Psychology in Nazi Germany*, trans. R. Holmes (Cambridge: Cambridge University Press, 1992; original German edition, 1984). See also, Ulfried Geuter, "German Psychology During the Nazi Period," in Ash and Woodward, *Psychology in Twentieth-Century Thought and Society*; and C. F. Graumann, ed., *Psychologie im Nationalsozialismus* (Berlin: Springer, 1985).

27. For this view of Klages, see Lukács, "Pre-Fascist and Fascist Vitalism," in his *The Destruction of Reason*, pp. 522–46.

28. C. G. Jung, "Psychologische Typen," *Zeitschrift für Menschenkunde. Blätter für Charakterologie* . . . 1 (1925): 45–65. This can be found in *Psychological Types*. The connection with Klages and his characterology is not mentioned in the *Collected Works*, which leaves out the identifying subtitle given above.

29. Fanny zu Reventlow's affair with Rilke is unfortunately only obliquely referred to in Wolfgang Leppmann, *Rilke: A Life* (New York: Fromm International Publishing, 1984), pp. 60–61. Leppmann does, however, acknowledge that except for his association with Reventlow, Rilke was not among the café society denizens of Schwabing.

30. Cited and translated by Green, *The von Richthofen Sisters*, p. 94. Her autobiography also contains descriptions of the ritual invocations of the Earth Mother by the Cosmic Circle. See Gräfin Franziska zu Reventlow, *Herrn Dames Aufzeichnungen oder Begebenheiten aus einem merkwürdigen Stadtteil* (Munich: Langen, 1913).

31. The goals of the Cosmic Circle were very much in tune with the neopagan sentiments that also stimulated Jung:

> The *Kosmiker* proceeded from the idea that the total decay of the soul of mankind through rationalism and believed in salvation by reawakening the myths of those cultural strata which had become lost through the history of Judeo-Christian Western civilization. Both Klages and Schuler believed that a re-establishment of man's mystical rapport with the ultimate forces of life could be brought about by an ecstatic embrace of paganism; in Klages's opinion that of the Germanic tribes before their conversion to Christianity, to Schuler that of the mystery religions practices in imperial Rome. (Metzger and Metzger, *Stefan George*, pp. 35–36).

32. Jung, *The Psychology of the Unconscious*, para. 290.

33. Ibid., para. 315.

34. Ibid., para. 316. The diagrams he then interprets in this text are between paras. 316 and 317 on p. 198.

35. Ellenberger, *The Discovery of the Unconscious*, p. 223.

36. McGuire, *Freud/Jung Letters*, p. 503 (letter 313 J).

37. Ibid., p. 504 (letter 314 F).

38. This citation and translation is by Ellenberger, *The Discovery of the Unconscious*, p. 816. The original reference is Sigmund Freud, "Gross ist die Diana der Epheser," *Zentralblatt für Psychoanalyse*, 2 (1912): 158–59. It is also included in Freud's *Standard Edition*, 12: 342–44.

39. Ellenberger, *The Discovery of the Unconscious*, p. 816.

40. Jung, *The Psychology of the Unconscious*, para. 317.

41. Ibid.

42. This is documented in the enlightening volume by Harold Jantz, *The Mothers in Faust: The Myth of Time and Creativity* (Baltimore: Johns Hopkins University Press, 1969).

43. This is translated and cited by Burkert in his exemplary book, *Ancient Mystery Cults*, p. 21. Of particular value for understanding the experience of the Hellenistic mysteries are his chapters on "Personal Needs" and "The Extraordinary Experience."

44. Cited in Jantz, *The Mothers in Faust*, p. 71.

45. Jung, *The Psychology of the Unconscious*, para. 458.

46. Ibid., para. 459.

47. Sombart, "Max Weber and Otto Gross," p. 139.

48. C. G. Jung, "The Significance of the Father in the Destiny of the Individual" (1909), *Freud and Psychoanalysis*, CW 4 (New York: Pantheon, 1961) para. 692n.

49. C. G. Jung, "The Content of the Psychoses," para. 160

50. Ibid., paras. 341–42.

Chapter Ten

1. *MDR*, pp. 158–60. Another version is found in E. A. Bennet, *Meetings with Jung: Conversations Recorded During the Years 1946–1961* (Zurich: Daimon, 1985), pp. 117–18. Rather than the usual transcendental interpretations of this dream by Jung, in Bennet's account Jung associates the supposedly "impersonal" material from collective unconscious sources with some very personal ones: "When he reflected on it later the house had some association in his mind with his uncle's very old house in Basel which was built in the old moat of the town and had two cellars; the lower one was very dark and like a cave."

2. Jung, *Analytical Psychology*, pp. 22–23.

3. Ibid., p. 23.

4. Ibid.

5. McGuire, *Freud/Jung Letters*, letter 157 J.

6. Ibid., letter 159 J.

7. Jung's *Bibliothek* catalog gives the dates 1810–1821 for the complete four volumes of Creuzer's work, which seems to indicate that Jung had some volumes from the first edition and some from the second. There is no more specific information to be found than this, which appears in the *C. G. Jung Bibliothek: Katalog*, p. 17. The particulars for the first two editions of Friedrich Creuzer, *Symbolik und Mythologie der alten Völker, besonders der Griechen*, are as follows: for the first edition, all of which were published in Leipzig and Darmstadt, the first volume of 1810 was published by Leske, and the following three, in 1811 and 1812, were published by Heyer and Leske. The entire second edition of four volumes was published in Darmstadt by Heyer and Leske, and they appeared in 1819, 1820, and 1821. The second editon was greatly expanded by hundreds of pages in volumes 1, 2, and 4.

8. Metzger, "Considerations of Methodology in the Study of the Mystery Religions and Early Christianity," p. 1. Metzger cites as the primary "precritical" works those of both Creuzer and of G.E.J. de Sainte Croix, whose *Recherches historiques et critiques sur les mystères du paganisme . . .* (Paris, 1784), also supported this same hierarchical "secret society" image of the ancient mysteries. Jung's *Bibliothek* lists these very early works by Creuzer and Sainte Croix among the volumes in his personal library.

9. *Goethe's Bibliothek: Katalog*, ed. Hans Ruppert (Weimar: Arion Verlag, 1958), pp. 280–81.

10. A chicken or the egg argument arises here, for in the opinion of Jung and his disciples, the transcendent archetypes worked through Goethe and Wagner, and it was Jung's genius to discover the imprint of these extramundane forces in *Faust* and in Wagnerian opera. Jungians dismiss the idea that Goethe and Wagner (and later Jung) could have been consulting the same German-language source materials for their mythological studies and that this could account for the similarity of motifs in their work instead of transpersonal archetypes. Jungian interpretations of Goethe and especially Wagner work backward in their logic by positing transcendental forces—the archetypes of the collective unconscious—as the true creative influence on these men. It does not occur to them that Creuzer, Goethe, and Wagner influenced Jung and that he only later claimed it was not these men per se, but transcendental forces working through them and through him that accounted for such similarities. This faulty logic, based on an essentially religious belief in the occult realm of the collective unconscious, permeates the Jungian literature and is evident, for example in analyses of the archetypal origins of Wagner's genius. See, e.g., Robert Donnington, *Wagner's "Ring" and Its Symbols: The Music and the Myth* (New

York: St. Martin's, 1974), and the recent work, Jean Shinoda Bolen, *The Ring of Power: The Abandoned Child and the Authoritarian Father* (San Francisco: Harper San Francisco, 1993).

11. Wagner, *Cosima Wagner's Diaries* 2:565.

12. The sobriquet "Solar Phallus Man" is the invention of Sonu Shamdasani.

13. Shamdasani, "A Woman Called Frank," p. 40.

14. See McGuire and Hull, *C. G. Jung Speaking*, pp. 433–35.

15. Jung, *The Psychology of the Unconscious*, para. 173.

16. Mead, *A Mithraic Ritual*.

17. Dieterich, *Eine Mithrasliturgie*. The first edition of this work appeared in 1903.

18. McGuire and Hull, *C. G. Jung Speaking*, p. 435.

19. For Jung's revised versions, see "The Structure of the Psyche" (1928/1931), *Structure and Dynamics of the Psyche*, para. 319; and especially "The Concept of the Collective Unconscious" (1936), *Archetypes and the Collective Unconscious*, para. 105. It is dismaying to note that so many of Jung's closest collaborators also repeated this story as a way of offering dramatic evidence for the collective unconscious without mentioning Honegger's role or the 1903 edition of Dieterich's book. Their repetition of this story should be seen more as acts of devout discipleship than as ignorance of the truth. See, e.g., von Franz, *C. G. Jung: His Myth in Our Time*, p. 124; and C. A. Maier, *Soul and Body: Essays on the Theories of C. G. Jung* (Santa Monica, Calif.: Lapis Press, 1986), p. 78.

20. I am indebted to William McGuire for this fact.

21. I am again indebted to McGuire for sharing this information with me. As these papers remain under restriction at the insistence of C. A. Maier, further examination of Honegger's papers and the case of the Solar Phallus Man must await future publications.

22. Jung, "The Concept of the Collective Unconscious," para. 105n.

23. Creuzer, *Symbolik und Mythologie der alten Völker*, 3:335.

24. Bachofen, *Myth, Religion, and Mother Right*, pp. 114–15.

25. McGuire, *Freud/Jung Letters*, letter 175J. Also see McGuire, introduction, to Jung, *Psychology of the Unconscious*, p. xviii.

26. The abstract is reprinted in full in Hans Walser, "An Early Psychoanalytical Tragedy: J. J. Honegger and the Beginnings of Training Analysis," *Spring* (1974): 253–54.

27. After the devastation of the First World War, the only persons with resources enough to pay for psychoanalysis were to be found outside of Continental Europe, the caseloads of both Freud and Jung were made up of predominantly English-speaking patients. By the 1920s Jung spoke and wrote English fluently, but Freud had great diffi-

culty mastering English in his sixties just to understand and talk to the majority of his patients, and this was not helped by his growing mouth cancer at this time. As persons from England and particularly America (even college-educated ones) did not have the sort of intensive classical education so prominent in Hellenized Germany, Jung's frequent claims that his patients "could not have possibly known" such material were far more believable to them. As for the mythological content of their own dreams, by the 1920s most of the well-to-do American and British patients who made the pilgrimage to see Jung had been involved in occult traditions such as Theosophy, had read Jung's works, or were attracted to his spiritual and mythological themes, and wanted more of the same. Hence, Jung's clinical evidence for a collective unconscious comes from a highly biased subject pool.

28. C. G. Jung, "A Study in the Process of Individuation," (1950), *Archetypes and the Collective Unconscious*, para. 542. For the record, Jung had indeed already begun his intense study of alchemical symbols earlier in the 1920s, and was quite familiar with them through other works as early as 1909.

29. For a discussion of Mann and her Swedenborgian family heritage and her possible exposure to alchemical ideas because of this, see Webb, *The Occult Establishment*, pp. 388–94.

30. Cited in McGuire, introduction to Jung, *The Psychology of the Unconscious*, p. xxiii. The original reference is Sigmund Freud, "Über einige Übereinstimmungen im Seelenleben der Wilden und der Neurotiker, I: Die Inzestscheu," *Imago* 1 (1912): 18.

31. Kerr, "Beyond the Pleasure Principle and Back Again."

32. Jung, *Analytical Psychology*, p. 99.

33. McGuire, *The Freud/Jung Letters*, p. 296 (letter 180J).

34. Homans gives psychoanalytic historian John Gedo the credit for astutely "[putting] his finger on a critical point in the Freud-Jung relationship" in an unpublished paper by Gedo. This critical point came in 1910 when, according to Homans, "Jung tried to endow Freud and psychoanalysis with religious powers" (*Jung in Context*, p. 56).

35. McGuire, *Freud/Jung Letters*, p. 288 (letter 174 F).

36. Ibid., p. 294 (letter 178 J).

37. Ibid.

38. Ibid.

39. Ibid.

40. Ibid., p. 295 (letter 179 F, 13 February 1910).

41. Ibid., p. 296.

42. Ibid.

43. Ibid., p. 308 (letter 186 J).

44. Ibid., p. 346 (letter 206 J).

45. Unlike Jung's own case histories claiming to support the phylogenetic hypothesis, these papers by his assistants provide much more information regarding personal history. Nelken cites Cumont and Dieterich on Mithras and amplifies the delusion of his patient with references to solar mythology, the tree of life, the snake, and other mythological symbols of interest to Jung during this period. At the very end of his paper, Nelken claims (like Jung) that it is "out of the question" (*"ausgeschlossen"*) that the patient was conscious of the meaning of his mythological symbolism, although Nelken does honestly admit that, after examining the patient in numerous interrogations concerning his prior knowledge of solar worship and the Mithras cult, "the knowledge of the patient in this regard has, however, proven itself to be more than superficial" ("Die kentnisse des Patienten in dieser Richtung haben sich aber mehr als oberflächlich erwiesen."). See Jan Nelken, "Analytische Beobachtungen über Phantasien eines Schizophrenen" ("Analytical Observations on the Fantasies of a Schizophrenic"), *Jahrbuch für psychoanalytische und psychopathologische Forschungen* 4 (1912): 504–62. See also Sabina Spielrein, "Über den psychologischen Inhalt eines Falls von Schizophrenie," *Jahrbuch für psychoanalytische und psychopathologische Forschungen* 3 (1912): 329–400.

46. Jung, *Letters: I. 1906–1950*, p. 24. Letter to Freud of 12 June 1911.

47. See Shamdasani, "A Woman Called Frank," pp. 26–55 .

48. Kerr, "Beyond the Pleasure Principle," p. 41.

49. Jung, *Analytical Psychology*, p. 27.

50. Paskauskas, *Freud/Jones Correspondence*, p. 160 (letter 94, 18 September 1912).

51. Fortunately, this is summarized for us in Ellenberger, *The Discovery of the Unconscious*, pp. 809–16.

52. Ibid., p. 813.

53. Ibid., p. 814.

54. McGuire, *Freud/Jung Letters*, p. 487 (letter 300 J).

55. Ibid., p. 478 (letter 291 J).

56. Ibid., p. 480 (letter 293 F of 10 January 1912).

57. See the excellent biography by Rudolph Binion, *Frau Lou: Nietzsche's Wayward Disciple* (Princeton: Princeton University Press, 1968), especially pp. 335–99.

58. A list of the programs of the society held between October 1912 and July 1913 appeared in the "Bulletins" section of the *Internationale Zeitschrift für ärztliche Psychoanalyse* 1 (1913): 635.

59. See McGuire, "Introduction," in Jung, *Dream Analysis*, p. vii.

60. Jung, *Freud and Psychoanalysis*.

61. See Noll, "Jung the *Leontocephalus*," pp. 12–60.

62. See Kerr, *A Most Dangerous Method*.

63. McGuire *Freud/Jung Letters*, p. 491 (letter 303 J).

64. See pp. 131–32, above.

65. Von Franz gives this date in her introduction to *The Zofingia Lectures*: "In 1912 he came to the conclusion that he personally could *not* return to the medieval or original Christian myth and set his foot on the path of finding his own myth by a form of meditation that he later called 'active imagination'" (p. xxiv).

66. Jung, *Two Essays*.

67. See Phyllis Grosskurth, "The Idyll in the Harz Mountains: Freud's Secret Committee," in Gelfand and Kerr, *Freud and the History of Psychoanalysis*, pp. 341–56.

68. Jung, "New Paths in Psychology," para. 430.

69. Ibid.

70. Ibid., para. 437.

71. Ibid., para. 438.

72. Ibid.

73. Ibid., para. 441.

74. C. G. Jung, "Preface to the First Edition (1917)," in *Two Essays*.

75. C. G. Jung, "Preface to the Second Edition (1918)," ibid.

76. Jung, *Analytical Psychology*, p. 42.

77. Ibid.

78. The speculation in the Jungian literature that the voice was Spielrein's. See William McGuire's footnote in ibid.

79. Ibid.

80. Ibid., p. 46.

81. Ibid., p. 33.

82. Ibid., p. 46.

83. The first compilation of works by Jung's group can be found in C. G. Jung, ed., *Psychologische Abhandlungen* (Leipzig and Vienna: Deuticke, 1914). It was to be the first of many volumes of this group, but further volumes under the name of this series did not appear until 1928. In the foreword to the book dated May 1914 Jung explains: "The present state of psychology seems to make it advisable that schools or movements have their own organs of publication." *The Symbolic Life: Miscellaneous Writings* CW 18, (Princeton: Princeton University Press, 1976), para. 1825. Jung clearly sees his group as a school or movement at this time.

84. Jones wrote to Freud from Rome on 29 December 1912 (Paskauskas, *Freud/Jones Correspondence*, p. 189, letter 112). This appeared as Ernest Jones, "Der Gottmensch-Komplex; der Glaube, Gott zu Sein, und die daraus folgenden Charactermerkmale," *Internationale Zeitschrift für ärtzliche Psychoanalyse* 1 (1913): 313–29. An English translation can be found under the title "The God Complex: The Belief That

One Is God and the Resulting Character Traits," in Ernest Jones, *Essays in Applied Psycho-analysis, Volume II* (New York: International Universities Press, 1964).

85. Ibid.

86. Jones, *Essays in Applied Psycho-Analysis, Volume II*, p. 255.

87. C. G. Jung, "Psychoanalysis and the Association Experiments" (1906), *Experimental Researches*, para. 727.

88. Jones, *Essays, Volume II*, p. 247.

89. Ibid., p. 248.

90. Ibid., p. 260.

91. Ibid., p. 261.

92. Jung, *Analytical Psychology*, p. 41.

93. Ibid., p. 44.

94. Ibid., p. 43.

95. See Homans, *Jung in Context*. Homans gives priority to an argument in an unpublished manuscript by John Gedo, "Magna est vis et veritatis tuae et praevalebit: Comments on the Freud-Jung correspondence" (1974).

96. Jones, *The Life and Work of Sigmund Freud*, 2:33

97. *MDR*, p. 176.

98. Jung, *Analytical Psychology*, pp. 43–44.

99. See Jaffé, "Introduction," *MDR*, p. vii.

100. Ibid.

101. *MDR*, pp. 181–84.

102. Jung, *Analytical Psychology*, pp. 63–64, 88–89.

103. *MDR*, p. 181.

104. He does not, however, examine possible personal sources of inspiration for these figures. For example, they may well have corresponded to concerns with Freud and Andreas-Salomé.

105. Jung, *Analytical Psychology*, p. 89.

106. *MDR*, p. 182.

107. Jung, *Analytical Psychology*, p. 89.

108. *MDR*, p. 182.

109. Jung, *Analytical Psychology*, p. 93.

110. Ibid., p. 95.

111. Franz Joseph Mone, *Geschichte des Heidenthums*, 2 vols. (Leipzig and Darmstadt: Carl Wilhelm Leske, 1822 and 1825). Although these two volumes by Mone are distinct from Creuzer's four volumes, Creuzer is responsible for having them published and it is Creuzer's name on the spines of these books. The individual volumes under Creuzer in Jung's *Bibliothek* are not listed.

112. Jung, *Analytical Psychology*, p. 96.

113. Ibid.

114. Ibid., p. 37.

115. Ibid., p. 98.

116. Ibid., p. 98.

117. Ibid., p. 99.

118. Ibid.

119. On the multiple interpretations of Aion, see the following: Howard Jackson, "The Meaning and Function of the Leontocephaline in Roman Mithraism," *Numen* 32 (1985): 17–45; R. L. Gordon, "Reality, Evocation, and Boundary in the Mysteries of Mithras," *Journal of Mithraic Studies* 3 (1980): 19–99; and Doro Levi, "Aion," *Hesperia* 13 (1944): 269–314; and Ulansey, *The Origins of the Mithraic Mysteries*.

120. Jung, therefore, never having set foot in Rome, never saw this actual statue of the lion-headed god in person.

121. See the following recent biographies that document this relationship: Forrest G. Robinson, *Love's Story Told: A Life of Henry A. Murray* (Cambridge, Mass.: Harvard University Press, 1992); and Claire Douglas, *Translate the Darkness: The Life of Christiana Morgan, the Veiled Woman in Jung's Circle* (New York: Simon and Schuster, 1993).

122. See McGuire, "Introduction," in Jung, *Dream Analysis*.

123. This is immediately clear when one closely examines Jung's pattern of publications, chronologically listed in the *General Bibliography* (CW 19; Princeton: Princeton University Press, 1979), especially for his publications in his native German.

124. These publications were somewhat akin to today's politically conservative *Reader's Digest*, and not at all similar to medical, professional, or scientific journals in any way.

Chapter Eleven

1. C. G. Jung, "La Structure de l'inconscient," *Archives de Psychologie* 16 (1916): 152–79. Jung's original manuscript was in German, and an English translation of this appeared in Long, *Collected Papers on Analytical Psychology*. It was subsequently revised and greatly expanded into an almost entirely new paper and published in 1928 as "The Relations Between the Ego and the Unconscious." The original German manuscript was found in 1961 after Jung's death, and forms the basis of the translation of the original that appears in the appendix of *Two Essays* as "The Structure of the Unconscious."

2. Jung, "The Structure of the Unconscious," para. 446.

3. Ibid., para. 450.

4. Ibid., para. 456.

5. Ibid., para. 455.

6. Ibid.

7. Ibid., para. 456.

8. Ibid., para. 454.

9. Ibid., para. 470.

10. See R.F.C. Hull, "Bibliographic Notes on Active Imagination in the Works of C. G. Jung," *Spring* (1971): 115–20.

11. Jung, "The Structure of the Unconscious," para. 464n.

12. Ibid., para. 466.

13. Ibid., para. 467.

14. Ibid.

15. There is much private speculation over whether the charges of Jones and Freud that Jung believed himself to be the "Aryan Christ" had a basis in Jung's subjective experience. There is an unsubstantiated report that the famous "Red Book" in which Jung inscribed and illustrated his active-imagination fantasies may contain just such evidence.

16. Jung, "The Structure of the Unconscious," para. 468.

17. Ibid.

18. C. G. Jung, *The Transcendent Function*, trans. A. R. Pope (Zurich: C. G. Jung Institute Students Association, 1957). This translation from Jung's original document is twenty-three pages long. Jung added material primarily to the end of this document in the version that appears as "The Transcendent Function" (1916/1958), in *The Structure and Dynamics of the Psyche*. A preface by James Hillman is included in the 1957 publication.

19. Ibid., p. 5.

20. Ibid., p. 6.

21. Ibid.

22. For a description of the use of "evolution" in the biological sciences to describe both embryological development and species change, see Richards, *The Meaning of Evolution*.

23. Jung, *The Transcendent Function*, p. 5.

24. Ibid.

25. Ibid., p. 6.

26. Ibid., p. 7.

27. Ibid.

28. Ibid., p. 10.

29. Ibid., p. 11.

30. Ibid.

31. Ibid., p. 23.

32. Ibid., p. 13.

33. Ibid.

34. Ibid., p. 22.

35. Ibid., p. 18. For a description of the role of Ascona in the birth of the modern dance movement, see Green, *The Mountain of Truth*.

36. Ibid., p. 22.

37. However, the English translation in the *Collected Works* appeared in Hull, "Bibliographic Notes."

38. C. G. Jung, "Adaptation, Individuation, Collectivity" (1916), *Miscellaneous Writings*, para. 1087.

39. Ibid., para. 1090.

40. Ibid., para. 1094.

41. Ibid.

42. Von Hartmann, devotes an entire section to *"Der Begriff der Individualität"* ("The Concept of Individuality") and its syncretic blend of Schopenhauerian philosophy and vitalistic evolutionary biology in *Philosophie des Unbewussten*, pp. 515–34. He also includes a chapter on *"Die Individuation"* ("Individuation") and its likelihood (rare) and resulting personality characteristics (Schopenhauerian) on pp. 612–32. Schopenhauer first mentions the *principium individuationis* (which he admits is an expression he borrowed from "the old scholasticism") in the first volume (1819) of *The World as Will and Representation*, trans. E.F.J. Payne (New York: Dover, 1969), 1:112. Nietzsche refers to it in the first section of his very first book (1872), *Die Geburt der Tragödie aus dem Geist der Musik* (*The Birth of Tragedy from the Spirit of Music*). See Friedrich Nietzsche, *The Birth of Tragedy and The Case of Wagner*, trans. Walter Kaufmann (New York: Vintage Books, 1967), p. 36.

43. Jung, "Adaptation, Individuation, Collectivity," para. 1103.

44. Ibid., para. 1094

45. Ibid., para. 1097.

46. Ibid.

47. Ibid., para. 1099.

48. On Alcoholics Anonymous as a charismatic group, see Galanter, *Cults: Faith, Healing and Coercion*.

49. Hugo Ball, *Hermann Hesse: Sein Leben und Werk* (Berlin: S. Fischer Verlag, 1927). A later special edition was Hugo Ball, *Hermann Hesse: Sein Leben und Werk* (Frankfurt: Suhrkamp Verlag, 1956). Ball's summary of these notes appear on pp. 142–45 of this later edition.

50. Ralph Freeman, *Hermann Hesse: Pilgrim of Crisis* (New York: Pantheon, 1978). Freeman is using the 1956 edition of Ball's biography.

51. This is my translation of the following: "23. X. 17. Du wirst Hören die Stimme, die aus den Urtiefen der Erde ruft, verkünden werde ich Dir die Gesetze des Magmas, in dessen Quellen ich throne, vernehmen sollst Du von mir die Gesetze der Toten, welches sein werden Satzungen der neuen Zeit." Ball, *Hermann Hesse*, pp. 158–59.

52. "Gehe ruhig zur Ruhe, ich bin Dir immer nahe, sende aber oft des Tages und während der Nacht die Strahlen Deiner Gedanken in den finsteren Schacht Deiner Seele, wo ich mich Du zu nahen suche, um Berührung zu gewinnen." Ball, *Hermann Hesse*, p. 159.

53. "Ich hämmere in Deinem Schachte, einmal wirst Du verstehen

und lesen die Runen, die ich im Gestein Deiner Seele herausgeschlagen habe, die Urschrift des Menschen, die Du sie lehren musst, die Gesetzestafeln des Kommenden." Ball, *Hermann Hesse*, p. 159. In reading this passage, it is difficult not to imagine the musical hammering of the subterranean Niebelungs in Wagner's *Das Reingold*, Jung's favorite opera.

54. Diederichs was the publisher of an early collection of Hesse's poetry. For an appreciation of the publisher by the author, see Hermann Hesse, "Der Verlag Eugen Diederichs," *März* 3 (1909): 318–20.

55. Freeman, *Hermann Hesse*, p. 109.

56. Guido von List, *Die Geheimnis der Runen*. Band 1, Guido von List Bücherei (Gross-Lichterfeld: P. Zillman, 1908). For an English translation and a biographical essay by Stephen Flowers, see Guido von List, *The Secret of the Runes* (Rochester, Vt.: Destiny Books, 1988).

57. Goodrick-Clarke, *The Occult Roots of Modern Nazism*, p. 49. The speculation about ancient mystery initiations among the Germanic tribes can be traced at least as far back as the work of Justus Möser (1720–1794). Möser argues in "Von den Mysterien und dem Volksglauben der alten Deutschen und Gallier" (*Sämtliche Werke*, 2, p. 402) that mystery initiations took place in secret underground churches in the form of ritual dramatic performances, much like the Mithraic and Dionysiac cults of the Greeks.

58. Jung, "On the Psychology of the Unconscious," *Two Essays*, para. 118.

59. Ibid.

60. Jules Verne, *A Journey to the Center of the Earth* (Pleasantville, N.Y.: The Reader's Digest Association, 1992), p. 1. This modern edition uses the same anonymous English translation of the work that has been used for over a century. For the purposes of convenience, all references will be from this easily accessible edition.

61. Ibid., p. 2.

62. Ibid., p. 5.

63. Ibid., p. 8.

64. Ibid., p. 16.

65. Ibid., pp. 21–22.

66. Jaffé, *C. G. Jung: Word and Image*, p. 76 Jung's detailed explanation of this mandala precedes it on p. 75.

67. *MDR*, pp. 189–92.

68. Jung, *Letters, I: 1906–1950*, p. 34.

69. On the real Basilides, see Gilles Quispel, "Gnostic Man: The Doctrine of Basilides," in Joseph Campbell, ed., *The Mystic Vision: Papers from the Eranos Yearbooks, Volume 6* (Princeton: Princeton University Press, 1968), 210–46. Also useful is Giovanni Filoramo, *A History of Gnosticism* (Oxford: Basil Blackwell, 1990), pp. 159–61.

70. *MDR*, p. 190.

71. The translation used for this summary can be found in Segal, *The Gnostic Jung*, pp. 181–93. The critical seventh sermon appears on pp. 192–93, which is the source of my references to the work that follow.

72. For a useful summary of perspectives and a comprehensive footnote citation of the interpretive literature on the "Seven Sermons," see ibid., pp. 35–48.

73. Metzger and Metzger, *Stefan George*, pp. 157–58.

74. See Peter Gay, "The Secret Germany: Poetry as Power," a chapter in *Weimar Culture*, pp. 46–69. According to Gay, "Stefan George was the king of a secret Germany" (p. 47).

75. See the poems "Templars" and "The Guardians of the Forecourt" in Stefan George, *The Works of Stefan George*, trans. Olga Marx and Ernst Morwitz (New York: AMS Press, 1966), pp. 177–79.

76. Stefan George, "The Star of the Covenant" (1913), in ibid., p. 248.

77. After years of teaching his disciples how to reach the god within, Jung formalized this idea as the "self" in his psychological theory in his 1928 essay on "The Relations Between the Ego and the Unconscious." Jung had, however, hinted at such a concept in 1921 in his *Psychological Types* (CW 6, para. 623) and, of course, in his 1916 exposition on "godlikeness" in his essay on "The Structure of the Unconscious."

Chapter Twelve

1. Jung, "Adaptation, Individuation, Collectivity," para. 1099.

2. Jung, "Introduction to Toni Wolff's 'Studies in Jungian Thought,'" para. 887.

3. See the discussion in chapter 7 of Jung, *Zofingia Lectures*.

4. Mosse, *The Crisis of German Ideology*, p. 43.

5. In "The Structure of the Unconscious," Jung says that "the faculty of imitation" is "most pernicious for individuation," and he condemns those who "are content to ape some eminent personality . . . thereby achieving an outward distinction from the circle in which they move" (para. 463). Jung was no doubt aiming this arrow at the Freudians, but was also no doubt warning those within his own circle that his official position on their own "imitation of Jung" was one of intolerance.

6. Jung, "The Relations Between the Ego and the Unconscious," para. 399.

7. Ibid., para. 401.

8. See, for example, the 26 May 1923 letter of Jung to Oskar Schmitz (chap. 6). Jung repeatedly warned his fellow Europeans about the dangers of pursuing spiritual paths originating in lands or from peoples who had a different geographical or especially biological heritage.

Jung persisted in this attitude even after studying Chinese alchemy with Richard Wilhelm. In his "Commentary on *The Secret of the Golden Flower*" (1929), a translation of an ancient Chinese alchemical text by Wilhelm, Jung devotes his entire first section to "Difficulties Encountered By A European in Trying to Understand the East" and includes the warning that, "It is not for us to imitate what is foreign to our organism or to play the missionary; our task is to build up our Western civilization, which sickens with a thousand ills" (para. 5). A further discussion of Jung's rejection of Eastern spirituality for Westerners on these völkisch grounds can be found in Harold Coward, *Jung and Eastern Thought* (New York: State University of New York Press, 1985), pp. 8–11.

9. These facts came to light during a seminar on "Jung and Anti-Semitism" at a conference of Jungian analysts in Paris in 1989. See Mary Ann Mattoon, ed., *Paris 89: Proceedings of the Eleventh International Congress for Analytical Psychology, August 28–September 2, 1989: Personal and Archetypal Dynamics in the Analytical Relationship* (Einsiedln, Switzerland: Daimon Verlag, 1991).

10. Nietzsche, "The Birth of Tragedy," in *The Birth of Tragedy and the Case of Wagner*, p. 123.

11. Ibid., p. 124.

12. Ferdinand Tönnies, *Gemeinschaft und Gesellschaft* (Darmstadt: Wissenschaftliche Buchgesellschaft, 1979; original edition, 1887). An English-language translation by Charles Loomis is *Community and Society* (New York: Harper & Row, 1963). However, perhaps the best summary of Tönnies' utopianism can be found in Liebersohn, *Fate and Utopia in German Sociology*, pp. 11–39.

13. Interestingly, in an unpublished essay written between 1920 and 1925, Tönnies proposed an apocalyptic vision of a coming new age of history in which Christianity would be overthrown and a cosmic oneness with the natural world would mark humankind's new spiritual freedom. Tönnies even entitled his prophetic essay *Die neue Botschaft* ("The New Gospel"). Tönnies was no doubt influenced by his participation in the monistic religion of Haeckel and Ostwald.

14. On the Rosicrucian influences on Goethe, and for information on the history of the construction of this poem, see the commentary to Goethe's "*Die Geheimnisse*" by Erich Trunz in *Goethes Werke, Band II*, 7th ed. (Hamburg: Christian Wegner Verlag, 1965), pp. 653–58.

15. The völkisch movement and especially Nazi Germany deliberately used similar fantasies of an elite order of Grail-Knights in their rhetoric. During the Nazi era Heinrich Himmler's elite SS corps comprised just such an organization. As Hermand tells it, "Pushing aside a semitic Christianity in favor of an Indo-Germanic religion, Himmler

wanted to construct a series of SS monasteries—a desire partly realized in the mid-1930s with the transformation of Wevelsburg castle near Paderborn into a racial cultic shrine—where those SS leaders who were especially 'adept' in the mysteries of the SS came together every year to participate in occult meditation practices" (*Old Dreams of a New Reich*, p. 243).

16. Cited in Aschheim, *The Nietzsche Legacy in Germany*, p. 8.

17. Kaufmann, *Nietzsche: Philosopher, Psychologist, Antichrist*, p. 272.

18. Ibid., p. 262.

19. Nietzsche, "Thus Spoke Zarathustra, First Part," in *The Portable Nietzsche*, p. 187.

20. Typical nineteenth-century views on the degenerate nature of genius can be found throughout the highly influential work of Cesare Lombroso, *The Man of Genius* (London: Walter Scott, 1910; original Italian edition, 1888). For an exemplary modern review of the issue, see George Becker, *The Mad Genius Controversy* (New York: Sage, 1978). A useful summary of the relationship between genius, IQ, and "eminence" is found in the collection by Robert S. Albert, ed., *Genius and Eminence: The Social Psychology of Creativity and Exceptional Achievement* (New York: Pergamon Press, 1983).

21. Jung, "Thoughts on the Interpretation of Christianity," para. 243.

22. See Becker, *The Mad Genius Controversy*.

23. C. G. Jung, "On the Psychology and Pathology of So-Called Occult Phenomena" (1902), *Psychiatric Studies*, para. 3.

24. Jung, "Cryptomnesia," para. 175. Jung's paper was originally published in the weekly Berlin journal *Die Zukunft* as one in a series of articles published in 1904–1905 that discussed a possible instance of plagiarism by a noted drama critic. Writing this article was a way for Jung to participate in the cultural dialogue of his day at the highest levels, for the previous discussant of the case in an earlier issue had been Arthur Schnitzler (1862–1931), the famous Viennese novelist, playwright, and physician.

25. Schopenhauer, *The World as Will and Representation*, 2:386. The first German edition of only the first volume appeared in 1819; the second German edition containing the additional second volume of supplements in which Schopenhauer's famous chapter "On Genius" first appeared was published in 1844.

26. Ibid., 2:379.

27. Carl Pletsch, "The Self-Sufficient Text in Nietzsche and Kierkegaard," in S. N. Godfrey, ed., *The Anxiety of Anticipation* (Yale French Studies, no. 66) (New Haven: Yale University Press, 1984). See also Pletsch's superb *Young Nietzsche*.

28. Schopenhauer, *The World as Will*, 2:385.

29. See R. B. Onians, *The Origins of European Thought about the Body, the Mind, the Soul, the World, Time and Fate* (Cambridge: Cambridge University Press, 1951), pp. 160–62, 168–73.

30. Benedict Augustin Morel, *Traité des Dégénérescences physiques, intellectuelles et morales de l'Espéce humaine et des Causes qui produiscent ces Variétes maladaptives* (Paris: Bailliére, 1857), p. 5. Cited and translated in Nordau, *Degeneration*, p. 16.

31. Jung, *Letters, I: 1906–1950*, p. 35.

32. Jung, "On the Psychology of the Unconscious," para. 186.

33. Beatrice M. Hinckle, *The Re-Creation of the Individual* (New York: Harcourt, Brace, 1923).

34. See the discussion at the beginning of chapter 3. Also see: Lenoir, "The Göttingen School," pp. 111–205.

35. Jung, "The Structure of the Unconscious," para. 495.

36. This antiscientific bias has been faithfully carried on by generations of Jungians, who in social interactions and Jungian publications often clearly use the adjective "scientific" in a devaluing, pejorative sense. Many of these same persons, however, would be equally offended if it were pointed out to them that their Jungian ideas were occultist or "New Age," despite Jung's open derivation of these ideas from such occultist sources.

37. This essay does not appear in the *Collected Works*. See C. G. Jung, "The Psychology of Unconscious Processes," in Long, *Collected Papers on Analytical Psychology*, pp. 352–444.

38. Ibid., p. 432.

39. C. G. Jung, "Instinct and the Unconscious," *British Journal of Psychology* 10 (1919): 15–26. This first reference to archetypes also appears in *Structure and Dynamics*, para. 270.

40. See Brigitte Hoppe, "Polarität, Stufung, und Metamorphose in der spekulative Biologie der Romantik," *Naturwissenschaftliche Rundschau* 20 (1967): 380–83. The explicit connection between Jung's archetypal theory and early nineteenth-century Naturphilosophie was noted by Poliakov: "Here, under the guise of spirituality, we see a complete return has been made to *Naturphilosophie*, in the wake of Haeckel's 'soul of the protista,' or of 'the soul of the world'" (*The Aryan Myth*, p. 288).

41. Lenoir, "The Göttingen School," p. 195.

42. Several of Jung's disciples did begin contact with him in the late 1920s, and of these Hannah and Meier are the most prominent.

43. For a sensitive explanation of the "pseudo-religious" nature of the National Socialist movement and its seductive appeal, see Stern, "National Socialism as Temptation," in his *Dreams and Delusions*, pp. 147–92.

Chapter Thirteen

1. Max Weber, *Economy and Society* (Berkeley and Los Angeles: University of California Press, 1978), pp. 246–99, 1111–56. For an overview of the extension of Weber's concept of charisma to contemporary historical events, leaders, movements, and organizations, see the selections in Ronald Glassman and William Swatos, eds., *Charisma, History, and Social Structure* (New York: Greenwood Press, 1986).

2. Gerald Gieson, "Scientific Change, Emerging Specialties, and Research Schools," *History of Science* 19 (1981): 20–40.

3. Max Weber, *The Theory of Social and Economic Organization* (New York: Macmillan, 1947), pp. 363–364.

4. Weber, *The Sociology of Religion*, p. 46.

5. For example, by 1920 Max Eitington (a "secret commitee" member) had set up the Psychoanalytic Clinic and Training Institute in Berlin with Freud's blessing. It was the first of its kind. A second such clinic was set up in Vienna in 1922. For Freud's own perspective on his movement in 1914, see his *On the History of the Psycho-Analytic Movement*, trans. James Strachey (New York: Norton, 1966). On the rise of psychoanalysis in America, see the useful volume by C. P. Oberndorf, *A History of Psychoanalysis in America* (New York: Grune & Stratton, 1953).

6. Michael Fordham, "Analytical Psychology in England," *Journal of Analytical Psychology* 24 (1979): 280.

7. Joseph Henderson, "Reflections on the History and Practice of Jungian Analysis," in Murray Stein, ed., *Jungian Analysis* (La Salle: Open Court, 1982), p. 11. Henderson makes much of the role of women in the growth of the Jungian movement in this century, but instead of looking at admittedly more mundane psychological or especially sociological hypotheses to explain the phenomenon, Henderson in true Jungian fashion attributes it to their desire to make men see the archetypal feminine in themselves, too, and thereby lessen male-female tensions in the Western world.

8. On the founding of Bollingen Foundation, see the useful memoirs of the editor of Bollingen Series for more than thirty years: William McGuire, *Bollingen: An Adventure in Collecting the Past* (Princeton: Princeton University Press, 1989).

9. Cited in McGuire and Hull, *C. G. Jung Speaking*, p. 29.

10. See Burkert, *Ancient Mystery Cults*, pp. 12–29.

11. Cited in McGuire and Hull, *C. G. Jung Speaking*, p. 29.

12. This pyramid-shaped economic system that places such a high emphasis on selling distributorships to others resembles those of other charismatic economic movements in the U.S. such as the Amway and Nu-Skin enterprises. There seem to be four levels of initiation in the

current Jungian movement, each increasingly smaller in size in this pyramid. They range from "interested nonpatient," who may attend Jungian programs, buy Jungian books, etc., to "patient of a Jungian analyst or trainee," to "trainee" (essentially an elevated status of patienthood) in one of the approved institutes, to finally "Jungian analyst." In 1991, based on an official list of approximately five hundred certified analysts and an estimated figure of about one thousand trainees, I found that Jungian analysis was indeed a major capitalist enterprise that had a total market size of almost $80 million. This is not including the countless workshops, publications, etc., that also go on in Jung's name. Thus, worldwide, the Jungian movement is generating income in the hundreds of millions of dollars annually.

13. C. G. Jung, "Analytical Psychology and *Weltanschauung*" (1928/1931), *Structure and Dynamics of the Psyche*, para. 740.

14. Jung, "The Role of the Unconscious," para. 13.

15. Ibid., para. 26.

16. Käthe Bügler, "Die Entwicklung der analytischen Psychologie in Deutschland," in Michael Fordham, ed., *Contact with Jung: Essays on the Influence of his Work and Personality* (Philadelphia: J.B. Lippincott, 1963), pp. 24–25.

17. McGuire and Hull, *C. G. Jung Speaking*, p. xvii.

18. The text of this fawning interview is reprinted in ibid., pp. 50–56.

19. Weber, *The Sociology of Religion*, p. 55.

20. *MDR*, p. 209.

21. This Eranos lecture formed the basis of sections of his 1944 book, *Psychology and Alchemy* (CW 12).

22. See Large and Weber, *Wagnerism in European Culture and Politics*.

23. C. G. Jung Institute of Los Angeles, *Matter of Heart*, p. 11.

24. Liliane Frey interview, Jung Oral Archives, p. 4.

25. Ibid., p. 8.

26. Jolande Jacobi interview, ibid., p. 27. Jacobi's interview makes fascinating reading. She is blunt about Jung's "contradictions" on the issue of anti-Semitism, but claims he once said to her, "you know, I would never like to have children from a person who has Jewish blood" (p. 19).

27. Ibid.

28. Ibid., p. 28.

29. See David Large, "Wagner's Bayreuth Disciples," in Large and Weber, *Wagnerism in European Culture and Politics*.

30. Max Weber, "The Nature of Charismatic Authority and its Routinization," in *On Charisma and Institution Building*, ed. S. N. Eisenstadt (Chicago: University of Chicago Press, 1968), p. 57.

31. Sheila Grimaldi-Craig, "Dirty Harry," *Spring* 54 (1993): 149.

32. Weber, *The Theory of Social and Economic Organization*, p. 366.

33. Jacobi interview, Jung Oral Archives, p. 81.

34. Aniela Jaffé, "From Jung's Last Years," in Jaffé, *From the Life and Work of C. G. Jung*, p. 99.

35. C. G. Jung, "Address On the Occasion of the Founding of the C. G. Jung Institute, Zurich, 24 April 1948," *Miscellaneous Writings*, para. 1129.

36. C. A. Maier, *Antike Inkubation und moderne Psychotherapie, Studien aus dem C. G. Jung Institut, Vol. I, Zurich* (Zurich: Rauscher Verlag, 1949). The English translation by Monica Curtis appeared as *Antique Incubation and Modern Psychotherapy* (Evanston: Illinois University Press, 1967). In his epilogue Maier could not help addressing the similarities between the ancient healing cult of Asclepius and the modern Jung cult, although he vehemently denies that Jung's psychology is a cult or an esoteric secret society as he says has been charged (English edition, p. 123).

37. C. A. Meier interview, September 1970, Jung Oral Archives, p. 80.

38. For the ancient phenomenon, see A. J. Festugière, *Personal Religion Among the Greeks* (Berkeley and Los Angeles: University of California Press, 1954). This view of the mystery cults of pagan antiquity is also found in Burkert, *Ancient Mystery Cults*. Burkert, a leading authority on Greek religion, notes: "Mysteries are a form of personal religion, depending on private decision and aiming at some form of closeness to the divine" (p. 12). Also useful is Arthur Darby Nock, *Conversion: The Old and New in Religion from Alexander the Great to Augustine of Hippo* (Oxford: Oxford University Press, 1933).

39. James Hall, *The Jungian Experience: Analysis and Individuation* (Toronto: Inner City Books, 1986).

40. On the classical, developmental, and archetypal schools of thought among Jungian analysts, see Andrew Samuels, *Jung and the Post-Jungians* (London: Routledge and Kegan Paul, 1985).

41. See Noll, "Multiple Personality and the Complex Theory," pp. 321–23.

42. For example, in a recent biography of one of Jung's most prominent patients, Christiana Morgan, the prominent Jungian analyst Claire Douglas makes the following blatantly incorrect series of statements: "In 1912 the younger man broke with Freud, ostensibly because Jung could not accept Freud's dogma of sexuality and because to Freud, Jung's idea of the collective unconscious was heresy. After a severe mental crisis brought about by this rupture, Jung emerged with his own theories in the form of *The Psychology of the Unconscious*, in which he postulated a collective as well as a personal unconscious, a

potentially optimistic view of the psyche rather than a pessimistic one, and an amplificatory as well as a reductive mode of treatment that aimed at individuation rather than a narrow adjustment to reality" (*Translate the Darkness: The Life of Christiana Morgan, the Veiled Woman in Jung's Life* [New York: Simon and Schuster, 1993], p. 129). Not only is the sequence of historical events wrong, the details are completely wrong as well. Such ignorance of the history of Jung's thought and life are typical among Jungian analysts.

43. Margot Adler, *Drawing Down the Moon* (New York: The Viking Press, 1979).

44. M. D. Faber, *Modern Witchcraft and Psychoanalysis* (Cranbury, N.J.: Farleigh Dickinson University Press, 1991).

45. Tanya Luhrmann, *Persuasions of the Witch's Craft: Ritual Magic in Contemporary England* (Cambridge, Mass.: Harvard University Press, 1989), p. 281.

46. Ibid., p. 282.

47. Flowers, "Revival of Germanic Religion in Contemporary Anglo-American Culture," pp. 279–94.

48. See Melton and Poggi, *Magic, Witchcraft, and Paganism in America: A Bibliography*, pp. 233–36.

49. Flowers, "Revival of Germanic Religion in Contemporary Anglo-American Culture," pp. 288–89.

50. Ibid., p. 292.

51. Ibid., p. 193.

52. Edward Edinger, *The Creation of Consciousness: Jung's Myth for Modern Man* (Toronto: Inner City Books, 1984), p. 90.

53. For an informative and scholarly hagiographic volume that contains much information about the continuing development of the Swedenborgian "New Life" Church (which has an actual cathedral in Bryn Athern, Pennsylvania), see Robin Larsen, ed., *Emanuel Swedenborg: A Continuing Vision* (New York: Swedenborg Foundation, 1988).

❈ *Index* ❈

Jung, C. G. (*cont.*)
  phie, 41–42, 269–273; on the necessity of
  the rejection of God as a prerequisite
  for individuation, 232; Ostwald's influence on, 50–51; and polygamy, 159–
  160, 216–217; pseudoliberational
  Nietzscheanism of, 257–259; Psychological Club inaugural lecture (1916), 250–
  254; racialist thinking of, 22; on racial
  psychology, 99; on rebirth, 99, 224;
  on the rejection of Freud's Oedipus-
  complex theory on the grounds of prehistoric matriarchy, 171–172; on
  Ritschl, 143, 147; routinization of cult
  in Küsnacht-Zurich, 286–291; self-
  deification, experience of, 209–215; self-
  identification with the German *Volk*,
  21–22; self-recognition as modern
  prophet of a new age, 206–208; six theories of, 9; on the Society for Psychoanalytic Endeavors, 194–199; and spiritualism, 63, 142, 144–146; "star complex"
  of, 149; on "star" or "sun" as the inner
  core of the human personality, 240–
  243; on sun worship in Africa and
  America, 283; theological study of the
  historical Jesus in student years, 36–37;
  utopian views of Freudian psychoanalytic movement as a religion, 187–190;
  Verne's influence on, 238–240; on vitalism, 142; völkisch interpretation of
  runic sword dream of female patient,
  227–228; völkisch utopianism of, 259–
  263; as a Wagnerite, 73–74; and Wilhelm, 95; and Wolff, 191; and Zurich research school investigations into the
  phylogenetic unconscious, 184–187
  —Works: "Adaptation, Individuation,
  Collectivity (1916)," 230–233; "Mind
  and Earth (1927)," 95–97; "New Paths
  in Psychology (1912)," 199–202; "The
  Role of the Unconscious (1918)," 97–99;
  "The Structure of the Unconscious
  (1916)," 219–224; "The Transcendent
  Function (1916)," 225–230; *Wandlungen
  und Symbole der Libido* (1911–1912): as
  Bachofenian theory, 169–175; as sci-

ence, 111–119; as solar mysticism, 111,
  119–122; as völkisch Aryanism, 123–
  137
Jung, C. G., the Elder, 20, 22, 41, 144
Jung, Emma, 148, 192
Jung Institute (Zurich), 225, 289–290, 333–
  334
Jung Oral Archives, 18, 285, 289, 308
Jung, Paul, 19, 22, 34, 142
Jungian analyst, fantasy of being, 281
Jungian movement, 6–7
Jungian university, 289
Jungism, 7–9, 13, 15, 272, 285; and neo-
  paganism, 294–297; as personal reli-
  gion, 291–294

Kafka, Franz, 108
Kahane, Max, 44
Kalthoff, Albert, 88, 132
Kant, Immanuel, 142
Katz, Fanny Bowditch, 250, 268
Kaufmann, Walter, 264, 304
Keller, Adolph, 87, 204
Kemnitz, Mathilde von, 79
Kepler-Bund, 146, 312, 349
Kerr, John, 43, 46, 109–110, 152, 191, 342
Keyserling, Count Hermann, 20, 39, 56–
  57, 92–97, 108, 134, 283, 336–337
Kielmeyer, Karl, 43
kinship libido, 21
Klages, Ludwig, 39, 57, 166–169, 205,
  356–357
Knapp, Alfred, 188
Köhler, Wolfgang, 345
Köngener, Die, 17
Kraepelin, Emil, 31, 46, 151–152
Kulturkampf, 49
Kundalini yoga, 33

Laban, Rudolph, 108, 229
Laennec, René-Théophile-Hyacinthe, 7–8
Lagarde, Paul Anton de, 39, 79, 85, 88,
  333
Lamarck, Jean-Baptiste, 87, 264
landscape mysticism, völkisch, 95–103,
  305
Lang, Andrew, 82, 343

social Darwinism, 35, 50, 312, 320–321
Society for Psychoanalytic Endeavors, 194–198, 249
Society of German Believers, 80
sociobiology, 159, 163, 354
soft inheritance, 85, 96
solar mythology, 81–84, 116, 172–173
Solar Phallus Man, 121, 126, 181–184
somatic treatments for mental disorders, 45–46
Sombart, Nicholas, 166, 175
Sonnenkinder (children of the sun), 92, 101
Spielrein, Sabina, 43, 73–74, 128, 149, 159, 181, 184, 191, 208, 219, 351
spiritualism, 30, 57, 59, 77, 142, 144–146, 148, 202, 203, 229–230, 256, 265, 269, 279, 312
Sprung, Helga, 299
star complex, 149–150
Stark, Gary, 87–89, 334
Stein, Frau von, 262
Stein, Gertrude, 310
Steiner, Rudolph, 50, 65, 77, 230, 320
Stekel, Wilhelm, 44
Stoker, Bram, 29
Strauss, David Friedrich, 35–36, 142, 311–312
Struve, Walter, 56, 323
Sturulson, Snorri, 75
subliminal self, 32
Sulloway, Frank, 42, 46
sun worship, 49, 75, 79, 80–94, 101–107, 109, 116–122, 128–129, 133, 136–137, 184, 210, 224, 240–246, 260, 283
suprapersonal unconscious, 97
swastika, 77, 89, 136, 335, 346–347
Swedenborg, Emmanuel, 186, 297, 361, 377

Tacitus, 75
Talbert, Charles, 302
Tannenberg Foundation, 79–80, 88
Tannhäuser, 254
Taylor, Eugene, 349
teleomechanists, 42, 316
Tennyson, Lord, 65

Terrible Mother, 174, 218–219, 250, 255, 268
Teutons, ancient, 75
theos aner (divine man), 14, 208
Theosophical publications, 67–69, 108, 183–184, 191
Theosophical Society, 59, 65, 78, 86, 133, 335
Theosophy, 30, 57, 59, 63–69, 72, 83, 86, 92, 104–106, 136, 215, 238, 270, 279, 320, 361
Thor's hammer, 79
Thule Society, 51, 80
Tillich, Paul, 108
Time Magazine, 7, 284
Tönnies, Ferdinand, 3–4, 59, 137, 257, 261, 299, 371
toxin theory of dementia praecox, 151–152
Transcendentalism, 313
transcendent function, 225–230, 252
transference, 21
Tübingen School of Theology, 33, 36, 130, 311
Tumarkin, Nina, 55
Turanian race, 84
Twain, Mark, 71

übermensch, 20, 263–264
Ulansey, David, 340
Unternährer, Anton, 339
Urbild, 41, 270
Urform, 267
Urtyp, 40–41, 269
U.S. News and World Report, 300
Usener, Hermann, 88
utopianism, völkisch, 49, 58, 75–108, 259–263

van der Post, Laurens, 73, 108, 328
Vatican Museum, 214
vegetarianism, 104–106
Verne, Jules, 234, 238–240
Viking Brotherhood, 295
vital force, 120
vitalism, 24, 42, 51, 129, 142–143, 150, 169, 348

RICHARD NOLL,

A CLINICAL PSYCHOLOGIST,

IS POSTDOCTORAL FELLOW IN

THE HISTORY OF SCIENCE AT

HARVARD UNIVERSITY.